Golem

Front Cover Photo: Golem Couple

SUNY Series in Judaica:
Hermeneutics, Mysticism, and Religion
Michael Fishbane, Robert Goldenberg, and Arthur Green, Editors

Golem

Jewish Magical and Mystical Traditions on the Artificial Anthropoid

Moshe Idel

State University of New York Press

Paintings on cover and in text
by Abraham Pincas.

Published by
State University of New York Press, Albany

Printed in the United States of America

For information, address State University of New York Press, State University Plaza, Albany, N.Y., 12246

Library of Congress Cataloging-in-Publication Data

Idel, Moshe, 1947–
Golem : Jewish magical and mystical traditions on the artificial anthropoid / Moshe Idel.
p. cm.—(SUNY series in Judaica)
Bibliography: p.
Includes index.
ISBN 0-7914-0160-X.—ISBN 0-7914-0161—8 (pbk.)
1. Golem. 2. Mysticism—Judaism—History. I. Title.
II. Series.
BM531.I34 1989 *89-30042*
296.1'9—dc19 *CIP*

10 9 8 7 6 5 4 3

To Abraham,
who created Golems

Contents

Acknowledgments *ix*

Abbreviations *xi*

Introduction *xv*

Part One
Ancient Traditions

1. Ancient Parallels *3*
2. Sefer Yeẓirah *9*
3. Talmud and Midrash *27*

Part Two
Medieval Elaborations

4. Tempering Magic: Geonic and Rationalistic Attitudes *47*
5. Ashkenazi Ḥasidic Views on the Golem *54*
6. The Northern France Discussions *81*
7. The Golem in Ecstatic Kabbalah *96*
8. R. Joseph ben Shalom Ashkenazi *119*
9. Psychological Implications of the Golem *127*
10. Theosophical Interpretations of the Golem *134*

Part Three
Renaissance Period

11. Sixteenth and Seventeenth Century Discussions in the West *165*

12. R. Moses ben Jacob Cordovero's View *196*

Part Four
Early-Modern and Modern Reverberations

13. R. Eliyahu, the Master of the Name, of Helm *207*

14. Golem in the Halakhah *213*

15. Golem and Sex *232*

16. Vicissitudes of the Golem Techniques *242*

17. Golem and Ḥasidic Mysticism *247*

18. Modern Reverberations *251*

19. Golem: Imaginaire, Anomian, and Silent *259*

20. Summary *269*

Part Five
Appendixes

A. Golem and Ẓelem *285*

B. Golem: Some Semantic Remarks *296*

C. Was There a Macranthropos Named 'Emet? *306*

Subject Index *315*

Author Index *319*

Acknowledgments

My interest in the topic of the Golem commenced in 1975, when I was preparing my Ph. D. on the Kabbalah of Abraham Abulafia. His original treatment of this theme aroused my curiosity and despite the fact that I devoted to this issue only a few pages in the thesis, I continued for years to collect related material from manuscripts. My return to this issue in a more concrete manner was catalyzed by an invitation from the Jewish Museum to contribute an essay to the catalogue of an exhibition on the Golem in 1988, organized by Mrs. Emily Bilski. The essay in that catalogue treated a few new texts and exposed briefly new ideas concerning the concepts of the Golem, which are elaborated here in detail.

The need to explore an immense range of material, covering factually almost the whole of Jewish literature renders an exhaustive treatment of the Golem impossible. I learned about material neglected by modern scholarship not only from the study of manuscripts; conversations with friends and colleagues were very helpful both in detecting new material and understanding various aspects of its content. I would like to mention here those persons whose help contributed substantially to enrich the present book: Professors Joseph Hacker, Yehuda Liebes, Shlomo Pines, Israel Ta-Shma and Sara Zfatman from the Hebrew University, and Professors Sid Z. Leiman, Menaḥem Schmelzer and Elliot R. Wolfson from New York. The Institute of Microfilms of Hebrew Manuscripts of the National and University Library in Jerusalem helped me, in numerous ways, to peruse the pertinent material.

Professor Elliot Wolfson also kindly accepted to revise the first version. Thanks are due to Mr. William Eastman, the director of SUNY Press, whose interest in this work facilitated its accomplishment.

Abbreviations

Altmann, "The Delphic Maxim"; Alexander Altmann, "The Delphic Maxim in Mediaeval Islam and Judaism," ed. A. Altmann, *Biblical and Other Studies* (Cambridge, Mass. 1963), pp. 196–231.

Cohen, *Shi'ur Qomah: Texts and Recensions;* Martin S. Cohen, *Shi'ur Qomah: Texts and Recensions'* (Tuebingen, 1985).

Cohen-Alloro, *The Secret of the Garment*; Dorit Cohen-Alloro, *The Secret of the Garment in the Zohar* (The Hebrew University of Jerusalem, Research Projects of the Institute of Jewish Studies, Monograph Series, 13, Jerusalem, 1987). (Hebrew)

Commentary on Genesis Rabbah; *Kabbalistic Commentary of Rabbi Yoseph ben Shalom Ashkenazi on Genesis Rabbah,* ed. Moshe Hallamish (Jerusalem, 1984).

Dan, *The Esoteric Theology*; Joseph Dan, *The Esoteric Theology of Ashkenazi Hasidism* (Jerusalem, 1968). (Hebrew)

Dan, *Studies*; Joseph Dan, *Studies in Ashkenazi-Hasidic Literature,* (Givatayim Ramat Gan, 1968). (Hebrew)

Eleazar of Worms, *Commentary on Sefer Yeẓirah,* according to ed. Przesmysl (1883).

Eleazar of Worms, *Sefer ha-Ḥokhmah* according to the ed. of Chaim Konyevsky, in *Roqeaḥ, A Commentary on the Bible,* (Bnei Berak, 1986), vol. 1, pp. 11–51.

Eleazar of Worms, *Ḥokhmat ha-Nefesh,* according to ed. Safed, (1913).

Fossum, *The Name of God and the Angel of the Lord*; Jarl E. Fossum, *The Name of God and the Angel of the Lord* (Tuebingen, 1985).

Gottlieb, *Studies*; Ephraim Gottlieb, *Studies in Kabbalah Literature,* ed. Joseph Hacker (Tel Aviv, 1976) (Hebrew).

Gruenwald, *Apocalyptic and Merkavah Mysticism*; Ithamar Gruenwald, *Apocalyptic and Merkavah Mysticism* (Leiden, 1980).

Gruenwald, *SY*; Ithamar Gruenwald, "A Preliminary Critical Edition of Sefer Yeẓira," *Israel Oriental Studies,* vol. 1 (1971), pp. 132–177.

Halperin, *The Faces of the Chariot*; David J. Halperin, *The Faces of the Chariot* (Tuebingen, 1988).

Hyman, "Some Observations"; Peter Hyman, "Observations on Sefer Yeṣira: (1) Its Use of Scripture," *JJS,* vol. 36 (1984), pp. 168–184.

Idel, *Abraham Abulafia*; Moshe Idel, *The Doctrine and Works of R. Abraham Abulafia* (Ph. D. Thesis, Hebrew University, Jerusalem, 1976). (Hebrew)

Idel, "Enoch is Metatron"; Moshe Idel, "Enoch is Metatron," ed. Joseph Dan, *Early Jewish Mysticism* (Jerusalem, 1987) *JSJT,* vol. 6: 1–2, pp. 151-170. (Hebrew)

Idel, "Hermeticism and Judaism"; Moshe Idel, "Hermeticism and Judaism" in eds. I. Merkel and A. G. Debus, *Hermeticism and the Renaissance* (Folger Books: Associated University Presses, 1988), pp. 59–76.

Idel, *Kabbalah: New Perspectives*; M. Idel, *Kabbalah: New Perspectives* (New Haven-London, 1988).

Idel, *Language, Torah and Hermeneutics*; M. Idel, *Language, Torah and Hermeneutics in Abraham Abulafia* (Albany, NY, SUNY: 1988).

Idel, "Reification of Language," M. Idel, "Reification of Language in Jewish Mysticism;" ed. Steven Katz, *Language and Mysticism* (forthcoming).

Idel, "The Magical and Neoplatonic Interpretations"; Moshe Idel, "The Magical and Mystical Interpretations of the Kabbalah in the Renaissance," ed. Bernard D. Cooperman, *Jewish Thought in the Sixteenth Century* (Cambridge, Mass., 1983), pp. 186–242.

Idel, *The Mystical Experience*; M. Idel, *The Mystical Experience in Abraham Abulafia* (Albany, NY: SUNY, 1987).

Idel, *Studies in Ecstatic Kabbalah*; M. Idel, *Studies in Ecstatic Kabbalah* (Albany, NY: SUNY, 1988).

Idel, "The Concept of the Torah"; M. Idel, "The Concept of the Torah in the Heikhalot Literature and Its Metamorphosis in Kabbalah," *JSJT,* vol. 1:1 (1981), pp. 23–84. (Hebrew)

Idel, "The World of the Angels"; Moshe Idel, "The World of Angels in Human Form," eds. J. Dan, and J. Hacker, *Studies in Jewish Mysticism, Philosopy and Ethical Literature Presented to Isaiah Tishby* (Jerusalem, 1986), pp. 1–66. (Hebrew)

Jellinek, *Bet ha-Midrasch*; Adolph Jellinek, *Bet ha-Midrasch,* vol. 6 (Vienna, 1877).

Joseph ben Shalom Ashkenazi, *Commentary on Sefer Yeẓirah* according to ed. (Jerusalem, 1961) of *Sefer Yeẓirah.*

Lewy, *Chaldean Oracles*; Hans Lewy, *Chaldean Oracles and Theurgy* ed., M. Tardieu (Paris, 1978).

Liebes, "Christian Influences"; Yehuda Liebes, "Christian Influences in the Zohar," *JSJT,* vol. 2:1, (1983), pp. 43–74. (Hebrew)

Liebes, *The Sin of Elisha*; Yehuda Liebes, *The Sin of Elisha, The Four Who Entered Paradise and The Nature of Talmudic Mysticism,* (Research Projects of the Institute of Jewish Studies, Hebrew University of Jerusalem, Monograph Series, 9, 1986) (Hebrew).

Mueller, "Die Golemsage"; Konrad Mueller, "Die Golemsage und die Sage von der lebenden Statue" *Mitteilungen der Schleischen Gesellschaft fuer Volkskunde,* vol. 20 (1919), pp. 1–40.

Nifla'ot Maharal; *Nifla'ot Maharal,* ed. Judel Rosenberg (Petrokov, 1909).

Pagel, *Paracelsus*; Walter Pagel, *Paracelsus, An Introduction to Philosophical Medicine in the Era of the Renaissance* (Karger, Basel etc. 1982).

Pedaya, "'Flaw' and 'Correction'"; Ḥaviva Pedaya, "'Flaw' and 'Correction'" in the Concept of Godhead in the Teaching of Rabbi Isaac the Blind," ed. Joseph Dan, *The Beginnings of Jewish Mysticism in Medieval Europe* (Jerusalem, 1987), *JSJT,* vol. 6:3–4, pp. 157–285. (Hebrew)

Pseudo-Sa 'adyah, *Commentary on Sefer Yeẓirah* according to the ed. (Jerusalem, 1961) of *Sefer Yeẓirah.*

Schaeffer, *Synopse*; Peter Schaefer, *Synopse zur Hekhalot Literatur* (Tuebingen, 1981).

Scholem, *Kabbalah*; Gershom G. Scholem, *Kabbalah* (Jerusalem, 1974).

Scholem, *On the Kabbalah*; Gershom G. Scholem, *On the Kabbalah and Its Symbolism* (New York, 1969).

Scholem, *Origins of the Kabbalah*; Gershom Scholem, *Origins of the Kabbalah,* Trans. A. Arkush, ed. R. J. Z. Werblowsky, (JPS & Princeton University Press, 1987).

Scholem, "The Idea of the Golem"; Gershom Scholem, "The Idea of the Golem," in *On the Kabbalah and its Symbolism,* Trans. by R. Manheim, Schocken, (New York), pp. 158–204.

Scholem, "The Image of the Golem"; Gershom Scholem, "The Image of the Golem in Its Tellurian and Magical Context," in *Elements of the Kabbalah and Its Symbolism* Trans. Joseph ben Shelomo (Jerusalem, 1976), pp. 381–424. (Hebrew).

Scholem, "The Name of God"; Gershom G. Scholem, "The Name of God and the Linguistic of the Kabbala," *Diogenes,* vol. 79 (1972), pp. 59–80, vol. 80 (1973), pp. 164–194.

Scholem, "Ẓelem"; Gershom G. Scholem, "Ẓelem" in *Elements of the Kabbalah and Its Symbolism,* pp. 358–380.

Sherwin, *The Legend of the Golem*; Byron L. Sherwin, *The Legend of the Golem: Origins and Implications* (University Press of America, 1985).

Sirat, *Les Theories des visions surnaturelles*; Colette Sirat, *Les theories des visions surnaturelles dans la pensee juive du Moyen-Age,* (Leiden, 1969).

Tishby, *Mishnat ha-Zohar*; Isaiah Tishby, *Mishnat ha-Zohar,* vol. 2 (Jerusalem, 1957, 1961). (Hebrew)

Tishby, *Torat ha-Ra'*; Isaiah Tishby, *Torah ha-Ra' ve-ha-Qelippah be-Qabbalat ha-'Ari* (Jerusalem, 1984). (Hebrew)

Wolfson, "The Anthropomorphic Image"; Elliot Wolfson, "The Anthropomorphic Image and Symbolism of Letters in the *Zohar*" (forthcoming).

Journals

AJS Review—Association of Jewish Studies Review

HUCA—Hebrew Union College Annual

JJS—Journal of Jewish Studies

JSJT—Jerusalem Studies in Jewish Thought

JQR—Jewish Quarterly Review

MGWJ—Monatschrift fuer die Geschichte und Wissenschaft des Judentums

REJ—Revue des Études Juives

Introduction

> "We have lived too long under the terror of the matchless perfection of the demiurge" my father said. "For too long perfection of his creation has paralysed our own creative instinct. We don't wish to compete with him. We have no ambition to emulate him. We wish to be creators in our own, lower sphere; we want to have the privilege of creation, we want creative delights; we want—in one word—Demiurgy"
>
> *The Street of the Crocodiles* translation Celina Wieniewska. (New York, 1977) pp. 60–61.

Bruno Schulz's "mad father", whose monologue was quoted above, seems to aspire to Faustian claims by his request of Demiurgy; the longing for creative powers, even on a smaller degree, is however much more modest when we peruse the context of the above quotation: "We wish to create a second time—in the shape and resemblance of a tailor's dummy," says the father to his daughters. The modest request implies a capability which does not imperil the divine superiority, recognising as it does the perfection of the divine creation in comparison to the second creation. Describing the dummies, the father continues: "Their roles will be short, concise, their characters—without a background. Sometimes, for one gesture, for one word alone, we shall make the effort to bring them to life."

The medieval predecessors of Schulz's father were much more pretentious; their interest was not in a dummy, a creature for a short instance, but in a creation that indeed reflects the divine creation much more than the twentieth century Polish tailor could dare. The medieval masters intended an experience that is much more than witnessing a unique theatrical gesture. For them, magical creation and experience were conceived as a continuum that sometimes testifies to the attainment of their spiritual perfection. In other words, between the medieval masters who exposed the doctrine of the creation of the Golem, and modern Jewish and non-Jewish literature, a profound change has taken place. Modern man, alienated as he is from the divine, is afraid of the inherent theological implications of his creative powers; the medieval masters, probably because of their sense of closeness to God, were able to strive toward and, according to their feeling, achieve aims that are beyond the modern frame of mind. Kafka's alienation, just as Schulz's spiritual paralysis inhibiting creativity, are symptoms of more general sentiments that avenues once open are no longer accessible to man. Without question, inhibitions regarding creative urges are part of this loss of direction, of the disorientation which characterizes modern figures. Our modern awareness of the imaginary nature of medieval spiritual universes caused a more skeptical attitude to the patrimony of the past, awakening, at the same time, the optimistic, activistic and resourceful approach that characterized some forms of magic and mysticism. Let us now study one magical-mystical technique out of the many to be found in Jewish mysticism, one that shows the way to a creative contact with the divine: the creation of the Golem.

Before embarking on the detailed discussions of the Golem texts, a short survey on the scholarly understanding of this issue is pertinent. This survey is not intended to be an exhaustive one, as the various attitudes toward some details will be referred to in due time in the separate chapters. Here I shall confine my discussion mostly to the details of the theses of the most important scholar who treated this subject, Gershom Scholem. I shall refrain from summarizing the discussions of authors preceding Scholem as their knowledge of the relevant texts was partial, and their approach was motivated by an attempt to relate the origins or the influences of the concepts they were dealing with to alien sources, rather than an attempt to understand the texts themselves. Afterwards, the treatment of two others scholars, Byron Sherwin and Andre Neher, who wrote after the publication of Scholem's essay, will be presented in a concise manner.

Gershom Scholem's View of the Golem

I

Whoever is involved in the study of Kabbalah, or Jewish mysticism and magic in general, has a duty to express his debt to the important contribution of Gershom Scholem with respect to many of the particular topics he is going to research; such a debt is especially obvious in the case of the contribution of Scholem to a critical evaluation of traditions regarding the complex of ideas concerning the Golem. Since 1933, he continued to be interested in this topic, to write and rewrite about it and, indeed, the final version of his views of the Golem is a masterpiece of erudition. His major contribution to this topic was an essay presented in 1955 at an

Eranos meeting, which was published in its German original and in an English translation. Twenty years later, a Hebrew version was prepared by Prof. Joseph ben Shelomo, a former student of Scholem, who under his supervision has rendered the paper into Hebrew and added additional material, and here and there some minor errors were corrected. The Hebrew version is the most elaborate statement of Scholem on this issue. We shall regularly refer in the following to the English translation when it does not differ from the later Hebrew version, but we shall take advantage of all the additions found in this version, which will be indicated by the abbreviation of the title, "The Image of the Golem." It should be mentioned that the crystallization of the idea of the Golem was part of an attempt by Scholem to present Jewish mysticism to a wider audience, the Eranos participants, who were not interested or even able to absorb Hebrew philological and historical treatments of any topic. Thus, Scholem preferred the notion of one "idea of the Golem" to what seems to me to be a more complex topic. Although this approach had the advantage of having pushed the scholar to adopt a more phenomenological attitude, I fear that its limitation in scope, a presentation limited by the circumstances, served as a Procrustean bed for the treatment of this issue.

Towering far beyond the amateurish writings on this topic produced in the early twentieth century, Scholem was able to unearth the extant material which contributes to the history of the idea of the Golem, to analyze it for the first time in a scholarly manner, tracing its development until its latest manifestations. The greatest contribution of this scholar was his ability to place this peculiar issue in the framework of Jewish mysticism, allowing an insight into the shift of a magico-mystical topic into a popular legend. The quintessence of Scholem's view of the Golem seems to be contained in his introductory lines to the entry on the Golem in the *Encyclopedia Judaica*:

> The golem is a creature, particularly a human being, made in an artificial way by the virtue of a magic art, through the use of holy names. The idea that it is possible to create living beings in this manner is widespread in the magic of many people. Especially well known are the idols and images to which the ancients claimed to have given the power of speech. Among the Greeks and the Arabs these activities are sometimes connected with astrological speculations related to the possibility of "drawing the spirituality of the stars" to lower being. The development of the idea of the golem in Judaism, however, is remote from astrology; it is connected, rather with the magical exegesis of the *Sefer Yeẓirah* and with the ideas of the creative power of speech and of letters".[1]

Scholem's formulation that the artificial creation of the Golem is "connected . . . with the magical exegesis of the *Sefer Yeẓirah*" betrays his historical understanding of the history of the Golem practices. It is not a topic of *Sefer Yeẓirah* per se, but rather a magical interpretation of it, namely a later development. Elsewhere in the same book, he offers a more cautious formulation; when dealing with the creation of the Golem he indicates that: "Whether *Sefer Yeẓirah* itself initially was aimed at magical ideas of this type is a subject on which opinions differ, but it is not impossible".[2] Thus it seems that Scholem preferred a later, rather than an earlier dating of the techniques to create the Golem. How late it is is difficult to assert in a precise manner. On the basis of a statement of his, however, it is possible to conclude that he envisioned the writings of R. Eleazar of Worms as the earliest occurrence. In his article on "Tradition and New Creation in the Ritual of the Kabbalists," he stated that "the oldest instructions for making a Golem must be regarded as a theurgical ritual. . . . These instructions are contained in the writings of the same Kabbalist to whom we owe the preservation of the above-mentioned rites."[3] By these rites Scholem means the rite of the transmission of the Divine Name, preserved by R. Eleazar of Worms, conceived here as a Kabbalist. Thus, according to this scholar, the magical use of *Sefer Yeẓirah* is indeed a later interpretation, as late as the early thirteenth century. Only in one case a statement of Scholem explicitly contradicts the conclusion we may draw from the above sentences.[4] Implicitly, another view on the problem of the dating can be found where Scholem characterises Rashi's understanding of the Talmudic passage dealing with the creation of an artificial man by the means of the divine name as follows: "In general Rashi reflects a much older learned tradition."[5] I cannot explain this implicit contradiction, and I assume that Scholem simply waivered between two different views.

Two other issues recurring in Scholem's analyses are the existence of what he calls the "tellurian" elements in the Golem, namely those powers inherent in the brute material which enter into the constitution of the Golem, the dangers that emerge from these powers being a leitmotif in Scholem's analysis.[6] According to some statements of Scholem, there was in existence in ancient Judaism a view that the earth had a spirit of itself;[7] this concept, whose influence is, according to Scholem, also visible in Gnosticism,[8] can explain the independent and uncontrolled growth of the Golem and its becoming a dangerous being. Scholem does not specify how exactly this ancient view reached the medieval Jewish authors; even, according to him, the motif of the dangerous Golem is a late one, as late as the seventeenth century, though he remarks that it is also present in an implicit way in the view of R. Moses Cordovero.[9]

Another main assumption of Scholem is that the creation of the Golem served, in the twelfth and thirteenth centuries, mainly mystical purposes, i.e., the ritual of creating the Golem was intended to achieve a mystical experience. This last point was formulated in an explicit way in his last overall survey of Kabbalah where he states in connection with the Ashkenazi Hasidim: "The study of the book [of *Yeẓirah*] was considered successful when the mystic attained the vision of the Golem, which was connected with a specific ritual of a remarkably ecstatic character."[10] It seems that Scholem had attenuated an early formulation of the meaning of the Golem ritual in Ashkenazi esotericism. In his essay "Tradition and New Creation in the Ritual of the Kabbalists" he preferred two foci for the Golem ritual: "the oldest instructions for making a golem must be regarded as a theurgical ritual, in which the adept becomes aware of wielding a certain creative power . . . these specifications for the making of a golem are . . . a description of a precise ritual, calculated to induce a very definite vision, namely a vision of the creative animation of the golem."[11] In comparison to the view that the Golem ritual had only a symbolic meaning, this formulation allows for a more magical and realistic interpretation of the ritual. I assume that Scholem envisioned the Golem practice as containing the formation of the body out of dust and then the entrance into an ecstatic experience, when the magician experiences, symbolically—i.e., as an inner experience alone—the animation of the body. A terminological observation is pertinent in relation to Scholem's use of the term "rite" or "ritual" in order to describe the practice of creating a Golem.[12] We shall prefer in the following the term "technique" or "techniques" in order to emphasize the more magical character of these devices. I propose to use this term also in order to distinguish the magical, and even the mystical practices, from the regular Jewish ritual as it was sanctified in the Halakhic and custom literature. This distinction will help one discriminate between modes of behaviour that were recognized as religiously obligatory or, at least as recommended practices, in comparison to the magical behaviour which was voluntary. "Technique" also seems to be more neutral from the religious point of view.

Finally, Scholem has attempted to solve the problem of the semantic transformation of the biblical Golem into the magical anthropoid; his view on this issue will be described and examined separately.[13] Here I would like to stress that his conviction that the semantic mutation from the significance "unformed" to the magically created man occurred, according to Scholem, in R. Eleazar of Worms' *Commentary on Sefer Yeẓirah.* Thus both the technique of creating an anthropoid and the new meaning of the Golem were understood as appearing at the same time, at the beginning of the thirteenth century.

In 1965, Scholem addressed a speech on the Golem and the first computer in Israel, which were reminiscent of the remarks of Norbert Wiener written a year earlier.[14] Going beyond the technical and historical discussions in his earlier essay, Scholem opened a series of approaches to the topic in the context of modern science.[15] The most important of them is that of Byron Sherwin.

The study by Sherwin printed in 1985 treats two major issues; the legend of the Golem and the modern implications of this legend. In the first part he surveys the basic texts related to the legendary aspect of the Golem, introducing also texts which were not treated by Scholem; thus, for example, he discusses the passage of R. Isaiah Horwitz and that of R. Gershom Ḥanokh Leiner. Subsequently, the juridical and medical implications of these legends were exposed. The major effort in this study is to relate modern developments in matters of medicine, mostly genetic engineering, to the Rabbinic attitude to the humanity of the Golem.

In a recent book, the Jewish philosopher, André Neher, has considered the myth of the Golem according to the version which attributed the creation of the Golem to the Maharal, as contemporary to the formation of the myth of Faustus in the eighties of the sixteenth century. These two myths, conceived as twin myths, reflect different aspects of magic; the Jewish one, associated ultimately with God, culminated with the creation of the modern cibernetics by a Jew, Norbert Wiener, who openly mentioned the Golem as a precedent of the modern automata. The Christian one, related to Satan especially by Thomas Mann, will culminate ultimately with the destructive processes of Auschwitz and Hiroshima.[16] Neher bases his reflections on the significance of the divergences between these two parallel myths on the fact that they appeared simultaneously, an event fraught with a profound meaning for the whole range of speculations which constitutes the essence of the book. He is inclined to accept the attribution of the legend to the Maharal as authentic, though in his earlier studies on the Maharal he rejected this attribution. Neher did not intend to deal with the medieval texts and consequently his contribution to the material dealt with below is not significant. As to the speculation on the relationship between the two myths and their evolution in history, they perhaps belong to the domain of historiosophy which remains beyond the scope of this study.

II

The present study aims at presenting fresh material concerning the nature and history of the Golem and, at the same time, to offer some other views related to this topic, some of them differing substantially from

Scholem's approach. I have reexamined the whole range of the texts adduced by Scholem and I have attempted to rethink their content anew. In some instances the results of these second readings are different. However, beyond the novel suggestions as to the significance of the material also presented by Scholem, I have endeavoured to cover all the printed and manuscript material available. This sustained effort yielded a series of highly significant sources which discuss the Golem in Jewish mysticism. In some cases these are texts of authors already dealt with by Scholem who, nevertheless, did not exhaust the analysis of the views of certain authors. This is the case as far as R. Eleazar of Worms and R. Abraham Abulafia are concerned. However, in the following pages the reader will find a long series of texts which are discussed for the first time, some of them authored by the most important figures in Kabbalistic literature. So, for example, I shall discuss the views of R. Isaac of Acre, R. Joseph ben Shalom Ashkenazi and those found in the nineteenth-century Hasidic material, ignored in the extant studies of the Golem. A whole period with a marked interest in the Golem, the Jewish and Christian Renaissance, was dealt with by Scholem only incidentally. I am confident that, notwithstanding the fact that in the present situation of the study of Kabbalah it is impossible to exhaust any given theme because of the great mass of material still in manuscript, this study does contribute a substantial amount of major texts which enriches the understanding of this topic. The perusal of hundreds of manuscripts has permitted me to form a more adequate picture of the history of Kabbalah in general and, I believe, a more mature approach to the analyzed texts when they are presented in the framework of the speculative system of their authors and against the background of their intellectual ambiance.

III

By presenting here a new discussion of an issue already dealt with in detail by Scholem, the reader will become aware that despite the genial work invested by this scholar, we still are only at the beginning of the study of Jewish mysticism and magic; this study can be advanced not by the repetition of Scholem's conclusions, as is the custom in the prevalent scholarship of Kabbalah, but by a sustained effort to reexamine the subject under discussion with the help of a larger perspective which is the result of the accumulative study of material unknown to Scholem. The fact that Scholem's descriptions of the Golem remained unexamined or that new material was not added after Scholem's publication of his article in 1955 by his followers, testify to the nature of the post-Scholemian research. I am confident that the reexamination of the material which served

Scholem as the starting-point for his conclusion in matters of specific themes or on general topics will enable us to reach different conclusions from those advanced by the founder of modern Kabbalah scholarship. This is the only way to overcome the conformist attitude of most of the disciples of Scholem. The detailed examination of this scholar's theses related to the Golem undertaken here is, to my knowledge, the first attempt to approach a major theme treated by Scholem *in extenso* on the basis of different methodology and documents, and in a critical way. The prevailing assumption of the followers of Scholem, generally implicitly but sometimes even explicitly, is that the major outlines of the history and characteristic of Jewish mysticism were already formulated in the studies of the master. I hope that the present discussion will show that much can be done also in a different way.

IV

Though I cannot enter in this introduction into the details of all the differences between the way Scholem understood the one "idea" of the Golem and the findings of the present writer, I would like to emphasize that Scholem's attempt to differentiate the Jewish practice of the Golem from the pagan practices of drawing down spirituality onto statues is too sharp, for there are texts which relate this drawing down to astrological views.[17] If our observation is correct, then part of the Golem traditions is to be envisioned as the result of the encounter of Jewish mystical and magical traditions with other types of cultures, which fertilized Jewish thought also in other domains, and produced a variety of understandings of the nature of the Golem. As we shall see below, the impact of Neoplatonic and Aristotelian views on the concepts of the Golem is to be added to that of the magical astrology; the Golem is, therefore, one more example of the different results of the various encounters of ancient Jewish traditions and alien types of thought. Therefore, in contrast to the implicit assumption of the existence of one "idea" of the Golem, as advocated by Scholem, we shall deal with different syntheses between ancient Jewish magical traditions and alien types of thought. In principle, the different conception of the history of Jewish mysticism advocated by the present author, in comparison to that espoused by Scholem and his followers, can be exemplified by the findings of the following analysis. As we have seen above, Scholem was ostensibly inclined to consider the existence of one basic technique for the creation of the Golem shared, with minor differences, by all the German and Northern French texts, and also by Abulafia. In principle, these were conceived as medieval creations, which are to be considered as novel interpretations of *Sefer Yeẓirah.* This is concurred, though Scholem does not explicitly mention this correlation, by an alleged semantic change of Golem to a magically created anthropoid. Only in very rare instances, the reader will detect some hesitations as to the medieval nature of these techniques.

V

In contrast, the findings of the present study, especially the suggestions with regard to the interpretation of *Sefer Yeẓirah,* open the strong possibility that this ancient work is to be seen as including a main discussion of the creation of a man by the combination of letters by God, and the imitation of this process by Abraham. Consequently the medieval authors exposing elaborate and different techniques testify to the existence of an older practice, congruent to the teachings of *Sefer Yeẓirah*; this hypothetical practice had ramifications in subsequent generations. In addition to the differentiation of the technique, some interpretations of the nature of the Golem emerged as the result of the encounter with different speculative systems. Thus, I assume that at least in this case, it is plausible that though basic components of Jewish mysticism and magic are ancient, the process of transmission caused an enrichment of their content. This process was, at least partially, provoked by cultural encounters with alien types of thought. Whatever may be the ultimate origin of the elements constituting Jewish mysticism and magic, in general and in our particular case the idea and techniques to create an anthropoid, some of them were in existence in Judaism in antiquity. The unfolding of Jewish mysticism, as we shall see below in the case of the discussion of the macranthropos and the combinations of two letters, discloses curious examples of similarities, which are, in my opinion, not only an issue of phenomenological affinity but also of historical connections. Thus I am hesitant to conceive the history of Kabbalah as it appears in the written documents as a "progressive" evolution alone. It seems that alongside this category we shall better be aware of the possibility that later strata of Kabbalistic literature may contain also older elements or structures, not so visible in the earlier bodies of literature. In other words, I allow a greater role to the subterranean transmission than Scholem and his followers did.[18] In one of the chapters below, I shall propose the possibility that what was considered to be a late sixteenth century Kabbalistic innovation indeed predates this period and can be reasonably traced to at least as early as the second half of the thirteenth century.[19] On the basis of some similarities, I further assume that it is possible that the late sixteenth century Kabbalistic discussion of a macranthropos reveals a very ancient mystical view, stemming from Jewish sources but extant in a Gnostic text.

VI

Our working hypothesis requires a methodological clarification as to the nature of the Jewish magical and mystical traditions. The attempts to reconstruct earlier speculative structures on the ground of later material is a complex endeavour, involving the danger of misconstruction.[20] Our assumption is that if the same theme occurs in texts which do not depend on each other, it is reasonable to consider the possibility that a common source, or sources, generated the later discussions. The reconstruction is a reasonable requirement if parts of the later theme or structure, disparate motifs or phrases, are found in the earlier period. Thus I propose to resort to a reconstruction of an earlier stage of existence of a certain speculative structure only when a minimum of evidence, fragmentary or obscure, can be elucidated by applying a later scheme which includes components in existence in the earlier periods. I do not recommend the reconstruction of ancient patterns of thought or comprehensive systems unless this minimum is extant.

Since texts are the only reliable testimonies as to the possibility of the existence of more comprehensive views treated in a certain text in a truncated or nebulous way, I avoid the assumption of propelling into the remote past later concepts; however, the austere attitude which is content only with the philological discussion of texts, as if their authors had nothing to say in domains of theology or mysticism, is in my eyes an easy way to avoid the confrontation with vital aspects of some types of texts. Though I believe that magical and mystical traditions were transmitted also in oral fashion, and it is even possible that crucial issues were deliberately handed down in this way, I prefer not to speculate about Jewish magic and mysticism beyond texts, since these speculations cannot contribute solid findings which will advance the understanding of the development of culture. In our case, the situation seems to be extraordinarily complex. Elements connected to the medieval techniques and other discussions related to the Golem are in existence in hoary antiquity, but in a more elaborate manner they occur only in later periods. Since the assumptions of the portents of these traditions is that the material is ancient, we are in a curious situation as to the development of the material under discussion. Are the Jewish masters right when they assume that their traditions are ancient, or is the more cautious and sceptical attitude of the academic more productive? In general, the study of Jewish magic and mysticism has preferred a more sure, and easy, approach; to deny the assessment of the traditional portents of these traditions. There is no question that such a sceptical attitude is a necessary requirement in order not to succumb to an uncritical vision of the history and the evolution of religious traditions. However, modern scholarship in the field of Jewish mysticism has not been open enough in order to carefully examine the pretensions of the medieval mystics, before it ignores them as unhistorical.

In the case of the Golem, the attempt to approach the text of *Sefer Yeẓirah* as dealing with the creation of man by God by means of the combination of letters, as it was understood in the medieval sources, proved to be constructive and was corroborated by a linguistic analysis of the text. To summarize this point; reconstruction on the basis of some elements in earlier sources, which require a more elaborate discussion, may be highly productive when it is based upon texts or, at least, some indirect evidence.

VII

Another emphasis of the present discussion will be the analysis of the mystical and magical techniques employed, or at least exposed, by the Jewish masters; this issue was only tangentially referred to by Scholem, and it may contribute toward a better understanding of some issues related to the technical facets of Jewish magic and mysticism in general. I shall attempt to delve into this issue as it seems to be a neglected area of scholarship; the very fact that we shall be able to point out the existence of a variety of techniques seems to be crucial for a new understanding of the experiential nature of some aspects of Jewish esoteric discussions. Though I am inclined to minimize the visionary nature of the Golem experiences in those discussions where this aspect is not mentioned explicitly,[21] I still assume that the magical technique is not devoid of an experimental facet. This statement is directly related to the nature of the following discussions. Whereas Scholem would assume that despite the magical aspects of the topic, the ultimate goal of the creation of an anthropoid was a mystical experience, I am inclined to stress more the technical part of the practice and its theological implications. However, what is conspicuous is that most of the material discussed below stems from writings conceived to constitute the mystical literature of Judaism. This fact opens at least one major question; since this literature was written by the elite, at least up to the end of the eighteenth century, what was the status of magic in this stratum of Jewish society. As we shall see below, the so-called rationalists either ignored the topic of the Golem altogether, or attenuated its magical aspects. However, this approach is statistically marginal; most of the authors who discussed the topic of the Golem did it in a positive tone. Thus the examination of this matter may help to clarify an aspect of Jewish mystical literature; its attitude to magic is far from negative in several circles. However, we should be aware of the fact that too sharp a distinction between magic and mysticism does not do justice to the categories of thought of the authors under discussion.[22]

What can be regularly conceived as a magical operation, can be understood not so much as an attempt to confront the divinity by the accumulation of an independent power, but an attempt to imitate Him by verifying the *modus operandi* and so testifying to the grandeur of the creator. Thus it is possible that in some Jewish texts, already beginning with antiquity, magic and mysticism can be regarded as two faces of the same coin. This is obvious in the Heikhalot literature, and it runs through some other types of literature up to the Renaissance, in the writings of Yoḥanan Alemanno and Abraham Yagel. In the case of the creation of the Golem, the practical implications of such an operation were never emphasized, up to the seventeenth-century legends. Thus we may conclude that most of the following texts, whose magical facet is obvious insofar as the technical aspect is concerned, are after all less interested in a practical goal. Thus, it seems that we can define the subject of our study as the magical component of mystical literature; the context of the appearance of these discussions mitigated the more practical possibilities inherent in this type of operation.

The above conclusion may be the result of the fact that we are dealing not with the entire corpus of concepts related to the Golem in existence, but with the written one, which is *ipso facto* the creation of the learned persons. The popular attitude to the artificial creation of an anthropoid remains beyond our reach. Thus we shall be aware that most of the generalizations regarding our topic hold only as far as the elite discussions and interest are concerned. It may well be that in the popular strata, less complex and more colorful approaches were in circulation already in the Middle Ages and they ultimately surfaced only later, at the beginning of the seventeenth century.

VIII

I would like to address now a question that is crucial for the understanding of most of the following discussions. Scholem, as we have seen above, emphasized the mystical, or visionary goal of the creation of the Golem; in the following I shall present a more moderate approach which will limit this goal mostly to the ecstatic Kabbalah. In the cases of the other discussions I prefer the epithet of magic, to be restricted as we have already indicated above. However, if the goal was neither the attainment of a mystical experience nor a "practical" magical purpose, how can we understand the intention of the masters who indulged in these practices? Details of my view will be found below. Here I would like to suggest the term "ergetic" coined by Amos Funkenstein,[23] in order to indicate a type of knowledge attained by action. By creating an anthropoid the Jewish master is not only able to display his creative forces, but may attain the experience of the creative moment of God, who also has created man in a similar way to that found in the recipes used by the mystics and magicians. Paraphrasing a statement of Glanvill,[24] we may describe the Golem practices as an attempt of man to know God by the art He uses in order to create man. On the other hand, the creation of the calf in the Middle Ages can be explained as a peculiar case of the general view that the combinations of letters are the sources of all the creatures. If our description of the meaning of the mystico-magical practices is adequate, then the creation of the Golem can be considered as anticipating the ergetic mode of knowledge, which consolidated only in the seventeenth century.

IX

The Jewish discussions concerning the creation of an artificial man can be divided into three main categories; two of them concern the creation of an entity called, roughly speaking, a Golem, while the third basically stems from alien sources and can be described as magical Hermeticism, dealing with the creation of living statues. The two types of Golem-discussions which are dominant in the Hebrew material are:

a) The descriptions of the nature of the Golem, which are not focused on the instructions or the techniques by which it was created;
b) The techniques of creating a Golem which may or may not include detailed discussions of the nature of the artificial man.

These two categories, in clear distinction from the Hermetical magic constructions of human-like statues, are of Jewish origin, and can be traced to much earlier traditions. Whether they are Jewish in their inception is a question that cannot be answered in a conclusive way. In the first chapter we shall survey parallels to the later Jewish discussions which may point to the adoption of certain elements from alien sources. In any case, it will be presumptuous to attempt to establish a "pure" Jewish origin for such a widespread practice. However, given the fact that the creation of an anthropoid was expressed in a canonical Jewish writing and no substantial opposition to it is extant, I consider the first two types of discussions as a category apart from the third one which is quoted in order to criticize it.

There are five main types of techniques which describe how to produce a Golem; three of them are evidently Ashkenazi and Northern French by their extraction; the fourth, that of R. Abraham Galante, seems to stem from the same circles, though it was committed to writing only at the end of the sixteenth century. The fifth, that of R. Abraham Abulafia, is apparently influenced by an Ashkenazi tradition, components of it being still extant in the various Ashkenazi versions of the Golem creation. The four basic techniques are:

a) The technique of R. Eleazar of Worms, disclosed in his *Commentary on Sefer Yeẓirah,* and corroborated by some discussions recurring in his other mystical writings.
b) Closely related to [a] is an anonymous text, which will be referred to in the following discussions as *Pe'ulat ha-Yeẓirah,* found in several manuscripts and still unprinted in its entirety. This is the most elaborate text dealing with this issue, and its influence is to be found beyond the Ashkenazi areas, in the Renaissance period.
c) The Pseudo-Sa'adyan *Commentary on Sefer Yeẓirah,* in print, though in a rather corrupt version. This seems to stem from the beginning of the second half of the thirteenth century and it is, apparently, of Northern French extraction.
d) Last but not least, the version preserved by R. Abraham Galante, which includes other elements, as we shall see below, may also be of Ashkenazi extraction.

X

All these techniques were committed to writing in the thirteenth century or later on, though the basic components might, and in my opinion they indeed did, predate this period. The common elements of these techniques are twofold: the material employed to create the Golem is dust, eventually kneaded with water, and the pronunciation of combinations of letters on the shaped body, in order to animate it. Indubitably, these two practices constitute the core of the Golem creation. Beyond these common elements, each of the four techniques include several details that are unique to it. Given the slight differences between these techniques, we may assume that one basic technique was the *Vorlage* which generated the various versions, that developed during the hidden period of the evolution of Jewish mysticism. The large gap of time which separates the period of the composition of *Sefer Yeẓirah* and the writing down of the different versions of the techniques to create an anthropoid, may be one of the reasons for the differentiation of what apparently was one basic tradition of the use of *Sefer Yeẓirah* as a magical composition. As we shall attempt to demonstrate in our discussion of the view of *Sefer Yeẓirah,* it is possible that the creation of man by the combination of letters was part of the original view of the book, and subsequently, the tradition related to the creation of the Golem emerged from this understanding of this mystical writing. If this assumption is correct, then we must allow for an ancient tradition which might serve as the common denominator for the medieval versions of the creation of an anthropoid.

The fact that the thirteenth century is the period when the most important techniques of creating a Golem were committed to writing is not a matter of accident. This is the period of the emergence of some major mystical phenomena which did not play any role on the scene of history beforehand. It is as part of the appearance of the massive corpora of mystical literature that the Golem techniques were committed to writing. Thus, we may assume that also in the earlier period, when the techniques were not written down, or at least not disseminated, those techniques were, nevertheless, part of a mystical literature, or literatures.

XI

The present study attempts to analyze the material related to the Golem in the speculative literature: magical and mystical. I shall not enter the often discussed reverberations of the Golem theme in the legends of the late eighteenth and early nineteenth centuries, but only to the extent that they reflect issues that help us gain a better understanding of the description of the nature of this anthropoid and its technique. Thus, the legendary and folkloristic material remains basically beyond the scope of our presentation. I attempt to cover in the following survey the pertinent discussions on the Golem since *Sefer Yeẓirah,* viz., those of the Ashkenazi Hasidism, Northern French texts, Kabbalistic and Hasidic descriptions of this being and the way of its fabrication. Likewise I have attempted to cover the most relevant occurrence of the Golem in the Halakhic literature. No doubt, as I have already remarked above, even after an intensive perusal of the wealth of manuscripts and huge quantity of printed material, it is impossible to exhaust the whole realm of the treatments of this topic. However, I hope that the following discussion will contribute a more variegated picture of the spectrum of concepts related to the theme of the Golem, both by the broadening of the relevant material and by contributing new perspectives as to the complexity and the problems involved in this topic. The need to cope with a variety of literary corpora, each one having a peculiar speculative frame of mind, and each of them constituting hundreds of texts is a great impediment to a more incisive analysis of part of the texts. Though I have attempted to present them by taking into consideration the intellectual framework of the tens of authors mentioned below, it is obvious that I could not survey the whole range of Jewish literature in an appropriate manner.

A substantial part of the material dealt with here is still in manuscript, some of the texts in several manuscripts. Though an examination of these manuscripts was done toward the completion of this work, and the manuscripts are mentioned here, the publication of the Golem texts in a critical way will contribute to a fuller encounter between the reader and the relevant material. I have adduced here only the passage related to the subject under discussion. I hope to publish the whole range of this material, manuscript and printed texts, in a critical edition which will constitute a series of appendixes to the Hebrew version of this book.

Notes

1. *Encyclopedia Judaica* (1971), vol. 7, col. 753, *Kabbalah,* p. 351.

2. Ibid., p. 26. Compare to the similar formulation of Joseph Dan in his *Three Types of Ancient Jewish Mysticism* (University of Cincinnati, 1984) p. 23: "it is not conclusively established that it [the creation of the Golem by combination of letters] is connected with our text of *Sefer Yeẓira.*" In his earlier *Esoteric Theology,* p. 53, Dan assumes that the Ashkenazi Hasidim used *Sefer Yeẓirah* only as a pretext in order to endow their interest in creating a Golem with the aura of antiquity and authority.

3. *On the Kabbalah,* p. 137.

4. "The Idea of the Golem," p. 175.

5. "The Idea of the Golem," p. 169, n.1.

6. This point is obvious in the title of the Hebrew version of the paper on the Golem; in English, this title should be translated: "The Image of the Golem in Its Tellurian and Magical Context."

7. "The Idea of the Golem," pp. 163–164.

8. Ibid., pp. 164, 165.

9. Ibid., pp. 191, 194–195. On this issue see also below, chapter 12.

10. *Kabbalah,* p. 40. Compare ibid., p. 352 where he states that the ritual of the Golem was "used, apparently, to symbolize the level of their achievement at the conclusion of their studies," referring again to the Ashkenazi Hasidim. Furthermore, he goes on to say there that "in the opinion of the mystics, the creation of the Golem has not a real, but only a symbolic meaning." See also below, *Summary* for a discussion of this thesis of Scholem.

11. *On the Kabbalah,* p. 137.

12. Ibid., p. 137.

13. See below Appendix B.

14. See *God & Golem, Inc.* (Cambridge, Mass. 1964). The relationship between cybernetics and the Golem are obvious already in the first book of Wiener, *Cybernetics or Control and Communication in the Animal and the Machine,* (New York, 1948).

15. "The Golem of Prague and the Golem of Rehovot," in his collection of articles, *The Messianic Idea in Judaism* (New York, Schocken 1971), pp. 335–340.

16. André Neher, *Faust et le Maharal de Prague, Le mythe et le Réel,* (Presse Universitaire de France, 1987).

17. See below, ch. 5, par. 3.

18. See Idel, *Kabbalah: New Perspectives,* pp. 20–22.

19. Cf. ch. 10, par. 7 a,b,c.

20. Idel, *Kabbalah: New Perspectives,* pp. 32–34, idem, "Enoch is Metatron," ed. J. Dan, *Early Jewish Mysticism* (Jerusalem, Hebrew University of Jerusalem, 1987), pp. 159–161. (Hebrew)

21. See below *Summary.*

22. Compare Idel, "The Concept of the Torah," p. 37, n.39.

23. See his *Theology and the Scientific Imagination from the Middle Ages to the Seventeenth Century* (Princeton, Princeton University Press, 1986), pp. 296–299.

24. Ibid., p. 298.

PART ONE

Ancient Traditions

1

Ancient Parallels

Creating artificial anthropoids was part of the early layers of magic. Some of them were simple automata, others were speaking statues, and only a few of them were entities fraught with spiritual capabilities. In the following remarks I shall limit the discussion only to those phenomena which could, and indeed I believe did, influence the subsequent Jewish material. Thus we shall shortly discuss Egyptian, Roman, and patristic views, dealing with the concept of an anthropoid and its functions in the Near East. Other similar phenomena, like the Chinese living statues,[1] must remain beyond the scope of our treatment.

I

"Small figures, usually of wax or clay, were an integral part of Egyptian magical practices."[2] At a certain phase of the "development" of these figures, they were designated as *ushabti,* a term translated as "answerer". The statue, located in the coffin, was conceived as capable of "answering" in lieu of the dead, in the moment the deceased was called to a certain work. Thus, the minuscule figurines were considered also as living statues, able to perform some tasks, and likewise to answer. This role of "answering" seems to be especially important for the understanding of the classical passage in the Talmudic tradition dealing with the creation of an anthropoid. As we shall see below, it was the silence of the anthropoid which served as a touchstone of his being a nonhuman entity, and thus liable to be destroyed by R. Zeira. Another intriguing feature of some of these *ushabti* is the inscriptions (magical spells) on their torso. As we shall see below, correspondences between letters and limbs will play an important role in the Jewish techniques of creating anthropoids.[3] Although this affinity is indeed very general, it may reflect a common ancient source as to the correspondence between language and organism.

II

According to several medieval versions of the creation of the anthropoid, this creature appears when the word *'emet,* truth, is written on its forehead.[4] All these versions are from the high Middle Ages and I am not acquainted with any ancient Jewish tradition related to this detail. Nevertheless, it seems that the fact that this word appears on the forehead is of extreme importance for establishing the antiquity of the source of the Golem legend. Let me start with the occurrence of the dictum "Truth has a *locus standi,* whereas Falsehood had no foothold."[5] As pointed out by Alexander Schreiber and Haim Schwarzbaum, this statement is reminiscent of a tradition found in Phaedrus's fable on Prometheus and Dolus, entitled *De Veritas et Mendacio.*[6] According to this ancient fable, Prometheus has formed Truth, an anthropoid female, out of fine clay. This figure was copied by his apprentice, Dolus, the Cunning. However, the latter did not have enough material to finish the copy of Truth, and his figure remained without feet. After the two statues had been baked and life had been breathed into them, Truth was able to walk, whereas the copy did not; this is the reason why it was conceived as Mendacity, the name of the imperfect copy: it has no feet.[7] It is pertinent to recall that Prometheus is, according to Greek mythology, the titan who created the first man,[8] and the creation of "Truth" is presumably part of his endeavour to establish a better society guided by truth.

The similarity between the Jewish dictum and the Greek description of mendacity is striking: the conception of falsehood as lacking feet is sufficient in order to assume a certain relationship between the two discussions. However, the scholars who have pointed out the surprising affinity between these texts, have ignored the similarity between the context of the occurrence of the dictum in the respective discussions: in the Greek fable it is connected to the fabrication of an artificial entity, in the medieval Hebrew sources Truth is inscribed on the forehead of an anthropoid, which apparently was supposed to walk, at least according to the Talmudic passage. Thus, two aspects of the Greek fable can be found in separate contexts in different Hebrew sources, one ancient and the other medieval;

these sources have, nevertheless, something in common, for they deal with the word *'emet.* Consequently, I would like to propose an hypothesis regarding the occurrence of the two elements in Jewish sources: a tradition similar to that inherited by Phaedrus, apparently of Greek extraction, and presumably predating the composition of the fable in Rome in the first century C. E., was known by Palestinian Jewish masters. The fact that only a part of it, that dealing with mendacity, was integrated in ancient Jewish material, may indicate that the entire story was already known to Jews in ancient times, though the part connected to the Truth was not written down, for unknown reasons. Prometheus' creation of the Truth out of clay and his breathing into it might have reminded some Jews of the creation of man out of dust and the induction of life by God, a fact which possibly facilitated the absorption of this tradition in Jewish sources.[9]

III

As Scholem has already mentioned, another striking parallel to the Jewish traditions on the artificial creation of an anthropoid is found in a legend related to the notorious Simon Magus, as he was described in the *Clementine Recognitiones.* There he was reported as boasting that he "can render statues animated, so that those who see them suppose that they are men."[10] However, the apex of his alleged achievements was the creation of a boy by a series of transformations of the air:

> 'Once upon a time, I, by my power, turning air into water, and water again into blood, and solidifying it into flesh, formed a new human creature—a boy—and produced a much nobler work than God the Creator. For He created a man from the earth, but I from air—a far more difficult matter; and again I unmade him and restored him in to air, but not until I had placed his picture and image in my bedchamber, as a proof and memorial of my work.' Then we understood that he spake concerning that boy, whose soul, after he had been slain by violence,[11] he made use of those services which he requires.[12]

The background for this attainment is the attempt to concur with the divine creation of man. In comparison to the creation out of a solid element, earth, used by God in his creation of Adam, Simon Magus, conceiving himself as the representative of the divine on earth, argues that he could form a human creature even from the air, which is condensed so as to become ultimately a human-like being. Thus, the material attainment is the main subject of this passage. However, according to the statement of his former followers, Simon used the soul of the boy in order to perform magical operations; the violent death of the boy is mentioned, and it is possible that there is a relationship between the violent death and the magical usage of the soul. According to some medieval texts, if someone is killed suddenly when thinking about a certain issue, his soul will continue to think, and act, according to the specific thought in the moment of his death. Is there here an implicit criticism of Simon that he killed the artificial boy in order to employ his soul for magical aims?

For our purpose, there are two issues of some possible importance for further discussions on the Golem. The matter used by Simon is air, which was transformed into a body by several transformations.[13] Ultimately, Simon will restore the body to air. Obviously, this body is not to be mistaken with the soul, which is reported as still serving the magical demands of the magician.[14] This etheral body is reminiscent of a much later Jewish tradition where the *Ẓelem,* identical with the term Golem, is conceived as an etheral body. Now, the same term, Golem, refers in medieval Hebrew both to a magically created body out of dust, and, in other contexts, to the spiritual body that differs from the soul, and is formed out of the air of Paradise. This overlapping of meaning may well be a matter of sheer coincidence; although this indeed may be a reasonable explanation, it is nonetheless worthwhile to mention another solution, which, though it cannot be presently proven, may be substantiated by the discovery of new material.

An hypothetical archaic Jewish tradition, dealing with the creation of a man, as exposed by Simon, used the term Golem. The meaning of this term was the external form of a human body, either created by God, as in the case of Adam, or by man. The possible elements of creation of this form were not important; they could include dust, air or other possibilities. Later on, a split occurred in the way this term was used in Hebrew; the basic sources dealing with the creation of an artificial man of dust continued to use the term Golem, and in such cases the material out of which man was created was dust; in other circles, the term designated also the bodily form, but it was connected to the structure of the body as represented by the term *Ẓelem,* the hidden image, which was paralleled in some texts by the Golem.[15] If this hypothesis will be substantiated by new data, then the testimony of Simon will demonstrate the existence of a deep concern in ancient Jewish magic and mysticism with the divine creative powers as exercized by expert magicians. As we shall see below in our discussion of *Sefer Yeẓirah,* such a concern was in existence at a slightly later period, when *Sefer Yeẓirah* was redacted. However, as some scholars have already remarked, there is a certain affinity between the Pseudo-Clementine texts and Jewish material, including *Sefer Yeẓirah.*[16]

On the other hand, the phrase used by the Pseudo-Clementine passage in relation to the created boy, "a new human creature," is reminiscent of the term "new man" used in relationship to the creation of man by Rava, as it was related and interpreted by R. Yehudah Barceloni.[17]

Notes

1. See Weynants-Ronday, *Les statues vivants* (Bruxelles, 1926), p. 26; E. M. Butler, *The Myth of the Magus* (Cambridge, Cambridge University Press, 1980), p. 80; Mueller, "Die Golemsage," pp. 1–3.

2. See Bob Brier, *Ancient Egyptian Magic* (New York, Quil, 1981), p. 170. The following discussion is based on the description of Brier.

3. See below ch. 2, pars. 3, 13; ch. 5, par. 5 and ch. 7, par. 1.

4. See below ch. 5, par. 8 and n. 58.

5. *BT Shabbat,* fol. 104a. Additional occurrences, in the versions of the *Alphabet of R. 'Aqiva'* were indicated by Haim Schwarzbaum, *Studies in Jewish and World Folklore* (Berlin, 1968), p. 379. See also Liebes, "Christian Influences," p. 60 n. 55.

6. Alexander Schreiber, "Die Luege hat keine Fuesse, zu den antiken Zusammenhaengen der Aggada," *Acta Antiqua,* vol. 9 (1961), pp. 305–306. Schwarzbaum, ibid., pp. 378–379.

7. Ben Edwin Perry, *Babrius and Phaedrus,* (London-Cambridge, Mass., Harvard University Press, 1965), pp. 376–379. On the similarity between the description of Prometheus as "figulus" and the conception of God as a potter in Isa. 29:16; see Ernst R. Curtius, *European Literature and the Latin Middle Ages,* trans. W. R. Trask (London, 1953), p. 544. See also below, ch. 3, n. 29. Compare also to R. Eleazar of Worms, *Sefer ha-Ḥokhmah,* p. 18.

8. Ovid, *Metamorphoses* 1–2.

9. In some other cases as well it is plausible that Prometheus-myths influenced ancient Jewish legends; see e.g., Jellinek, *Bet ha-Midrasch,* vol. 5, pp. XLVIII–XLIX.

10. *The Recognitions of Clement,* Book 2, ch. 9, *The Ante-Nicene Fathers,* vol. 8 (Grand Rapids, Michigan, 1951), p. 99. Compare also ibid., Book 3, chapter 57, p. 126; *The Clementine Homilies,* Homily 2, chapters 32, 34, p. 235; Homily 4, ch. 4, p. 252. See also Butler, (n. 1 above), pp. 80–82; Fossum, *The Name of God and the Angel of the Lord,* pp. 113–114 and Scholem, "The Idea of the Golem," p. 172.

11. A violent death was conceived as a way to prepare the soul of the murdered person to accomplish magical acts. Yoḥanan Alemanno mentioned the view

of some magicians who indicated that by killing someone condemned to a death penalty, when the murdered individual thought about a certain issue, his soul would continue to perform that issue, a fact that was used in order to manipulate the dead. Cf. *Sha 'ar ha-Ḥesheq,* fol. 43a, idem, *Collectanaea,* Ms. Oxford 2234, fol. 15a.

12. *Ante-Nicene Fathers* Book 2, Ch. 15, p. 101. Compare also *The Clementine Homilies,* Homily 2, ch. 26, pp. 233–234.

13. The term used for these transformations is *theiai tropai,* theurgical transformations. Scholem, "The Idea of the Golem," p. 172 guessed that this phrase corresponds to the later instructions to create a Golem, with the difference that the medieval Jews used letters in lieu of air. However, this opinion seems to be incorrect; the medieval Jewish Golem was created by the transformation induced into earth, not only in the letters. For the Jews the earth played the same role as the air in Simon Magus.

14. The distinction between the creation of the body, which is described in the Pseudo-Clementine text, and the soul, whose creation is not mentioned, apparently was implicit in the minds of those who composed these sermons. See a similar distinction in the text of *Genesis Rabbah* to be discussed below ch. 2, n. 44.

15. See below, Appendix A.

16. See Heinrich Graetz, *Gnosticizmus und Judentum* (Krotoschin, 1846) pp. 110–115; Epstein, *Mi-Qadmoniyot ha-Yehudim,* pp. 43–44, p. 200; Scholem, "The Idea of the Golem," pp. 172–173; Fossum, *The Name of God and the Angel of the Lord,* pp. 113–114; see now Shlomo Pines, "Points of Similarity between the Doctrine of the *Sefirot* in *Sefer Yeẓirah* and a Text from the Pseudo-Clementine *Homilies:* The Implications of this Resemblance," *Proceedings of the Israeli Academy of Science and Humanities*, vol. vii (1989) pp. 63–142.

17. See below ch. 4, and the discussions of Yoḥanan Alemanno, below ch. 11, nn. 11, 28.

2

Sefer Yeẓirah

I

The most influential text which shaped most of the later versions of the creation of the Golem is *Sefer Yeẓirah.*[1] This short text is an ancient cosmogonical and cosmological treatise,[2] which, as we shall see below, has also other important topics to offer, particularly pertinent to our discussion though they were presented in a concise and enigmatic way. Almost all the medieval and modern authors who dealt with the Golem issues have mentioned this text, the Golem being one of the most famous topics connected to *Sefer Yeẓirah.* Nevertheless, the creation of an anthropoid is not mentioned explicitly in this text, though many of the elements which constitute the later techniques for creation of a Golem were extracted from *Sefer Yeẓirah.* Therefore, before embarking on a larger investigation based on a literature which consists of various commentaries and interpretations of this work, let us attempt a survey of the pertinent passages in *Sefer Yeẓirah* itself.

More than any other text of ancient Jewish mysticism, *Sefer Yeẓirah* presented an elaborate cosmology which is grounded in the assumption that combinations of letters are both the technique to create the world and the material for this creation. Though in this process of creation there are also other components, namely, the *sefirot,* standing for the numerical infrastructure of the cosmos, the letters and their combinations preoccupied the ancient author of this treatise more than any other topic. Nevertheless, it is quite difficult to extract a systematic theory of the creative language from the condensed statements of *Sefer Yeẓirah.* We shall try to analyze here those parts of the book which served as *loci probantes* for the descriptions of the creation of the Golem in late medieval literature, in order to enable the reader to encounter the classical substratum of the later authors.[1] There are some discussions which, when combined, support the view that *Sefer Yeẓirah* indeed referred to the creation of a Golem; one deals with the theory of combinations of letters, and the other with the achievement of Abraham.

II

The first occurs in the second chapter of the book, which is devoted to linguistic theory:

> Twenty-two letters, He engraved [*ḥaqaq*] them and He extracted (or carved) [*ḥaẓav*] them and weighed them and permutated them and combined them, and He created by them the soul [*nefesh*] of all the formation [*yeẓur*] and the soul of all the speech [*dibbur*], which will be formed in the future. . . . Twenty-two basic[2] letters, fixed in the wheel, in the 231 gates.[3] And the wheel turns forward and backward, and the proof of it is that there is no greater of the good [things] than the delight [*'oneg*], and no worse [thing] than plague [*nega'*]. How did He weigh them and permutate them? *'Alpeh* [was combined] with all [the other letters] and all with *'aleph. Bet* with all [the other] and all with *Bet.* And so [the wheel] turns again and again [*ḥozeret ḥalilah*]. All the formation [*yeẓur*] and the whole speech [*vekhol ha-dibbur*] emerges out of one name.[4]

The emergence of the universe is described as related to all the possible permutations of the letters. Exploiting these combinations is tantamount to the exhaustion of all the possible formations and of all the possible languages. Thus the letters are conceived as the potential matter and the investigation of the possibilities immanent in the consonants of the Hebrew language is tantamount to the exploration of the elements which form the creation. The focus of the speculation is now the linguistic world presented as more important than the other universe, that of the three elements, air, water and fire. On the other hand, the way of creating the letters and arranging them in various ways is considered to be the clue to creation. The more obvious technique of combining the letters is the use of one wheel, or possibly two, in the ancient text, and several wheels in some of the medieval interpretations of this technique of combining letters. It is plausible that the combination was performed by the use of more than one wheel, which were moved in the two directions, forward and backward; as a result all the various combinations of the alphabet-letters were produced. The forward movement was considered to be the positive process, namely the combinations of letters extracted in this manner being the creative permutations, whereas the backward movement produced the negative combinations, which were considered as noxious, or destructive combinations.

A comparison of the descriptions of the effects of the combinations of letters as they appear in the above text may allow a distinction which will illuminate the view of *Sefer Yeẓirah.* At the beginning we are told that the permutations and the combinations of letters produce the "soul of the formation and the soul of the speech," whereas at the end, the book mentions only "all the formation and speech." The word *nefesh,* soul,[5] has disappeared. In the first case we are not told about the peculiar way of the permutation and combination of the letters, whereas in the second instance the technique was presented as the combination of each and every letter with the other letters. It is possible to assume that the second discussion elaborates a topic which was presented in detail at the beginning, and therefore there is no divergence between the techniques of combination as they were understood in the two cases. However, in order to accept such an explanation, we must ignore the difference between the effects of the two presentations. However, following a medieval commentary, we may assume that in the first case the combination produced the soul, or the essence of all the beings, whereas the second description presents the creation of the beings themselves. This distinction may account for the different formulations of the techniques: at the beginning the *ẓeruf,* the combination of letters, was mentioned, whereas in the second discussion it is absent. According to the medieval commentary, the first discussion deals indeed with the spiritual part of formation, the second one dealing only with the more material aspect. This distinction is reminiscent of another one, occurring in some techniques of creating a Golem in medieval sources, which assumes two stages of creation: one dealing with the combination of the twenty-two letters as described in *Sefer Yeẓirah,* and a second one dealing with the combination between the letters of the divine name, the Tetragrammaton, and the twenty-two letters.[6] The second type of combination is not mentioned in *Sefer Yeẓirah.* However, this book discusses the various combinations of the three letters of the Tetragrammaton, Y,H,W as part of the creative process, as sealing the extremities of the created cosmos. Therefore, we may assume that in the final stage of creating, the theory of *Sefer Yeẓirah* included, in one way or another, the combinations of the letters of the Tetragrammaton.

Whether a third type of combination, between the regular letters and those of the Tetragrammaton, was also hinted at in *Sefer Yeẓirah,* is not clear. If indeed such a mode of combination was in existence it could account for the formation of the soul versus the regular combinations which are responsible for the formation of the bodies. Again, such a distinction between the creation, or formation, of the souls at the beginning and that of the bodies later on, is partially corroborated by the Midrashic assumption that the souls of the righteous were created before the creation of the world.[7] The Midrashic statements dealing with this topic were already adduced in connection to the text of *Sefer Yeẓirah* by R. Yehudah Barceloni.[8]

III

The term translated as formation is *yeẓur*; this word appears several times in *Sefer Yeẓirah* in connection to the results of the combinations or permutations. Our translation is literal, and the question has to be raised as to what is the precise meaning of the word in our context. Regularly, this word stands for creatures, or as Scholem proposed, for creation in general; as such the sentences in *Sefer Yeẓirah* using this term may convey the creation of all creatures in general.[9] However, this possible reading is not the only probable one; at least in some cases in the Midrash, *yeẓur* designates a human being. In *Bereshit Rabba* we learn that God knows the thought which arises in the heart of man before it surfaces; this view is expressed immediately afterwards as a tradition in the name of R. Isaac in the following formulation: "Before the *yeẓur* was formed, his thought was already manifest to Him".[10] Here, the parallelism between the *yeẓur* and man is conspicuous. Even more explicit is the context of another Midrashic treatment of the term *yeẓur.* In *Pesiqta Rabbati,* we learn that four men were called *yeẓurim,* Adam, Jacob, Isaiah and Jeremiah, because in connection to their creation the verb *YẒR* was used in the Bible.[11] It seems that such a significance of the term *yeẓur* is consonant to the contexts of some liturgical texts, like the sentence in the *Nishmat* prayer where it is said that "the duty of all the *yeẓurim* . . . is to praise [God]." Consequently, an attempt to understand the *Sefer Yeẓirah* texts as dealing with the creation of a human creature, is not a linguistic innovation but can be supported by other material.[12]

It would be in order thus to look again at the relevant contexts in our treatise: by combining letters God created all the *yeẓur* and the speech. The distinction between creatures in general and speech is, logically, not better than the distinction between the creation of men and their languages. On the other hand, the phrase "the soul of all the formation" can be better understood when translated the soul of men than the souls of creatures.

We must recall that extensive passages in *Sefer Yeẓirah* deal with the correspondence between limbs, apparently designating the *yeẓur,* and the letters, conspicuously designating the *dibbur.* The several detailed discussions of the correspondence between these two topics and the pair *yeẓur-dibbur* allow the understanding of the *yeẓur* as a reference to an anthropoid. Moreover, this pair seems to be reflected also in the dichotomy between the two covenants which are unique to *Sefer Yeẓirah*: the covenant of the circumcision (*berit ha-ma'or*) and the covenant of tongue or language (*berit ha-lashon*).[13] The first term may reflect the creation of man by the penis, the second covenant being explicitly related to speech.[14] *Sefer Yeẓirah* indicates immediately after the mentioning of the second covenant that God "bound twenty-two letters into his language". According to another passage in *Sefer Yeẓirah,* occurring in several good manuscripts, God "created all the *yeẓur* and all the *dibbur,* in one name, and the proof-sign for this are the twenty-two things in one body".[15] The body referred to here is not described in this context, and, in principle it may be any sort of body; however, in *Sefer Yeẓirah* there is only one body which is mentioned in the context of the number twenty-two, viz., the human body. I assume that the one name is a divine name formed out of the twenty-two letters, and it stands for the unified crystallization of the alphabet,[16] whereas the body stands for the anthropomorphic formation which emerges as the result of the application of a technique related to the twenty-two letters. This view of the whole range of the alphabet as forming a divine name and at the same time a body, according to our assumption, an anthropomorphical structure, is paralleled by an ancient text, probably influenced by Jewish concepts.[17] In Irenaeus' *Adversus Haereses* I, 14:1–3, Marcos the Gnostic describes an anthropomorphic body whose limbs correspond to a divine name. As scholars have already pointed out, there are some striking correspondences between the text quoted in the name of Marcos and Jewish views,[18] and these correspondences seem to be more numerous than scholars have assumed.[19] I would like to add to the already known affinities the correspondence between the text of *Sefer Yeẓirah,* as interpreted above, and Marcos' parallelism between letters and limbs, as well as the fact that the whole alphabet constitutes a divine name and at the same time corresponds to an anthropomorphic structure. It should be mentioned that in the description of Marcos two letters correspond to each of the limbs. This is not the case in the correspondence between letters and limbs in *Sefer Yeẓirah*; however, just as in the descriptions of Marcos, the later interpretation of *Sefer Yeẓirah* emphasizes the combinations of two letters as part of the creative processes of the anthropoid.[20] Moreover, as we shall see below, in our discussion of the Sarugian Kabbalah and its possible sources, [21] there is a correlation between the combinations of letters of *Sefer Yeẓirah* and an anthropomorphical figure, which is connected to the gigantic *Shi'ur Qomah* of ancient Jewish mysticism.[22] It should also be noted that both Marcos and *Sefer Yeẓirah* refer to a body, *soma* and *guf,* in the case of the former, the body of truth.[23]

We may therefore conclude that from the philological point of view, it is reasonable to assume that a reading of the texts of *Sefer Yeẓirah* as discussions of the creation of men is a possibility which makes sense; consequently, the understanding of the medieval commentators who extracted the creation of the Golem from the sentences which include the term *yeẓur* is not problematic, at least not from the philological point of view.[24]

IV

Let us examine another topic which is pertinent to the question of creating a Golem. At the end of *Sefer Yeẓirah* there are several sentences which occur only in some of the versions of the treatise, dealing with the activity of Abraham:

> Because Abraham our ancestor, blessed be his memory, contemplated and looked, saw and investigated, understood and engraved, extracted and combined and formed, and succeeded, the Master of the Universe was revealed to him and He made him sit [*hoshivo*][25] in His bosom and He kissed him upon his head and called him My beloved and put him [as] his son.[26]

The acts of Abraham seem to reflect the acts of God, who is portrayed as combining letters in order to create; however, at least in one instance it is obvious that the last statement is related also to the imperative of the book, as it was stated in the discussion of the ten *sefirot*:

> Understand by [your] wisdom, and be wise by your understanding, observe them and investigate them and know, and think and form,[27] and set up [*leha'amido*] the thing on the [proper] place and return [*hashev*] the Former to His throne[28] [*mekhono*].[29]

It is not so much the repetition of the verbs in the two texts which concern us here as the fact that in the last quotation the student of the book was requested to understand the constitutive numbers, the *sefirot,* then to investigate them, and afterward, to act in a certain way which is not clear, that is, to place the thing on its proper place. In other words, *Sefer Yeẓirah* was, according to some statements, not only a cosmogonic treatise, explaining what happens in *illo tempore,* but also a directive to certain types of actions which are explicitly connected to the actions of God, and also, apparently, have an influence on God Himself. As to the meaning of the return of God to His throne, it is interesting to elaborate upon the possible implications of the enigmatic remark of the author of *Sefer Yeẓirah.* I assume that the author's understanding was that an inadequate vision of the creative processes was tantamount to the displacement of God from His throne of glory. Only when someone understands appropriately the course of creation is he able to mend the situation, apparently by a certain repetition of the acts of God which will prove, by the effectiveness of these acts, that God is indeed the Former. He, apparently, can convince the sceptics, or the idolaters, as to the correct religious faith.[30] In this context, it would be interesting to discuss the possible implication of the term *mekhono.* This term, and the whole context quoted above, was important enough that the author of *Sefer Yeẓirah* used it again when referring to the seven double letters.[31] Immediately afterwards the holy palace is mentioned, as located in the centre of the six cosmic directions.[32]

It is possible, from the philological point of view, to interpret this word metaphorically, on the basis of the expression found in Ezra 2:68 in connection with the house of God, "to set it up in its place," *leha'amido 'al mekhono.* This interpretation fits our proposal above as to the restoration of God as the Former, in an hypothetical controversy with persons who would deny it. However, even if this is a correct interpretation of the intention of the ancient treatise, I believe that here there is still a more precise significance to *makhon.* In several biblical verses, *makhon* occurs in the context of alluding to the presence of the divine in a certain place, specifically in the phrase *makhon shivto.*[33] Therefore it will not be an overemphasis to conclude that the word *makhon* here refers to something similar to the concept of divine throne, or *merkavah* in the Heikhalot literature. Such a reading is corroborated by the interest in the divine throne in *Sefer Yeẓirah,* in the *Heikhal,* namely the divine palace which is located in the middle of the universe. As Baeck has already remarked, the concept of the center was crucial for the theory of *Sefer Yeẓirah,* and the different terms referring to it, like *makhon, kisse' ha-kavod, ma'on* or *heikhal ha-Qodesh* are synonyms.[34]

Moreover, scholars have given attention to an obvious affinity between the description of Abraham at the end of *Sefer Yeẓirah*, and the description of an important ancient Jewish mystic, R. Eleazar ben 'Arakh[35]. In the two cases some identical verbs recur, and even the other verbs in these contexts have similar meanings. To this important observation should be added the fact that at the end of the eulogy of R. Eleazar ben 'Arakh, R. Yoḥanan ben Zakkai mentions his ability "to deal with the account of the Chariot," *lidrosh be-ma'aseh merkavah.* This mentioning of the account of *merkavah* is reminiscent of the mentioning of the *makhon* in *Sefer Yeẓirah*.[36] In both cases the two places of residence occur after an enumeration of verbs which are similar. Moreover, if the hypothesis of Liebes[37] regarding the meaning of the term *ma'aseh* as having a theurgical connotation will be corroborated by additional material, then the significance of the return of the Former to His throne will be easily understood not only as the recognition of the real Former, but also as the restoration of God to His throne after an hypothetical displacement. Abraham, therefore, was portrayed as the first person who investigated the lore of the book and was able to succeed. The exact nature of this success was not explained in the book. Modern scholars considered, correctly I believe, that this success was that of an operator who was able to accomplish his act,[38] not simply an achievement of someone interested in contemplation or meditation alone.[39] Accordingly, the mention of the making of souls by Abraham in this context was understood by medieval authors and modern scholars as the creation of man, i.e., the creation of man by the technique of combination of letters.[40] It would be interesting to add in this context a polemical nuance which may be detected in the activity of Abraham in Haran. According to several Midrashic texts, Haran was considered to be the place of idolatry, understood as the worship of statues.[41] This may be the background of the unity of God which is emphasized time and again in *Sefer Yeẓirah*, which was perceived as the Book of Abraham. This figure was portrayed already in the Midrash as the prototype of the person who was able to discover the unity of God from the contemplation of the processes going on in the universe.[42] Moreover, according to a certain commentator on *Sefer Yeẓirah*, the creation of the souls is to be understood as the attempt of a beloved to present in public the powers of his lover;[43] in other words, the creation of the souls in Haran can be understood as the counteraction to idolatry by presenting the powerful letters which bear witness to the Creator of the world, as against the beliefs of the idolaters. In opposition to the statues of the idolaters, Abraham created men; according to the medieval understanding of *Sefer Yeẓirah*, "men" refer to anthropoids created by the means of *Sefer Yeẓirah*. The question is: when exactly was the biblical verse related to Abraham and when did the "souls" become a slogan for magical creation? This understanding is crucial for a clearer interpretation of the end of *Sefer Yeẓirah*. Another context, already pointed out by Scholem, is important for a more appropriate understanding of our issue. A second century Tanna, R. Yosei ben Zimra[44] asserted, in relation to the verse in Gen. 12:5, that Abraham and Sarah made souls, "if all the creatures in the world gathered together to make a single gnat and put a soul into it, they would not succeed."[45] Scholem understood this statement as an indication that it was impossible to create a gnat at all.[46] However, at least in some versions of this dictum, which follow the formulation adduced above, there is a clear distinction between the creation of the gnat and the act of imparting a soul into it. The term used in order to negate the possibility to impart a spiritual entity into the gnat is in all the versions *neshamah*; in the biblical verse dealing with the activity of Abraham, the term is *nefesh.* The passage of R. Yosei can be understood as pointing to a position similar to that of the text in the *Sanhedrin* discussion. In both cases the assumption is that the higher spiritual faculty cannot be conferred upon the artificial being. In lieu of the reading of Scholem, which emphasized the impossibility to create the gnat, what should be stressed is the impossibility to confer a soul upon it. The implication of this Midrashic text would accordingly be that an artificial body cannot be bestowed with a soul, be it an anthropoid or a gnat. The use of the word *neshamah* negates the human capacity to confer the highest spiritual faculty upon an artificial body. Thus a reading of the Midrash permits a view of the *Sanhedrin* text, to be discussed in the next chapter, as dealing with the limitation of man insofar as the spiritual facet of the creation is concerned. If a second century author had already distinguished between the corporeal and spiritual creations, then it may have served as a background for allowing Abraham a creation of an anthropoid which does not possess a *neshamah.*

V

Another pertinent treatment connected to Abraham is found in *Genesis Rabbah*; Abraham was given the letter *he,* which changed his name from Abram to Abraham.[47] This addition can be interpreted as the addition of the name of God as summarized by the letter *he,* it being the letter by which the earth was created.[48] Does it imply that Abraham became a potential creator of earth, or of a world, as in the case of the righteous mentioned in the *Sanhedrin* passage? This assumption seems to be endorsed by another passage found in the same Midrash:

> And he [Melkhiẓedeq] blessed him [Abraham] and said:[49] "Blessed be Abram by God the Most High, Creator of heaven and earth." From whom did he acquire them? . . . R. Isaac said: "Abraham used to entertain wayfarers and, after they had eaten, he would say to them, 'Say a blessing!' They would ask, 'What should we say'?" He replied: "[Say:] Blessed be the God of the universe of whose bounty we have eaten." Then the Holy One, blessed be He, said to him, "My name was not known among My creatures, and you have made it known among them. I will regard you as though you were associated

> with Me in the creation of the world." Hence it is written: "And he blessed him and said: Blessed be Abram by God the Most High, who has created heaven and earth!"[50]

This view of the patriarch as an associate to the act of creation is reminiscent, as Fossum has correctly proposed, of the theory of *Sefer Yeẓirah.*[51] It implies that Abraham was conceived not only as the person who was able to create souls, or persons, by the means of the combination of letters, but also was considered as a potential creator. This view of the patriarch is corroborated by the homiletic interpretation through a transposition of the letters of the form *behibar'am,* "as they were created," stated in the context of heaven and earth, as *be-'Avraham,* namely "by Abraham." This interpretation is also found in *Genesis Rabbah.*[52]

A question to be addressed in detail in this context is the meaning of the biblical verse adduced by *Sefer Yeẓirah* dealing with the creation of souls by Abraham and Sarah. As Scholem has already remarked, the common interpretation of the verse in the ancient Jewish literature, with the exception of *Sefer Yeẓirah,* is that this pair converted people to Judaism. Thus, the mystical treatise seems to be an exception in the way it understands this verse.[53] However, it is of interest to mention here a Talmudic statement commenting upon this verse. In *Sanhedrin* it is written that whoever teaches Torah to the son of his friend can be conceived of as if he made him, *'asa'*o.[54] As we shall see later on, this verb will occur also in the case of the creation of Adam as a Golem in the Midrashic literature and in the medieval sources in connection to the creation of the Golem itself.[55] The ground for this interpretation is the verse about Abraham's activity in Haran. No doubt, the intention of the Talmudic masters was that instruction in matters of religion is tantamount to creation, whereas the preceding stage of the child, or of the idolater, is that of an imperfect man. Thus, the verb *'sh* and the verse of Gen. 12:5 were understood as expressions for the addition of the spiritual to the material aspect of a human being.

VI

In any case, at least in one instance, it seems that the anonymous author of *Sefer Yeẓirah* hinted at a certain relationship between the knowledge of the content of this book, a certain operation and the unity of God: "Know, and think and form, that the Master is Unique and the Former is one, without a second."[56] Here, the recognition of the unity of the creator is explicitly included in the same sequel of acts with knowledge and action. The assumption that *Sefer Yeẓirah* serves the purposes of asserting the uniqueness of God is indicated in a lengthy discussion of the relationship between Abraham and the cosmological gnosis included in this book. Abraham, according to this late Midrashic source:

> sat alone and meditated on it, but could understand nothing until a heavenly voice went forth and said to him: "Are you trying to set yourself up as my equal? I am one and have created the *Sefer Yeẓirah* and studied it; but you by yourself cannot understand it. Therefore take a companion, and meditate on it together, and you will understand it." Thereupon, Abraham went to his teacher Shem, the son of Noah, and sat with him for three years and they meditated on it until they knew how to create a world. And to this day, there is no one who can understand it alone, two scholars [are needed], and even they understand it only after three years, whereupon they can make everything their hearts desire. Rava, too, wished to understand the book alone. Then Rabbi Zeira said to him: It is written,[57] "A sword is upon the single, and they shall dote," that is to say: a sword is upon the scholars who sit individually, each by himself, and concern themselves with the Torah. Let us then meet and busy ourselves with *Sefer Yeẓirah*. And so they sat and meditated on it for three years and came to understand it. As they did so, a calf was created by them and they slaughtered it in order to celebrate their conclusion of the treatise."[58]

The understanding of *Sefer Yeẓirah* by oneself, without a companion, is conceived here as the prerogative of God. Man can achieve the utmost knowledge of the creative powers included in it, even to create a world, but it must be done with a companion. In any case, in the above book there is at least one sentence regarding the inference of the unity of God from the study of *Sefer Yeẓirah*; Abraham is portrayed as being able to innovate the content of the Torah and of *Sefer Yeẓirah* out of his own profoundity. In connection to statements of *Sefer Yeẓirah*, it is said that "He studied them and announced them to his disciples so that they will believe in the unity of God."[59]

The fact that the creation of the world is mentioned just before the mentioning of the names of the two Amoraim indicates that the whole context of the *Sanhedrin* passage was before the author of this passage; in the former the righteous are portrayed as being able to create a world, just before the sentences concerning the creation of a man and a calf. The probability of a relationship between the Talmudic text on the creation of the Golem and the view of *Sefer Yeẓirah* itself on the success of Abraham seems to be enhanced by (1) the fact that just before the discussion of the creation of man, the Talmudic text mentions the possibility of creating a world, and (2) the Midrashic view that Abraham was connected, even if only by the homiletic interpretation of his name, to the creation of heaven and earth. As we know, the major topic of *Sefer Yeẓirah* is the exposition of the way the world was created.

VII

The affinity between the creation of the world and the creation of the Golem is apparently reflected in the sequel of some recipes extant in manuscripts. The first of these two recipes deal with the creation of the Golem according to R. Eleazar of Worms, the second with the creation of heaven and then again with the creation of an anthropoid.[60] Though there is a surprising discrepancy between the knowledge of how to create a world and how to create a calf, as in the text quoted above from R. Yehudah Barceloni, it seems unreasonable to assume, as Scholem does,[61] that the creation of the world is "purely contemplative". As the recipe describing the creation of heaven demonstrates, it was not contemplative in its nature, but a magical act.[62]

Last but not least: the later part of *Sefer Yeẓirah* deals with the detailed relationship between Hebrew letters and human limbs, on one hand, and planets, constellations and the Zodiac, on the other. The precise significance of these double relations is not explicitly indicated in the book, but the assumption that the book deals also with the creation of an artificial man, not only with the creation of the world, allows the possibility that there is a hidden affinity between the letters as combined as part of the process of permutations and the letters as related to the human body.[63] If we may follow the assumption of the medieval commentators, such an affinity is crucial for the understanding of the creation of an artificial man. If this hidden relationship was in existence as part of the system of the book, it must have implied also something more; the astronomical relationship between letters and heavenly bodies would allow an assumption that the creation of man by letters, explicitly indicated in *Sefer Yeẓirah*, implies also an operation of an astrological nature. To this point we shall turn later on.[64]

VIII

Some more general reflections on *Sefer Yeẓirah* may help us understand the following discussions better. The attribution of the work to Abraham, found in several manuscripts and repeated by several medieval authors, seems to have an affinity to the conception of Abraham in the Midrash as an exalted individual. Indeed, such an affinity may be understood as implying that the unique status of this patriarch fascinated early Tannaitic figures, like R. Isaac of Napḥa, and these traditions were probably cultivated by the anonymous author, or authors, of *Sefer Yeẓirah.* In any case, the conception of Abraham as the beloved of God, emphasized at the end of this treatise, seems to parallel the importance of Moses, the legislator. The image of Abraham the progenitor versus his descendant, the legislator, corresponds also to the difference between the Bible, less interested in cosmogony and more in religious behaviour, and *Sefer Yeẓirah*, focused as it is on the question of the divine and human creation. The fact that the latter is not even mentioned in the former is relevant for our discussion.[65] The later traditions, where Abraham is commanded to study *Sefer Yeẓirah* with a companion, and thus to avoid a possible comparison between him and God, may indicate that an attempt was made in these sources to attenuate the exalted status of Abraham as expressed in *Sefer Yeẓirah* itself.

Notes

1. We cannot adduce here the whole literature pertinent to this work. As for the most recent discussions of the antiquity of the book, whose ideas may have originated already in the second century C. E., see Liebes, *The Sin of 'Elisha',* p. 116; A. P. Hayman "Sefer Yeṣira and the Heikhalot Literature," ed. J. Dan, *Early Jewish Mysticism* (Jerusalem, Hebrew University of Jerusalem, 1987), pp. 82–83; J. Dan, *Three Types of Ancient Jewish Mysticism* (University of Cincinnati, 1984), pp. 20–24 and the article of Shlomo Pines, see ch. 1, n. 16.

2. *'Otiyyot Yesod.* The other possible translation would be the twenty-two fundamental or elemental letters. In any case, the intention was the formative nature of the letters, which by their combinations, will constitute the fabric of the universe. See Gruenwald, "Critical Notes," p. 489.

3. On the issue of these 231 combinations of twenty-two letters, see David R. Blumenthal, "The Creator and the Computer" in ed., M. Wohlgelernter, *History, Religion, and Spiritual Democracy: Essays in Honor of Joseph L. Blau* (New York: Columbia University Press, 1980), pp. 114–129. Each of the combinations of two letters is called a gate, *sha'ar.*

4. According to the regular division of the book, these sentences are the last two dicta of the second chapter. However, there is evidence that the last words of the above quote were connected to the statements that constitute the beginning of the third chapter. See e.g. R. Yehudah Barceloni's *Commentary on Sefer Yeẓirah,* p. 211. For another translation and explanation, see Scholem, "The Idea of the Golem," p. 198.

5. The meaning of the term *nefesh* in *Sefer Yeẓirah* is not so clear; in several

instances it stands, just as in Biblical Hebrew, for the whole human person, or organism. However, in our context, when the *nefesh* of the speech or of the formation, i.e., the creature, is meant, it seems that the soul is intended.

6. On the two stages of creation see below ch. 5, par. 1; ch. 7, par. 1.

7. On the pre-existence of souls in ancient Jewish literature, see, e.g., *Genesis Rabbah,* section 8, par. 7, p. 61.

8. See his *Commentary on Sefer Yeẓirah*, p. 208, and Georges Vajda, *Recherches sur la philosophie et la kabbale dans la pensée juive du Moyen Age* (Paris, Mouton & Co. 1962) p. 375, n. 1.

9. Scholem, "The Idea of the Golem," p. 168.

10. Section 9: par. 3, p. 69.

11. M. Friedmann, ed., *Pesiqta Rabbati* (Wien, 1880), fol. 129a. See also ch. 8 n. 17.

12. See, e.g., the poetic material printed by Daniel Goldschmidt, *Maḥzor Yamim Nora' im* vol. 1 (Jerusalem, 1980), pp. 89, 92, 103, 225; ibid., vol. 2, p. 497. For the use of *yeẓur* in the sense of an anthropoid, see below in our discussion of the Pseudo-Sa'adiyan *Commentary on Sefer Yeẓirah*, and Abraham Abulafia's view in his *'Imrei Shefer,* Ms. Münich 40, fol. 247b: "The power of imagination [*koaḥ ha-ẓiyyur*] is mingled with the creative power [*koaḥ ha-yoẓer*] and the creaturely power [*koaḥ ha-yeẓur*], until the fortieth year, which is in the image of the forty days." It is obvious from the general context, (see Idel, *The Mystical Experience,* pp. 198–199, 222) that the figure forty refers to the development of man, and thus the *yeẓur,* is not a creature in general, but a human being.

13. Gruenwald, *SY* par. 61, p. 174; Hyman, "Some Observations," p. 178. It should be emphasized that the occurrence of the covenant of circumcision in this work has something to do with the alleged authorship of this book, Abraham who was the first biblical figure who was circumcised. On the two covenants, see Nicolas Sed, "Le Memar samaritain, Le Sefer Yeṣira et les trente-deux sentiers de la sagesse," *Revue d'histoire des religions,* vol. 170 (1966), pp. 174–175.

14. See Elliot Wolfson, "Circumcision, Vision of God and Textual Interpretation: From Midrashic Trope to Mystical Symbol," *History of Religions,* vol. 27 (1987), pp. 206–207. In Hebrew *'ot* stands for both circumcision and letter. The relationship between phonocentric and phallocentric conceptions has been recently discussed by Jacques Derrida; see Richard Rotry, "Derrida on Language, Being and Abnormal Philosophy," *Journal of Philosophy,* vol. 74 (1977) pp. 673–681; Robert Solomon, "Sexual Paradigms," ed. Alan Soble, *The Philosophy of Sex: Contemporary Readings* (Totawa, New Jersey: Rowman and Littlefield, 1980), pp. 89–98 and the rejoinder of Hugh T. Wilder, ibid., pp. 98–109. See also below ch. 5, n. 88.

15. Gruenwald, *SY,* p. 150, par. 22; see also ibid., p. 148, par. 19.

16. See Scholem, "The Name of God", p. 75.

17. See, however, the opinion of Cohen, *The Shi'ur Qomah, Liturgy and Theurgy,* p. 39 who proposes to see in the Hebrew material of *shi'ur qomah* a response to the Gnostic treatment of the gigantic anthropos and the letters inscribed on it. The opposite view was expressed in the studies referred to below in nn. 19–20.

18. Gruenwald, *SY,* p. 149, par. 20, in the *varia lectiones* and p. 150, par. 22.

19. Moses Gaster "Das Schiur Komah" in *Studies and Texts,* (London, 1925–1928), pp. 1342–1345; Scholem, "Shi'ur Qomah—The Mystical Image of the Divinity," in *Elements of the Kabbalah and Its Symbolism,* pp. 161–163, Gedaliahu G. Stroumsa, "Form(s) of God: Some Notes on Metatron and Christ," *Harvard Theological Review,* vol. 76:3 (1983), p. 281.

20. See Idel, "The World of the Angels," pp. 2–15.

21. See below ch. 10, par. 7c and especially n. 99.

22. See above n. 3 and Stroumsa (n. 19 above), p. 280 n. 55.

23. See Idel, (n. 20 above), pp. 2–6.

24. It should be noted that ancient Jewish liturgical literature, the *piyyuṭ,* also uses the term *yeẓur* with the meaning man. See Aharon Mirsky, ed., *R. Yosse ben Yosse, Poems* (Jerusalem, 1977), p. 221: *nishmot ha-yeẓurim* which refer to the souls of the righteous. Thanks are due to Professor Menaḥem Schmelzer who kindly drew my attention to this phrase.

25. This verb is one of the passive forms of the root *yshv,* which recurs in another context of *Sefer Yeẓirah,* to be quoted and analyzed below. The use of the verb in this book can be summarized as follows: man enthrones God by the use of the technique that God used; God enthrones Abraham because of his successful use of the device used by God Himself.

26. Gruenwald, *SY,* p. 174, par. 61. See also Scholem, "The Idea of the Golem," pp. 169–170.

27. On the last three verbs, see the discussions referred to in n. 35 below, where these verbs occur again.

28. For the reason of this translation see our discussion below.

29. Gruenwald, *SY,* p. 141, par. 4; idem, "Some Critical Notes on the First Part of *Sefer Yeẓirah,*" *REJ,* vol. 132 (1973), pp. 488–489. See also below, on the discussion in par. 6.

30. See *Genesis Rabbah* section 63: par. 7 to be quoted below in this chapter, where the sequel of recognition and creative power is rather different: there

the recognition of the unity of divinity culminates with the transformation of Abraham into a cooperator in the act of creation, whereas in our case the act of creation is the avenue for the recognition of the divine unity.

31. Gruenwald, *SY,* p. 157, par. 38.

32. Ibid.

33. See Ex., 15:17; I Kings 8:13, etc.

34. See Leo Baeck, "Zum Sefer Jezira," *MGJW,* vol. 70 (1926), p. 375, n. 8. This author considered the idea of the center as the result of the influence of Neoplatonism on *Sefer Yeẓirah.* See also Nicolas Sed, "Le Sefer Yesira: L'edition critique, le texte primitif, la grammaire et la metaphysique," *REJ,* vol. 132 (1973), pp. 521–522.

35. See Josef Gugenheimer, "Ueber Einen in der Koeniglichen Bibliothek zu Muenchen handschriftlich sich befinden Commentar zu Sefer Jezira," *Literaturblatt des Orients,* vol. 19 (1848), p. 294; Liebes, *The Sin of 'Elisha',* pp. 117–118.

36. Ibid., pp. 119–120, where Liebes adduced also the passage from *Sefer Yeẓirah* on *hashev 'al mekhono,* without, however, emphasizing the possible affinity between the *merkavah* and the *makhon.* Compare also Gruenwald, "Critical Notes," p. 489.

37. Liebes, ibid., pp. 121–122.

38. Scholem, "The Idea of the Golem," pp. 169–170; Liebes, ibid., pp. 117–118.

39. It seems that there can be no question as to the contemplative and mystical significance implied in the description of Abraham at the end of *Sefer Yeẓirah*; the parallel suggested by Gugenheimer and Liebes strongly corroborates this reading. Compare, however, Dan, *Three Types,* (n. 1 above), p. 23.

40. Scholem, "The Idea of the Golem," pp. 170–171.

41. Louis Ginsburg, *The Legends of the Jews* (Philadelphia, 1968), vol. 1, pp. 213-217.

42. Ibid. See David Flusser, "Abraham and the Upanishads," *Immanuel,* vol. 20 (1986), pp. 53–61 where the author discusses the fact that the revelation of God occurred after Abraham's investigation; this sequel is also evident in *Sefer Yeẓirah,* which concurs on this point with the similar stand in the Midrash.

43. See the view of the Pseudo-Sa'adiyan *Commentary on Sefer Yeẓirah* Ms. Münich, 40, fol. 77a and the view quoted in R. Moses Botarel's *Commentary on Sefer Yeẓirah* from a spurious work of R. Sa'adyah Gaon, fol. 13a.

44. The version of this passage in *Genesis Rabbah* is faulty since there is no second century Tanna named Eleazar ben Zimra; this version was accepted by

Scholem, "The Image of the Golem," p. 393. I have therefore preferred the name R. Yosei ben Zimra on the grounds of the parallel found in *Genesis Rabbah,* section 84: par. 4, p. 1004. Though Scholem is not correct about the identity of the name of the Tanna, it seems that he is correct about the antiquity of the dictum, as it is mentioned already in L. Finkelstein, ed., *Sifre ad Deuteronomium,* 6:5 (Berlin, 1939), p. 54.

45. See *Genesis Rabbah,* section 39: par. 13, pp. 378–379.

46. Scholem, "The Idea of the Golem," p. 171.

47. *Genesis Rabbah,* 39:11, p. 375.

48. Ibid. 12:10, pp. 108–109.

49. Gen. 14:19.

50. *Genesis Rabbah,* section 63: par. 19, p. 421 (and the parallels quoted by the editors there.)

51. See Fossum, *The Name of God and the Angel of the Lord,* pp. 246–247.

52. Gen. 2:4; *Genesis Rabbah,* section 12: par. 9; Fossum, ibid., pp. 253–254.

53. See "The Idea of the Golem," pp. 171–172.

54. *Sanhedrin,* fol. 97b.

55. See below ch. 3, par. 4 and n. 54.

56. Gruenwald, *SY,* par. 6, p. 142.

57. Jer. 50:36. See also below ch. 9, n. 34 and ch. 15 n. 16. The relationship between the imperative of studying issues related to cosmology and the uniqueness of God is implied in R. Eleazar of Worms, *Sefer ha-Ḥokhmah,* p. 26.

58. See R. Yehudah Barceloni's *Commentary on Sefer Yeẓirah*, p. 268, according to the translation in Scholem, "The Idea of the Golem," p. 176. See also Scholem, ibid., pp. 177–178.

59. Barceloni, *Commentary on Sefer Yeẓirah,* p. 100.

60. See Ms. British Library, 753 fol. 66a–67a; Ms. Cambridge, Add. 647, fol. 18a–19a and below *Summary.*

61. "The Idea of the Golem," p. 178.

62. See above n. 60 and below *Summary.*

63. On the affinity between the relationship of the letters to the human limbs in *Sefer Yeẓirah* and the similar relationship in a Mandaean text, see Dan

Cohn-Sherbok, "The Alphabet in Mandean and Jewish Gnosticism," *Religion,* vol. II (1981), pp. 227–234.

64. See ch. 6, par. 1–2.

65. See Hyman, "Some Observations," pp. 180–183.

3

Talmud and Midrash

The Talmud

I

The most influential passage treating the possibility to create an artificial human being is found in a Talmudic passage:

> Rava said: If the righteous wished, they could create a world, for it is written,[1] "Your iniquities have been a barrier between you and your God." For Rava created a man[2] and sent him to R. Zeira. The Rabbi spoke to him but he did not answer. Then he said: "You are [coming] from the pietists: Return to your dust."[3]

Two points seem to be pertinent to the proper understanding of this passage: though the magical powers of the righteous are extraordinary, their being able to create a world, Rava himself was not able to create a creature who could speak. I assume that the term describing those who may create a mute creature, *ḥavrayya,* is not to be understood, as some scholars have suggested, as "magicians"[4] but as pietists. Such an understanding is corroborated by the parallel between the righteous who are able to create worlds and those who create an artificial man, and by the significance of the term, *ḥaver,* in some Talmudic texts, where it refers to those persons who meticulously perform the minutia of Halakhic prescriptions.[5] The juxtaposition of the first passage to the second one seems to be helpful also in the deliniation of these two related categories of persons; in both cases a certain obstacle is present which prevents the righteous from actualizing their potentialities. In the first case this hindrance is mentioned explicitly, the "iniquities", whereas in the second the limitation is implicit in the impossibility to create a speaking creature.[6] If Rava was presented as the person who is aware of the limitations of the righteous, the second passage can be envisioned as an illustration of such a shortcoming *de facto.* The creation of the artificial man would, presumably, be a touchstone not only for the creative powers of a pietist, but also a test for his religious perfection. Would he be able to create a speaking man, he would perform an operation similar to the creation of Adam by God, this similarity being, presumably, a sign that there are no iniquities which separate him from God. We may summarise our attempt to explain the Talmudic text as follows: the pietists, or the righteous, are endowed indeed with extraordinary powers which are, however, apparently limited by the inescapable iniquities of these persons. A major argument which fosters the present understanding of the *ḥavrayya* can be adduced from the Palestinian Talmud where R. Zeira is mentioned several times in direct connection with the *ḥavrayya,* probably having the sense of junior scholars of the Talmudic academy in Tiberias. Thus, the occurrence of the phrase, *min ḥavrayya,* which appears in the above passage when discussing R. Zeira's incident of destroying the anthropoid, is also characteristic of the relationship between R. Zeira and the Tiberian scholars.[7]

Our reading of the meaning of the *Sanhedrin* passage is corroborated by the episode of Simon Magus, discussed above,[8] who created a man out of air, in order to demonstrate his powers, possibly as part of his pretention to be the hypostasis of the Great Power. *Imitatio Dei* via magic seems to underlie both the Talmudic text and the text of Simon.

An essential issue in the Talmudic text is the fact that the artificial man was not able to speak; ostensibly, this is the result of some iniquities of its creator, Rava. However, it is worthwhile to attempt a more detailed analysis of the possible implications of the power to speak in the context of the Talmudic discussion. Taking into account the immediate context of the passage will reveal, I believe, the connotations of the silence of the artificial man. In the Baraita that precedes our passage we read:

> 'Or that consulteth the dead'[9] — this refers to one who starves himself and goes and spends the night in a cemetery, so that an unclean spirit may rest upon him. When R. Aqiba reached this verse, he wept, saying: "If one starves himself so that the spirit of uncleanness

> should rest upon him, he who fasts, so that the spirit of purity should rest upon him, how much more so! But what is one to do, seeing that his iniquities have brought this upon him, as it is said, 'But your iniquities have separated between you and your God'?[10]

The terms "spirit of uncleanness" and "spirit of cleanness" refer, it is reasonable to assume, not only to the dwelling of these forces upon men but more specifically to their revelations. In other words, a righteous individual, who will fast in order to obtain the spirit of cleanness, will, in principle, be able to attain it. On the basis of this passage, which is an organic part of the Talmudic discussion in this page, the statement on Rava's creation of a man is adduced. Consequently, it seems adequate to read the two texts from the perspective of the possibility of inducing speech, either on the holy and unholy persons, or on an artificial man. In the case of inducing the pure spirit and in the story of the silent anthropoid, there is a failure to achieve the goal.[11] However, if the essential issue is not speech in general, but some revelatory speech, magically obtained, as we can learn from the larger context of the *Sanhedrin* discussion, the story of an artificially created man can be understood as part of an endeavour to create a speaking man, in particular a creature upon whom a spirit will dwell in order to reveal something. Such an hypothetical reading is corroborated by the existence of a similar practice in magic circles during the period of the Talmudic discussion. I refer to the speaking statues which were created in order to induce demons and gods in them, who reveal to pagan priests future events.[12] If this practice is the background of the "silent" man, we may consider the Talmudic discussion as a polemic against the belief in the revelation of gods and demons by means of created anthropoid structures.

The assumption that the Talmudic passage is a polemic against the animation of the statues involves a certain problem; it occurs in the Babylonian Talmud, but not in the Palestinian one. In principle, the probability that an encounter between the pagan magic connected to the fabrication of statues and their animation, widespread in the Hellenistic culture, and the Babylonian Rabbi is not a great one. It is much more probable to assume that such an encounter would have taken place in Palestine. Moreover, we must remember that at least some of the figures mentioned in the *Sanhedrin* passage were of Palestinian extraction, R. Ḥanina and R. Oshaya. They were described as dealing with the *Hilkhot Yeẓirah* and thus it may imply, if we shall accept the evidence of the Talmud as historically accurate, that the peculiar gnosis related to artificial creation of creatures stems from Palestinian rather than Babylonian sources. Such an explanation, hypothetical as it is, seems to be corroborated also by another example; the name Meṭaṭron, part of the mystical literature of Heikhalot speculation, is mentioned in the Babylonian Talmud alone, but not in the Palestinian one, although its genesis seems to be related to the Greek language.[13] However, the most decisive argument in favor of a Palestinian stage of the anthropoid story is to be found in details related to R. Zeira. This figure had close relations with the Tiberian scholars, and it is widely accepted that he was also a resident of this city for a certain time.[14] Thus, the fact that he was involved in the later part of the story of the anthropoid may point to a Palestinian origin of this incident. Moreover, the phrase *min ḥavrayya* is considered by scholars to be characteristic of the Palestinian Talmud, in the specific context of Tiberian figures.[15] Thus, the fact that R. Zeira uses this phase may be understood as evidence of the Palestinian background. It is possible that when employing this phrase R. Zeira referred not to a Babylonian circle, but to his acquaintances in Palestine. Moreover, in the Palestinian Talmud the name of R. Zeira occurs together with the two other names mentioned in the *Sanhedrin* passage, R. Ḥanina and R. Oshaya.[16]

If our inference is correct, then the arrival of the Palestinian material to Babylonia and its integration into Babylonian practices, or traditions, may point to a relatively earlier period of the emergence of this sort of magical practices in Palestine. This assumption is supported also by the existence of similar practices in Samaria, as the later legend related to Simon Magus demonstrates.

Another topic that is relevant to the passage under examination is the Gnostic description of the creation of man by the angels, who were incapable of infusing a soul in the lifeless body, a situation vivified only by the intervention of a divine spirit.[17] This problem of infusing the soul into a body may be reflected as well in the Talmudic passage. In our case the lower creator, the Rabbi, is able to create the body but is unable to infuse the soul into it.

II

Let me address another issue connected to the story. In the passage dealing with the creation of the artificial man there is no indication as to the technique of this performance. It only implies that man was created out of dust to where he is returned by R. Zeira. However, one of the earliest commentators on this passage, Rashi, explains that Rava did it "by means of *Sefer Yeẓirah*, they [!] studied the combination of the letters of the [divine] name."[18] Therefore, according to the medieval commentator, the magical act was performed by the combination of the letters of the divine name, a fact that is not corroborated by the version in the Talmud.

Indeed, it seems that the commentator could impose the statement found in the immediate proximity to Rava's text, according to which R. Ḥanina and R. Oshaya were sitting and studying *Hilkhot Yeẓirah,* and a calf of three years old was created by them.[19] Therefore, it is possible, and probable that the study of topics related to *Yeẓirah,* either according to the version *Hilkhot* or to that of *Sefer,* was conflated with the creation of man, though in the original it is related only to the creation of the calf. However, this hypothesis regarding the emergence of the interpretation of Rashi seems to be simplistic. Immediately before the man-creation passage, Rava relates to the creation of the world, an act which may be performed also by the righteous. According to some Midrashic and Talmudic statements, the world was created by the combination of the letters, apparently the letters of the divine name.[20] This operation was repeated by Beẓalel when he created the Tabernacle.[21] Moreover, Rava is portrayed as someone acquainted with the divine name, and even willing to discuss it in the *Beit ha-Midrash.*[22] If the redactors of the Talmud intended to say that the righteous may create a world, they may, though it is not obvious, have had in mind the letter-combination technique.[23] If this hypothesis is correct, then the Talmudic passage under discussion may contain a sequence of three creations: the world, the artificial man and the calf. The first could be related to letter-combinations, the last, if the version *Sefer Yeẓirah* is correct, did imply such a technique. The middle one, the man-creation passage, may, therefore, be related to the combination of letters as Rashi explicitly explained.[24] Moreover, there are some Jewish traditions, totally independent of the *Sanhedrin* passage, which indicate the possibility of reviving a dead person by inserting the divine name in his mouth, a practice mentioned also in connection with the vivification of statues.

Let me summarize my proposal of the meaning of Rava's creation passage: a tradition dealing with the magical practices attributed to Rava was understood as a test-case for someone's righteousness. This operation was, presumably, performed by the means of combinations of the letters of the divine name. This tradition was used by the redactors of the Babylonian Talmud in their discussion of the variety of idolatry, mainly that connected to divinatory practices. The significance of this insertion was, presumably, to show that even the pietists are not able to create a speaking creature, an argument which may be conceived as part of the polemic with the pagan practices of creating speaking statues.

III

Another issue to be addressed here is the possibility that the ancient Rabbis were acquainted with the pagan practices of animating statues; the awareness of these practices may have fostered the polemical overtones of the Talmudic text. Scholem found in a medieval manuscript an important version of the creation of a human creature by Enosh, which is relevant to our point. When pushed by his contemporary to demonstrate the way of creation of man by God, he told them:

> He collected dust and kneaded it [*gibbelo*] and He breathed into it the spirit of life. They told him: How is it possible to do such a thing? Show it [to us] by the deed of [your] hands in its form and structure, [just] as He did. And they compelled him, so that he took dust and kneaded it and made it in the likeness of man and its image, and afterward he breathed into it the spirit of life, in order to show them the deed of the Holy One, blessed be He. Then Satan came to show [himself ?] [*lehizdaqqer*] in this deed, and the statue became alive. And a demon entered it and all the generation erred because of it and they made it an idolatruos worship. Then idolatry began to be designated by the name of God, and since then all those who sinned because of it [the statue, or perhaps "he," that is, Enosh] make statues in the image of man".[25]

Idolatry as the worship of animated statues is therefore known by Jews; the question is at what time in history can we be sure that this view was considered part of the pagan patrimony by the Jews. The preceding text is attributed to R. Yehudah he-Ḥasid, one of the founding fathers of Ashkenazi Ḥasidism, and therefore it may be considered a medieval elaboration. However, it seems that the core of the story may indeed be much earlier, as the following parallel found in the Heikhalot literature possibly testifies:

> . . . until the time of the generation of Enosh who was the head of idol worshippers of the world. And what did the generation of Enosh do? They went from one end of the world to the other, and each one brought silver, precious stones and pearls in heaps like upon mountains and hills making idols out of them throughout the world. And they erected idols in every quarter of the world; the size of each idol was 1,000 parasangs. And they brought down the sun, the moon, the planets and the constellations, and placed them before the idols on their right hand and on their left, to attend them even as they attend the Holy One, blessed be He, as it is written,[26] "And all the host of heaven was standing by him on His right hand and on His

> left." What power was in them that they were able to bring them down? They would not have been able to bring them down but for Uzza, Azza and Azaziel who taught them sorceries whereby they brought them down and made use of them.[27]

This passage includes not only a description of idolatry in the vein of biblical criticism; here the ancient Jewish authors oppose a specific type of idolatry which is the result of the construction of a gigantic anthropoid structure from special material which is, apparently, related to the astral bodies. I assume that this passage should be seen as a polemic against the astro-magical statues in existence in the contemporary pagan Hermeticism and Neoplatonism. Since the Heikhalot passage, and its parallel found in *Midrash Tanḥuma,* may reflect an awareness of and a reaction to the pagan practices, it seems that the Talmudic passage may also reflect the same situation.

Last but not least. The Talmud did not elaborate on the technique of creating the artificial man. We may infer that it was made out of dust, but the details of the device were not even alluded to in the *Sanhedrin* text. However, the mention of the *Hilkhot* or *Sefer Yeẓirah* in the context of the creation of the calf allows us to surmise that the technique of *Sefer Yeẓirah*, or one of its sources, was known to the redactors of the Talmudic passage. That the technique was not mentioned may be conceived as part of the overall tendency of the Talmud not to indulge in details concerning esoteric issues. An interesting parallel to this reticence is the mentioning of the "Four who entered the Pardes" in *Ḥagigah* (fol. 14b), without describing exactly what this Pardes is and especially what technique is used to attain such an entrance. It is only by a comparison to the Heikhalot literature that we may ascertain the meaning of the Pardes as the contemplation of the Divine Chariot, and only this literature preserved the details of the technique for reaching such an experience; the Talmud remained silent on this point. Thus, the discussion in *Sanhedrin* can be plausibly supplemented by the details of God's creating man in *Sefer Yeẓirah*, and even of Abraham's creating "souls" at the end of this treatise. I believe that the fact that medieval authors "conflated" the topics related in these two texts is to be considered interesting evidence for how to deal with the disparate material in this case. Their combination of sources cannot alone demonstrate the affinity between the sources under discussion; however, their collation of sources may betray the genuine affinity between those sources and it may alert us to a possible reading to be corroborated by an independent analysis on the content of each and every passage.

The Midrashic Adam as Golem

IV

The act of creating an anthropoid has several features in common with the creation of Adam by God. In this context it is interesting to analyze the description of the creation of Adam in a text that has escaped the notice of scholars who have dealt with the idea of the Golem. I refer to the description of the creation of Adam in *Leviticus Rabbah* which includes, as we shall see immediately, a sequel of divine actions related to the various stages in the creation of man according to the different hours. Similar descriptions recur in several Rabbinical texts,[28] but it seems that the passage in *Leviticus Rabbah* includes some elements which are particularly germane for several reasons to the understanding of the later recipes for creating a Golem.

> In the first hour, he [Adam] ascended in the thought [of God]. In the second [hour] He discussed [the creation of man] with the ministering angels. In the third, He collected his dust. In the fourth, He kneaded him [*gibbelo*].[29] In the fifth, He formed [his limbs] [*riqqemo*].[30] In the sixth, He made him a Golem [*'asa'o golem*]. In the seventh, He blew in him the soul. In the eighth, He put him in Paradise, etc.[31]

For our topic, only the activities of the third to seventh hours are relevant; the collection of the dust, the kneading, the formation of the limbs, the transformation of man into a Golem, and, finally, the infusion of the soul. The first three acts are clear; they reflect the primary acts related to the emergence of the human organism out of dust and water, the latter being implied in the usage of the verb *gbl.* However, between the formation of the limbs and the infusion of the soul stands the stage of the transformation of the aggregatum into an intermediary status of Golem, i.e., an entity which is more than a structure in the form of man, but less than a being endowed with a soul. The status of Golem as a fully structured creature preceding the reception of the soul is also found in another context. In *Genesis Rabbah* we learn that: "[God] rose him [as] a Golem from the earth to heaven[32] and cast the soul in him."[33] It seems that the Golem here stands for an already formed being, in the penultimate stage of creation which culminates with the infusion of the soul. This view is also shared by a mystical midrash, *Midrash Avkir,* where Adam is said to have been created before the creation of the world; then God:

> made him [*'asa'o*] as a Golem. And when He was about to cast[34] a soul into him, He said, "If I set him down now, it will be said that he was my companion in the work of Creation; so I will leave him a Golem until I have created everything else." When He had created everything . . . He cast the soul into him and set him down.[35]

The phrase used in this midrash, "made him [as] a Golem" is identical to that occuring in *Leviticus Rabbah*; in both cases, in distinction from some other Rabbinical sources, the stage of being a Golem is tantamount to being shaped already in a human form, just before receiving the soul. Another text that is pertinent for our discussion is found in *Pirqei R. Eliezer,*[36] where the sequence of actions is 1) the collection of the dust, 2) the kneading, 3) the formation (*rqm*); between this last stage and the infusion of the soul, another action is mentioned by the use of the term "*vetiqqeno*" without, however, mentioning the Golem stage. In any case, it is obvious that an additional operation was performed after the formation but before the casting of the soul. This analysis is corroborated by the meaning of the term Golem is several Rabbinical sources, where it signifies the simpleton in distinction from the wise, as is the case, for example, in *'Avot,* ch. 5 and in the medieval material dealing with this text.[37] The simpleton, as the embryo qua Golem, is a living entity which needs the final quality that will transform him into a fulfledged human being, viz., wisdom; corporeally, he is already a structured human creature.

The similarity between *Leviticus Rabbah* and *Midrash Avkir* concerning the status of the Golem as the last stage before the complete human status does not necessarily constitute an argument for the antiquity of this view of the Golem in comparison to the other formulations, where between the Golem stage and the blowing of the soul there is one, or more, intermediary stages. The version of *Leviticus Rabbah* may, indeed, preserve an ancient tradition rather than express a later view.[38] This assumption of the antiquity of the sequel of actions as they were described in this Midrash is corroborated by the parallelism between the acts described therein and those occuring in the context of the verse in Psalms that is the *locus probans* for the discussions of the Golem. In Ps. 139:15–16 we read:

> My bone[39] was not hidden from Thee, when I was made in secret, and formed in the lowest part of the earth. Thy eyes did see my Golem; for in Thy book all things are written: the days also in which they are to be fashioned, and for it too there was one of them.

The biblical verses use the verb *rqm* just before the noun Golem occurs, exactly as the passage from *Leviticus Rabbah* does. Since the term Golem is a biblical *hapax legomenon,*[40] it is doubtless that this biblical sequence of words is reiterated in a more precise manner in this Midrash, in comparison to other Rabbinical discussions where the verb *rqm* does not occur at all,[41] or does not occur in immediate proximity to the term Golem.[42] Moreover, the fact that the "earth" is mentioned as the locus of the creation, according to the verses from Psalms, immediately before the mentioning of the Golem, was influential for the later interpretation of the Golem as a creature emerging from the dust, just as Adam in Genesis. Furthermore, the biblical verse uses the verb *'sh*, which recurs in *Leviticus Rabbah,* whereas in other sources, the verb *br'* is to be found.

V

Let me address now the possible meaning of the Golem in the Midrashic literature. According to Scholem,[43] the fact that God revealed the future generations to the Golem before he was given a soul, allows an interpretation of this being as having "tellurian" powers, namely, powers stemming from the earth, irrational or harmful in their essence, a leitmotif of Scholem's reading of the Golem even in later medieval texts. Indeed, according *Genesis Rabbah,*[44] while still being in the stage of Golem, namely before he was given a soul by God, this being was shown future things. This power of perception, even if we regard the text of the Midrash as a careful formulation, does not assume explicitly, and I assume even not implicitly, that the power of the vision emerged from the tellurian component of the Golem; it may, with the same degree of probability, be the result of the advanced stage of the formation of the dust by God. Such a capacity could be part of the structuring of the matter into the peculiar form of man, or be the infused capacity connected to the intention of God to display the future things to the newly created being. On the basis of a comparison to the usage of the term Golem in *Piyyuṭ,* chronologically the closest type of literature to the Midrash, it seems that Golem is understood as the embryonic stage. This understanding is consonant with the biblical meaning of the term and it is corroborated by some other sources.

As we know from several Rabbinical texts, the embryo has a distinct cognitive power, which is similar, and presumably also influenced by, a Platonic-like view of the knowledge of souls before their descent to this world.[45] The Golem in the *Genesis Rabbah* passage is not different from the embryonic Golem in the *Piyyuṭ* genre, both of them sharing an extraordinary cognitive faculty. Thus, for example, we read in one of Yannai's poems:

> The texture of the limbs, [*'arigat*[46] *'eivarim*] You have opened the orifices [*'avarim*], which are [the limbs] *gelumim* and squared [*merubba'im*], in the forty [or fortieth] days [day].[47]

The meaning of the form *gelumim* is not clear; it has been explained, however, as referring to the amorphous phase of the limbs of the embryo, an understanding that contradicts the meaning of the Golem as a relatively advanced being, on its way to receiving the soul, as we attempted to prove above. However, it seems that this understanding of the *piyyuṭ,* which emphasizes the amorphousness of the Golem, is not necessary, for by comparing the above verses to others of the same poet, we may reach a different conclusion about the significance of the form *gelumim.* Yannai wrote in a similar context: "You have cut [*gizartah*] and You have *galamtah* bodies and corpses [*geviot*]."[48] Now, the cutting of the bodies is presented as preceding the second act of preparing the embryo. This may be substantiated on the grounds of the verb *tqn* occurring in *Pirqei R. Eliezer* chapter 11, after *rqm,* and of the description found in *Avot dē-R. Natan* chapter 1, where we learn that after the collection of the dust, the form of man was created (*nivra' ẓurato*), and it is only then the author mentions "*na'asah Golem.*" Regarding the Midrash, a passage in *Leviticus Rabbah*[49] seems to strengthen the interpretation of the Golem as referring to an embryonic form that already has limbs; as part of the description of the form of the embryo an anonymous master enumerates the small size of the eyes, nose, ears, arms, face, and body as distinct limbs, and then it is said, "and the other limbs are comprised in him [*meẓumẓamim bo*] as a Golem[50], concerning which it is said, "Thy eyes did see my Golem". This description is to be compared to the above text from the same Midrash where the Golem is mentioned after the limbs were formed. It is possible that the mention of Golem in this last quote refers not only to the comprised limbs, but to the whole embryo, though such a reading is not certain.

Thus both in the Midrash and in the *Piyyuṭ,* Golem stands for an advanced stage of the formation of the embryo, as apparently we may learn also from the biblical verses. If the embryo is not conceived of as having any tellurian powers, and I am not aware of such a conception, why shall we invest the Golem with such a power? In any case, the conjecture regarding the existence of tellurian powers, independent of the divine activity, in the Golem is an interesting thesis that requires substantiation by some corroborating material before it becomes a cornerstone of the interpretation of the Golem legend. For the time being, the only sentence which may have any relevance to this issue is the interpretation of the verse from Gen. 1:24 "Let the earth bring forth living creatures [*nefesh*] after their kind," which is understood as referring to the spirit of Adam.[51] However interesting this statement may be,[52] it was not uttered in the context of the creation of Adam or of a Golem.

Let me summarize the above discussion. The biblical verse from Psalms was reinterpreted by Rabbinic sources as dealing with the creation of Adam. The motifs related to the creation of Adam include also mythical material, as the creation out of virgin dust or the collection of dust out of the four corners of the world. Therefore, we may consider the discussions of the creation of man as conflating the episode related in Genesis, the view expressed in Psalms, which served mainly as homiletic material, and eventually even also extra-biblical material.[53] To these elements the concept of creation by the combinations of letters was superimposed at a later stage.

For the history of the idea of the Golem, it is important to point out that it is possible to find in its sequel of actions a pattern similar to the later discussion of creating an artificial man. The pertinent actions as occurring in *Leviticus Rabbah* are: the collection of the dust; the kneading and the making of this entity into a Golem. Beyond these actions, to be found in some Ashkenazi Hasidic prescriptions there are also terminological similarities; the verb *gbl* occurs in the Midrashic and Ashkenazi texts, as well as the connection between the verb *'sh* and Golem.[54]

Notes

1. Isa. 59:2.

2. In Aramaic: *rava' bera' gavra'.* The consonants of this phrase are almost identical, the only difference being the order in which they were arranged. It seems that this use of the combination of letters in the classical text dealing with the creation of the artificial man, may intimate the method of this creation, which is not specified in Talmud, namely the combination of letters. Such a reading is consonant with the later interpretations of this text even by non-Kabbalists. The verb *tuv,* namely return, reflects the return of man qua man to his dust according to the Bible; cf. Gen., 3:19. Using it together with the verb *bera',* which describes the act of creation here and in the case of God's creation of Adam, the editors of the Talmud hint to the similarity between the artificial and the primeval man.

3. *TB, Sanhedrin,* fol. 65b. The following analysis is based on the assumption that a careful redactor, or redactors, arranged the various topics which occur as a continuum on this page of Talmud, though originally they may have been part of disparate traditions. I cannot confirm or negate the historicity of the connection between the masters mentioned here and the legends whose heroes they are.

4. Jacob Neusner, *The Wonder-Working Laywers of Talmudic Babylonia,* (Lanham, New York, London, University Press of America, 1987), p. 218; Fossum, *The Name of God and the Angel of the Lord,* p. 242.

5. *Mishnah, Damai* ch. 2, par. 3; *BT, Pesahim,* fol. 9a. Interestingly, the *ḥaver* is described in this source as someone who did not do anything in a deficient way. See E. E. Urbach, *The Sages: Their Concepts and Beliefs* (Jerusalem, 1979) pp. 581–589 (Hebrew).

6. Though this may indeed be a conjecture, the silence of the creature brings to mind the silence of Adam after his sin, when he did not answer the voice of God in Paradise, but hid himself amongst the trees. If this intertextual reading is indeed correct, it may have something to do with the iniquities that prevent a righteous individual from being similar to God, their creation being deficient.

7. Moshe Baer, "On the Havrayya", *Bar-Ilan: Annual of Bar-Ilan University* (Ramat Gan, 1983), vol. 20–21, pp. 83–86 (Hebrew).

8. See ch. 1, par. 3.

9. Deut. 18:11.

10. *TB, Sanhedrin,* fol. 65b.

11. For another understanding of the meaning of the relationship between the first quotation from *Sanhedrin* and the second part quoted here, see Morton Smith, *Clement of Alexandria and a Secret Gospel of Mark* (Cambridge, Mass., Harvard University Press, 1973), p. 220. Smith proposes to see the dwelling of the spirit mentioned by R. Aqiva, as the fact in the case of Rava, as the spirit revealing to the Amora the details of the creation of the artificial man.

12. See the material collected by Paul Krauss, "Jabir ibn Hayyan et la science grecque," *Memoires presentées a l'Institute d'Egypte,* vol. 4–5 (1942), pp. 127–134; Mueller, "Die Golemsage", *passim.* On the acquaintence of Jews, since the second century, with pagan practices of inducing spirits into idols, see Saul Lieberman, *Hellenism in Jewish Palestine* (New York, 1950), p. 121, n. 33.

13. See Saul Lieberman's appendix to Gruenwald, *Apocalyptic and Merkavah Mysticism,* pp. 241–244.

14. See Baer (note 7 above) p. 83, n. 51.

15. Ibid., pp. 83–89. See especially ibid. pp. 90–91 where Baer discusses some passages in the Babylonian Talmud where the term *ḥavrayya'* may refer to a single person, and not to a group, as in the case of the Palestinian Talmud. In this case, it is possible that R. Zeira has in mind Rava.

16. Ibid., p. 84, referring to *PT, Shabbat* 3, 5, fol. 5d.

17. Fossum, *The Name of God and the Angel of the Lord,* pp. 242–243. R. Van den Broek, "The Creation of Adam's Psychic Body in the Apocryphon of

John"; eds. R. Van der Broek and M. J. Vermaseren, *Studies in Gnosticism and Hellenistic Religions* (Leiden, Brill 1981), pp. 38–57; Birger A. Pearson, "Biblical Exegesis in Gnostic Literature" ed. M. E. Stone, *Armenian and Biblical Studies* (Jerusalem, 1976) pp. 70–80.

18. Rashi on *Sanhedrin,* fol. 65b. It seems highly probable that Rashi did not express only his own opinion; an explanation of the creation of the calf by means of the combination of the letters of the divine name was exposed by an anonymous contemporary of Rashi, in a text brought to my attention by Professor I. Ta-Shma; see Ms. Oxford, 1207, fol. 193b.

19. The magical creation of calves was considered by some Palestinian Rabbis as a fact they themselves witnessed; see *PT, Sanhedrin,* ch. 7. It should be mentioned that the discussions on creating calves did not embarrass the Amoraim; this fact seems to complicate the argument of Halperin, *The Faces of the Chariot,* pp. 157-193, concerning the calf as the dark side of the Merkavah.

20. *BT, Berakhot,* fol. 55a.

21. Scholem, "The Name of God," p. 71.

22. *BT, Pesaḥim,* fol. 51a.

23. Compare to the view, adduced in this context already by Scholem, "The Idea of the Golem," p. 167 expressed in *Midrash Tehillim* on Psalm 3, that had the Torah been revealed in its original sequel of letters, the readers would be able to create a world. On the magical implications of this view see Scholem, *On the Kabbalah,* p. 37, and Idel, "The Concept of the Torah," pp. 52–54.

24. Compare to the view of an anonymous Kabbalist who wrote, apparently as late as the seventeenth century, that the combinations of letters of the divine name which were instrumental in the creation of the world were the same as those studied by R. Ḥanina and R. Oshaya, according to the *Sanhedrin* passage, as understood by Rashi. See *Ẓuf Devash,* Part 2, ch. 1, in a manuscript found in the possession of Mr. Norman Gorman, New Jersey.

25. See Scholem, "The Image of the Golem," p. 402, "The Idea of the Golem," p. 181. Compare to the other version of this event, noticed already by Scholem, ibid., found in *The Chronicles of Jerahmeel or the Hebrew Bible Historiale,* translated by Moses Gaster, (New York, 1971), pp. 49–50:

> Male and female He created them. "But how?" asked they [Enosh's questioners]. He answered, "God took water and earth and moulded it together in the form of man." They asked, "But how?" Enosh then took six clods of earth, mixed them, and moulded them and formed an image of dust and clay. "But" said they, "this image does not walk, nor does it possess any breath of life. But when He began to breathe into it, Satan entered the image so that it walked, and they went astray after it, saying, "What is the difference between the bowing down before this image and before man?" That

is what is meant when it is said, "Then they began to apply the name of the Lord;" that is they gave this name to other gods. On this account Enosh is mentioned in Scripture immediately before the word "his image."

For more on the question of the sin of Enosh, see Steven D. Fraade, *Enosh and His Generation: Pre-Israelite Hero and History in Postbiblical Interpretation* (California: Scholar Press, 1984), pp. 141, 166.

26. I Kings 22: 19.

27. *Hebrew Enoch* ed. H. Odeberg (New York, 1973), pp. 15–16, Hebrew text pp. ix–x. See also Idel, "Hermeticism and Judaism," pp. 61–62; Fraade, ibid., pp. 163–164. See also below ch. 15 beside n. 29.

28. See *BT, Sanhedrin,* fol. 38b, *'Avot de-R. Nathan* ch. 1 version A, *Pirqei R. Eliezer,* ch. 11 and *Leviticus Rabbah* 29 to be discussed in detail below, par. 4.

29. See the use of this verb in the context of the creation of the embryo in Yannai's poem, ed. Z. M. Rabinovitz, *The Liturgical Poems of Rabbi Yannai* (Jerusalem, 1985), p. 391, line 19. It is pertinent to mention here that this verb is connected to the concept of pottery; see especially R. Eleazar of Worms, *Commentary on the Pentateuch,* vol. 1, p. 153. See also ch. 1, n. 7.

30. Compare to *Song of Songs Rabbah* 1: 22, ed. S. Dunski, (Jerusalem, 1980), p. 23, where Abraham and Sarah's metaphorical act of creating the gentiles by converting them to Judaism, is described using the verbs, *bera'o, yiẓaro, reqamo.* It seems that the mention of the forming, *reqamo,* as the third stage, points to an advanced phase in the creation process.

31. *Leviticus Rabbah* par. 29, ed. M. Margaliot, *Midrash WaYYiqra' Rabbah* (Jerusalem, 1956), vol. 3, pp. 668–669.

32. On the huge stature of the primordial man, see Susan Niditch, "The Cosmic Man: Man as Mediator in Rabbinic Literature," *JJS,* vol. 34 (1983), pp. 137–146; Idel, "Enoch is Metatron," pp. 153–154, 163, n. 16.

33. *Genesis Rabbah,* section 8, par. 1, Theodor-Albeck, ed. pp. 55–56, where the numerous parallels are noted.

34. *Lizroq;* this verb occurs several times as an alternative to the biblical *npḥ.* On the casting of the soul into the body, compare the Mandaean view discussed by Hans Jonas, *The Gnostic Religion* (Boston, 1963), pp. 63–65.

35. In *Yalqut Shim 'oni* on Gen., par. 34. See Scholem, "The Idea of the Golem," pp. 162–163; Idel, *Kabbalah: New Perspectives,* pp. 117–118.

36. Ch. 1, version A.

37. S. Horovitz, ed., *Maḥzor Vitri,* (Jerusalem, 1963), p. 541 and Rashi on *BT, Ḥullin,* fol. 25a. This meaning is reflected also in the passage of the *Zohar,* 1 fol. 121a–b (*Midrash ha-Ne'elam*) and R. Joseph Giqatilla, *Ginnat 'Egoz* (Hanau, 1615), fol. 33c. Compare to Scholem, "The Idea of the Golem," p. 191, n. 1, where he assumes that the *Zohar* and Giqatilla were influenced by the German Pietistic use of the term Golem.

38. For more on this issue see below, Appendix A.

39. *'Azmi.*

40. As to the meaning of this term in the biblical context there are various explanations. Scholem, "The Idea of the Golem," p. 161, is however, sure that "there is no evidence as to the effect that it means 'embryo'." See also below Appendix B.

41. E.g., *Pirqei R. Eliezer,* ch. 11.

42. *BT, Sanhedrin,* fol. 38b.

43. "The Idea of the Golem," pp. 161–165.

44. *Genesis Rabbah,* section 24: par. 2, p. 230.

45. See *BT, Niddah,* fol. 30b where the embryo is conceived as seeing from the beginning of the world to its end. This description is reminiscent of the size of Adam who, as a Golem, filled the whole world. On the similarities and divergences between Plato's epistemology and the Jewish conception of the embryo, see Urbach, *The Sages* (note 5 above), pp. 246–248.

46. See the use of the verb *rqm* whose basic meaning is to embroider, therefore pointing to an act that is more advanced than the producing of the texture, *'arigah.*

47. Rabinovitch, (note 29 above), p. 389. My understanding of the text, as reflected in the translation, differs from that of the editor, who based his interpretation on the assumption that *gelumim* stands for amorphous. Moreover, *pataḥtah,* translated here as "You have opened" was vocalized by the editor as *pitaḥtah,* and understood as creating the body from the center to the periphery. See Ibid., p. 389 in footnotes. Compare also to R. Amitai's verse discussed below, Appendix B.

48. *Ibid.* p. 482.

49. *Leviticus Rabbah,* section 15, par. 8. The minute size of the Golem as described here does not preclude an influence of the embryonic understanding of the magical Golem, who may also have been of a minute size, as is attested by the quantity of dust employed by the operator. See below, par. 6 and the discussion of the bitter water, constituted from the dust of the soil of the tabernacle, water and the ink stemming from the verses of the Bible related to the curse of the suspected *soṭah.* In this case as well the quantity of the dust is a small one.

50. In the parallel discussion in *PT, Niddah,* ch. 3, par. 3 the version is different. After mentioning the discernible limbs as in *Leviticus Rabbah,* the Talmud says: "all the other limbs are a kind of Golem, sticked [*mezummatim*], and the cutting [*pittuaḥ*] of the hands and feet is not [evident]". According to this version, the separation of the feet and hands is not clearcut, whereas the other limbs seem to be discernible. It seems that even in this case, the meaning of the Golem cannot be the amorphous stage of the embryo, but a more developed phase. My interpretation is a rather moderate one; according to a classical interpreter of the *PT ad locum,* R. Moses Margaliot, *mezummatim* means *meḥubbarim,* namely linked to each other, and the *pittuaḥ* means the separation of the fingers of hands and feet, not the separation of the feet and hands themselves.

An important attestation for the understanding of the Golem as a small, though already formed, entity, is found in R. Yosse ben Yosse, a fifth century Palestinian poet, who wrote in one of his verses: "To form [*lirqom*] the Golem and to cause it to grow, in the image of its Awesome [Creator]." See Aharon Mirsky, ed., *R. Yosse ben Yosse, Poems* (Jerusalem, 1977), p. 221. Thus the Golem is described as formed in the image of God. See also ibid., p. 175, where the formation of the Golem is mentioned, again in relation to the *zelem.* My thanks to Professor Menaḥem Schmelzer for this reference.

51. *Genesis Rabbah,* 7: 5, p. 54.

52. The main evidence that Scholem brings to strengthen his thesis is the discussion of the creation of man in a gnostic text, where man is created from the marriage between Edem, a mythical figure named also Earth, which has a pneumatic element, and God. See "The Idea of the Golem," pp. 164-165. The text quoted by Hypolitus considers Edem, the feminine counterpart of *'Elohim,* as confering to man the soul whereas *'Elohim* begets the spirit. Edem is referred to several times as earth. However, the gnostic text deals with a personification of earth rather than with earth as a material. Edem is a virgin, half-human and half-serpent, whose name is earth; the extent to which she is literally earth is unclear. Thus, the interesting evidence of Scholem for the existence of a tellurian theory of the soul in ancient Judaism—since the text quoted by Hypolitus seems indeed to reflect a Jewish version of Gnosticism—is less evident than it appears from his presentation. The whole matter needs a detailed analysis, which will confirm, modify or refute the hypothesis of Scholem. See also Rivkah Shatz, "Gnostic Literature as a Source of Shlomo Molcho's Sefer ha-Mefoar" in J. Dan ed. *Early Jewish Mysticism, JSJT,* vol. 6 (1987) pp. 237-242, 246-247. [Hebrew]

53. See ch. 1, par. 1.

54. See, e.g., the beginning of the quotation in ch. 5, par. 2.

PART TWO

Medieval Elaborations

4

Tempering Magic: Geonic and Rationalistic Attitudes

I

The story of the artificial man in the *Sanhedrin* passage was presented above as part of a polemical attitude.[1] The supernaturalism of the pagan magic was combated by the assumption that revelations by means of statues cannot be achieved, since even the most accomplished masters cannot create a speaking man, let alone a speaking statue. Nevertheless, the assumption was that the righteous were able to create at least an imperfect man. Such a creature does not satisfy the requirement of a fullfledged human being according to the *halakhah*, a question which will be discussed below.[2] However, those editors who included the story in the Talmud were living in a society which assumed that wonderful powers were the prerogative of the very few, who are capable of imitating the acts of the divine, even if their actions are not perfect.

The belief in such supernatural powers of language waned, however, in certain circles which flourished in the ambiance of the rationalistic theology regnant since the ninth century in the former Babylonian area. In the atmosphere of relatively open religious disputations, some leaders of oriental Judaism adopted a rather rationalistic approach to the content of the sacred scriptures, as well as post-biblical canonic texts. Some of the Geonim, like R. Sa'adyah and R. Hai oscillated between their allegiance to the Jewish literary patrimony which included also magical, mythical and mystical elements and their novel theological convinctions. This intellectual disonance was resolved by an attenuation of the "inconvenient" elements which were presented in such a light that their idiosyncracy was substantially mitigated. Such anthropomorphic elements as included in *Shi'ur Qomah*[3] or the ecstatic experiences of the descenders to the *merkavah*[4] were explained away so as to permit the formulation of a more "respectable" version of Judaism. In this context the reticent attitude to the problem of artificially creating a man is natural. Expressed by persons immersed in the study of the Talmud, this reticence began to be evident and influential since the tenth century, and it has remained an ingredient of Jewish thought until our days. Interestingly enough, the extant material of the Geonim does not address the question of their understanding of the passage on the artificial man. Thus evidence for a rationalistic attack on the *Sanhedrin* passage is absent from the known texts. In comparison to the explanations offered in the mystical texts since the early thirteenth century, the rationalistic attitude is statistically marginal in its expressions. To the extent that it was influential, the rationalistic view influenced Jewish masters by reducing the discussion of the *Sanhedrin* text to silence. However, though there is no direct testimony concerning the Geonic interpretation of the Golem passage, an indirect evidence may help us fathom the possible way that one of the Geonim would have treated this passage. R. Ḥananel ben Ḥushiel, a mid-eleventh-century Halakhist, commented upon the *Sanhedrin* story, in the following way:

> Would the righteous desire to request grace from God, that He should create another world, God would accomplish their will . . . Rava, by the [technique of] illusion ['*aḥizat 'einayim*] created a man, and he wanted to expose [*lehodi'a*] the deed of the Egyptian sorcerers, who made, by their magic, a serpent from a staff. This is the way he did it.[5]

There are two basic assumptions in this passage as to the content of the Talmudic discussions. The righteous are capable of creating a new world, though not directly, but rather as a result of their prayer, or as a response to their request from God. God, rather than the righteous, is the primary creative agent; the righteous individual does not exercise a decisive influence on the very act of creation, though he may be regarded as the initiator of the process. However, in the case of Rava, the assumption is that the creation of man is the entire achievement of this figure, though the nature of this achievement is not sufficiently clear. The emergence of the artificial man was understood as part of a magical illusion, not as a substantial entity, even if an imperfect one. The Amora is presented here as performing a magical practice that does not differ in principle from the magical deeds of the Egyptian magicians. No need of an address to God is mentioned here as part of the creation of this man, as in the case of the righteous individual willing to create a world. God does not intervene in the creation of the illusionary anthropoid. Language, or *Sefer Yeẓirah,* is not involved in this commentary on the Talmud. The whole passage seems to be understood as part of a polemic between Jewish and pagan magicians; both of them are able to transform matter into unexpected types of forms. The emphasis here is on the superiority of the achievement of the righteous, who can attain a higher spiritual status by inducing a divine act, which is also materially superior to that achieved by the magician. We may also assume that the difference between the creation of a man in comparison to the creation of a serpent was understood here as proving the superiority of the Jewish magician, at least as far as the issue of the level of the created being is concerned. It would appear that R. Ḥananel's approach illustrates the possible interpretation of earlier authors, because this author is known as someone who reflects faithfully the views of Geonim, mostly those of R. Hai Gaon.

In this context it is important to remark that in the first commentaries on *Sefer Yeẓirah*, the topics related to the creation of the Golem are absent. This is the case in the commentaries of R. Sa'adyah Gaon[6], R. Shabbatai Donnolo[7] and R. Dunash ibn Tamim.[8]

II

In the twelfth century such a reticence is still visible in the voluminous *Commentary on Sefer Yeẓirah* authored by R. Yehudah ben Barzilai of Barcelona. Written under the weighty impact of R. Sa'adyah, this work tries to reduce the magical significance of the *Sanhedrin* passage, and proposes a rather conservative solution, apparently influenced by the view of R. Ḥananel or his sources. According to the Catalan author, the study of the *Hilkhot Yeẓirah* by the various Amoraic authorities was requited by God through the appearance of "a new man," namely, a quasi-real being whose appearance serves as a proof for the scholarly and religious achievement of the students.[9] The different degrees of spiritual achievements were externalized by the proportional natures of creatures sent by God. The highest creature was an anthropoid, whereas a less perfect achievement was rewarded by the appearance of a calf or another animal. Therefore, neither the creative power of the righteous, nor the forces inherent in the language, are the ultimate reason for the creation of the new man, but rather the divine act, which responds to the acts of an accomplished scholar. Thus the extraordinary story of the Talmud was integrated into the conservative view regarding the relation of achievement and retribution, rather than allowing the penetration of magic into the classical text of the Rabbinic lore.

The dumbness of the new man was not related to the limitation of the human creator, but to the intention of the Creator to distinguish the appearance from real men, and allow thereby the perception of the retribution. According to R. Yehudah, this appearance is a vision which takes place in the imaginative power of man, "*'ela' shehayah mar'ehu ha-Bore' be-dimyon.*"[10] Notwithstanding this imaginative nature, the creatures are endowed with motive and sensitive qualities, this being the reason why these creatures could be consummated by the scholars. R. Yehudah compares the Golem to the manna which descended from heaven, for this was not produced by any human activity but, nevertheless, was eaten by the children of Israel. The supernatural was transfered from man to God, and the actual creative achievement to the imaginative status; magic was understood here as the externalisation of a hidden religious law.

After proposing this interpretation of the Talmudic story, R. Yehudah mentions the view of other persons, who maintained that the practice of the Talmudic masters was a licit type of magic, similar to witchcraft, *ḥokhmat ha-makhshefot,* or a way to induce illusions or phantasma, *'aḥizat 'einayim,* which transcends the achievements of the alien magic. It is obvious that the occurence of the Talmudic term *'aḥizat 'einayim* in the context of the creation of man, demonstrates the affinity of those persons to the explanation offered by R. Ḥananel. The attempt to use the *'aḥizat 'einayim* explanation for the interpretation of the Talmudic text was known also by a late twelfth, early thirteenth century Castilian Talmudist, R. Meir ha-Levi Abulafia, who rejects it, arguing that the illusive phenomenon is possible only when the operator and the person who is supposed to be influenced are together in the same place. In the case of the Talmudic situation, R. Zeira was apparently remote from Rava, as the artificial man was sent to the former by the latter. Thus, argues R. Meir, this explanation is improbable, and he prefers the one suggested by Rashi.[11]

The attenuation of the magical elements inherent in the *Sanhedrin* passage is also obvious in the interpretation proposed by R. Yehudah of the achievement of Abraham according to the end of *Sefer Yeẓirah.* As seen above, Abraham used the linguistic gnosis of *Sefer Yeẓirah* in order to create something, and he was highly praised by God for his achievement. This passage is interpreted by the twelfth-century commentator as referring to the religious activity of Abraham, who was able to convince his contemporaries about the truth of monotheism, and thus to improve the status of the world in the eyes of God. Abraham's creation was one of a religious nature, converting the idolators to the true religion; the making of souls at Haran was understood, following the Midrash, as a religious conversion.[12]

III

The suggestion that the practice of the Talmudic masters included a capacity to induce illusive visions recurs later on in R. Shem Tov ibn Shaprut, a fourteenth century commentator on the Talmudic *'aggadot.* In his *Pardes Rimmonim,* the author states that the production of the illusions, *'aḥizat 'einayim,* is not prohibited by Jewish lore. Rava produced an illusion in the form of a man in order to test R. Zeira, who was capable of perceiving the real nature of the creature and thus commanded it to return to dust.[13]

IV

In the nineteenth century, a discussion on the possible implications of the study of *Sefer Yeẓirah* is found in a dialoque on the Kabbalah by Samuel David Luzzatto. In his *Dialogues sur la Kabbale et le Zohar,* the imaginary Polish guest, who is the critic of Kabbalah and its antiquity, addresses the question of the creation of a man by means of the study of *Sefer Yeẓirah.*[14] He does not reject the possibility that such a creation was indeed a reality, in the vein of the *Sanhedrin* passage, but he offers an explanation that is reminiscent of R. Yehudah Barceloni.[15] The positive result of the study of this book has, according to this critique, nothing to do with creative powers inherent in the letters, but rather with the divine will which fulfills the desires of the righteous. If there are any external effects to the study of the mystical treatise, they are solely the act of God. The role of the combinations of letters in this book is to help the mystic to concentrate his thought in order to ask his question, or, in other words, to structure human thought in a certain way. This psychological explanation of the study of *Sefer Yeẓirah* was criticized immediately after the printing of the *Dialoques* of Luzzatto by his compatriot, R. Eliyahu ben Amozegh; in his *Nouveaux Dialogues sur la Kabbale,* ben Amozegh argues that the psychological explanation is insufficient because any other type of books could function in the same way as *Sefer Yeẓirah* by inducing some intention in the soul of the student. However, he continues, it is in this book alone that the creative processes are mentioned, and a more substantial affinity between creation and *Sefer Yeẓirah* has to be surmised.[16]

Notes

1. Ch. 3, par. 1.

2. See ch. 14 below.

3. See Dan, *Esoteric Theology,* pp. 104–110.

4. See Idel, *Kabbalah: New Perspectives,* pp. 90–91.

5. See *'Ozar ha-Geonim, Sanhedrin,* ed. H. Z. Taubes (Jerusalem, 1966), p. 557. On this author see Sirat, *Les theories des visions surnaturelles,* p. 92.

6. On the general anti-mythical attitude of Sa'adyah to *Sefer Yeẓirah* see Haggai Ben-Shammai, "Saadya's Goal in his *Commentary on Sefer Yeẓira,"* in: ed., Ruth Link-Salinger, *A Straight Path: Essays in Honor of Arthur Hyman* (Washington D.C., Catholic University of America, 1988), pp. 1–9.

7. On the philosophical basis of this author, see Giuseppe Sermoneta, "Il Neo-platonismo nel pensiero dei nuclei Ebraici stanziati nell'occidente latino [Riflessioni sul 'Commento al Libro della Creazione' di Rabbi Sabbetai Donnolo]," *Settimane di studio del Centro italiano di studi sull'alto medioevo,* vol. 26 (1980), pp. 867–925.

8. See Georges Vajda, "Le Commentaire Kairouanais sur le Livre de la Creation," *REJ,* vol. 107 (1946–1947), pp. 99–116; idem, "Nouveaux Fragments arabes du Commentaire de Dunash ibn Tamim sur le Livre de Creation", *REJ,* vol. 113 (1954), pp. 37–61.

9. *Commentary on Sefer Yeẓirah*, ed. S. Z. H. Halberstam (Berlin, 1885), p. 102.

10. *Commentary on Sefer Yeẓirah*, p. 103.

11. See *Yad Ramah,* Sanhedrin, (Warsaw, 1895), fol. 63b.

12. *Commentary on Sefer Yeẓirah*, pp. 99–100.

13. *Pardes Rimmonim* (Sabionetta, 1554), fol. 13a.

14. *Dialogue sur la kabbale et le Zohar* (Gorice, 1852), pp. 18–20. The critique of the Polish guest reflects, undoubtedly, the views of Luzzatto himself, as the comparison to the content of some of Luzzatto's letters demonstrates. See his *Hebraeische Briefe* (Cracau, 1892), pp. 693–694, which is but another version of the critique elaborated later on in the *Dialogues.* Since the letter was addressed to a real Polish correspondent, Gedeon Brecher of Prossnitz, who was a fervent admirer of Kabbalah, I assume that the persona of critique is an ironic transposition of the admirer into a critic.

15. The similarity of the explanations of the effectiveness of *Sefer Yeẓirah* proposed by Barceloni and Luzzatto are the result of the reading of the former's

Commentary on Sefer Yeẓirah by the nineteenth century scholar. Though by 1840, when Luzzatto was composing his *Dialogues,* the *Commentary* of Barceloni was not in print, Luzzatto had the opportunity to examine the manuscript, and I assume that he was deeply impressed by the rationalistic approach of this, and other commentaries, on *Sefer Yeẓirah.* This was obviously one of the major reasons for the later anti-Kabbalistic attitude of Luzzatto, who was in his youth more sympathetic to this lore. See S. D. Luzzatto, *Hebraeische Briefe,* pp. 693–694, 792–793, 925, 935, 966, 1031–1032.

Regarding the acquaintance of Luzzatto with the specific views of Barceloni, it is sufficient to note that the unique manuscript of this *Commentary on Sefer Yeẓirah* was found in Padua, the residence of Luzzatto.

16. *Nouveaux Dialogues sur la Kabbale* (Livorno, 1863), pp. 182–183.

5

Ashkenazi Ḥasidic Views on the Golem

I

As was seen above, the peculiar type of creating the artificial man by Rava was conceived by some Jewish authors as revolving around *Sefer Yeẓirah*.[1] However, besides this statement it is difficult to find any substantial description regarding the details of the use of *Sefer Yeẓirah* as part of a creative human process. Indeed, this tract explicitly alludes to the creative potentialities already inherent in the book, by the very fact that the world was created according to the devices which are central to the theory of this book. The correspondence between the Hebrew letters and the human limbs is a clue for the application of the combinatory technique to the creation of man, as the correspondences are conceived as the guiding lines for this activity. Nevertheless, the extant commentaries on *Sefer Yeẓirah*, composed before the beginning of the thirteenth century, seem to ignore these possibilities.[2] However, we should consider seriously the possibility that techniques exposed by the Ashkenazi masters since the beginning of the thirteenth century are their innovation. At least two commentaries on *Sefer Yeẓirah*, composed in the twelfth century and still available in the second half of the thirteenth century, might have included these techniques or, at least, substantial parts of them, which were subsequently elaborated in the writings of their followers in the thirteenth century. I refer to the commentaries of R. Abraham ibn Ezra and R. Yehudah he-Ḥasid, which may have contributed to the emergence of the techniques that surfaced some few generations after their composition. The probability of such an hypothesis is great; the two authors who offered in the thirteenth century the most detailed discussions of the technique to create an artificial man were R. Eleazar of Worms and R. Abraham Abulafia: the first one was in close relationship with R. Yehudah he-Ḥasid, the other admitted that he studied the commentaries on *Sefer Yeẓirah* composed by the first three.[3] Last but not least: after the discussion of the creation of the artificial man and its destruction, R. Eleazar writes, "so we received concerning this secret."[4] This statement may refer to a tradition inherited from R. Yehudah he-Ḥasid, his main master.

Moreover, a certain legend, committed to writing apparently in the mid-fifteenth century, presents R. Shemuel he-Ḥasid, the father of R. Yehudah he-Ḥasid, as a creator of an artificial man, which accompanied him in his wanderings.[5] What seems to be important in this legend is, however, not only the details of the relationship between the Golem and its creator, but a sentence describing the Golem as mute since "Intelligence and speech are (the prerogative) of the Life of the Worlds."[6] This sentence is a quotation from a famous hymn known as "*Ha-'Aderet veha-'Emunah.*" Originally, this verse had, as it seems, no connection to the story of the Golem; however, it was related to the artificial creation of a man in a commentary on this hymn, which constantly quotes traditions in the name of R. Eleazar of Worms:

> Speech was mentioned together with intelligence, since man has the knowledge to create a new creature by the means of *Sefer Yeẓirah*; but he cannot confer speech upon it, only God alone.[7]

It is possible that the primary source of this statement was indeed the commentary to *Ha-'Aderet veha-'Emunah,* and the apparently late legend used this statement in relation to R. Shemuel he-Ḥasid; this assumption, however, though possible, is not necessary, for it is equally possible that R. Eleazar, who is referred as the source of the tradition, indeed received from his predecessors traditions concerning the nature of artificial creation, and he incorporated it in his commentary. The legend on R. Shemuel he-Ḥasid, therefore, may preserve a much earlier tradition.

II

R. Eleazar of Worms was the main inheritor of some esoteric traditions passed onto him by his teacher, R. Yehudah ha-Ḥasid and his own father. It is he who committed to writing the greater part of the Ashkenazi esotericism and it is no wonder that in his writings we find also the most extensive description of the Golem. Let us cite the discussion of R. Eleazar of Worms on the creation of the artificial man:

> Whoever studies *Sefer Yeẓirah* has to purify himself [and] don white clothes.[8] It is forbidden to study [*Sefer Yeẓirah*] alone, but only [in groups of] two or three, as it is written:[9] "and the souls they made in Ḥaran." And it is written[10]: "Two are better than one [alone]", and it is written[11]: "It is not good for man to be alone; I will make a fitting helper for him." Therefore, [Scripture] begins with a *bet, bereshit bara,* He created. It is incumbent upon him to take virgin soil[12] from a place in the mountains where no one has plowed. And he shall knead[13] the dust with living water,[14] and he shall make a body [Golem] and shall begin to permutate the alphabets of 221 gates, each limb separately, each limb with the corresponding letter mentioned in *Sefer Yeẓirah*. And the alphabets will be permutated at the beginning, and afterwards he shall permutate with the vowel A, A̱, A̤, Ạ, Ạ, Ạ. And always, the letter of the [divine] name with them, and all the alphabet; afterward A̱I, then ẠI, and then A̤I, and then AỊ. Afterward [the permutation of] AV, and similarly AḢ in its entirety. Afterward, he shall appoint B and likewise C, and each limb with the letter designated to it. He shall do all this when he is pure. These are the 221 gates.[15]

Before entering into the details of the creation of the artificial man, let me address a semantic question. The operator is supposed to create a figure, or a body out of dust; this form is called Golem and this term ostensibly refers to an entity which is not created in a magical way, but it is only the starting point for the magical creation. Therefore, the proposal of Scholem to see in this term the earliest occurrence of the word as signifying a magically created being is doubtful.[16] Conspicuously, the operation which involves the pronunciation of the letters of the alphabet begins only after the preparation of the form. An important proof for the standard meaning of the term Golem in the above text is found in another passage of R. Eleazar's commentary on *Sefer Yeẓirah*; when explaining the meaning of the term *sefer* he writes: "It is the writing of the Golem of the letter, in order to teach them. . . ."[17] I assume that the "Golem of the letter" here has nothing magical implied and it simply refers to the form of the letter. Such an understanding is completely coherent with both the context of its occurrence and the terminological tradition related to the term Golem as external form.

The material having been prepared, the operator begins the process wherein the recitation of letters is involved; until now, no use of them seems to be necessary. A comparison between the stages of creation here and those in the following texts penned by R. Eleazar or patterned on his views, and the above discussion of the midrash, will prove that the Ashkenazi author, like the Midrashic Rabbi, did not envision the Golem as the result of any act connected to permutations of letters. This latter act, absent in the ancient descriptions of the creation of Adam, seems to parallel the divine infusion of a certain spiritual essence into the motionless Golem. The basic magical activity begins with the combinations of the letters after the Golem is already structured.

The first stage of creation by permutation is related solely to the combination of letters of the alphabet; the operator combines 221 combinations of two letters, each of them named "gate". Therefore, the correspondence of letters to limbs is operative at this stage. Following the directives of *Sefer Yeẓirah*, the operator is combining it with all the other letters of the alphabet, so that all the limbs mentioned in *Sefer Yeẓirah* are related to these combinations. The permutation of letters is described in the *Commentary* at length, where the tables explaining the combinations of letters were supplied.

III

Similar discussions of the creation of the creature recur in another writing of R. Eleazar, *Sefer ha-Shem.*[18] According to one of these discussions, the Torah that preexisted the world and was the blueprint of its creation comprised "the permutations of the letters in order to create by them whatever He wants."[19] Immediately afterwards the author adduces a table of the permutations of the letters identical to that found in the *Commentary on Sefer Yeẓirah.*[20] Therefore, the creativeness of the permutations of the alphabets, which served God in order to create the world, is also used in order to create a creature. Indeed, immediately afterward he refers to the permutations of each letter with the first half of the alphabet which are creative, and those of the letters with the second half of the alphabet, which are to be used when someone "desires to return it to dust". This issue of returning the creation to dust will concern us later on. Here it is pertinent to remark that the technique of creating the creature is the combinations of the letters appointed to the limbs with the alphabets alone, i.e., only the first step according to the *Commentary on Sefer Yeẓirah.*

In the latter work, R. Eleazar also mentions a second step, when the letters corresponding to the limbs are combined with the letters of the divine name, namely with Y, H, V, H and pronounced according to the six vowels mentioned in the *Commentary.* In the first phase, the combinations involve consonants alone; it seems reasonable to assume that the combinations were also recited but the vocalization is not mentioned. Therefore all the letters of the alphabet are combined with the four letters of the Tetragrammaton, and vocalized according to a certain order to be discussed below. This operation is also performed in relationship to the limbs of the man. At this stage, the emphasis is on the permutations of the vowels much more than on the letters. What R. Eleazar of Worms exactly intended when he refers to the vowel-permutation is not elaborated in the *Commentary on Sefer Yeẓirah,* but the tables containing the combinations of the letters of the alphabet with the letters of the divine name and with the various vowels were preserved in *Sefer ha-Shem.* Without referring to the creation of the Golem, these tables exemplify the principle underlying the statement regarding the permutation in the second stage of the creation of the creature.[21]

What may have been the source of the combinations of the letters of the Tetragrammaton with each letter of the alphabet in the context of the creation of a creature? It seems that R. Eleazar did not invent such a device, or at least he did not invent it out of the blue. Already Rashi, in his commentary on the *Sanhedrin* passage, remarked that: "by the means of *Sefer Yeẓirah,* they (!) studied the combination of the letters of the (divine) Name."[22] The assumption of this statement is that the divine name was involved in the creative process of the Golem, but its letters were combined according to a device found, according to Rashi, in *Sefer Yeẓirah.* This treatise does not, however, discuss the creation of man by the combination of letters of the Tetragrammaton. Therefore, Rashi's view is neither a direct conclusion from the Talmudic passage nor from the text of *Sefer Yeẓirah* as it is formulated in the extant editions. It may include, therefore, a certain interpretation of this treatise in line with that elaborated later on by R. Eleazar of Worms. In any case, it is important to remark that one of the teachers of Rashi, R. Jacob ben Yaqar, was interested in *Sefer Yeẓirah,* as short discussions related to this text testify.[23] R. Eleazar also indicated other elements which are part of this second stage of creating the creature, as for example, vowel-permutation. But even if this is a later Ashkenazi addition, an issue that is open to dispute,[24] a short remark of Rashi seems to contain, *in ovo,* the device of R. Eleazar's second stage.

Another possible indication of the existence of a two-stage technique of creation by the combinations of letters is found in the writing of the most bitter opponent of R. Eleazar, R. Moses Taqu[25] in his *Ketav Tamim.*

In a fierce critique of the Ḥasidei Ashkenaz theology as exposed by the circle of R. Yehudah he-Ḥasid, Taqu writes in connection to the creation of the calf as described in the *Sanhedrin* passage:

> They were pronouncing the names that emerge from the verses of the [pericope of] formation [*yeẓirah*][26] or they were permutating at the beginning of the 231 gates of the alphabet and pronounce the names which emerge from them[27], as it is written in *Sefer Yeẓirah.*[28]

Two types of creation by linguistic techniques are indicated here; the use of the creative forces inherent in the letters of the first chapter of Genesis, or, alternatively, a technique which includes as a first stage the combinations of the letters of the alphabets and, afterwards, of the divine names that emerge from these combinations. In the very least, the two stages of linguistic creation outlined here are similar to the technique exposed by R. Eleazar.

IV

Let me address a recurring theme in R. Eleazar's treatment of the creation of the Golem by combination of letters; the operator is said to use 221 combinations that are the combinations of the twenty-one letters, appointed over the various limbs, with the first eleven letters of the alphabet; these combinations are the forward, creative permutations whereas the combinations of the twenty-two letters with the last eleven letters of the alphabet are conceived as destructive, annihilating the creature that emerged previously. This issue, mentioned several times in the writings of R. Eleazar, may, or may not, immediately precede the creation. Nowhere does this master prescribe an immediate destruction of the creature; the usage of phrases like "if he desires to destroy" when introducing the inverse technique, points to the possibility that the Golem will not be reduced to dust at all or, at least, not immediately after its creation. If this reading of the statements is accurate, then the ecstatic element of the rite[29] will become, even in the case where it indeed was part of the rite, secondary. The material, rather than the spiritual, achievement will preoccupy the operator. Such a conclusion is corroborated by a discussion on the creative powers of the righteous found in another writing of R. Eleazar. In his *Sefer Tagi,* we learn that:

> In the future, the righteous will cause the resurrection of the dead, [like] Eliyahu, Elisha [and] Ezekiel as it is written[30] "The seal [*ḥotam*][31] will be changed into clay". . . . Why is it not written "made"[32] [instead of changed]? Because it [the verse] hints at the righteous

> who know how to create by means of the combination of letters, and they created a man by means of *Sefer Yeẓirah*, but he was not similar to the man created by God in His wisdom . . . this is the reason of the fact that if he will sin, he [apparently the Golem] will return to the dust.[33]

The meaning of the passage is far from being clear; I assume that the author refers to the extraordinary power of the righteous to create, by means of combinations of letters, a man, i.e., the Golem, which will be changed into clay, or return to dust if the righteous will sin. If this explanation is correct, the assumption of the author is that the creature was supposed to have a rather lasting existence, stopped only by the sin of the human creator.

V

Let us address another text extant in several manuscript versions which incorporates the two stages of R. Eleazar, adding some new details:

> This creature that you want to create: with regard to each and every particular limb [of it], look inside and see what letter you must appoint to it, and combine it as I shall instruct you. And you must take virgin soil from underneath virgin earth and seed it here and there upon your holy Temple in a state of [ritual] purity. Purify yourself and form from this soil a Golem which you want to create and imbue with the spirit of life. See what letter you must appoint to it, and what proceeds from it. Do so also with the letters of the Tetragrammaton, by means of which the entire world was created. Formulate a *notariqon,* and recite each of its letters with the vowels O A I E EI U, and that limb will immediately be animated.[34]

The sentence beginning with the words "do so" indicates another type of action, distinct from that mentioned earlier. Thus, the first action is related to the limb of the man and the letters in general; then the letters of the Tetragrammaton are mentioned which, like in the case of the above technique of R. Eleazar of Worms, are to be pronounced according to a certain vocalization, *notariqon,* that refers to the six vowels also in the case of R. Eleazar.[35] If we may infer from this quotation the views of R. Eleazar as well, then the role of the letters of the divine name is to animate the organs of the artificial man. Thus, the two-stage process ends in the vivification of man, but it leaves the reader without any clear indication as to the experience of the operator himself, who, according to

Scholem, is supposed to undergo a mystical experience as part of, or as the culmination of, the emergence of the Golem.[36]

The above text includes a detail that is important for understanding the concept of the creation of the creature. At the beginning, the operator is supposed to bring the virgin soil to his "Temple"—*miqdashekha* or the House of your Temple, *beit miqdashekha,* or, according to other versions, to the house of study, *beit midrashekha.*[37] Then, he is supposed to spread it in this room and only afterwards is he said to create the body out of this soil. The question which arises is: why is someone supposed to seed the virgin soil before he creates the artificial man? I assume that by means of this ritual one imitates the creation of Adam by God according to the Midrashic literature. According to several sources, Adam was created out of the dust collected from the four corners of the world. At the same time several Jewish sources, occurring at least in one occassion together with the view that Adam was created from the earth of the four corners[38], maintain that man was created from the earth of the altar or, according to other sources, from the dust of the Temple.[39] The fact that the operator is performing a ritual connected to the Temple is corroborated by the prerequisite of purity; likewise, the recitation of the letters of the divine name is reminiscent of the role of the great priest, the only person who was permitted to pronounce the divine name. Therefore, it seems highly probable that the Ashkenazi author proposed a ritual that is ostensibly reiterating the primordial creation on one side and acts related to the temple on the other side. At least the mention of the creative quality of the letters of the Tetragrammaton is indicative of the imitative nature of the Golem rite. In this connection it is noteworthy that as part of the creation of the embryo, the seed of the couple is spread all over the storehouse (*goren*) according to two sources dealing with this topic. In the earlier texts, the way this seed is restored so as to enter the process of development in the womb of the mother is not mentioned at all.[40]

VI

The connection to the temple being evident, both because of the explicit mentioning of the Temple and because of the creative aspect of the dust of the Temple in sources that predate the Golem practice, let me address another connotation which this version of the technique recalls, and to a certain extent the other three versions of the technique as well. I refer to the ritual of testing the *Soṭah,* a woman suspected of adultery; according to the biblical verses, the bitter water, that is the touch-stone for her integrity or adultery, is to be prepared in the following way: "and the priest shall take holy water in an earthen vessel; and of the dust that is on the floor [literally, the soil, *qarqa*'][41] of the tabernacle shall the priest take, and put it into the water."[42] Here we have a clear reference to dust and water in connection to the tabernacle, which in the later texts was changed to the Temple.[43] Though the ritual is conspicuously connected to a suspicion of illicit sexual relations, no evidence can be adduced from the biblical text as to the creative outcome of this ritual.[44] However, in the Midrash and the Talmud, such a connotation can be found. According to Rava, if the *soṭah* undergoes the test positively, her compensation will be "a son who will be like Abraham, on whom it is written,[45] 'I, [who am] dust and ashes.'[46] If she did not gain [the test] she will return to her dust".[47] The two alternatives, to give birth to a son or to return to the dust, are similar to the two acts of the magical operator, to create the Golem and to return him to the dust. Interestingly, the Amora who formulated this explanation of the ritual of the so*ṭah* is the same person who is the hero of the creation of the first Golem, in the famous passage in *Sanhedrin.*

According to another discussion of the *soṭah,* attributed to R. Meir, a second century Tanna, the so*ṭah* is tested by dust because "out of it Adam was created, and this is the reason why she is given to drink from it, since if she is pure, she conceives and gives birth to a son in his image."[48] If the attribution of this statement to R. Meir is correct, then the statement of Rava has some polemical implications, for he prefers Abraham to Adam, the former being a less mythical figure in comparison to the legendary hero.

It is possible that here the use of the materials mentioned in connection with the creation of Adam has some mythical implications. Thus, for example, R. Isaiah Horwitz proposed in *Shenei Luḥot ha-Berit* that the reason the dust of the tabernacle is used is reminiscent of the creation of Adam from the dust of the altar, and that the first sin of Adam was the reason for Eve's sexual transgression with the serpent.[49] In one way or another, it seems that the connections between the primordial couple and the so*ṭah* ritual may, indeed, be productive for the understanding of the mythical background of the amoraic interpretation of the *soṭah* ritual, but we cannot enter this rather speculative domain here as it does not, presumably, contribute to the understanding of the Golem ritual.

Moreover, in the same Talmudic context, the biblical mention of water is understood as "living water" an expression found in another technique of creating the Golem out of dust.[50] It seems that the pouring of the living water in the dust of the soil of the Tabernacle, together with the formula written down by the priest which includes also the Tetragrammaton, may have, in the case of the woman's integrity, a creative effect in the form of the birth of a son. These Tannaitic and Amoraic understandings of the outcome of the ritual are indeed reminiscent of the ritual of creating an anthropoid out of the same materials used in preparation of the bitter water. Indeed, in medieval times, a magical practice is found which stands between the ancient biblical prescription related to the rite of the *soṭah* and the medieval technique of creating a Golem. G. Scholem has remarked, in connection to the Ashkenazi prescriptions for creating a Golem, that a similar ritual related to the *soṭah* is found in Jewish medieval magic.[51] According to this recipe, a pure man, playing the role of the ancient priest, will take water from an overflowing spring, in lieu of the "holy water" of the old times, and instead of the dust of the tabernacle, he shall go to the Synagogue and take therefrom dust from the four corners of the arch of the Torah. Then he shall throw that dust in the waters of the spring, and write the divine names mentioned beforehand, and give the waters which dissolved the names to the *soṭah*. How the divine names were written down we do not know. Since no additional instruments are mentioned, I assume that the names were written down on the dust, already found on the surface of the water, and then additional water was used in order to dissolve the names. If so, we may have in this magical text a first evidence of writing down something on the dust as part of an oracular ordeal. As we shall see below, a technique of preparing a Golem by writing on the dust is extant, and it may indeed be connected to the present magical text.[52]

VII

According to another version, whose authorship is obscure, it is not the Temple (*miqdashekha*) of someone where the Golem is created but his house of study, *beit Midrashekha* or *midrashekha*. The later form appears in a passage extant in R. Menaḥem Ẓiyoni's *Commentary to the Pentateuch*; when discussing the powers of the name of seventy-two groups of letters he wrote:

> And whoever wishes to perform an operation using it [namely the divine name] shall do so: He shall bring virgin soil, which was never plowed and scatter it in your study [*midrashekha*], or in the place where we will do the [magical] signs ['*otot*], and you shall wash yourself and immerse [yourself] in water and cloth yourself with white clothes and shall pronounce with awe . . .[53]

The author continues to describe the magical operations which can be performed by this preparation which are curative in nature and the issue of an artificial man in not even mentioned. Nevertheless, I assume that the above quotation is related to the creation of the Golem for several reasons:

a) the preparations described above are closely parallel to those we have met in the *Commentary on Sefer Yeẓirah* of R. Eleazar of Worms; they include the condition to don white clothes and to collect earth from a virgin soil which was not plowed.
b) the mention of the study occurs in one of the above texts which presumably is reflecting the views of R. Eleazar or, at least, of his school.
c) the name of seventy-two mentioned here is related to the creation of the Golem by R. Abraham Abulafia.[54] Since there is no reason to assume that R. Menaḥem Ẓiyoni was influenced by Abulafia's Kabbalah, it seems reasonable to surmise the existence of a common source in which there was a link between this divine name and the creation of the Golem.
d) Ẓiyoni preserved material from Ashkenazi Ḥasidism, especially from R. Eleazar of Worms, some of it still unidentified, and therefore it is possible that this is the case here as well.[55]

VIII

Another version of creating a Golem extant in the Ashkenazi circles is found in *Sefer ha-Gemaṭri'ot,* a collectanaea of traditions stemming from the disciples of R. Yehudah he-Ḥasid, composed, it is reasonable to assume, in the second third of the thirteenth century.[56] According to this version:

> Ben Sira wanted to study *Sefer Yeẓirah.* A voice [bat qol] came out and said, "You cannot do it alone." He went to Jeremiah his father. Ben Sira is [numerically equivalent to] Ben Jeremiah,[57] [the son of Jeremiah] and they studied it and after three years, a man was created to them, upon whose forehead it was written *'Emet,* as on the forehead of Adam.[58] And the created one said to them: If the Unique One, the Holy One, Blessed be He, created Adam, when he wanted to kill [*lehamit*] Adam, He erased a letter from *'emet* and what remained is *MeT* [dead], even more so I would like to do it and you shall no longer create a man, so that people shall not err concerning him, as it happened in the generation of Enosh.[59] This is why Jeremiah said:[60] Cursed is the man who relies on Adam. The created man said to them: Reverse the combination of the letters backwards. And they erased the letter *'aleph* from his forehead and he immediately turned into ashes.[61]

This version includes two different ways to annihilate the Golem; the first, mentioned by the Golem itself in connection with the death of Adam, is the erasing of the *'aleph* of *'emet.* Accordingly, this act alone is sufficient to turn the creature to dust or ashes. The other one, indicated also by the Golem, consists in the reversal of the combinations of the letters of the alphabets, which is not, however, mentioned as actually performed by the two operators. I assume that the two ways to reduce the creature to ashes reflect two different traditions which were combined together. The one transmitted in the introduction to the *Commentary on Sefer Yeẓirah* of Pseudo-Sa'adyah, where it stands alone, without the specification of the need to reverse the combinations of letters. This author adduces this tradition as a Midrashic concept:

> As it is said in the Midrash, Jeremiah and Ben Sira have created a man by means of *Sefer Yeẓirah*, and on his forehead it was written *'Emet* just as the name which was pronounced on the Formation [*yeẓirah*] [in the verse] as Elohim created and performed. And this man was erasing the 'aleph, namely the Holy, Blessed be He alone, and the man had to die for the sake of the man whom they created by the name of God, and it is none besides Him.[62]

Therefore, this way of undoing the created man is similar to the tradition adduced in *Sefer ha-Gemaṭri'ot.* On the other hand, the technique to reverse the combination of letters is existent independently of the former one, as we shall see later.[63]

IX

Another discussion stemming from Ashkenazi circles is found in R. Shimeon ben Shemuel's *Hadrat Qodesh* also called *'Adam Sikhli.* This tract, composed in 1400, preserves some mystical traditions of the Ashkenazi school, and this seems, as Scholem has already proposed, to be the case also in this instance:

> It is known that whoever is expert in *Sefer Yeẓirah* is able to perform operations by the holy names, and out of the elements, dust of a virgin soil and water, a body [Golem] and form will emerge. Even though [this body] has vitality, it is called dead [met] since he cannot confer upon it knowledge of divine issues and speech, for knowledge and speech are [the prerogative of] the Life of the Worlds[64]. The Holy One, Blessed be He, has sealed man, [by the sign of] *'Emet* [truth], which is hinted at in the verse,[65] "And He breathed into his nostrils the breath of life", the end-letters of these words being *ḥo-*

> *tam* [seal] since man was the seal of the Formation in the Account of Creation, and His seal is the creation of man.[66] And this is said in the verse[67] "God has created and performed."[68]

Several details are reminiscent of the technique proposed by R. Eleazar of Worms: the virgin soil, the use of the holy names and the reference to the verse from *Ha'-aderet veha-'Emunah.* It appears, then, that the above passage includes only one element that is absent in the classical Ashkenazi versions of the production of the Golem, namely, the philosophical use of Golem and *ẓurah* as found in the Spanish philosophers.[69] Basically, it deals with the *'emet-met* phases as in the previous texts. Thus we may conclude that the version of the creation of the Golem by Jeremiah and Ben Sira as related by *Sefer ha-Gemaṭri'ot* includes two distinct traditions, which were associated in the circle of R. Yehudah he-Ḥasid.

X

This conclusion may help us to reexamine the relationship between one of the most influential traditions on the Golem, that found in the circle of Kabbalists who produced treatises constituting the literature close to *Sefer ha-'Iyyun,* and the traditions from the circle of R. Yehudah he-Ḥasid. In his article on the Golem, Scholem presented the text to be analyzed below as written under the influence of the Ashkenazi Hasidim, and he pointed to the excerpt from *Sefer ha-Gemaṭri'ot* and the passage from Pseudo-Sa'adyiah's *Commentary on Sefer Yeẓirah* as the possible sources.[70] Later on, J. Dan proposed to see in the version found in the circle of *'Iyyun* the result of the influence of Pseudo-Sa'adyah's commentary, implicitly rejecting the possible influence of the circle of R. Yehudah he-Ḥasid[71]. He subsequently even predated the text to the writings of R. Isaac Sagi-Nahor, considered by the Kabbalists to be the father of the Kabbalah, and to the period of the *Bahir.* As an illustration of this early dating, he posited this text on the Golem as one of the first among the earliest Kabbalistic texts.[72] Such a far-reaching conclusion, when stated without appropriate evidence, invites meticulous inspection of all the relevant material which, unfortunately, was not undertaken.[73] So, for example, only the material found in the Pseudo-Sa'adyah was taken into consideration in this context, neglecting the elements included in the version in *Sefer ha-Gemaṭri'ot.* Given the absence of a philological examination of this important issue, let me elaborate upon what was presented as the earliest of the early Kabbalistic texts. In a manuscript treatise named *The Secret of the Name of 42 Letters,* the anonymous Kabbalist introduces the following version of the Golem creation by some sentences that did not draw the attention of scholars:

This [divine] name is unknown and incomprehensible but by the thought, and it is not comprehended but by five things,[74] which are *Tiqqun* and *Ẓeruf* and *Ma'amar* and *Mikhlol* and *Ḥeshbon. Tiqqun* [proper order][75], is to know the name from its beginning to its end, as it is written. *Ẓeruf* is when you combine it with the 22 alphabets of *Sefer Yeẓirah*; and you shall know how to make from each and every combination [*Ẓeruf*] and *Ma'amar* and afterwards to comprise [*likhlol*] all of them together, which is the meaning of *Mikhlol*. Afterwards [you] have to know the calculation so as not to err when you join the letters and their vowels. All these things are comprised in *Sefer Yeẓirah*, and this is the reason why the Sages opened [*Sefer Yeẓirah*] with LB, and it is the essence of the written Torah, as we said B of *Bereshit* [and] L of Israel.[76] And on this issue the Torah said,[77] "Man cannot know its order [literally, value], nor is it found in the land of the living." On this the Sages O. B. M. said: If man knew its order, he could create worlds like the Holy One, Blessed be He.[78] We found in *Sefer ha-Biṭṭaḥon* written by R. Yehudah (ben Bateirah)[79] that Jeremiah, O. B. M. was studying *Sefer Yeẓirah* alone: A voice came out and said to him: Take a companion. He went to Sira his son and they studied [together] for three years in order to accomplish what was written.[80] Then they that feared the Lord spoke one with the other. At the end of the three years, when they wanted to combine the alphabets, according to the *Ẓeruf*, [combination] the *Mikhlol* and the *Ma'amar*, a man was created, and on his forhead it was written, *YHVH 'Elohim 'Emet*. In the hand of that man there was a knife, and he was erasing the *aleph* of the word 'emet and there remained met. Jeremiah rent his garment and said to him, Why did you erase the *'aleph* of *'emet*?" He answered him, "I will tell you a parable[81]. . . . Thus is God, when He created you in the image, likeness and form. Now, when you created a man like Him, the people will say that there is no God in the world but you." Jeremiah told him, "If so, how can we repair it?" [*Ma'y taqanateh?*] He answered them, "Write the letters backwards on the dust that was thrown, by the intention of your heart and do not think about the way of [its] honor or of its order [*tiqquno*][82] but do all this backwards."[83] And they also did so and that man became before their eyes dust and ashes. Then, Jeremiah said,[84] "Indeed it is worthwhile to study these matters for the sake of knowing the power and dynamis of the creator of the world, but not in order to do [them]. You shall study them in order to comprehend and teach."[85]

It is evident that the story of the Golem illustrated the potential inherent in the mystical techniques mentioned at the beginning of the above passage. The study of *Sefer Yeẓirah* by the two figures is described as focused on the *ẓeruf,* one of the categories enumerated beforehand. By virtue of the combination of the letters in a peculiar way, to be dealt with immediately, the man was created. In the moment the two heroes of the story wanted to annihilate the man, they used the same technique, in an inversed order. Therefore, the anonymous Kabbalist uses the story of the Golem in order to exemplify by means of a practical example the possibilities of the mystical techniques. He uses the story of the Golem since it includes the process of combinations of letters, their pronunciation, understood as the *ma'amar;* even the *tiqqun* is mentioned, by using a pun "order" as understood at the beginning of the text, and repair by the reversal of the order, hinted at in the question and answer "*ma'y taqanateih*?." However, it is obvious that this reinterpretation of the five linguistic techniques is an artificial one, intended to exemplify the application of the various stages of the techniques as one continuous process. Therefore, it seems reasonable to assume that the Golem story is an adaptation of an already existing story to the conceptual requirements of the '*Iyyun* circle, and therefore it is to be understood as a certain development in this circle.

What is the source of the Golem legend adopted by the anonymous Kabbalist? It is obvious that the *vorlage* which stood before the eyes of the anonymous Kabbalist, included the technique of annihilating the Golem by the reversal of the combinations of the letters; moreover, the definition of the combination of the alphabets is, according to this text, the combination of the letters of the divine name with the combinations of the letters of the alphabets. This peculiar understanding of the creative process as the association of the letters of the divine names with the combinations of the letters of the alphabets is characteristic, as far as we know, of R. Eleazar of Worms, and it is part of the second stage of the creation of the Golem, as we described it above. On the other hand, the technique to annihilate the Golem is not identical to that of R. Eleazar but it is the same as that found in *Sefer ha-Gemaṭri'ot.* The prescription for the annihilation of the artificial man in the so-called *Sefer ha-Biṭṭaḥon* is completely different from that of the Pseudo-Sa'adyah, where the operator has to walk backward in order to undo the Golem. In addition, the description of the annihilation of the Golem in the *Sefer ha-Biṭṭaḥon* is similar to that of *Sefer Gemaṭri'ot.* In both cases the artificial anthropoid is described as returning to ashes, a motif completely different from the Pseudo-Sa'adyah's view on the sinking of the creature. Therefore, the version of the Golem creation in the circle of '*Iyyun* incorporated elements from the circle of R. Yehudah he-Ḥasid and R. Eleazar of Worms, whereas the similarity to the Pseudo-Sa'adyah concerns the same material included as well in *Sefer ha-Gematri'ot.* If these conclusions are correct, then we must defer the dating of the version of the Golem creation in the *'Iyyun* literature from the late twelfth century, as proposed by Dan, or early thirteenth century, as proposed by Scholem, to a later period.[86] How late it is, is a matter of debate.

Let me turn to the specific way the inverse combinations are to be performed; the writing of the letters on the dust, which was spread in order to create the Golem. It would appear that this device is not original with the *'Iyyun* text, but is to be found in a larger discussion preserved by a later Kabbalist, R. Abraham Galante.

XI

A separate technique of creating a Golem, apparently of Ashkenazi extraction, though possibly including in its present form also later elements, was preserved, as Scholem has remarked,[87] by R. Abraham Galante. He was a sixteenth century Safedian Kabbalist, a disciple of R. Moses Cordovero, and his view was quoted by R. Abraham Azulai, in the latter's commentary on the *Zohar, 'Or ha-Ḥamah,* as follows:

> The creation of all the worlds was [accomplished] by the twenty-two letters, and so also the creation of man by the twenty-two letters. The father, when he engenders his son, engraves the twenty-two letters which his father engraved in him . . . at the time of his [own] engendering. By the virtue of these twenty-two letters the foetus emerges and develops. Likewise the existence of the creature created by the ancients, as it is indicated in the Gemara that R. Hoshayah created a man, and similar things, [these] were by means of the twenty-two letters. And they were doing it in the following way: They took new dust, which was not wrought, and spread it on the earth in a homogenuous way [*beshaveh*]. Then they engraved in this dust the name of the thing they wanted to create, and with each and every letter they were combining all the alphabets. How [was it done]? [In the case of the creation of] a man [*'Adam*] they were combining the letter 'A with all the alphabets, then the letter D with all the alphabets and likewise the letter M with all the alphabets, all this together with other conditions that they were doing. Then that thing was created. And if they wanted to wipe it out and destroy its structure (*binyano*), they were turned the alphabets backwards, together with the letters of that thing they had created, and it was wiped out by itself. This is the reason that when [the creature] came in the presence of R. Ḥanina, he turned the letters, as mentioned above, this being [the meaning] of his saying to him: "Return to your dust. . . .

Since all the combinations which are backwards are pointing to [strict] judgement and destruction."[88]

The affinities between this text and the other Ashkenazi practices are evident: a) the combination of the use of dust and pronunciation of the combinations of the alphabets; b) the way to annihilate the creature is similar to that in the text of R. Eleazar. However, some important elements shared by the Ashkenazi recipes are absent here: the dust is not kneaded and the formation of the human form is not done manually, but firstly by the writing down, and then by combining the letters which form the name of the entity to be created. Therefore, it seems that the dust was spread over the floor, and the anthropoid form was created by itself; this view seems to be consonant to the version of the Golem as it appears in the *Sefer ha-Biṭṭaḥon* version, where the annihilation of the Golem is accomplished by the writing down in an inverse order in the dust that which "was cast." The terms used for this act are identical; there also the alphabets alone are written down. It is possible that this version, though preserved in a very late source, contains the technique which lays behind the vague indications of the text formulated in the circle of *Sefer ha-'Iyyun.* This assumption is corroborated by the magical text dealing with the test of the *soṭah*, where it is possible that the divine names, which according to the Bible were written down on a scroll, instead were written down on the dust.[89]

XII

The emphasis on the role of the name of the being to be created is presented here in a clear way; it has to be written down on the earth and also pronounced when combined with the letters of the alphabets. This indication seems to imply that there is a creative power inherent in the letters in general, and in the particular combination which constitutes the name of a particular thing in Hebrew. This assumption occurs also in the writing of a contemporary of Galante, R. Joseph Ashkenazi, the Tanna of Safed.[90] In his attack on the philosophical and Kabbalistic-philosophical literary productions in the Middle Ages, R. Joseph discusses the relationship between the calling of the names of all the beings by Adam and the animation of the beings after the names were pronounced. He indicates that the order of the biblical treatment of these two issues reveals a significant fact: the relationship between the expression of the name and the lower soul, *nefesh ḥayyah,* mentioned in the Bible.[91] In this context R. Joseph mentions that the above issue is similar to the tradition that

> a man can make a Golem[92] which possesses a living soul [*nefesh ḥayyah*] by the power of his speech, but the [higher] soul [*neshamah*] cannot be conferred by man because it is from the divine speech. Behold, [you can] understand the issue of the [higher] souls [*neshamot*] which are in the body [*guf*][93], hewn from the throne of glory,[94] which are but their names[95], which are [identical to] their [higher] souls.[96]

R. Joseph assumes, that the pronunciation of the name is tantamount to a certain manipulation of the soul; thus, someone who pronounces the name can create a Golem, which has the lower soul. This Kabbalist apparently distinguishes between the divine speech which confers the higher soul (*nishmat ḥayyim*) to man, according to Gen. 2:7 and the human one, which is able to confer only the lower soul, *nefesh ḥayyah.* The creative power of the name of a certain being is conspicuous here as in the case of the recipe of Galante's tradition. It is possible to assume that the affinity between the two explanations of the creation of the Golem, issued by two contemporary authors dwelling in the same town, are related to each other; such an explanation would enable us to envision this affinity in a simple way: the authors followed similar traditions that were extant in Safed. However, as far as we know, the text of R. Joseph quoted above was composed in Northern Italy, before his emigration to Safed. Thus, a direct relationship between the two texts seems implausible. An alternative explanation would be that the two Kabbalists inherited similar traditions, apparently of Ashkenazi extraction.

Notably conspicuous is the absence of the use of the divine names in the device of Abraham Galante. The indications found in this recipe, which make it so singular are, however, more important than its affinities to the Ashkenazi parallels. The motif of the embryo, which was neglected by the other Ashkenazi devices, is here presented in a very explicit way. It may be that the specific explanation of the similarity between the emergence of the foetus and the Golem is late; this, indeed, may be possible but it is not necessary.[97] In any case the very comparison between them is highly instructive, since it points out, from a new angle, the affinity between the natural and the artificial creation. As to the technique employed in order to structure the peculiar nature of the creature, it is of utmost importance to remark that the above prescription is not specifically one intended to create a man but a device that can be used for the creation of any kind of creature, provided its name is known. The Golem is only one particular case of a larger range of creation, which is based upon the magical powers inherent in the name of a certain entity, instead of that of the divine name in the regular techniques.

XIII

The classical description of the creation of the Golem includes the combination of letters according to *Sefer Yeẓirah*. On the other hand, the same combinations are used by God in order to create the *yeẓur* and *dibbur.* If, according to our interpretation, *yeẓur* refers to a human being, we may assume that man also was created by God using the technique of combining the 231 gates. However, this implicit reading of *Sefer Yeẓirah* is not found in the standard commentaries of this work where the creation of the Golem by man is mentioned. However, at least in one text, the combination of the twenty-two letters, in relation to *Sefer Yeẓirah*, is conceived of as the manner in which man was created by God. In R. Menaḥem Ẓiyoni's *Commentary on the Torah,* we read that:

> I shall explain [the creation of man] according to the way of *Sefer Yeẓirah*. Know that by the combination of the twenty-two holy letters, inscribed on the arm of God,[98] He formed man. By three words[99]: *'AMSh,* by means of them He created the essence of the body, by the combination of 'A. *'AShM,* by means of it He created the air, created out of the wind. By it He created the body of Adam and Eve. Male by *'AMSh,* female by *'AShM.* M, through which He formed earth out of water, and with it He created the belly in man. Sh by which He formed heaven out of fire, by it He formed the head in man. The ones in the first day, and the others in the sixth day. By the seven double consonants, BGD KPRT, He formed the seven gates in the body and the seven stars on the fourth day . . . By twelve simple letters HV ZH LN S' ZQ He formed the twelve signs of the Zodiac and the twelve servants in the body. . . .[100]

I did not quote all the details of the correspondence between the creation of man by letters and that of the world. What is important for our theme is the very fact that the correspondence between letters, limbs and cosmological things is treated here in the frame of a creative process. Thus *Sefer Yeẓirah* is conceived to be the directory of both the creation of the world and that of man. An inspection of the material presented by Ẓiyoni in the entire description demonstrates that it is based upon the views of *Sefer Yeẓirah*, arranged in a different order, and the most significant addition being the ideas that the creation was done by means of the combination of these letters.

With respect to the origins of this emphasis on the combination of letters, we have no definite answer. It is possible that the whole text is an innovation of the Ashkenazi author; however, it is equally possible that this Kabbalist preserved an earlier tradition. This possibility is enforced by the fact that this author had at his disposal other earlier material from the circle of the Ashkenazi Ḥasidim, quoted throughout this commentary.

Notes

1. See ch. 3, par. 2; ch. 4, par. 2. See also par. 3 below.

2. See ch. 4, par. 1.

3. See Jellinek, *Bet ha-Midrasch,* vol. 3, pp. 42–43. (German part).

4. *Perush Sefer Yeẓirah,* fol. 5b.

5. N. Bruell, *Jahrbuch fur Jüdische Geschichte und Literatur,* vol. 9, (1889), p. 27; Scholem, "The Idea of the Golem," pp. 198–199.

6. Ms., Jerusalem, 3182, fol. 109b: "*Lefi sheha-dibbur le-ḥay ha-'olamim*". On this manuscript and another one stemming from the fifteenth century, see Sara Zfatman, "The Mayse-Buch: an Old Yiddish Literary Genre", *Ha-Sifrut,* vol. 28 (1979), pp. 126–152. (Hebrew) See especially p. 140 where the Hebrew and Yiddish versions were presented. Her suggestions that the material preserved in the fifteenth century may be earlier seems to me very plausible and it is quite possible that the legend stems from the circle of the Ashkenazi Ḥasidism, rather than being a late, popular invention.

7. *Siddur R. Naftali Zvi Herz* (Thiengen, 1560), fol. 28, b,2. See also Scholem, *Origins of the Kabbalah,* p. 122 n. 125. R. Abraham ben Azriel's, *'Arugat ha-Bosem,* ed. E. E. Urbach, vol. 4 (Jerusalem, 1963), p. 478. On this commentary, see J. Dan, "Perushei 'Ha-'Aderet ve-ha-'Emunah' shel Ḥasidei Ashkenaz", *Tarbiẓ,* vol. 50 (1981), pp. 396–404. (Hebrew)

8. This is a commonplace in magic devices; see Idel, *The Mystical Experience,* p. 39.

9. Gen. 12:5.

10. Eccles. 4:9.

11. Gen. 2:18.

12. *Qarqa' betulah.* This expression occurs also in other recipes to create a Golem to be studied below. See par. 5, 9 and ch. 9 par. 4.

13. *Vayigabbel he-'afar.* On the verb *gbl* in connection to the creation of Adam see our discussion above of *Leviticus Rabbah* 29, in ch. 3, par. 4–5.

14. *Mayyim ḥayyim.* See n. 50 below.

15. *Commentary on Sefer Yeẓirah,* fol. 15d.

16. "The Idea of the Golem," p. 174. On the whole issue, see the detailed discussion in Appendix B below.

17. *Commentary on Sefer Yeẓirah*, fol. 2b.

18. Ms. Oxford, 1566, fol. 46b–47a.

19. Ibid. fol. 46ab. This view is reminiscent of Sarug's theory of the primordial Torah as the *malbush.* See below ch. 10, par. 7a.

20. Ibid., fol. 46b.

21. Ibid., fol. 117b–118a.

22. See *Sanhedrin,* fol. 65b.

23. I hope to elaborate on this in a separate study.

24. See, e.g., the contemporary technique of the Pseudo-Sa'adiyan *Commentary on Sefer Yeẓirah*, ch. 6, par. 1.

25. On this author, see Dan, *The Esoteric Theology,* pp. 143ff.

26. A widespread view in Jewish mysticism maintained that divine names, especially the name of forty-two letters, can be extracted from the first chapter of the Bible. See also below par. 10.

27. I assume that also the names emerge as part of a process of permutation; compare to ibid., p. 58, where he mentions the combinations of the great divine name.

28. *'Oẓar Neḥmad,* vol. 3 (1860), p. 85.

29. On this issue see below, Summary.

30. Job, 30:14. Compare also the understanding of this verse in *TB, Sanhedrin,* fol. 38a.

31. I have translated the biblical verse in accordance with the understanding of the medieval mystic. I assume that the term *ḥotam* stands here for an anthropoid, as we shall see later on, in the discussion on R. Isaac Sagi Nahor, ch. 10, par. 1 n. 9. See also R. Eleazar of Worms, *Ḥokhmat ha-Nefesh,* fol. 17d–18a.

32. The question why the verb *hithapekh,* change or transformed into, occurs instead of the verb *'sh,* to do, seems to imply that the latter verb was understood as creative, apparently in connection to the creation of man, whereas the former, *hpkh,* was understood as destructive. This verb recurs in R. Eleazar's, *Commentary on Sefer Yeẓirah*, in the context of the undoing of the anthropoid; see fol. 5d, 15d.

33. Ms., Oxford, 1566, fol. 243a.

34. Ms. Cambridge, Add. 647, fol. 18a; Ms. Bologna University Library, 2914,

fol. 178b–180b; Ms. Oxford, 1638, fol. 59a etc. A detailed discussion of this text will accompany the edition of the Hebrew original, now in preparation. See also below Appendix C.

35. See *Commentary on Sefer Yeẓirah*, fol. 4d and above par. 2; cf. Idel, *The Mystical Experience,* p. 45 n. 39. A crucial topic, which cannot be treated here in detail, is the question of the date of the technique of vocalization of the combinations of letters related to the creation of the Golem.

It seems that in principle it is plausible to assume that the combinations of vowels related to the combinations of letters in *Sefer Yeẓirah* were already known by R. Sabbatai Donnolo; see his *Commentary on Sefer Yeẓirah*, fol. 69c: "He [God] permuted the speech according to its letters and its vocalizations [*niqqudav*]."

36. "The Idea of the Golem," pp. 185–187. See also Summary.

37. Ms., Oxford, 1638, fol. 59a.

38. See the Targum Yerushalmi to Gen., 2:7, "God created man with two inclinations and collected dust from the place of the Temple [*beit ha-miqdash*] and from the four corners of the world." Compare also Rashi's comment ad locum. On the whole question of creation of Adam from dust, see Raphael Patai, *Man and Earth in Hebrew Custom, Belief and Legend* (Jerusalem, 1942), pp. 155–156. (Hebrew)

39. See Patai, *ibid.,* pp. 160–162.

40. See *Sefer Yeẓirat ha-Valad,* Jellinek, *Bet ha-Midrasch,* vol. 1, p. 135. See also the comparison between seed and dust in R. Eleazar of Worms' *Sefer ha-Ḥokhmah,* p. 27.

41. Compare R. Abraham ibn Ezra's commentary on Num. 5:17 where the word *qarqa'* is explained as "underneath the soil", "*taḥat ha-qarqa'*" exactly as the phrase occurring in the device to produce a Golem! It is noteworthy that the soil of the Temple was conceived as a virgin one; see *Midrash Shemuel,* ch. 26, p. 125.

42. Num. 5:17.

43. See already *Mishnah, Soṭah,* 2:2 where it is obvious that the temple is referred to in connection with the dust to be used in this context; cf. Jacob Licht, *A Commentary on the Book of Numbers, 1–9* (Jerusalem, 1985), p. 77. On the ordeal of the *soṭah* in general, see his remarks, ibid., pp. 67–74, 168–169.

44. However, there are some clear statements on the productive nature of the Temple in general, having explicit sexual connotations; see Raphael Patai, *Man and Temple* (New York, 1967), pp. 89–92 and M. Idel, "Metaphores et pratiques mystiques dans la Kabbale" in ed. Ch. Mopsik, *Lettre sur la Sainteté* (Lagrasse, Verdier, 1986), pp. 339–341

45. Gen. 11:27.

46. Compare the discussion below of the return of the Golem to dust and ashes in the circle of R. Yehudah he-Ḥasid.

47. *BT Soṭah* 17a, *Yalqut Shime'oni,* parashat *naso'* n. 707. Cf. Num. 5:28, where it is written that if the woman proves to be innocent, then she shall conceive seed. However, the precise connection between the dust and the son, proposed by Rava, cannot be extracted from the biblical material. See, however, the commentary of *Sifre* ad locum, *Sifre d'be Rab,* ed. H. S. Horowitz (Jerusalem, 1966), pp. 22–23; *Yalqut Shim'oni,* ibid. n. 709, where the undefiled woman who drank the bitter water is promised retributions that are related to fertility in general, without mentioning the connection to dust found in the BT in the name of Rava.

48. *Midrash ha-Gadol,* on Numbers, ed. Sh. Fish (London, 1958), vol. 1, p. 96. See also n. 150 there.

49. Part 3, fol. 65a. See also *Midrash ha-Gadol,* ibid., p. 97 where the dust and the water involved in testing the *soṭah* are related to earth and heaven as two witnesses.

50. See n. 14 above.

51. See "The Idea of the Golem," p. 185, n. 3. There he refers to A. Marmorstein, "Beitraege zum Religionsgeschichte und Volkskunde," *Jahrbuch fuer Juedische Volkskunde* ed. Max Gründwald (1924/5), p. 381.

52. On writing a biblical text on dust for a magical reason, see also *Shimmushei Tehilim,* on the Ps. 19 and especially Ps. 16, where we read:

> This psalm is appropriate for unfolding the name of the thief. Take clay from the shore of the river and sand of the sea and mix them and knead, and write the names of the suspects and take an earthen cup and fill it with "drawn" water and put all the names of the suspects in the cup, each one separately etc. . . .

53. *Shimmushei Tehilim* (Jerusalem, 1934), p. 4. Printed in Menaḥem Ẓiyoni, *Ẓefunei Ẓiyoni,* ed. Sh. Weiss (Brooklyn, 1985), p. 88. Here the editor printed a section from Ẓiyoni's *Commentary on the Pentateuch* which was not printed in its proper place in parashat *beshalaḥ.* Another version of this text is found in R. Eleazar of Worms' *Sefer ha-Shem,* Ms. Münich, 81, fol. 127b; but it seems that this is not an organic part of this work. The copyist mentions that this is the name, namely the name of seventy-two letters, that he has written down on the verso of this page. See also Scholem, "The Idea of the Golem," p. 185, n. 3.

54. See below ch. 7, par. 1.

55. See also below par. 13.

56. The bibliographical problems related to this work are very complex and this text deserves a detailed study in itself.

57. *Ben Yeremiyahu* is numerically equivalent to 323 as is the phrase *Ben Sira'*. On Ben Sira in medieval Jewish literature, see Eli Yassif, *The Tales of Ben Sira in the Middle Ages* (Jerusalem, 1984), pp. 17, 33–34. (Hebrew)

58. On this issue see ch. 1, par. 1. See also below ch. 8.

59. See above, ch. 3, par. 3, our discussion of the sin of Enosh as it is related to the creation of an artificial man. However, it appears that the medieval author refers there to the Midrashic tradition, where Adam is presented as a huge being before whom men prostrated, believing that he was God. It seems also that the fact that the *'emet* was enscribed on his forehead was understood as hinting to the seal of God.

60. Jer. 17:5.

61. Printed by Abraham Epstein, *Miqadmoniyot ha-Yehudim* (Jerusalem, 1967), pp. 113–114, and see Scholem, "The Idea of the Golem," p. 179; Joseph Dan, *The Hebrew Story in the Middle Ages* (Jerusalem, Keter, 1974), pp. 76–77 (Hebrew).

62. Printed by M. Steinschneider, *Magazin fuer die Wissenschaft des Judentums,* vol. 9 (1892); p. 83, and see Scholem, "The Idea of the Golem," p. 178, ch. 9, n. 58.

63. See ch. 6, par. 1.

64. This is the interpretation of R. Eleazar of Worms on *Ha-'Aderet ve-ha-'Emunah*; see above n. 7.

65. Gen. 2:7.

66. On the term *Ḥotam* see below ch. 10, n. 9; ch. 8 besides n. 6 and Appendix C.

67. Gen. 2:3.

68. Warsau, 1910, fol. 2a. This text was quoted in the seventeenth century version of the creation of the Golem by R. Eliyahu of Helm. See below ch. 8.

69. See Scholem, "The Idea of the Golem," p. 193, n. 4.

70. Ibid., pp. 178–181.

71. Joseph Dan, *Ḥugei ha-Meqqubalim ha-Rishonim* (Jerusalem, 1978), pp. 65–66. (Hebrew)

72. Joseph Dan, *The Early Kabbalah* (New York, Mahwah, Toronto, Paulist Press, 1986), pp. 24–28, 54–56.

73. Dan, for example, does not mention that there are different datings of the *'Iyyun* literature in Scholem's writings, and that the later dating, the middle of the thirteenth century was sometimes accepted by Scholem, when he thought

that this literature was composed not in Provence, but in Castile. This later view was recently proposed in Verman's monograph on *Sefer ha-'Iyyun.* See Mark Verman, *Sifrei ha-Iyyun* (Ph. D. Thesis, Harvard University, 1984), pp. 163–178. However, even according to Dan's own criterion (ibid., p. 27) our text cannot be considered as part of the early phase of the *'Iyyun* literature, as Dan argues. He asserts that the writings belonging to this stratum, which includes according to him also the *Commentary on the Tetragrammaton,* do not contain the symbolism of ten *sefirot.* It seems that he was in possession of a unique version in an unknown manuscript, since all the manuscripts I could consult discuss not only one system of ten sefirot but two! This text was printed and discussed in my article "Sefirot sheme'al ha-Sefirot," *Tarbiz,* vol. 51 (1982), pp. 247–248 (Hebrew). I should like to emphasize that for the time being no evidence for the early dating of the *'Iyyun* literature has surfaced, and the attempts to consider it as the earliest type of medieval Jewish mysticism, are based on no evidence at all.

74. This list of five successive devices recurres in the *'Iyyun* literature; see Hallamish, *The Commentary on Genesis Rabbah,* p. 255, n. 10 and Scholem, *Origins of the Kabbalah,* p. 313.

75. See also the occurence of this term below, where it is used in the same way. The translation "restoration" in Dan-Kiener does not fit the precise meaning of this term in this context; see Ibid., p. 55. However, in the text of the *Secret of the Tetragrammaton,* immediately after the end of the discussion of the Golem, the term *tiqqun* occurs having another meaning, congenial to the usual understanding of this term in the literature of the *'Iyyun* circle; see Ms., New York JTS, 1887, fol. 8a, and compare to *Sefer Ma'ayan ha-Ḥokhmah* printed in *Yalqut ha-Ro'im* (Jerusalem, 1973), fol. 2c. etc., This shift in the use of the same term seems to be important for the argument that the text dealing with the Tetragramaton is a later composition which combines the terminology of the *'Iyyun* circle with material connected to the creation of the Golem by permutations. For a third meaning of this term in this circle, that of "mental preparation and concentration," see Verman, Ibid., pp. 206–207.

76. This relationship between the beginning of *Sefer Yeẓirah* and the beginning and end of the Torah was already mentioned by Naḥmanides, in his authentic *Commentary on Sefer Yeẓirah*; see G. Scholem, "The Authentical Commentary on *Sefer Yeẓirah* and Other Kabbalistic Material Attributed to Naḥmanides," *Qiryat Sefer,* vol. 6 (1930), p. 401 (Hebrew).

77. Job 28:13.

78. Compare to the discussion of Scholem of the similar Midrashic material in his *On the Kabbalah,* pp. 37–38. Here, however, the mention of the creation of the world just before the creation of the artificial man is indebted to the sequel of these issues in the *Sanhedrin* passage analyzed above or that of the *Book of Bahir.*

79. On this work see Scholem, *Origins of the Kabbalah,* p. 322. The attribu-

tion of the magical discussion to R. Yehudah ben Bateirah is exceptional in the writings of this circle. It possibly has something to do with the legend on the relationship between the birth of this figure and magic; see *TJ, Sanhedrin* 8:13, fol. 25d.

80. Mal. 3:17.

81. This parable was translated by Scholem, "The Idea of the Golem," p. 180 and Dan, *The Early Kabbalah,* pp. 54–55.

82. Namely, do not be afraid of the honor of the divine name and its order.

83. In Ms. New York, *"Ky'im bdrkh kll"*, but I preferred the version of the Florentine Ms. and that of *Sefer ha-Peli'ah,* which indicate *"Ki'im hkl"*. Ms., Moscow-Guensburg, 607, fol. 51b indicates *"Derekh ha-kelal."* Scholem ignores this phrase in his translation; Dan-Kiener, p. 55 translate "Only do not meditate with the intention of honor and restoration, but rather the complete opposite."

84. Compare to our discussion of Abraham Abulafia's use of this statement below ch. 8, n. 10.

85. Part of the material was translated by Scholem and Dan-Kiener, but for various reasons I have decided to translate differently the parts already translated. I used as the base manuscript Ms. New York, *JTS,* 1887, fol. 7b–8a, the version of Ms. Florence-Laurentiana II, 41, fol. 200 and *Sefer ha-Peli'ah* 1, fol. 51cd. This text was also printed by David de Guenzburg, "La Cabale a la veille de l'apparition du Zohar," *Ha-Qedem,* vol. 1 (1907), p. 115. On the context of this version see below. On the Latin version of this text see below ch. 11, par. 5, and n. 58.

86. See n. 76 above.

87. "The Idea of the Golem," p. 196, n. 1.

88. Quoted in Abraham Azulai's *'Or ha-Ḥamah* (Premyzlany, 1886), vol. 1, fol. 62d. It is interesting to mention that just before this quotation, the version of the creation of the Golem according to *Sefer ha-Biṭṭaḥon* is also quoted. As to the relationship between letters and inception, see R. Azriel of Gerona's *Commentary on Sefer Yeẓirah, Kitvei ha-Ramban,* vol. 2, pp. 453–454, and Wolfson, "The Anthropomorphic Image," n. 28 and above ch. 2, n. 14.

89. See above the magical text concerning the soṭah, where it seems that the curses are also written on the dust, spread over the space where the magical practice is accomplished. Compare also R. Joseph Ashkenazi's *Commentary on Genesis Rabbah,* p. 275.

90. On this author see Gershom Scholem, "New Information on R. Joseph Ashkenazi, the "Tanna" of Safed," *Tarbiẓ,* vol. 28 (1959), pp. 59–89, 201–235 (Hebrew); Isadore Twersky, "R. Joseph Ashkenazi and Maimonides', *Sefer Mishneh Torah,"* in *Salo Baron Jubilee Volume* (Jerusalem, 1975), vol. 3, pp. 183–194. (Hebrew)

91. Gen. 2:19–20, ". . . brought them to the man to see what he would call them; and whatever the man called each living creature [literally soul, *nefesh ḥayyah*] that would be its name. And the man gave names to all the cattle etc."

92. Golem in the original.

93. See *TB, Yebamot,* fol. 62a; R. Eleazar of Worms, *Ḥokhmat ha-Nefesh,* fols. 2c, 7c.

94. On this view of the origin of the soul, see M. Idel, "A Speculative Fragment of R. Asher ben Meshullam of Lunel," *Qiriat Sefer,* vol. 50 (1975), p. 150 (Hebrew).

95. *Shemotam,* their names, is a pun on *nishmotam,* their souls. On the letters engraved on the throne of glory see *The Hebrew Enoch,* chapter 41.

96. Scholem, (n. 90 above) p. 221. See also *ibid.,* p. 68.

97. See for example the statement of R. Isaac Sagi Nahor in his *Commentary on Sefer Yeẓirah* below ch. 10, par. 1.

98. On divine names inscribed on the arm of God see *Midrash Konen,* Jellinek, *Bet ha-Midrasch* vol. 2, p. 23. See also Ẓiyoni's discussion, ibid., fol. 1d–2a, and Idel, "The Concept of the Torah," pp. 43–45.

99. The three words are the letters which constitute the three types of consonants according to the phonetics of *Sefer Yeẓirah.*

100. Menahem Ẓiyoni, *Commentary on the Torah* (Jerusalem, 1964), fol. 4c–d.

6

The Northern France Discussions

The Pseudo-Sa'adyah Text

I

One of the most interesting descriptions of the creation of a Golem is found in a *Commentary on Sefer Yeẓirah*, written by an unknown thirteenth century author, presumably of French extraction, and attributed in print to R. Sa'adyah Gaon.[1] Commenting upon the passage in *Sefer Yeẓirah* in which the 231 gates are mentioned, the anonymous author wrote:

> . . . they are founded altogether so as to make a formation [*la'asot yeẓirah*]. They make a wheel [*galgal*] and a circle [*'iggul*] around the creature [*beri'ah*] and they go around the circle and say the alphabets . . . 231 [times]. . . . There are persons who explain [the words] "the wheel going frontward and backward," that the Creator has given power to the letters, [so that when] someone creates his creature [*beriyato*] out of virgin soil, and he kneads it [*megabbelo*] and buries it in the soil, and makes a circle and wheel around the crea-

> ture, and says at each and every circumference one alphabet, and so three and four [until he does it] 462 times. And if he goes forward, the creature rises to life by the power of the utterance of the letters, since God gave them power.[2] If he wants to destroy what he created, he returns backwards [going] around pronouncing the letters,[3] and the creature will sink by itself and it shall die. So it happened once to R. Y. ben A.[4] and his disciples who were studying *Sefer Yeẓirah*. They wanted to create a creature but they erred in [the direction] of their walking, and they went backwards until they sank in the earth up to their navels, by means of the letters. They were not able to go out, and they screamed. R. Y. ben A. heard their voice and told them, "Say the letters of the alphabets going forwards, just as you went backwards." They did so and went out . . . R. Sa'adyah explained that by the saying [the letters] forwards a form [*ẓurah*] emerges and by turning backwards, anytime, the form will sink in the earth.[5]

After the description of the specific way of combining the letters of the alphabets, we read in the same text:

> R. Sa'adyah explained that dance [*maḥol*] means when someone goes as in a dance [movement] when he wants to create and it [the creature] turns to its primal state by the backward dance. And I have heard that ibn Ezra created a creature in the presence of R. Tam and said, "'See what [power] God gave to the holy letters; and he said: 'Turn backwards' and it turned to its primal state. . . ." there is no speech but through the pronunciation[6] [of] the letters AH AY AV, and they emerge from the letters HVY, which are the soul as we explained above.[7] This is why they and their pronunciation are fraught by God with power to make a formation [*yeẓur*][8] and give it [that is, the Golem] vitality [*ḥiyyut*] and a soul [*neshamah*]".[9]

For the first time since the Talmudic passage, we learn about the application of the techniques of letter-combination in order to create a creature by medieval figures. This is not a recommendation as in the case of R. Eleazar of Worms, who did not specify if he did use this technique de facto,[10] but the peculiar device is described, at least twice, as having been put into practice. The fact that the two stories occur here, in comparison to the absence of similar material in the discussions of R. Eleazar of Worms, point to the later date of the Pseudo-Sa'adyan commentary. It would be strange to assume that, had the legends on the creation of the Golem by ibn Ezra already been in existence and widespread, they would not have been included by R. Eleazar in his discussions. Compelling evidence for the later date of this commentary and the tradition connected to the Golem is the fact that it is not included in the list of the commentaries of *Sefer Yeẓirah* studied by Abraham Abulafia in 1270; since the details concerning the creation did not reach Abulafia, who indeed was interested both in commentaries on *Sefer Yeẓirah* and techniques similar to those exposed by R. Eleazar of Worms, we may assume that the commentary was composed as late as the beginning of the second half of the thirteenth century, if not later.[11]

Let us discuss the details included in the above passages. As we have seen in the case of R. Eleazar, and as we shall see later on with respect to Abraham Abulafia,[12] there are two stages in the creational process: the combinations of the alphabets and that of the letters of the divine name. In the present text, the second stage is not so clear, the passage from the first to the second being an inferrence of mine on the basis of the existence of similar divisions of the creation in other cases and because of the mentioning of the special quality of the letters of the divine name in connection to the infusing vitality [*ḥiyyut*] and soul [*neshamah*]. Thus far the similarity between the commentary of R. Eleazar and that of Pseudo-Sa'adyah appears to be significant, though it alone cannot constitute a proof for a substantial affinity between them.[13] The divergences between the two texts are, as we shall see below, greater than the affinities, and it seems that a common source could provide the shared views, namely the use of virgin soil and the existence of two stages connected to recitations of the letters.

II

The uniqueness of this text is obvious in its introduction of the device of dancing. Nowhere else in the extant Golem practices did this device occur and it seems that here it is of especial importance. As seen above, the operator can reduce the Golem to dust by the recitation of a certain part of the combined alphabets, the L to T combinations. Here, the assumption is that the same combinations of letters have different impacts depending on the direction of the movement of the operators. Basic for the productiveness of the letters is not only their inherent powers but the bodily actions of the persons involved in the process.[14] The use of the circles in magical operations is well-known in several practices. By and large, it is the preventive role of the circle that is emphasized. Here, however, the movement, not the circle, is essential. What may be the rationale behind it? The term used by the Pseudo-Sa'adyan source is *maḥol.* The situation of circling around an entity intended to be destroyed is well-known from the biblical episode of Jericho. Reverberations of this practice are found in the Middle Ages,[15] but it seems that only in one case a significant parallel may be drawn between the practice of undoing the Golem and a ritualistic dance. I refer to the custom of ten righteous persons circumambulating the dead before he is buried in order to undo the evil spirits which originate from his seed.[16] According to some late versions of this practice, the persons performed this ritual while pronouncing divine names, mainly the name of forty-two letters, which was divided between seven circumambulations.[17] In both cases a human figure is found at the center of the circumambulation; in both cases it is a dead body; and divine names are recited in the two cases. The effects are, however, different. Notwithstanding this crucial discrepancy, it seems that the basic structure of the ritual is similar. Moreover, at least in one text dealing with the circumambulation, the term used is that which is used in Pseudo-Sa'adyah, *maḥol.* I refer to R. Aharon Berakhiah of Modena's *Ma'avar Yaboq,* where it is written:

> And the secret of this going around is in the form [*dugma*] of that dance [*ḥolah*] that God will prepare for the righteous in the Garden of Eden, since then the Maiden of Israel will be delighted, in that dance [*maḥol*].[18]

The dance of the ten Righteous below has a paradigm in the future dance prepared by God in the next world,[19] but nothing creative is mentioned in this supernal dance. Although nothing definitive can be deduced from the early seventeenth century view of the circumambulances of the dead to explain the thirteenth century practice of the Golem, it seems that a common structural denominator might be found that will attest to a deeper meaning of the going around as a creative operation.[20] However, it is possible that the dance may have some influence upon the consciousness of the operator. As we know from a series of examples in different religious traditions, dance may be a part of a technique to induce an ecstatic trance. If the purpose of the operation as understood in the Pseudo-Sa'adian text was not only a material creation, but also a mystical experience, as Scholem has already proposed, it may well be that the mentioning of the dance as part of the operation is an indication in this direction; for the time being, however, this interesting possibility must remain in the domain of probabilities that cannot be corroborated by hard evidence. As in the case of R. Eleazar, where the question of the ecstatic nature of the magical operation of the Golem in his technique is an open issue,[21] so also here we must wait for further evidence before the ritual of the creation of a material creature will be transformed, by scholarly analysis, into an ecstatic technique.

The appearance of the dance in the presumably French source on one side, and the separate discussions of the ritual of the burial in other sources seems to be connected, if at all, only by some structural parallels. However, a direct link between them is found in the famous version of the "Prague Golem" possibly penned by Judel Rosenberg. This author, or his hypothetical sources, adduces the spurious epistle of the Maharal, who describes the creation of the Golem out of clay, and then the following passage is found:

> And I commanded my son-in-law, R. Isaac ha-Kohen, to be the first to circumambulate the Golem seven times, beginning from the right side [of the feet] and up to the head, and from the head to the feet on the left side; and I gave him the combinations of letters to recite during the circumambulation. And he did so seven times, and when he finished the circumambulations the body of the Golem became red, as a burning coal of fire. Afterwards I commanded my disciple, Rabbi Ya'aqov Sason ha-Levi, to do seven circumambulations as well, similar [to the preceding ones] and I also gave him other combinations of letters. When he finished the circumambulations, his [the Golem's] appearance had hairs, as [a person of] thirty and the nails grew at the extremities of the fingers. Then I also did the seven circumambulations, and after the end of the circumambulations we said together the verse:[22] "and God blew the soul of life in his nostrils and man became a living being."[23]

The affinities between this description of the creation of the Golem and the rite of the burial are outstanding: the number seven in connection to the circumambulations, the recitations of special formulas during these acts, and the situation of a body found in the center of the circle. The version of R. Judel Rosenberg is the single version which adduces the circumambulations of the dead in the context of the creation of the Golem, and the question arises as to the existence of a source for this link: was it innovated in the early twentieth century by the Ḥasid, or does his version reflect an older tradition? I cannot presently answer this question in a decisive way, but I should like to point out the implications of the different answers for the hypothetical history of the development of the Golem traditions. If a tradition preceding the time of R. Judel Rosenberg, will be discovered, where the circumambulations are mentioned in connection to the Golem, it will be important evidence for the transmission of important details concerning the technique of creating this creature which may have escaped modern scholarship: Furthermore, the version of R. Judel, though not the attribution of the creation of the Golem to the Maharal, will turn out to be a more reliable source than it is considered to be by modern scholarship. On the other hand, the failure to find a source for such a major detail of the ritual will cast a great doubt upon the credibility of other details in the version of the modern Ḥasid, which are not corroborated by independent sources.

III

Let us address another unique feature of the version of the creation in the Pseudo-Sa'adyan text: the Golem is buried before the beginning of the magical process of permutating letters. It seems that only after its burial is the Golem capable of developing into the more elaborate anthropoid. The regular interpretation of this procedure is that we witness a practice of renewal or rebirth. However, some other connotations related to more substantial elements in Jewish traditions may assist us in decoding the meaning of this practice. First and foremost, we must recall the biblical verses in Ps. 139 where the Golem is introduced in the context of an embryonic status in the "lowest part of the earth." This phrase must have been influential on the device whereby the Golem is buried in order to enable it to emerge as a more advanced form of being. The earth serves, according to this parallel, as the womb of the embryo[24]; the procedure which follows the burial is concerned, at the beginning, with causing the Golem to emerge from the earth, i.e., with a process of extracting it from the womb, and, only later on, with the animation of this body.[25]

Sefer ha-Ḥayyim

IV

In the second third of the twelfth century, an interest in astrology and magic shaped the interpretation of Judaism found in the writings of the famous R. Abraham ibn Ezra.[26] In our context it is pertinent to quote only a reference he made to animating statues; describing the biblical *teraphim* of Lavan, this commentator wrote:

> The *teraphim* are built according to the forms of men and this form is made [in such a way as] to receive the power of the superior [beings].[27]

This view is also related by ibn Ezra to the construction of the golden calf, which was intended to serve as a surrogate for the missing Moses; according to the commentator, the calf was construed as imitating an astral form and it captured the supernal glory.[28] What is surprising in these expositions is the fact that these practices were not presented as idolatrous; thus we have an interesting background for the reinterpretation of the creation of the calf and the man according to the passage from *Sanhedrin,* though I am not acquainted with such a juxtaposition in ibn Ezra himself. With respect to the sources of this reinterpretation of the biblical episodes, I propose the so-called hermetical views, with their interest in astral magic, as the main channel of the penetration of this conception in medieval Judaism.[29]

These magical reinterpretations of passages in the Bible, as well as the meaning of some commandments, do not depend upon *Sefer Yeẓirah* and are not conspicuous in the few cases wherein ibn Ezra quotes from this book.[30] Nevertheless, it is quite possible that such a magical interpretation of this book was actually included in a commentary on this ancient treatise authored by ibn Ezra, still extant as late as 1270,[31] but now lost. According to Abraham Abulafia, the greatest part of it was devoted to philosophical issues, and a part of it contained "Kabbalistic" topics.[32] We cannot be sure what Abulafia exactly intended when he used this term, and it is possible that non-philosophical issues regarding the special status of the Hebrew letters in astrological and magical contexts was described by Abulafia as Kabbalistic. This assumption concurs with the interpretation of *Sefer Yeẓirah* of a contemporary and friend of ibn Ezra, R. Yehudah ha-Levi. In his *Sefer ha-Kuzari* he elaborates upon the uniqueness of the Hebrew language[33] and he compares the combinations of the letters by the means of the wheel, as indicated in *Sefer Yeẓirah*, to the emergence of the diversity in the universe by the movement of the sphere.[34] This comparison opens the door to a philosophical understanding of creation, similar to the theory of combinations of letters in *Sefer Yeẓirah*. In both cases, a circular devise, the wheel and the sphere, are involved in generating compound entities by their movements. In this context, the existence of the legend of the creation of a Golem by ibn Ezra, adduced already in the thirteenth century by the Northern French author of the Pseudo-Sa'adyan *Commentary on Sefer Yeẓirah*, may testify that an interest in *Sefer Yeẓirah* as a magical textbook was connected to the name of ibn Ezra shortly after his death.[35]

Around 1200 a treatise entitled *Sefer ha-Ḥayyim* was composed by an anonymous author, with manifest mystical leanings.[36] It was attributed to R. Abraham ibn Ezra, presumably because of the profound influence of the latter's theories on the content of the book. This book contains a passage concerning the creation of the artificial man which has been discussed by several scholars; however, it seems to me that the peculiar understanding of the meaning of this creation, as will be discussed below, has escaped the scholars and therefore a detailed presentation of the passage is in order at this point. Let me start by citing a few lines before the beginning of the text quoted by Scholem[37]:

> The thoughts of men change each and every hour, in accordance to the structure of their nature [*matkonet toladetam*], and according to the supernal [power] which is above the head of the recipient.[38] In this way the learned person will be able to understand all the deeds and all the creatures, blessed be the name of the Creator and the name of His unity forever. And all the witches and magicians of Egypt, who create creatures, were acquainted through demons or other lore with the order of the *merkavah* and they took dust under the feet of that constellation [*ma'arakhah*] and created whatever they wished. But our sages say that R. N. N. created a man. R. N. N. sent to him a three-year old calf on the eve of Shabbat; he knew the secret and took dust from under the feet of the *merkavah,* and recited the name of God on it, and it was created. In this way Mikhah[39] made the golden calf that could dance. "For he had seen, like all Israel, in the exodus from Egypt the *merkavah* in the Reed Sea." But whereas the other Israelites did not pay attention to this vision, he did so, as is indicated in [the verse][40] "My soul set me among the chariots of a princely people." When the bull in the *merkavah* [moved] to the left[41] he quickly took some of the dust from under its feet and kept it. And in the same way in India and in the Ishmaelite [i.e., Islamic] countries they made animals of men by conjuring a demon to bring them dust from under the corresponding constellation [*ma'arakhah*] and give it to the witch, and that witch gives it to the man to drink, whereupon the man is immediately [transformed into] [an animal] like it [i.e., the constellation]. And R. Sa'adyah[42] was acquainted with it, [carried out] either by means of angels or by the Name . . . Since every image [*demut*] that is above is [also] below. And in a similar way the holy angels are seen in the image of men or any other image, according to the will of the Creator or their will; they take dust from under the *supernal* constellation [*ma'arakhah 'elyonah*] and they are clothed by dust.[43]

The main difference between the translation and the interpretation offered by Scholem and the present one is connected to one important word; the Hebrew word *ma'arakhah* is translated by Scholem "order" and here as "constellation". This divergence is, however, much more than an issue of semantics; the exclusion of the idea of the constellation seems to be related to Scholem's axiom that in Hebrew sources the creation of artificial men is not connected to astrology; this text, and others which will be discussed below, unfortunately contradict Scholem's view. Regarding the sources of the astrological views of the anonymous author, it is obvious that one of the major influences is to be found in the writings of ibn Ezra; indeed, the view of the glory that dwells in the created forms is quoted verbatim from ibn Ezra.[44]

The extent of the importance of astrology for the understanding of this passage can be seen from several other statements in *Sefer ha-Ḥayyim*:

> From the dust under the constellation of the stars man is created[45] and from the dust under the constellation of the Lion the beast is created, and from dust under the constellation of the bull the animal is created, and from the dust under the constellation of the eagle, the birds are created.[46]

The peculiar choice of the four entities is conspicuous; they are the four living creatures that support the divine chariot, namely the *merkavah.* Therefore, according to the anonymous author, there is no substantial difference between the *merkavah* and the constellations. Thus, the astrological overtones of the passage seem to be well-established. What are the specific implications of an astrological reading which the author of *Sefer ha-Ḥayyim* offers to the creation of an artificial man? First and foremost, those Rabbinic figures who created the calf and the man combined their astrological knowledge with the recitation of the divine name; *Sefer Yeẓirah* is not mentioned in this context by the anonymous author and it is possible that this is not an accident.[47] In sharp contrast to his Ashkenazi contemporaries, who envisioned the recitation of the combinations of the letters of the alphabets as a sine qua non condition for the creation of the creature, this unknown author seems to ignore this technique. His reference to the divine name may be easily understood on the basis of traditions already in existence, where a dead man is animated by the use of a divine name.[48] Therefore, we have here a unique version of the creation of an artificial man which is basically independent of the mysticism of *Sefer Yeẓirah*. It is obvious that the theory of *Sefer Yeẓirah* regarding the creative feature of the combination of letters as the main instrument for creation was neglected in favour of a technique consonant with the views of ibn Ezra, based upon a strong astrological component. The correspondence between the higher and the lower, the affinity between peculiar elements and supernal entities, is the ground of this technique of creation, rather than the magical power inherent in the nature of the combinations of the Hebrew letters. Moreover, it seems that the pronunciation of the very name of the creature to be created was sufficient for the emergence of such a being; the anonymous author compares the divine creative speech, which operates by the transmission of letters to the "air of life", to the similar process in the case of the holy men; in their case also, "whatever they say appears immediately because the vapour which goes out of their mouth is pure and holy and it is combined with the air of the world and the thing is made and so do they create. R.N.N. created a man and R.N.N. created a three-year-old calf."[49] The basic assumption here differs from the previous astrological conception; the purity of the human breathing is the central factor of the creative process and it impresses on the air, which sustains all the creatures,[50] the requested form which is thereby substantiated.

As for the origin of this astrological knowledge, it is significant that, according to the author of *Sefer ha-Ḥayyim,* the non-Jewish magicians draw it from demonic sources whereas the Jews, in our case Mikhah and presumably also the later Rabbis, draws it from the contemplation of the *Merkavah,* a uniquely mystical activity. The mystical implication of Mikhah's contemplation is much more evident in the Midrash quoted by R. Menaḥem Ẓiyoni where Mikhah's activity is described in terms reminiscent of Enoch according to the first chapter of the *Hebrew Enoch.*[51] Before leaving this text, it is important to remark that the author had no problem interpreting the activity of the ancient rabbis in terms of regular magic, comparing them to the Indian and Arab magicians; like ibn Ezra before him, and under his strong influence, this author could present two types of activities that follow the same astrological pattern, one of them viewed in positive terms whereas the other conceived of as a negative activity. It is important to mention that in *Sefer ha-Ḥayyim* we can find some Hermetic motifs beyond those which entered Abraham ibn Ezra's writings.[52] This awareness may strengthen our proposal that in the case of the medieval interpretations of the Golem a confluence of different cultural trends produced new understandings of ancient Jewish practices.

The existence of a thirteenth century astrological interpretation of the Talmudic passage, apparently independent of the techniques of *Sefer Yeẓirah*, is also significant for another reason. According to an important textual evidence stemming from the middle of the thirteenth century,[53] *Sefer Yeẓirah* was studied together with a version of *Sefer Raziel.*[54] According to the testimony of R. Yehudah ben Nissim ibn Malka, who transmitted this information, the latter work is based upon the assumption that the divine names mentioned in it are related to the astral bodies and forces, and the possibility to succeed, when operating according to the instructions given by this work, depends upon the knowledge of the relationship between the peculiar time and the operation someone intends to perform. Therefore, a fullfledged astrological understanding of *Sefer Raziel* accompanied, according to this Morrocan Kabbalist, the study of *Sefer*

Yeẓirah. Moreover, the combination of letters in *Sefer Yeẓirah* is explicitly understood as a reference to the melothesia, the combination of the astrological forces involved in the magical operation.[55] Thus we may assume that an astrological interpretation of *Sefer Yeẓirah*, having some magical connotations,[56] was in existence in the middle of the thirteenth century, although there is no indication that in the works of ibn Malka a creation of an artificial man is intended; by the same token, nowhere is such an operation negated. In any case, the evidence of ibn Malka opens the way for an astrological interpretation of the combinations of letters as they are included in *Sefer Yeẓirah*.

Notes

1. On the group of writings to which this text belongs, see Dan, *The Esoteric Theology*, pp. 52–59, 156–164. See also n. 4, 11 below.

2. See the *Commentary on Sefer Yeẓirah*, fol. 30b–31a where the view of the letters as instruments of creation, used by God and man, is mentioned.

3. *'Amirat ha-'otiyyot*. Later on in this treatise, on fol. 43a, this phrase describes the way God created the creatures, for it is stated that God conferred life upon the creatures by the "vapor of the pronunciation of the letters." This explains the peculiar role of the pronunciation of the letters, viz., to induce vitality into the dust, even when men perform this practice; see ibid., fol. 42b. Especially important for our discussion is the statement on fols. 31a:

> The letters were created from the spirit of God and by their pronunciation He created the world, and you also will be able to create a creature by the power of the pronunciation of the alphabets.

Therefore, God infused a creative feature into the letters, which can be exploited by man through the pronunciation of the letters. See also the very end of the commentary, still in manuscript, trans. by Scholem, "The Idea of the Golem," p. 171, n. 1 and the view of *Sefer ha-Ḥayyim* par. 2 below.

4. Who exactly this Y. ben A. is we do not know. Scholem, *Kabbalah*, p. 352 and "The Idea of the Golem," p. 186, n. 3, suggested that these are the initials of the ancient master, R. Ishmael ben Elisha. However, it seems that this conjecture is highly speculative, since no tradition related to the Golem is mentioned in connection with this figure. I would opt for later persons. Among the French halakhists there are three figures who may be referred to as R.Y.B.A.; two of them are called R. Isaac ben Asher ha-Levi. I am inclined, however, to the third author known by these initials; it seems that we are on firmer ground if we identify this figure as R. Isaac ben Abraham of Dampierre, who flourished at the end of the twelfth century, and was famous as a master of several authors, just as the figure portrayed in the above legend. His initials were, indeed, R.Y.B.A.; see E. E. Ur-

bach, *The Tosaphists: Their History, Writings and Methods,* 4th edition (Jerusalem 1980), p. 261, n. 4 (Hebrew). Moreover, there is interesting evidence linking this figure with mystical traditions; see Scholem, *Origins of Kabbalah,* pp. 250–251. According to some evidence pointed out by Scholem, it is possible that traditions connected to *Sefer Yeẓirah,* are to be attributed to this author. It may well be that the fact that the author of the Pseudo-Sa‘adyan commentary mentions R. Tam and immediately afterwards R.Y.B.A. has to do with the fact that the latter was the disciple of the former.

Since there is little doubt as to the identity of Y ben A., R. Isaac of Dampierre is, apparently, the latest among the figures mentioned in the circle of the Special Cherub. See, by contrast, the observation of Dan, *Studies,* p. 103, who mentions R. Abraham ibn Ezra in this context. If our identification is correct, I assume that the legend about R. Isaac of Dampierre the younger, emerged only after his death in 1210. (See I. Ta'-Shma‘, "A New Chronography on the 13th Century Tosaphists," *Shalem,* ed. J. Hacker, vol. 3, (Jerusalem, 1981), p. 323. This may strengthen the later, rather than the earlier, dating of the circle of the Special Cherub. See also below n. 11.

On the other hand, there is a manuscript that indicates the initials R. Z. in lieu of R.Y.B.A.'; Scholem decodes these initials as R. Ẓadoq, whose identity was unknown to him. See Scholem, ibid. However, as Prof. I. Ta'-Shma‘ has kindly suggested, this initial can reasonably be understood as referring to R. Isaac, as this way of decoding R. Ẓ. was in use in the circle of R. Isaac the Old, the teacher of R. Isaac ben Abraham.

5. See *Commentary on Sefer Yeẓirah,* fols. 40b–40c.

6. *Havarat ha-'otiyyot.* The term *havarah* for the vocalisation of the consonants occurs in the same context in the short passage, stemming from the circle of the Special Cherub, to be discussed below, ch. 10, n. 98.

7. The conception that the letters HWY are the souls of the other letters is found already in the twelfth century and was widespread in the doctrine of another member of the circle of the Special Cherub, R. Elḥanan ben Yaqar. See the latter's *Commentary on Sefer Yeẓirah,* ed. J. Dan (Jerusalem, 1973), pp. 36–37. According to this author (ibid., p. 37) God blew the spirit of life in man using these letters. As a possible inference we may indicate that the two stages of the creation of the Golem, the combination of the regular letters of the alphabet and the combinations of the letters of divine names, may respectively reflect the formation of the limbs, or their animation, and the infusing of the soul in the Golem. Such a reading, which is to be understood as merely a suggestion, is reinforced by the occurence of the terms *ḥiyyut and neshamah,* which may refer to the two different stages. See also Pedaya, "'Flaw'" and "'Correction'", p. 182.

8. For the term *yeẓur* as a man, see above ch. 2, par. 3.

9. *Commentary on Sefer Yeẓirah,* fol. 42b.

10. *Commentary on Sefer Yeẓirah,* fol. 16d.

11. See the chronology of the texts pertaining to the school of the Special Cherub, compiled by Dan, *Studies,* p. 105, where he locates the Pseudo-Sa'adyan *Commentary to Sefer Yeẓirah* in the third stratum of treatises of this school, apparently in the middle of the thirteenth century.

12. See above ch. 5, par. 2 and below ch. 7, par. 1.

13. Scholem, "'Golem' and '*dibbuk*' in the Hebrew Dictionary," *Leshonenu,* vol. 6 (1934), p. 40 [Hebrew] argues, without bringing any proofs, that the author of this *Commentary* was a student of R. Eleazar of Worms. Scholem quotes a text, from manuscript, that does not constitute, in my opinion, part of the commentary attributed to Sa'adyah. On the other hand, Dan has shown that this commentary is part of a group of writings which depart from the views of the central school of the Ashkenazi Ḥasidism; see n. 11 above.

14. Compare to the combination of recitation of letters and bodily movements in the ecstatic technique of Abraham Abulafia; Idel, *The Mystical Experience,* pp. 28–30.

15. See e.g., R. Abraham ben Natan of Lunel's, *Sefer ha-Manhig,* ed. I. Rafael, vol. 2 (Jerusalem, 1978), pp. 402–403; Pedayah, "'Flaw'" and "'Correction'", p. 274.

16. See Meir Benayahu, *Studies in Memory of the Rishon Le-Ẓion R. Yitzḥaq Nissim* (Jerusalem, 1985), pp. 120–125, especially p. 121, n. 69. (Hebrew)

17. See M. Idel, "Shelomo Molkho as Magician," *Sefunot,* vol. 3 (1985), pp. 195–198. (Hebrew)

18. *Ma'avar Yaboq,* (Wilna, 1896), fol. 108b.

19. See TB, *Ta'anit,* fol. 31a.

20. The entire question is connected with the history of the dance macabre, a topic to be studied elsewhere.

21. See above ch. 5 and below Summary.

22. Gen. 2:7.

23. *Nifla'ot ha-Maharal,* p. 69.

24. On the Golem as embryo see above ch. 3, par. 4; ch. 5 par. 5, 11 and below ch. 10, par. 1 and Appendix B.

25. The description of the emergence of the Golem is reminiscent of a rite of rebirth: see Mircea Eliade, *Rites and Symbols of Initiation,* (Harper and Row, 1978), pp. 51–53.

26. On this issue see Idel, "Hermeticism and Judaism," pp. 62–64.

27. See *ibid.,* especially the material collected in n. 41.

28. Ibid., the sources referred at in n. 36–37. On this term in *Sefer ha-Ḥayyim* see also below Appendix A.

29. *Ibid.,* passim.

30. The existence of this work, now lost, seems to me probable, inspite of the attempt of Israel Weinstok to argue that it never was written, the whole issue being an invention of Abulafia. See the preface of his edition of Abraham Abulafia's *Commentary on Sefer Yeẓirah* (Jerusalem, 1984), pp. 16–20 (Hebrew). Elsewhere I shall demonstrate in detail why such an assumption is implausible.

31. See the text printed by Jellinek, *Bet ha-Midrasch,* vol. 3, German part p. 62.

32. *Ibid.,* pp. 62–63.

33. On this issue see also below ch. 11, n. 16.

34. *Kuzari* 4, 25. See ch. 11, n. 2.

35. I suppose that this is the situation also in the case of R. Shemuel he-Ḥasid; see ch. 5, n. 5.

36. See Dan, *The Esoteric Theology,* pp. 133–156, 230–235.

37. "The Idea of the Golem," pp. 183–184.

38. Most of this phrase occurs also in *Sefer ha-Ḥayyim,* ed., Dan, p. 6, where it is part of an unacknowledged quotation from Abraham ibn Ezra's *Commentary on Exodus 26:1.* The astrological meaning of it is obvious in both ibn Ezra and *Sefer ha-Ḥayyim.* The correlation between operations and the precise time in astrologically biased types of magic is a common phenomenon. Nevertheless, compare our discussion below on Ibn Malka's views.

39. For the sources of the view that Mikhah took the dust from under the *merkavah,* see S. Lieberman's important remarks in *Yemenite Midrashim* (Jerusalem, 1970), pp. 17–18 [Hebrew]. The quotation he brought from R. Menaḥem Ẓiyoni, from an unknown Midrash on Song of Songs is very similar to the wording of *Sefer ha-Ḥayyim*; see also S. Lieberman, *Greek and Hellenism in Jewish Palestine* (Jerusalem, 1962), pp. 85–86. It is important to note, that the astrological implications of the sources adduced by Lieberman for Mikhah's activity, was combined by the author of *Sefer ha-Ḥayyim* with medieval astrology, mostly that of ibn Ezra, and the mention of the creation of man which is absent in the earlier sources. See also now Halperin, *The Faces of the Chariot,* pp. 178–180.

40. Song of Songs 6:12.

41. Cf. Ezek. 1:10. On the relation between the calf and the *merkavah* traditions see Halperin, *The Faces of the Chariot,* pp. 157–193.

42. This image of Sa'adyah may have something to do with the Pseudo-Sa'adian prescription to create a Golem discussed above.

43. I checked a number of manuscripts, since the printed edition seems to be very corrupt here; See Joseph Dan, *Sefer ha-Ḥayyim* (Jerusalem, 1972), p. 24 (a mimeotyped copy of Ms., British Library, 1055), Ms. Oxford, 1569 and the version of Scholem, "The Image of the Golem," pp. 404–405, Sirat, *Les visions surnaturelles,* pp. 109–110.

44. See Dan's edition pp. 6, 29.

45. Man is presented here as the result of the confluence of the influence of the stars in general, in contrast to the manner the animals and birds who were created only under the aegis of one constellation alone. Man is accordingly more complex than the other created beings. This astrological conclusion occurs also in another passage in *Sefer ha-Ḥayyim,* p. 31, to be discussed below Appendix A.

46. Dan's edition p. 23 corrected according to Ms., Oxford, 1569.

47. Scholem, "The Idea of the Golem," p. 185 assumes that the author refers to the technique of *Sefer Yeẓirah*, without bringing any evidence.

48. See Scholem, Ibid., pp. 182–183 and Appendix B below.

49. *Sefer ha-Ḥayyim,* p. 15, corrected according to the manuscript.

50. On the theory of the air, which is closely connected to God, see ibid., pp. 19–20.

51. See Lieberman, *Yemenite Midrashim,* p. 17, "*histakkel bi-ẓefiyat ha-merkavah*" and H. Odeberg, *Hebrew Enoch,* (Hebrew part), p. 3 and Halperin, *The Faces of the Chariot,* pp. 179–180.

52. See Idel, "Hermeticism and Judaism," p. 64.

53. The regular dating of the flourishing of Ibn Malka, established by G. Vajda, in the middle of the fourteenth century is erroneous. Elsewhere I shall supply full evidence for a mid-thirteenth century dating.

54. See Georges Vajda, *Juda ben Nissim ibn Malka, philosophe juive marocain,* (Paris, 1954), pp. 170–172. Vajda translates and comments upon the Arabic original of Ibn Malka's treatise dealing with this subject. The Hebrew medieval translation of this passage, printed by G. Vajda, *A Hebrew Abridgement of R. Judah ben Nissim ibn Malka's Commentary on the Book of Creation* (Ramat Gan, 1974), pp. 52–53, gives a totally different impression regarding the attitude to *Sefer Raziel*; whereas in the Arabic original there is no negative attitude toward this book, in Hebrew this magical book is sharply criticised.

55. On this topic see Nicolas Sed, "Le Sefer ha-Razim et la methode de 'Combinaison des lettres'", *REJ,* vol. 130 (1971), pp. 296–297. See especially Ibn Malka's view in Vajda, *A Hebrew Abridgement,* pp. 45–46.

56. A magical understanding of *Sefer Yeẓirah* is explicitly indicated in Ibn Malka's *Commentary on Sefer Yeẓirah*; see Vajda, *A Hebrew Abridgement,* p. 27.

7

The Golem in Ecstatic Kabbalah

Abraham Abulafia (1240–ca. 1292)

I

As we shall see later on, the early Provençal and Catalan Kabbalists were not especially interested either in the nature of the artificial man or in the technique of its creation. With the exception of few statements, always related to passages in the Talmud or the *Book Bahir,* they simply ignore this issue, either because they believed that it was not an actual subject, or, what seems to be less probable, because it was conceived to be a topic too esoteric to be discussed in written form.[1] Among the Spanish Kabbalists, it seems that no one was more interested in this issue than R. Abraham Abulafia. He seems to be the only Spaniard who adduced a detailed recipe to create a "creature" which included not only explanatory remarks on the nature of the creature but also on the way to perform the practice that culminates in the emergence of an artificial being. In the classical works of Abulafia, there is no explicit reference to the Golem. However, in an anonymous fragment, whose affinity to his major mystical handbook, *Ḥayyei ha-'Olam ha-Ba'* is undeniable,[2] we find the following statements:

> And the fourth way is built up in a solid manner, [*banui le-talpiyyot*] as it is designed beforehand in the twenty-four circles and in its proper vocalization, in order to receive the influx of wisdom, and [the act of] formation [*yeẓirah*] too. . . . The end of the end[3] aims to create a creature [*livro' beri'ah*][4] and to recite on each and every thing.[5] And the essential thing is to be acquainted with the pronunciation of its recitation, since each and every letter is to be recited loudly in one breath, as the spirit of man goes out the person who recites. He shall recite in a remote and pure place, where there is no one there,[6] and he will succeed.[7]

There are two cardinal themes which occur in the text; the reception of wisdom, expressed in philosophical terminology, "the influx of wisdom" (*shefa' ha-ḥokhmah*) and the creation of a creature. Although the nature of the linkage between the reception of the influx and the creative act is not explicitly specified, the order of their mentioning may indicate the appearance of wisdom before someone attains the stage of creating a creature. This sequel occurs also in another description of creating a creature, whose author is, in my opinion, Abraham Abulafia himself. Because of the importance of this text, to be refered to as *Teḥilat ha-Yeẓirah,* an extensive translation is provided herein:

> At the beginning of the [act of] formation [*yeẓirah*], the person has to be acquainted with the quality of the weight [*ṭuv ha-mishqal*], the combination [*ẓeruf*] and the variation [*ḥilluf*].[8] And he has to be acquainted with the construction [*binyan*] and all the alphabets, the two hundred and thirty one gates of the alphabets, which are engraved in the ninth sphere, [or wheel] divided into sixty parts.[9] And [he] has to be acquainted with the combination of all the letters, and all the alphabets, each one per se, until all the gates will be completed. And he shall take pure dust and flour, turn the wheel in the middle, and begin to combine until the two hundreds and thirty one gates [are computed], and [then] he will receive the influx of wisdom. When he receives the influx, let him [then] recite speedily the circle of velocity, which is the divine spirit. Afterwards let him take a cup full of pure water and a small spoon, and fill it with dust. He should be acquainted with the weight of all the dust before he begins to stir it, and also with the size of the spoon which [serves him] to measure. And after he will fill it, he shall pour it in the water, and he will gently blow during his pouring onto the surface of the water. And when he begins to blow on the first spoonful, he should recite loudly a letter of the divine name with one breath, until his spirit

> will go out i.e., it will be exhausted] by [his] breathing, his face being [turned] to the earth. And he shall begin with the head of the head, until he will end the first eight houses [i.e., lines], [in order to] preserve the head. And he shall recite the eight second houses, to preserve the body, according to the order. And he shall recite the eight houses of the third [order] [in order to preserve] the end and the spirit [*ruaḥ*]. And [then] an image [*demut*] will emerge . . . it is forbidden to do like the deed of the Creator, and you shall not learn it in order to perform it, but you shall learn it in order to understand and to teach[10] and to cleave to the great name of God,[11] praised be He.[12]

This passage ends in three manuscripts with the sentence "Peace, power, Abram." According to a fourth manuscript the name is a certain Menaḥem. On the basis of several resemblances between this text and Abulafia's views, some of them to be mentioned in the following discussion, I would suggest that "Abram" mentioned here is indeed Abraham Abulafia. The above text is based upon the recitation of the combinations of the alphabets, in order to receive the influx of wisdom, and the letters of the divine name in order to create the image.[13] The alphabets mentioned here are, presumably, themselves conceived as a divine name, as we learn from Abraham Abulafia's statement:

> The God of Israel means, secretly, YS Ra' eL gates, and it was taught that this name is attributed to our nation because of our knowledge of the [divine] name [or God] that created *ex nihilo,*[14] by the means of the two hundred and thirty one gates, which He combined in [or by] His wisdom.[15]

The numerical value of the letters Ra' eL is two hundred and thirty one. Thus, the name Israel is understood as indicating that there are [*yeSh*] two hundred and thirty one gates, connected to the divine wisdom, a remark strikingly reminiscent of the reception of the influx of wisdom by these combinations of letters. These combinations are conceived here as representing the divine creative activity; knowledge of them is tantamount to that theological gnosis which is characteristic of the people of Israel.

What precisely the divine name is, Abulafia does not indicate; however, it is obvious that the three times eight houses are twenty-four houses, i.e., the twenty-four combinations of letters. The figure "twenty-four" is reminiscent of the twenty-four circles mentioned in the first anonymous quotation. Now, each of these circles includes nine letters, making a total of two hundred and sixteen letters, i.e., the letters of the divine name of seventy-two combinations of three letters each. Assuming that the core of the process of creating an image is a combination of the pouring of dust and flour into pure water serving as the material substratum and the recitation of the name of seventy-two combinations of letters, we may identify the closest parallel to the second quotation; as in the case of the first citation it is found in Abulafia's *Ḥayyei ha-'Olam ha-Ba'.* This treatise is dedicated in its entirety, as the author explictly indicates in his preface, to the divine name of seventy-two.[16] Moreover, in this work we learn that the pronunciation of the name is done for five reasons, the first and last being ostensibly relevant to our discussion:

> The first intention of pronouncing the name of God is to receive from it the influx of wisdom and knowledge [*shefa' ḥokhmah ve-da'at*] . . . and the fifth [intention] is to write and learn signs and wonders, to change the parts of nature in the hour of need, as God commanded it to you.[17]

The formulation of the first intention is identical to the phrase used in the second anonymous quotation cited above. The fifth intention consists of a magical operation which is formulated in a much more general manner than the specific aim of creating a creature. Notwithstanding this difference, the formulation in *Ḥayyei ha-'Olam ha-Ba'* includes the change of the nature of a certain kind, which is similar to the change implicit in the transformation of dust into an image. It is conspicuous that both Abulafia's mystical handbook and the quotation in the name of "Abram" share the same basic sequel: first, the acquisition of wisdom by recitation of letters and, finally, the magical operation. Moreover, in the second text, cleaving to the name of God is mentioned in connection with the operation; this mystical ideal is absent in the Ashkenazi recipes to create a Golem, but is fully consonant with the emphasis on the centrality of cleaving to the divine name characteristic of Abulafia's mystical system.[18] As we shall see below, R. Nathan, a Kabbalist who apparently had been a disciple of Abulafia, posits the necessity of an experience of union with the divine intellect as the precondition to the creation of the artificial man. Whether this is also the case in Abulafia's view is not clear; nevertheless, in general, the relationship of these two processes seems to be shared by these two mystics.

Let me now address the details of the creation of the image (*demut*). According to *Teḥilat ha-Yeẓirah,* there are three basic combinations of letters, whose recitation is related to the "head" (*rosh*), the body, which is a translation of the form *qama,* which I consider to be a variation of *qomah,* namely, body; and finally *sof,* which means end. These three terms refer to the three locations of letters in each of the combinations of the name of seventy-two. The first letter is, accordingly, the head, the second, the middle, and the third the end. This is the specific method of Abulafia in *Ḥayyei ha-'Olam ha-Ba'*, apparently without precedent in any other author.[19] However, in this work Abulafia refers to the pronunciation of the letters of the name of seventy-two in connection to the limbs of the mystic; he indicates that:

> He has to be very cautious not to change a letter or a vowel from its place because the limb created by the means of this letter will change its natural place in your body . . . Know that there are three issues created in man . . . the head, created out of fire . . . the belly [created out of] water . . . and the torso, [created out of] wind[20] [*ruaḥ*][21]

This tripartite division of the human body is mentioned in direct connection to the technique of pronunciation; here Abulafia indicates that there is an organic affinity between letters and limbs, so that the proper pronunciation of the order of the letters is strictly necessary for the well-being of the mystic. The warning implied in this citation is repeated elsewhere in Abulafia's book:

> And if the person who recites the letter errs, God save us, in his pronunciation of the letter that is appointed upon the limb that is in the head of the person who reads, that limb is separated [from its place] and changes its place, its nature being immediately transformed, another form being conferred to it [and] the person becoming injured [*ba'al mum*], this being the reason that the name *whw* is sealed by the word *mum* [injury]."[22]

The name that begins with the letters *whw* is the name of seventy-two; therefore, we have clean evidence for the positive relationship of letters and limbs as part of the creation of man and a negative relationship between them which may occur during the pronunciation process. What is not stated explicitly is the nature of the actual relationship between the pronounced letters, when such an act is performed accurately, and the limbs of the mystic. Does he recreate his body during the pronunciation? Indeed this seems to be the possible answer according to another passage in *Ḥayyei ha-'Olam ha-Ba'*:

> Head and belly and torso, that is, the head, end, middle. The head is the first point that you imagine in it; the end is the final point of

the head, and it is like a tail to it and the belly is likewise like a tail to the head, . . . And the middle is the middle of the body and is the image of the torso wherein the heart is located. And the image that you ought to imagine at the time of pronunciation, in order to change within that image the nature of [one] part of the bodies, alone or with others, is . . . And pronounce in this manner whatever you pronounce and thus you will first say, "*heh*" [and envision it] in the middle of your head, and draw it within your head as if you were contemplating and seeing the center of your brain and its central point in your thoughts, and envision the letter inscribed above it, which safeguards the existence of the points of your brain.[23]

Thus, the pronunciation of the letters is accompanied by a practice of imagining the limbs of the mystic himself which correspond to these letters. Abulafia assumes that the pronunciation also includes a process of self-contemplation, the recited letters being appointed to the various limbs. We have, therefore, a technique which combines pronunciation and introspection as powerful tools, and which may be pernicious if inaccurate. On the basis of the above citations, it seems that the recitation of the letters of the name of seventy-two was connected to an elaborate view of the organic link between letters and limbs. This may explain the meaning of *Teḥilat ha-Yeẓirah* as a concise instruction for the creation of an image, whose details can be found in Abulafia's *Ḥayyei ha-'Olam ha-Ba'*. A basic difference between these texts is, however, the fact that in *Teḥilat ha-Yeẓirah* the image is constituted by the combination of dust and the recitation of the letters, and the emerging image seems to be independent of the mystic, whereas in *Ḥayyei ha-'Olam ha-Ba'* one probably has to imagine his inner constitution. In other words, whereas in the first case recitation is a creative process, in the second case it seems to be recreative. Whether the image emerging from the mixture of water and dust has something in common with the spiritual or corporeal constitution of the mystic himself is a matter that cannot be answered in a definitive way; in any case, it is significant to note that in Abulafia's ecstatic experiences a spiritual human form, which is the double of the mystic, emerges and communicates with him, an experience which seems to be parallel to that of the image created out of dust.[24]

What is important in the above discussions is the fact that no significant references to the Talmudic or Bahiric passages are to be found; in Abulafia's handbook the past or tradition is only the starting point for the present experience, interpretative proclivities, per se, being secondary in his literary activity. When they occur, these interpretations are of the nature of a "strong" hermeneutics, i.e., they dramatically change the meaning of the text. The story of Rava was, so I assume, marginal for a spiritualist like Abulafia who was basically interested in an experience of his own rather than in an interpretation of meaning of the corporeal creation of an artificial man. For him, the real creation was the spiritual one, which infinitely transcends any production of bodies. In his *Ḥayyei ha-'Olam ha-Ba'* the ecstatic Kabbalist writes:

> The greatest of all deeds is to make souls, [this being] the secret [of the verse][25] . . . "And the souls they made in Haran" . . . God has made man literally "in the image [*bi-demut*] of God he made him". And this deed is, according to our opinion, the culmination of all the good deeds. Therefore, every wise person ought to make souls much more than he ought to make bodies, since the duty of making bodies is [solely] intended to make souls. Thereby man will imitate his maker, since the prophet said on the issue of the deed of God,[26] "But the spirit and the soul which I have made should faint before me."[27]

Like his Ashkenazi predecessors, Abulafia exploits the classical interpretation of the verse referring to Abraham and Sarah's activity in Haran as a spiritual instruction of the gentiles, understood as a metaphorical creation of their souls. The Kabbalist does not contrast the creation of an artificial man to a spiritualistic teaching which alone is considered by him to be the creative par excellence; here corporeal procreation is compared to the intellectual one. However, we may infer from his formulation that the creation of a soulless Golem will be a meaningless activity; in any case, it is evidently inferior to the creation of the intellect of the mystic himself, by his reception of the intellectual influx as the result of the combination of the letters, or to the spiritual direction of the disciples. If, nevertheless, the creation of the creature and the appearance of the image are posited at a higher level than the perception of the influx, it seems that we must understand the vision of the creature and image as basically a spiritual experience. This reading of Abulafia is fostered by the occurrence of the term *demut* also in the passage from *Ḥayyei ha-'Olam ha-Ba'* where its meaning is explicitly a spiritual one because it functions as a synonym for the souls made by Abraham and Sarah. Moreover, Abulafia repeatedly uses this term in order to refer to the imaginative faculty, which is active during the ecstatic experience. Indeed, in one instance *demut* is presented not only as an inner force, but also one connected to the divine name which is inscribed in the inner constitution of man: "And I looked and I saw there [in the heart] my image (*ẓalmi*) and my likeness (*demuti*) moving in two paths, in a vision in the form (*bi-temunat*) of two Tetragrammata (*terei KW*)"[28]. Therefore, the image is conspicuously presented as an object of a vision, whose affinity to the divine name is obvious. According to the Abulafian terminology, the image stands for the intellect whereas the likeness stands for the imagination. With this clue in mind, let us cite a pertinent quotation from Abulafia's *Ḥayyei ha-'Olam ha-Ba'*:

> Whoever pursues the lore transmitted to us, in accordance with the [divine] name, in order to use it in operations of every kind for the glory of God, he is sanctifying the Name [of God]. But if he pursues the lore of the name in order to operate thereby corporeal issues, useful for wealth or longevity or for [the birth of] sons and daughters, or for love and hate, or in order to kill an enemy, and he intends, while doing this, his own glory or the glory of men or his benefit or theirs, without any true reason, and not for the glory of God, and he does it before he received from God an influx or [divine] spirit by [means of] the Tetragrammaton, even if he expresses by his mouth or things in his heart that he recites the name for the glory of God, it is not so, and though the operation is performed by the recitation of the aweful name, this man is wicked and a sinner who defiles the name of God.[29]

Therefore, the reception of the influx of wisdom is a prerequisite of the operation which, if intended to reveal the glory of God, is allowable. What is the meaning of this sequel, the influx of wisdom before the operation, which is parallel to the recipe for creation the image quoted above? I assume that if the influx of wisdom is identical to the *ẓelem,* the intellect, and the likeness or the creature to *demut* or imagination, we may understand the relationship between the two events in terms of the Maimonidean psychology of prophecy. Maimonides' definition of prophecy assumes the descent of the influx, which is manifestly intellectual in nature, first on the human intellect and afterward on the imaginative faculty.[30] The creation of the likeness therefore, can, be understood as the imaginative expression of the intellectual content of revelation; this view is cardinal for Abulafia's mystical experience, as I tried to explain elsewhere,[31] and it perfectly fits the occurrence of the *demut* in his revelatory experiences. Furthermore, we may better understand the rationale behind the anticipation of the influx to the imagination if we bear in mind Abulafia's view regarding the rule of intellect over the activity of imagination, a sine qua non condition for the attainment of true perceptions or visions. If this understanding of the recipe is correct, then we may consider it an intellectualistic interpretation, in the vein of medieval Aristotelianism, of a technique and religious ideal of Ashkenazi extraction.[32]

Abulafia's discussions of the creation of the creature or the likeness deal exclusively with the technique of its appearance; in opposition to the texts of the Ashkenazi Hasidism and those of R. Joseph Ashkenazi, to be discussed later on, which explicitly indicate as well the operation that will undo the creature. Abulafia and his followers ignore the need to annihilate the creature. Although it is dangerous to learn *ex absentia,* it would appear that the ignorance of this subject by the large corpus of ecstatic Kabbalah is highly significant. On the basis of the extant corpus we may conclude that Abulafia did not conceive the image as a lasting entity and therefore there was no need to worry about its ontological status after the end of the mystical experience involved in its creation. Insofar as the creature acts on the level of human imagination, it apparently disipates when the Kabbalist returns from the paranormal state of consciousness produced by the techniques described above.[33]

Last but not least, in all the descriptions of the creation of the anthropoid, Abulafia does not mention the necessity of having other participants present during this operation. In conspicuous opposition to some of the crucial medieval texts dealing with the study of *Sefer Yeẓirah* and the formation of an artificial man, where the imperative to cooperate with one or two people is explicitly mentioned, in some of the texts of Abulafia there are indications that the operator is expected to be alone. This is a major departure from the previous recommendations and it bears evidence to the strictly individualistic nature of the ecstatic Kabbalah in comparison to most of the important forms of Jewish mysticism.[34]

Post-Abulafian Views R. Reuven Ẓarfati

II

Let me now discuss the views on the creation of the artificial man in the writings of some authors who were particularly close to the theories of Abulafia, and who can be considered as belonging to the stream of ecstatic Kabbalah. The first one is R. Reuven Ẓarfati, an Italian Kabbalist who flourished in the fourteenth century.[35] Apparently drawing upon Abulafia's commentary on the *Guide of the Perplexed,* he wrote:

> . . . by the power of the Ineffable Name, which stems from the three verses that originates from *ḥesed,* [since] out of *ḥesed* was the world created.[36] And whoever is acquainted with them in a thorough way has the capability of making a creature and linking the composed [entities;[37]] and he will comprehend the comprehension that is worthwhile to be comprehended *in potentia,* and it will turn to be *in actu.*

> This is the ultimate perfection of man, who has to know this knowledge, as Rava has created a man. And the other sages of our generation comprehended this divine wisdom.[38]

Like Abulafia this Kabbalist refers to the name of seventy-two letters as the instrument of both comprehension and creation. Significant for our discussion is the assumption that the technique of creating a creature is in the possession of contemporary medieval sages, and presumably it is also applicable.

The Anonymous Sefer Ner 'Elohim

III

One of the most outstanding attempts to cope with the magical implications of the Talmudic discussions in *Sanhedrin* is to be found in the anonymous treatise *Ner 'Elohim,* written in the circle of Abraham Abulafia.[39] The author envisions the essential activity described by *Sefer Yeẓirah* as the combination of letters which culminates in the attainment of an ecstatic experience of prophecy. Immediately after stating this, he wrote:

> Do not believe the craziness of those who study *Sefer Yeẓirah* in order to create a three-year old calf, since those who strive to do so are themselves calves. And if Rava created a man and returned it to dust, there is therein a secret, and it is not the plain meaning of the matter. And he who did this on the eve of Sabbath, did it for a great secret reason, and the wise shall not be like a simpleton who does not possess the scales of reason to weigh the truth by them, and the stupid man will believe everything . . . and if the sages said it, he shall know the secret of their saying so, [since] they spoke in parables and enigmas.[40] See those stupid persons who believed the issue of creation in its plain meaning, but did not want to believe that if a man creates many souls, lasting for ever, it [this spiritual creation] is more elevated than the creation of bodies, generated for an hour and corrupted immediately.[41]

The corporeal creation is presented by the anonymous Kabbalist as a story that only fools understand literally, whereas the "illuminati" are able to penetrate beyond the exoteric form of the text to its inner esoteric meaning. Presumably, this meaning is that the corporeal creation is temporal, this being the intention of the command given to the man after he reached R. Zeira to return to his dust. We may assume that the absence of the power of speech was interpreted by this ecstatic Kabbalist as a sign of the insignificance of this creature. The spiritual creation is the real creation because it alone is lasting. Therefore, the Talmudic legend does not refer, according to this anonymous Kabbalist, to a mystical process, as Scholem interprets this passage,[42] but it alludes to the inferiority of the material activity in comparison to the activity of Abraham who created souls, according to the other parts of *Sefer Yeẓirah*.[43] We must distinguish between the positive attitude of the anonymous Kabbalist to the activity described in *Sefer Yeẓirah* and his negative attitude toward the plain meaning of the Talmudic passage. It is important to emphasize that the discussion in *Ner 'Elohim* seems to be the only instance in the literature of ecstatic Kabbalah where the corporeal creation of the artificial man is explicitly presented in a disparaging way. However, we can infer from this passage that at the end of the thirteenth century there were persons who believed that the study of *Sefer Yeẓirah* was intended to achieve merely corporeal goals. Since this evidence occurs in a polemical context, we must be cautious before accepting it as a clear-cut proof for the purely magical attitude and practice of *Sefer Yeẓirah* by the contemporaries of the author; however, the existence of other evidences concuring with this text,[44] allows for the acceptance of this evidence as reliable.

R. Nathan, the Teacher of R. Isaac of Acre

IV

R. Nathan, a Kabbalist who flourished at the end of the thirteenth century,[45] was quoted by R. Isaac of Acre as follows:

> . . . And if she [the soul] will merit to cleave to the Divine Intellect, fortunate is she, for she has returned to her source and root, and she is called, literally, Divine Intellect. And that person is called the 'Man of God', that is to say, a Divine Man, who creates worlds. Behold Rava created a man, but did not yet merit to give him a speaking soul. And you have to understand that since the pure soul of man has attained a degree of the supernal degrees, his soul governs everything below this degree. There is no need to elaborate upon the explanation of this issue for it is an axiom for every enlightened person.[46]

It is reasonable to assume that introducing the case of Rava's creation of man serves as an example of a degree that can be transcended by certain persons, the Divine Men, who, by cleaving to the highest degree, are able to rule over everything inferior to this degree; this reading is corroborated by the word "yet", *'Adayin,* which implies the possibility of surpassing the achievement of the Talmudic master. If so, the man of God, or the Divine Man[47] can induce a speaking soul into the Golem, provided he has realized a state of union with the Divine Intellect. A perfect Golem therefore can be created by a perfect man who is in a state of perfect mystical union, i.e., in a state of union with the Divine Intellect. The contact between the mystic and the Divine Intellect is reminiscent of the view of Abulafia that the process of creating a creature is preceded by the reception of the influx of wisdom. In both cases the intellectual perfection is considered as a prerequisite for the creative process.

Let me mention two other examples that require the union with the divine as preceding the creation of an artificial man. At the beginning of the fourteenth century, a commentator on the *Bahir* passage on Rava's creation, wrote:

> They created the world: the explanation is that they created worlds since [or after] they cleaved to God, i.e., to the [attribute of] Righteousness, [which is] the foundation of the world.[48]

Magical activity is presented here as following a mystical state, or status, which itself generates the creative activity. Although the conditioning of creation by *devequt* in the above passage seems to be historically independent of R. Nathan's view, it is possible that the latter's view found its way to the thought of R. Yehudah Loew ben Bezalel of Prague. The famous Maharal, wrote in his commentary on the *Sanhedrin* passage:

> When he [Rava] purified himself and studied the divine names in the *Book of Yeẓirah,* he thereby cleaved to God, blessed be He, and he created an artificial man. But he [the artificial man] lacked the faculty of speech, since his [Rava's] power was not great enough to bring a speaking soul in man, so that he [the man] would do like him, since he is a man and how can he create [something] similar to himself, just as it is impossible for God, who surpasses everything, to create one [God] similar to Himself.[49]

The clue for the creation of Rava is his purity and union with God. The prerequisite of purity can be easily understood against the background of the passage of the *Bahir,* whereas that of union seems to have been influenced by the explanatory addition of the commentator on the Bahiric passage. So far the similarities between the Maharal, the commentator and R. Nathan[50] are clear. However, they differ regarding the possibility of producing a precise replica of man or God. The commentator evades the problem. Just before the above passage, the Maharal discusses the talmudic statement that the righteous can create worlds, explaining it by the "total cleaving to Him", which insures the possibility of creating worlds, as the commentator of the *Bahir* maintained. Therefore, this author negates, in principle, the possibility of achieving the creation of the perfect Golem, notwithstanding the spiritual perfection of the mystic in his unitive state, when he may create a world.[51]

R. Isaac ben Samuel of Acre

V

Let me now address a most important text written by R. Isaac ben Samuel of Acre, one of the most interesting Kabbalists at the turn of the thirteenth century. The following passage includes a discussion during a Kabbalistic seminary, apparently connected to ecstatic Kabbalah:[52]

> Once . . . I, the young, was sitting in the company of advanced students, lovers of wisdom. One of them opened his mouth and asked me as follows: "What is the difference between the Creation [*beri'ah*] and Formation [*yeẓirah*]?" I told him, "Why don't you also ask why Abraham, our ancestor, called his book [by the name] *yeẓirah,* which consists of wondrous deeds, by the means of which Rava created a man . . . for R. Ḥiyya and R. Hoshaiyah a three-year old calf has been created each time before the entrance of the Sabbath, and they ate it during the day of Sabbath; and Jeremiah and Ben Sira created from it a speaking, wise and intelligent man, as I have explained above. Why did he not [namely, Abraham] call it the book of *Beri'ah?*" And he [the student] was not able [to answer me] and none of them answered me, since they did not know what it was. But I, the young,[53] while I was speaking it, I have seen the correct rationale for it, which is as follows: You already know the secret of the [letter] *yod* of the *'Abya'* and the secret of the [letter] *bet.* Since the majority of men have no power to endow a speaking soul, a fortiori an intellective soul, upon the matter shaped either in the form of an animal or a beast or a bird or a fish or a reptile, even not in the form of man, [using the capacity of] the *Book of Yeẓirah,* but only the animal and appetitive soul [alone], as our sages said Rava created a man and he sent it to R. Zeira etc, the book was called *Sefer Yeẓirah* but not the book of *beri'ah.* The reason is that the animal and appetitive soul, which perishes with the death of the body when the combina-

tion of the four elements is undone, stems from the intermediary world, which is the *yod* of *'Abya'*. But the secret of the speaking [and] intellective soul is from the supernal world, which is the [letter] *bet* of *'Abya'*. By saying the majority [of men] and not all [men] I intended to exclude Jeremiah the prophet, the disciple of Moses our master, peace on him, and Ben Sira and all those similar to them, few in number, who attained a divine perfection, [so as] to create an animal, speaking intellective [being]. And if you shall argue that all the prophets . . . were the disciples of Moses, our master, peace on him, so why did you mention Jeremiah in particular as a disciple of Moses? The answer is that you must pursue the Kabbalists so that they may explain to you the secret of the verse[54], "The Lord your God will raise up for you a prophet from among your own people, like myself; him you shall heed," and then you will certainly understand my intention. However, concerning Jeremiah and ben Sira alone have I received [a tradition] that they have drawn downward a speaking soul from their root of bet of *'Abya'*, that is the *'alef* of *'Abya'*, out of their great degree and the perfection of their soul, being able to [perform] this wondorous deed. The reason is that their degree attained to *Metatron*, the Prince of the Face, and *San*[*dalfon*], about whom we say in the blessing of the Ancestors,[55] "And You bring a deliverer on the sons of their sons", and the wise will understand.[56]

R. Isaac of Acre presents the act creating the Golem in the frame of his peculiar Kabbalistic *Weltanschauung*, which consists, *inter alia*, of the view that there are four worlds: the highest one is that of *'azilut*, the world of Emanation, referred to by R. Isaac by the first *'a* of the *'Abya'* acronym; the next one is the world of *beri'ah*, Creation, which is the world of the divine chariot, alluded to in the letter *bet;* the third one is the world of *yezirah*, Formation, which is the world of the angels and corresponds to the letter *yod;* and, finally, the world of *'asiyah*, the lower world of Making which corresponds to the letter *'Ayin*.[57] The discussion of the Golem is focused upon the capability of the mystics to induce the animal and appetitive soul into matter. This soul stems from the world of *yezirah*, this being the reason, according to R. Isaac, that Abraham named his book *Sefer Yezirah*. This possibility is conceived as indisputable for a fair range of persons, including the Talmudic figures. However, we learn from the above passage that a higher spiritual faculty can be induced by the very few, specifically Jeremiah the prophet and Ben Sira, and by "those similar to them". Consequently, some few elite have the access to the higher world, that of *beri'ah*, Creation, being able to draw down the speaking and rational soul. However, the Kabbalist assumes that those few may even be able to reach the world of *'aẓilut*, as the phrase "*Bet* of *'Abya'* which is the *'aleph* of *'ABYA'*" implies. If this interpretation is correct, if follows that R. Isaac asserts that it is possible to create a Golem that includes elements from all the three highest worlds, and hence, it seems reasonable to assume, also from the lowest one, which apparently would supply the matter of the Golem.

The assumption that man can create using elements from all the four worlds is tantamount, as I shall try to show immediately, to the divine act of the creation of Adam. In other words, the above passage is an interesting replica to the Genesis discussion of the creation of man, as R. Isaac of Acre understood it. Thus, for example, we read in his commentary on the Kabbalistic secrets included in the Pentateuch, *Mei'rat 'Einayim*:

> The secret of creation of man [refers to] the speculative soul [*ha-neshamah ha-ḥakhamah*], which stands for ever. And the secret of his formation [refers to] the animal soul, which does nor stand for ever . . . And emanation and creation are more spiritual than formation.[58]

This is, *in nuce,* the doctrine of the above discussion of the creation of the Golem. The implications of the view of R. Isaac are, however, more radical than it appears at a prima facie reading. The assumption that the two masters were able to induce the spiritual element from the world of emanation implies that the magically created man has the highest spiritual capacity, which is not to be found, automatically, even in a normally created man. According to some Kabbalists, the highest soul is an achievement to be obtained by a mystical *regimen vitae;*[59] while the conclusion that the man created by Jeremiah and Ben Sira is endowed with a spiritual soul that is characteristic of a mystic, will be a far-reaching one; the sublime status of their creation is undeniable in comparison to the views of other authors who rejected the possibility that the Golem can even speak.

Moreover, the artificially created anthropoid comprises the whole range of creation, and therefore it is parallel to the divine creation of the world. This understanding is consonant with a view, found in R. Nathan's traditions collected by R. Isaac of Acre, that the macranthropos, identical with the intellectual man, comprises the whole cosmos, including its spiritual facets, whereas the material man is the microanthropos.[60] Moreover, this view corresponds to a midrashic tradition on Adam, whose creation began before the creation of the world, and ended after the accomplishment of the creation of the world, the whole universe thus being included in him.[61] The assumption that the artificial man includes in itself the whole universe, including the four worlds of the Kabbalists, is reminiscent of the theory of Lurianic Kabbalah, where *'Adam Qadmon,* the Primeval Man, includes the whole range of worlds, and is connected, as we shall show below, to the creation of an anthropoid.[62]

R. Yehudah Albotini

VI

The above authors belonging to the ecstatic Kabbalah assume that the achievement of Rava is not the patrimony of the past but an avenue open in the present; moreover, the Talmudic master is not, ex definitio, the paragon who cannot be surpassed in the present. This is also the attitude of R. Yehudah Albotini, an early sixteenth century Kabbalist writing in Jerusalem. Following the views of his predecessors, he asserts that:

> all the creatures were made from the twenty-two letters and their combinations and their permutations, and as fire by nature warms, and water cools, so do the letters by their nature create all sorts of creatures . . . the other prophets and pious men in each generation, by means of the combination and permutation of letters and their vocalisation, used to perform miracles and wonders and turn about the order of Creation, such as we find it explained in our Talmud that Rava created a man and sent him to R. Zeira.[63]

Therefore, the performance of the Talmudic master is not limited to the past but is possible, at least in principle, in each generation. Given the disclosure of the technique of creation by combination of letters—Albotini's *Sullam ha-'Aliyah* being one of the most systematic expositions of this issue—all those who are pious are capable of recreating the attainment of Rava.

The Gates of the Old Man

VII

In a late thirteenth or early fourteenth century Kabbalistic text, named the *Gates, She'arim,*[64] consisting of the discussions of the circle of the Old Man, *ha-zaqen,* we read:

> The gate of the secret of the *ẓeruf* [combination of letters], we asked the sage, "Anytime we ask you anything your answer is, 'Great is the

> power of the *zeruf.*'" He answered to us, "You know that by the combination of the letters of His names, God created everything. And our old ancestor,[65] blessed be his memory, out of the combination of the letters which he was taught . . . he achieved the entire gist of His unity and the strength of all the formations, and he almost reached the degree that he knew how to form excellent formations, namely formations of thought [*yezirot mahshaviyot*], and this is the reason he called his excellent book by the name *Sefer Yezirah*".[66]

Scholem, who cited part of the above quotation, understood it as pointing to the ecstatic nature of the ritual of the creation of the Golem. However, it is far from being clear whether or not the creation of a man is here intended, though such an interpretation cannot be excluded; even less obvious is the fact that there is an ecstatic experience implied in this text; creation of forms which have a mental characteristic, presented here as a great achievement, can be understood in various alternative ways, the ecstatic interpretation being no more than one possibility, not corroborated by additional material. On the contrary, it seems that the gradation of the achievements of Abraham is rather strange: Abraham was taught the combination of letters, then he attained the knowledge of the divine unity and only then he almost reached what seems to be the most sublime topic, the mental creative one.[67] These distinctions assume that the combination of letters will enable the theological attainment, whereas the last stage, the creative one was not achieved at all. In lack of substantial semantic material which may illuminate the significance of this passage in the *Gates* themselves, I would like to propose a comparison of this text to two other passages, which may contribute a different understanding of the above citation.

The attempt to explain the title of *Sefer Yezirah* by the emphasis on the creation by combination of letters which yields a mental formation is reminiscent of the similar attempt made by R. Isaac of Acre. In the passage we discussed above, R. Isaac mentioned that Jeremiah and Ben Sira had created "a speaking, wise and intelligent man, as I have explained above." Thus, by the means of *Sefer Yezirah* it was possible to create a being that is intelligent; unfortunately, the discussion of the perfect creation of man alluded to by R. Isaac is not extant. Such a discussion would have helped us clarify the question if there is any connection between the Old Man and circle of R. Isaac. Thus, for example, it would have been possible to understand to what extent the knowledge of the divine world was instrumental in the creation of the Golem in the school of R. Isaac. As we have seen above, the perfect creation involves the drawing down of the influx from the whole range of higher worlds, the worlds of *'aby'*. Is this similar, or identical, with the knowledge of God referred in the *Gates*?

In any case, it is perhaps pertinent to remark that, at least in one case, a certain R. Isaac the Old is mentioned in a manuscript which includes material authored by R. Isaac of Acre,[68] and some excerpts from the *Gates* of the Old Man are extant in a manuscript including a writing of R. Isaac of Acre.[69] Moreover, at the beginning of the quotation of R. Isaac adduced above, he mentions a group of students who discussed the issue of the Golem. This is the case also in the *Gates*. Is our Old man R. Isaac of Acre in his old age? Or, alternatively, did the circle of the students of the Old Man, include R. Isaac as one of its members?[70] We cannot enter here into a discussion of these fascinating problems. However, if one of these hypothesis will be proven correct, then the meaning of the formations of thought will more likely be an intelligent anthropoid and not visions obtained during an ecstatic experience. Thus the phrase "*Yeẓirot maḥshaviyot*" would reflect the intelligent creatures which Abraham almost had been able to create.

Another pertinent text to be compared to the passage of the Old Man is found in a collection of Kabbalistic material that includes also traditions stemming from ecstatic Kabbalistic writings and compiled by R. Joseph Ḥamiẓ in the middle of the seventeenth century; there we read, "Know that mental letter-combination performed in the heart brings forth a word, being (the result of) the letter-combination entirely mental and born from the sphere[71] of the intellect."[72] The Hebrew form for mental letter-combination is *Ẓeruf maḥshavti* or, according to the other epithet *sikhli,* i.e., an intellectual.[73] Thus, it may also be that in the case of the combinations of letters by the Old Man, the reference is to a process that is envisaged as a mental creation. However, according to this alternative as well, an ecstatic experience is not explicitly expressed by this phrase.

Notes

1. See below, chs. 10–11.

2. See Idel, *Abraham Abulafia,* pp. 130–132 and in the discussions below.

3. See below in this paragraph and n. 19.

4. Compare to the text quoted in n. 13 below.

5. Probably, the technique is not to be restricted to the creation of an anthropoid alone; see our summary below.

6. See Idel, *The Mystical Experience,* pp. 38–39.

7. Ms. Parma, 1390, fol. 91a–92a; this manuscript was copied in 1286, only six years after the composition of *Ḥayyei ha-'Olam ha-Ba'* in Italy. Ms. Milano-Ambrosiana 52, fol. 111a–118; Ms. Paris BN, 763, fol. 26a–28a. Ms. Paris BN, 776, on the margin of fol. 163a; this folio is part of *Ḥayyei ha-'Olam ha-Ba',* and this seems to be the only evidence that connects this passage with this book of Abulafia. In some of the manuscripts mentioned above, this recipe appears together with the other text to be attributed to Abulafia which will be discussed below. See n. 20 below.

8. On this term in the context of combining letters, see Idel, *Language Torah and Hermeneutics,* p. 100.

9. The mention of the ninth sphere, or wheel, seems to refer to an astronomic plane, where all the entities are engraved in one way or another. It is interesting to point out that the linguistic device of combining letters by means of the wheel is apparently compared here to the astronomical sphere, as it is implied already in R. Yehudah ha-Levi's *Kuzari*; see above ch. 6, par. 2.

10. Cf. *'Avodah Zarah,* fol. 17a; *Sanhedrin,* fol. 65a; Rashi on Deut. 18:9 and Maimonides, *Commentary on the Mishnah, Pesaḥim,* chapter 5. The same warning occurs also in other discussions of the creation of the Golem; see the end of the passage from the circle of the *'Iyyun* literature, above chapter 5 n. 84 and in the *Commentary on Sefer Yeẓirah* of R. Meir ibn Avi Sahulah, Ms. Roma-Angelica, 45, fol. 2a.

11. The mystical achievement is portrayed here as the result of the magical practice, whereas in *Sefer Yeẓirah* the situation is inverse. Compare below par. 4 the views of the disciple of Abulafia who envisaged the stage of mystical union as a condition for the creative stage.

12. Ms. Paris BN, 763, fol. 31a–31b; Ms. Parma, 1390, fol. 94b–95a; Parma Perreau, 92/8, fol. 117b; Ms. Hamburg-Levi 151, fol. 23b; Ms. Vatican, 528, fol. 71b; Ms. Munchen, 341, fol. 183b; Ms. Cambridge Add. 647, fol. 18b; Ms. Bar Ilan, 286, fol. 82a.

13. Cf. the anonymous text found in Ms. Moscow-Guensburg, 96, fol. 18b:

> Two hundred and thirty-one gates in the wheel, all of them handed down to him, and whoever knows how to recite them and to combine them and to turn them with the vowels, he will create a creature [*livro beri'ah*] like Rava, since a species had encountered its counterpart.

14. *Yesh me-'Ayin,* literally, existence out of nonexistence. There seems to be a pun here since the Hebrew phrase is the classical formulation for the *ex nihilo* creation, which is presented here as part of the belief of the people of Israel, whose name commenced with the letters YS.

15. *'Oẓar 'Eden Ganuz,* Ms. Oxford, 1580, fol. 159b. Compare the very similar discussion of R. Joseph Gikatilla, a student of Abulafia, who writes in *Gin-*

nat 'Egoz (Hannau, 1625), fol. 57b: "The wheel has 231 gates and from this issue you have to understand the secret of the name of the nation which alone is called by this name, this being the secret of Israel . . . and the secret of Israel is *Sekhel ha-Po'el.*" Israel is numerically equivalent to *Sekhel ha-Po'el,* namely, both of them are in *Gemaṭri'ah,* 541. This *Gemaṭri'ah* also occurs several times in the writings of Abulafia.

16. Ms. Oxford, 1582, fol. 3a.

17. Ms. Oxford, 1582, fol. 49b–50a. Compare also Ibid., fol. 10a:

> Whoever knows how to combine it [that is the name of seventy two] in a proper manner, the divine spirit will enwrap him in any case, or the influx of wisdom will flow onto him, in order to teach his intellect, the essence of reality, suddenly.

18. See Idel, *The Mystical Experience,* p. 125.

19. See *Ibid.,* pp. 34–37.

20. In Hebrew it means also spirit, here the basic meaning seems to be air. See the occurence of *ruaḥ* and "end", namely the third part of the pronunciation process, in the anonymous text referred in no. 6 above.

21. Ms. Oxford 1582, fol. 12b. See also ibid., fol. 13b.

22. Ms. Oxford 1582, fol. 14b.

23. Ms. Oxford, 1582, fol. 61a; See also Idel, *The Mystical Experience,* p. 36 where some other issues connected to this passage, as well as a slightly different translation of the context are found. In general it should be mentioned that Abulafia is very fond of the idea that the body of man, and sometimes he even refers to his soul, is created out of letters. See e.g., *'Oẓar 'Eden Ganuz,* Ms. Oxford 1580, fol. 24b. See also Wolfson, "The Anthropomorphic Image," par. II.

24. See Idel, ibid., pp. 95–100. In this context, it is instructive to mention the angels and the celestial mentors, who are created out of the words of the student of the Torah according to R. Ḥayyim Vital. In his *Sha'ar ha-Nevu'ah ve-Ruaḥ ha-Qodesh* ch. 2, the very pronunciation of the sacred scriptures might generate an entity which will later on serve as a source of revelation for this student. Since these entities are conceived as being connected to this mystic who originates them, there is a certain affinity between the view of Abulafia that out of the combinations of letters an entity which reveals itself emerges and the view of the 16th century Safedian mystic. On the view of the *Maggid,* see Werblowsky, *Karo,* pp. 77–83.

25. Gen. 12:5.

26. Isa. 57:16.

27. Ms. Oxford 1582, fol. 5ab.

28. *Sefer ha-'Ot,* ed., A. Jellinek, in *Jubelschrift zum siebzigsten Geburtstage des Prof. Dr. H. Graetz* (Breslau, 1887), p. 81. The text is based upon the numerical equivalence of the words included in it: *Ẓalmi ve- Demuti* = 636 = *Mitn'oe'a* = *Bi-Shenei Derakhim* = *terei KW. KW* is the numerical value of the letters of the Tetragrammaton.

29. Ms. Oxford, 1582, fol. 80a–80b, Ms. Paris BN, 777, fol. 132a–133b.

30. *The Guide of the Perplexed* II, 36.

31. Idel, *The Mystical Experience,* p. 17.

32. Since it is a strong interpretation of Ashkenazi-Hasidic views, Abulafia's conception cannot simply be considered as a mere continuation of earlier traditions, without any addition.

33. Compare also to the fact that Abulafia, who supplied several different techniques to attain a mystical experience, did not pay attention to the possible problems involved in the return from such experiences.

34. On the emphasis of the importance of isolation in the ecstatic Kabbalah see Idel, *The Mystical Experiences,* pp. 38–39.

35. On this author, see Gottlieb, *Studies,* pp. 357–369. Thanks are due to my student, Mr. Abraham Elqayyam, who has drawn my attention to the following text.

36. Cf. Ps. 89:3. *Ḥesed* is numerically equivalent to seventy-two, a clear hint to the name of seventy-two letters.

37. On the description of man as a composite being, see Idel, *Studies in Ecstatic Kabbalah,* p. 9.

38. Ms. Cambridge, Add. 505,7, fol. 25b.

39. See Idel, *Abraham Abulafia,* pp. 72–75 and see also n. 41 below.

40. The assumption that the ancient Jewish sages spoke in parables is part of the Maimonidean view accepted by the Abulafian school, which maintained the allegorical approach. The view that there are secrets in the legends of the sages is common also in the theosophical Kabbalah, where the legends where interpreted according to the theosophical system. However, the feeling that the plain meaning of the ancient texts is problematic is uncommon among the theosophical Kabbalists, whereas the theology of the ecstatic Kabbalah, influenced by Maimonides, was more sensitive to the discrepancy between the ancient Jewish magico-mythico theologumena and the medieval theology.

41. *Ner 'Elohim,* Ms. Münich, 10, fol. 172b–173a. See Scholem, "The Idea of the Golem", p. 188. Scholem considers Abraham Abulafia to be the author of this anonymous treatise, though no evidence for this assumption is to be found in the unique manuscript of this work.

42. Scholem, ibid., p. 188.

43. See above beside n. 27 the discussion of Abulafia's similar view in *'Oẓar 'Eden Ganuz*.

44. See below, the evidence from R. Abraham of Esquira's *Sefer Yesod 'Olam* in the *Summary* below, n. 17.

45. See Idel, *Studies in Ecstatic Kabbalah,* pp. 73–89.

46. Goldreich, *Me'irat 'Einayim,* p. 223, Vajda, *Recherches,* p. 397.

47. On this concept see Idel, *Studies in Ecstatic Kabbalah,* p. 146 n. 35; p. 151, n. 63.

48. See *Sefer Ha-Bahir,* ed. R. Margaliot (Jerusalem, 1978), p. 89.

49. *Sefer Ḥiddushei 'Aggadot Maharal Mi-Prague* (Benei Berak, 1980), vol. 2, p. 166.

50. On another possibility of the influence of a view of the *Collectanaea* of R. Nathan, see Idel, *The Mystical Experience,* p. 217, n. 81.

51. For Maharal's view of *devequt,* see Byron L. Sherwin, *Mystical Theology and Social Dissent. The Life and Works of Judah Loew of Prague* (London, Toronto, 1982), pp. 122–141. On the Golem, see his remarks on pp. 17–19.

52. See also Idel, *The Mystical Experience,* pp. 116–118.

53. This is a common epithet that R. Isaac uses in order to describe himself; see Idel, *Studies in Ecstatic Kabbalah* pp. 87–88, n. 43.

54. Deut. 18:15.

55. The explanation of the significance of "the sons of sons", an expression from the Eighteen Benediction Prayer, as two angels occurs already in the initial literary stages of Kabbalah in a manuscript passage of R. Isaac the Blind, and it is reflected in a series of texts, one of them quoted by R. Isaac of Acre in his *Me'irat 'Eynayim,* p. 86; however, it seems that only here the names of the angels are specified.

56. Ms. Sassoon 919, p. 217, Ms. Cambridge, Genizah, TS, K 12, 4 p. 22.

57. On this issue see Idel, *Studies in Ecstatic Kabbalah,* pp. 82, 88.

58. Goldreich, p. 20.

59. This view is widespread in the theosophical Kabbalah as formulated in the *Zohar* and in the books of R. Moses de Leon and R. Joseph of Hamadan. Later on it became a commonplace in Kabbalah.

60. See Idel, *Studies in Ecstatic Kabbalah,* p. 98 n. 21.

61. See Idel, *Kabbalah: New Perspectives,* pp. 117–118.

62. See ch. 10 below.

63. Printed by G. Scholem, *Qiryat Sefer,* vol. 22, (1945), p. 165, and Idel, *The Mystical Experience,* p. 37.

64. This text has not received the due attention of scholars; it appears in fragmentary form in several manuscripts which will be discussed in detail elsewhere. The relationship between this text and ecstatic Kabbalah seems to be limited to the themes discussed below and the "gates" cannot be considered a part of the literature of this brand of Kabbalah.

65. *Ve-ha-zaqen avinu.* Scholem proposed to identify this person with Abraham, see "The Idea of the Golem," p. 188.

66. Ms. Oxford, 2396, fol. 53b; already mentioned by Scholem, ibid.

67. This view differs from that of R. Isaac of Acre, who agreed that latter figures did succed in creating an artificial man.

68. Ms. Sassoon, 919.

69. See Ms. New York, JTS, 1777; Cf. M. Idel, "Kabbalistic Material from the Circle of R. David ben Yehudah he-Ḥasid," *JSJT,* vol. 4 (1983), p. 170, idem, *Studies in Ecstatic Kabbalah,* pp. 73–89.

70. Ms. Sasson 919, pp. 205–206. This manuscript contains also, on p. 217, the fragment on the Golem of R. Isaac of Acre, discussed above; see n. 56.

71. For another example of Kabbalistic discussions in a circle in which R. Isaac was one of its members, see Idel, *The Mystical Experience,* pp. 117–118.

72. Ms. Oxford 2239, fol. 113a.

73. See also Idel, *The Mystical Experience,* p. 20.

8

R. Joseph ben Shalom Ashkenazi

The influence of the technique of creating the Golem found in R. Eleazar of Worms' *Commentary on Sefer Yeẓirah* on the development of subsequent techniques was tremendous. Although ignored in the standard descriptions of the impact of the Ashkenazi theology on Kabbalah,[1] it played a crucial role in several important domains of this lore. As seen above, it exercised a deep influence on Abulafia, mostly in his technique of reaching a mystical experience, though also in the path of creating a Golem.[2] Now, we shall embark upon a description of the reverberations of this technique in the writings of an Ashkenazi Kabbalist who combined the Ashkenazi technique with theosophical speculations, a synthesis which had important repercussions on Lurianic theosophies.[3]

We may distinguish between three main phases of the metamorphosis of R. Eleazar's discussion on the creation of the Golem in the writings of R. Joseph. Although we cannot evaluate the exact sequence of the composition of the writings of this Kabbalist,[4] we will attempt to follow the discussions concerning the practice of creating a Golem from their simplest form to the most complex one, ignoring the complicated problems connected to the order of those writings. It seems that in his *Commentary on Sefer Yeẓirah,* R. Joseph follows the major assumptions of his Ashkenazi predecessor, when he chooses the 231 gates formula,[5] though he was evidently aware of the existence of a version which proposes 221 gates of the combinations of letters.[6]

Again, following the path exposed by R. Eleazar, he accepts the technique of undoing the Golem by using the combinations of the alphabets from 'AL to 'AT.[7] However, the Kabbalist included a new element in the framework of the Ashkenazi technique when he related the combinations dealing with the creation of the Golem to the *sefirah* of *ḥesed,* whereas the 231 gates which undo the Golem were linked with the *sefirah* of *din.*[8] This theosophical interpretation of the technique is part of a more comprehensive attitude of this Kabbalist to interpret the concept of the Golem, and other instances of such reinterpretations will be discussed below.[9] Interestingly, it is possible that the relationship between the creative and destructive processes and *sefirot,* the correspondence to the *sefirot ḥesed* and *gevurah,* reflects, a higher correspondence between the creative feature of the *sefirot keter* and the destructive one of *ḥokhmah.* The former hints at the existence, *hawwayah,* and construction, *ha-hawayah bonah,* whereas the latter points, implicitly, to inexistence, *he'eder,* and destruction, *ḥorban.*[10] The source of such an interpretation seems to be the *Commentary on Sefer Yeẓirah* of R. Azriel of Gerona, who had already suggested that the forward combinations of letters do create, whereas the reversed form of those combinations undo. The terms used in order to refer to creation by combinations of letters is "to build" *livnot,* whereas the undoing is referred to by the verb "to destroy", *listor.*[11] Shortly before this discussion, R. Azriel indicates that the forward combinations of letters are related to grace, *panim zeh raḥamim,* and the backward combinations are related to judgement, *'aḥor zeh din.*[12] R. Joseph Ashkenazi applied this principle to the two major division of the 231 combinations, referring to the 'AB to 'AK combinations to creation, *miẓad ha-ḥesed livriy'ato,* and the 231 combinations of letters to destruction: *miẓad ha-din veha-gevurah listor ulehaḥriv.*[13] Later on he writes that there is a certain order of letters for the process of creation and an inverse order for destruction.[14] Although this Kabbalist uses the term Golem[15], it is not in connection with the artificial creations; yet, it seems reasonable to assume that the artificial anthropoid is referred in the *Commentary on Sefer Yeẓirah* by the terms *beri'ah* (creation) and *beriyah* (creature) which occur in the context of creation and undoing.[16] It seems that these terms were chosen for their ambiguity, though I assume that the Kabbalist was interested in being understood as dealing with the creation of the artificial man.

In the *Commentary on Genesis Rabba* he repeats the major assumptions of creating by letters described above,[17] with one crucial addition. Following the way of vocalisation of the combinations of the letters of the alphabets and the letters of the divine names as proposed by R. Eleazar of Worms, R. Joseph copies the tables of vocalisation as they occur in R. Eleazar of Worms' *Sefer ha-Shem.*[18] Moreover, he adduces an interpretation of the five main types of operating with the letters, as they occur in the literature related to *Sefer ha-'Iyyun*: *shiqqul, ẓeruf, ma'amar, mikhlal* and *ḥeshbon.*[19] When elaborating on the first one as a technique of combining letters using concentric circles, he mentions the passage from *Sanhedrin* and the paragraph from *Sefer ha-Bahir.*[20]

However, the most important discussion of the technique for creating the Golem occurs in an anonymous text, extant in manuscript, which can be considered as the composition of R. Joseph or deeply influenced by his writings.[21] I shall not enter here into the details of demonstrating the authorship of this passage; I shall refer to it however as the last, and most elaborate, stage of R. Joseph's discussions of this topic. It is also possible that this short text was composed by R. David ben Yehudah he-Ḥasid. The author repeats most of the assumptions discussed above, but adds two main points, which seem to be the result of accepting some elements which do not occur in the Ashkenazi passages on the Golem presented above. Two of these new points seem to be unrelated, but a closer examination of the material will demonstrate that they are indeed related to each other.

The first innovation is the view that the vowels, which are related to certain combinations of the letters of the divine names, function as the sustaining element for those creatures related to the specific permutation of letters of the divine name. In other words, the vowels are the souls of the letters of the divine name, and the beings under the aegis of a certain combination of letters and a certain vocalisation will exist as long as this vocalisation will govern these letters. Without the decomposition of the vocalisation, no being can decay.[22] This view implicitly emphasizes the importance of the knowledge of the peculiar vocalisations. From this point of view, R. Joseph, or R. David, is close to the view of the Northern French school which produced the *Commentary on Sefer Yeẓirah* attributed to R. Sa'adyah.[23]

More important is the second innovation when compared to his earlier discussions on the creation of the Golem. In this text, the author mentions the relationship between creation and the *sefirah* of *tif'eret,* and not the sefirah of *ḥesed* as in the earlier sources, while the process of destruction is still related to *gevurah.*[24] However, when mentioning the *sefirot,* the Kabbalist adds the terms *mar'eh.* In classical Hebrew, this term denotes the appearance of a certain thing; however, in the context of the Kabbalah of R. Joseph and that of the school with which he was connected, this term has something to do with color.[25] In our text, the term *zeva'*, the common word for color, indeed appears in connection to the *sefirot*:

> The issue of the emergence of the vocalisation of *Notariqon*[26] is [related] to the issue of creation and to the [process of] undoing. The creation [refers] to the appearance [or nuance] of *t[if'ere]t*, by its color, and the destructions to the appearance of *gevurah*, in its color.[27]

The relation between colors and *sefirot* is not an innovation unique to this anonymous text; it occurs several times in the *Commentary on Sefer Yezirah* of R. Joseph[28] and in his *Commentary on Genesis Rabbah*.[29] However, with one outstanding exception, these discussions apparently deal only with the symbolic values of the relationship, without any practical implication. Only in one case, the author mentions color as part of a more experiential discussion, and this passage indicates that the colors enwrap the divine names in the moment of an ecstatic experience.[30] However, an analysis of material extant from the writings of R. David ben Yehudah he-Ḥasid, where the colors were mentioned, allows us to formulate a theory on the visualisation of colors during prayer as part of the mystical intention which has to accompany the pronunciation of the words of the regular prayer.[31] This visualisation is explicitly related to the divine names and the peculiar vocalisation of those letters. This visualisation has a creative effect and the letters which were visualised in the various colors, which correspond to the *sefirot*, ascend to the *sefirotic* realm.[32] In other words, visualisation of letters and colors was conceived as producing a certain entity, which was supposed to have an existence of its own. I assume that this is the meaning as well of mentioning the colors in the text dealing with the creation using the 231 gates. It is possible that the color of the *sefirah* of *tif'eret* was part of the creative process whereas that of *gevurah* was a component of the mystical intention of the Kabbalist who undoes the creature.

This hypothetical use of color as part of the creation of a Golem may explain the absence of any mentioning of the material out of which the Golem was supposed to be created. Though following the technique of R. Eleazar of Worms in principle, R. Joseph fails to mention the dust, or any similar alternative, to be used in order to build up a Golem. This absence may be a matter of accident, and new texts of R. Joseph may change this situation. However, it may also be that the fact that the dust is not mentioned at the beginning of the act of creation is part of an effort to shape another type of Golem different than that found in the classical versions of the techniques of creating one. Apparently, dust was partially replaced by color, which was visualized as part of the creation of the

Golem.[33] This assumption, interesting as it is, must remain, for the time being, in the domain of an hypothesis, until further material may substantiate it.

In any case, if our hypothesis is correct, the question arises as to the kind of relationship that pertains between the two first stages of the description of the technique and the last one. The adding of the color, and revealing the importance of the vowels, can be explained in two different ways: we may assume that the later stage is the result of a certain evolution in the technique known to R. Joseph at an earlier stage of his writing. Accordingly, a certain element was introduced by him in the older Ashkenazi material. The second possibility may assume that the fact that the issue of the color appears only in one of the versions of the technique reflects the esoteric nature of this element, which was not revealed except in a discussion dealing with the creation intended to remain the patrimony of a limited circle. I am inclined to accept the second of these two explanations, for two reasons: first, already in the works which contain the earlier versions of the techniques, colors are mentioned as symbols; therefore, it seems reasonable to assume that a certain affinity between the colors and their visualisation was suppressed in the earlier stage, and revealed only later on. The second reason is the fact that the visualization of colors during prayer was considered an esoteric issue which was not mentioned in *Sefer 'Or Zaru'a,* R. David ben Yehudah he-Ḥasid's *Commentary on the Prayer*; however, in fragments of his preserved in manuscripts, we can reconstruct the existence of an esoteric practice of visualisation of colors as part of prayer.[34] It seems, therefore, that the absence of the visualisation of colors during the combinations of letters may be but another example of suppressing an esoteric practice. In any case, there are some indications that using the colors during the prayer may imply a construction of an anthropomorphic structure, and therefore we may compare the divine anthropos formed out of the various visualised colors[35] to the anthropoid created by means of visualising letters. Last but not least: the creation of the Golem in the *Sanhedrin* passage was interpreted by R. Joseph as a symbol for the creation of the *sefirotic* structure in an anthropomorphic shape.[36] Our hypothesis is that the creation of the Golem using a certain color is parallel to the practice of creating a *sefirotic* colorful anthropoid during the prayer of the Kabbalist. I cannot demonstrate this hypothesis as a whole, but at least parts of it seem to be obvious. In the *Commentary on Genesis Rabbah* R. Joseph describes the creation of Adam as the goal of the whole creation, and the dust out of which he was created as having five colors and their mixture, which is explicitly related to the ten *sefirot,* understood here as the ten luminosities, *zoharim.*[37] These colors are presented as the components of the limbs of man.[38] As we have already mentioned, according to R. Joseph Ashkenazi, the artificial creation of an anthropoid is a symbol for the creation of the *sefirot*.[39] Thus, we may assume that the creation of man using *Sefer Yeẓirah* included, in the system of this Kabbalist, or of R. David ben Yehudah he-Ḥasid an important component, the colors, vizualised or in any other way.

Finally, I would like to compare the hypothetical elements of the technique to create a Golem as proposed above to that of Abraham Abulafia. In both cases we witness an encounter between Ashkenazi techniques and Sefardi speculative material. Abulafia reinterpreted the Golem using Maimonidean psychological categories, whereas R. Joseph or R. David were acquainted with both the philosophical views of Sefardi extraction, and apparently also with the views of Abraham Abulafia regarding the combinations of letters,[40] and with the theosophical interpretation of the *Sanhedrin* passage as proposed by the Provençal and Catalan Kabbalists.[41] R. Joseph chose the later interpretation as far as the possible theosophical symbolism of the creation of an artificial man was implied; moreover, he apparently accepted a theurgical assumption regarding the way of creating the creature: it is not a material being, emerging out of dust, but created, if our hypothesis is correct, out of the imagination of the mystic. Here lies the difference between the interpretation of Abulafia and that of the theosophical Kabbalist; in the case of the ecstatic Kabbalist, the source of the creation is the Agent Intellect, which pours upon the human actualized intellect the forms, which are subsequently translated by the imaginative faculty into visible apparitions. The imagination translates more than it creates. According to the interpretation proposed above, which, I would like to emphasize, includes a highly speculative component, active imagination, or visualisation, plays a major role in the formation of the Golem. It is not a vision coming from above, but a creation of the human faculty of inner vision. More than being an object of contemplation, as in the case of Abulafia, it is a way of symbolically imitating God on the lower plane.

Notes

1. Compare Joseph Dan, "The Vicissitude of the Esotericism of the German Hasidism", in *Studies in Mysticism and Religion Presented to Gershom Scholem* (Jerusalem, 1967), pp. 87–99. (Hebrew)

2. See ch. 7, par. 1.

3. See ch. 10, par. 6.

4. On the writings of this Kabbalist, see Gershom Scholem, "The true au-

thor of the *Commentary on Sefer Yeẓirah* attributed to Rabad and his Writings," *Qiryat Sefer,* vol. 4 (1928-1929), pp. 267-272 (Hebrew); Hallamish, Introduction to the *Commentary on Genesis Rabbah,* pp. 14-15.

5. *Commentary on Sefer Yeẓirah,* fols. 41d, 42d.

6. Ibid., fol. 42d. *Commentary on Genesis Rabbah,* p. 255.

7. *Commentary on Sefer Yeẓirah,* fol. 40c, 41d.

8. Fol. 42cd.

9. See below ch. 10, par. 3.

10. *Commentary on Genesis Rabbah,* pp. 32 and 186.

11. *Commentary on Sefer Yeẓirah,* in Chavel, *Kitvei Ramban,* vol. 2, p. 459.

12. Ibid.

13. *Commentary on Sefer Yeẓirah,* fol. 40c.

14. Ibid., fol. 40d.

15. See below ch. 10, par. 3.

16. *Commentary on Sefer Yeẓirah,* fols. 22d, 42c and 60a.

17. *Commentary on Genesis Rabbah,* pp. 254-255.

18. Ibid., p. 256. See also here above. These tables occur also in R. David ben Yehudah he-Ḥasid's writings, apparently under the influence of R. Joseph. See Idel, *The Mystical Experience,* p. 45, n. 38.

19. See below ch. 10, par. 3.

20. *Commentary on Genesis Rabbah,* p. 255. The use of the concentric circles in order to extract the 231 combinations occurs also in the *Commentary on Sefer Yeẓirah,* fol. 31a, and its sources are earlier than the end of the thirteenth century. This technique is important for understanding the emergence of Ramon Lull's logica nova; see M. Idel, "Ramon Lull and Ecstatic Kabbalah: A Preliminary Observation," *Journal of the Warburg and Courtland Institutes,* vol. 51 (1988), pp. 170-174.

21. Ms. Sasson, 290, pp. 198-202. In this manuscript there is more material of R. Joseph and R. David ben Yehudah he-Ḥasid; in addition to the philological affinity of this passage to R. Joseph, the fact that it occurs in a codex which includes also other passages stemming from the same Kabbalistic school, strengthens the probability that the anonymous text was penned by R. Joseph or R. David. At the end of this manuscript, the scribe copied, with some slight variations, the version of the creation of the Golem from R. Joseph's, *Commentary on Genesis Rabbah.* Compare Ms. Sasson, 290, pp. 650-651 to the *Commentary,* pp. 254-257.

22. Ms. Sasson, 290, p. 198.

23. See above ch. 6, par. 1.

24. Ms. Sasson, 290, pp. 199, 201.

25. See Idel, *Kabbalah: New Perspectives,* p. 326, n. 224.

26. See Idel, *The Mystical Experience,* p. 45 n. 39.

27. Ms. Sasson, 290, p. 199.

28. See fol. 27a, 30b etc.

29. See pp. 228–229.

30. Ibid., p. 223 and Idel, *Kabbalah: New Perspectives,* pp. 105–106.

31. See M. Idel, "Kabbalistic Prayer and Colors," ed. David Blumenthal, *Approaches to Judaism in Medieval Times,* vol. 3 (1988), pp. 17–27.

32. See Idel, *Kabbalah: New Perspectives,* pp. 109–110.

33. However, in the *Commentary on Genesis Rabbah,* p. 255, the author mentions the combination which will reduce the formation, *yeẓirah,* to its dust. Notwithstanding this fact, it is awkward that the dust is never mentioned at the beginning of the process as it happens in all the other versions of the technique.

34. Cf. Idel, "Kabbalistic Prayer and Colors," (n. 31 above), p. 23.

35. This very complex issue will be dealt with in my monograph on visualisation of colors in Kabbalah.

36. See below, ch. 10, par. 3.

37. *Commentary on Genesis Rabbah,* p. 228; see also ibid., p. 229.

38. Ibid.

39. See below ch. 10, par. 3.

40. One of Abulafia's apparently lost commentaries on *Sefer Yeẓirah* is quoted by R. Joseph in the text extant in Ms. Sasson, 290, p. 199.

41. See below ch. 10, par. 1–2.

9

Psychological Implications of the Golem

The Book of Bahir

I

The emergence of Kabbalah on the historical scene in Provence and Spain reflects, as scholars have already pointed out, only a marginal interest in the nature of an artificial man or the techniques of its creation.[1] Though deeply influenced by the Talmudic texts and profoundly excited by the content of *Sefer Yeẓirah*, it is only rarely that some remarks on the Golem can be found in their writings. The most important of these discussions is found in *Sefer ha-Bahir,* a seminal book whose influence is visible in the Geronese Kabbalah; however, this interest in the anthropoid cannot bear evidence for the spiritual concern of the Kabbalists either in Provence or in Spain, as the author, or authors, of this compilation of mystical and mythical traditions are unknown; even the origin of this collection of Kabbalistic views is obscure, and we may assume, following Scholem, that in its present form, the *Bahir* reflects earlier traditions.[2] Whether the Bahiric discussion of the text in *Sanhedrin* reflects an earlier tradition, or it is simply a late twelfth century elaboration on the Talmudic text, is a matter we cannot decide. No doubt, this work offered an audacious interpretation of the Talmudic text which, nevertheless, has its source in the juxtaposition of Talmudic views that seemed to the editors of the book relevant for an understanding of the *Sanhedrin* discussion:

> Rava said: If the Righteous desired to do so, they could create a world. What prevented [them]? Their iniquities, as it is written:[3] But your iniquities have been a barrier between you and your God. Behold, if not for your iniquities, there would be no separation between you and Him. Since Rava created a man and sent it to R. Zeira he was speaking to him, but he did not answer. Were it not for your iniquities, he would have answered. Whence would he answer? Out of his soul. And does a man have a soul to infuse into him? Yes, as it is written[4] "and He breathed into his nostrils the breath of life", and man was the soul of life. Were it not for our iniquities, [which caused] that the soul is not pure, which is the separation between you and Him, as it is written[5] "yet you have made him a little lower than Elohim." What is the meaning of "little?" That man commits iniquities and the Holy One, blessed be He does not; blessed be He and His name forever.[6]

The author of the *Bahir* introduced a specification which does not occur in the Talmudic version: iniquities are harmful for the purity of the soul, a purity which seems to be crucial for the ability to create a world or a speaking man. The phrase used in order to denote this purity is *ha-neshamah ṭehorah.* An identical phrase occurs in a Talmudic discussion on the same page where the inability of man to create a living man is mentioned. In *Berakhot* we read:

> What is [the meaning of] the verse[7] "Bless the Lord, O my soul: and all that is within me bless His Holy Name." He said to him: Come and see: the way of the Holy One, Blessed be He, is different from that of flesh and blood [namely, man]. Man operates by designing a form on the wall, but he cannot confer upon it a spirit and a soul, bowels and intestines. But God is different; he designs a form within a form[8] and confers upon it a spirit and a soul, bowels and intestines . . . Just as God is pure[9] so also is the soul pure [*ha-neshamah ṭehorah*].[10]

Therefore, the purity is one of the resemblances of the soul to God, and, according to the *Bahir,* the purity of the soul would safeguard the creative powers in man. It is possible that the author of the *Bahir* attempted to explain the *Sanhedrin* passage in a more detailed way, and he therefore introduced in Rava's passage the motif of purity. This emphasis may be connected to an understanding of the nature of the *ḥavrayya* similar to that proposed in our analysis of the Talmudic passage: they are the pious. According to a passage in Rashi, the *ḥaverim* are those who purify.[11] The interpretation of the *Bahir* changes the significance of the *Sanhedrin* passage in a radical way; according to the Talmud, it is impossible to confer speech since even the righteous are defiled by iniquities. Therefore, creativity in man cannot be developed beyond its theoretical limits. In the *Bahir,* the assumption is that the pure soul, which is given by God and is not defiled by iniquities, insures the possibility of the perfect creation. Consequently, man is endowed, *ex definitio,* with creative forces that are divine powers, and which cease to function only when he defiles his soul.

This reading of the *Bahir* emphasizes the magical powers of man far beyond what is mentioned in the Talmud. My understanding of the above passage as pointing to a strong magical capacity seems to be corroborated by the sequence of the discussion of the *Bahir* where the ritualistic study of Torah is portrayed as affecting the link between the two supernal kinds of Torah, the Written and the Oral, which symbolize the two divine powers corresponding in classical Kabbalah to the *sefirot* of *tiferet* and *malkhut.*[12] Therefore, in comparison to the Talmudic anthropology, that of the Kabbalah, as presented by the *Bahir,* emphasizes the potentialities of man as a magician[13] or, in the case of the theurgical significance of the influence of the study of the Torah on high, it continues the already existing theurgical views, though with some important changes.

Provençal Kabbalah

II

The general interest of the earlier Provençal Kabbalists in the passage from *Sanhedrin* is basically a matter of understanding the relationship between the divine anthropos and the divine spirit which pervades the structure of the sefirotic realm. The act of creating an artificial man in the terrestrial world was not discussed at all. In contrast to their Ashkenazi and Northern French contemporaries, theosophy rather than magic motivated their discussion.[14] A third focus of interest in the Talmudic text is found in Naḥmanides and his followers. Though he flourished in the same place and time as the other Geronese Kabbalists, whose views of the text of *Sanhedrin* was presented above,[15] he seems to disregard the theosophical implications of the *Sanhedrin* passage in favor of an attempt to conclude from the details of the Talmudic story, the implications for the understanding of human psychology. As we shall see below, R. Isaac the Blind, and those who followed his understanding of the *Sanhedrin* passage, assume that the artificial man was not able to respond to R. Zeira's question because he was not endowed with a certain spiritual faculty: *ruaḥ* according to R. Isaac, *neshamah* according to R. Ezra. The affinity between the possibility to infuse a certain spiritual element and the ability to speak is obvious in these texts as it was already in *Sefer ha-Bahir.* Naḥmanides deals also with the faculty of speech in the context of the Talmudic text. Explaining the verse on the inspiritment of breath into Adam, he writes:

> He was lain as a Golem, as a silent stone, and the Holy One, Blessed be He, breathed into his nostrils the soul of life; then Adam became a living soul . . . But Onqelos translated, "And there was in Adam a speaking soul."[16] His opinion seems to be similar to those who believe that there are in him [man] different souls, and this rational soul which God breathed into his nostrils became a speaking soul. And this seems to me to be also the view of our sages, from what they said that Rava created a man . . .[17]

The fact that the *Sanhedrin* passage describes a being who is able to move but not speak, was understood by Naḥmanides as evidence for the existence of distinct souls; the lower souls can act without the existence of the higher soul. So, for example, in our case, the Golem of Rava was able to move, without the cooperation of the higher rational soul; therefore, Naḥmanides concluded, God was able to infuse a soul which transformed the Golemic Adam into a rational being, though it was possible, in principle, to confer upon him only the lower, animate soul, *nefesh ha-tenu'ah.* This whole discussion reveals a bias for Platonic psychology, and an attempt to reject the Aristotelian psychology which does not differentiate between souls but assumes the existence of three faculties in one unified human soul. The incident of the Golem in the *Talmud* serves as an important piece of evidence for the adherence of the ancient Jewish sages to the Platonic psychology. This orientation towards Platonism is part of a larger conception of Naḥmanides regarding the nature of higher spiritual faculties, which are considered as divine and pre-existent, as they originate from the *sefirotic* realm.[18]

Spanish Kabbalah

III

Following the general lines of Naḥmanides' *Commentary on the Pentateuch,* we learn from R. Baḥya ben Asher, a late thirteenth century Catalan commentator on the Pentateuch, that the Talmudic passage demonstrates that there is a higher soul, which will survive death. The wise soul, *ha-nefesh ha-ḥakhamah,* is totally beyond the reach of a human creator like Rava, who was not able to produce a speaking being, which is dependent on the existence of the rational soul in a created being.[19] Though influenced by the philosophical view regarding the affinity of reason and human nature, the views of these two Kabbalists are intended to counteract the Aristotelian rationalism which emphasized the intellectual achievement as the sine qua non condition for spiritual survival.

IV

An interesting application of the above conclusions drawn by the early Kabbalists with respect to the affinity between the Talmudic artificial man and the Platonic psychology is found in a passage of R. Meir ibn Gabbai. In his *'Avodat ha-Qodesh,* he assumes that the lower human spiritual faculty, the *nefesh,* is the source of motion, the higher one, the *ruaḥ,* is the source of speech, and the highest one, the *neshamah* is the source of the intellectual activity.[20] Only when the *ruaḥ* descends on the *nefesh* will a person be able to speak even if he has no rational soul. According to this Kabbalist, the encounter between the *nefesh* and the *ruaḥ* in a body constitutes the *ḥiyyut,* the human vitality activating the human body.[21] Thus ibn Gabbai separated the speaking faculty from the intellective one,[22] thus far the "normal" psychology. In this context, the Kabbalist quotes the *Sanhedrin* passage and Rashi's interpretation of it, in order to demonstrate that it is possible to conceive a walking anthropoid, which has no speaking faculty.

Ibn Gabbai is, however, applying these assumptions in order to understand the paranormal post mortem states. The assumption that the dead are able to speak and walk, recurring in a variety of medieval sources, was understood as the descent of the *ruaḥ*, during the limited period of twelve months after death, upon the *nefesh* which remained with the corpse for the whole period.[23] The intermitent descent of the *ruaḥ* enables the emergence of the *Ḥiyyut*[24]; they animate the body and cause it to speak. According to ibn Gabbai, this is the explanation of the biblical episode of the summoning of Samuel at 'Eiyn Dor.[25] A juxtaposition of this text of Ibn Gabbai to another, to be discussed below,[26] demonstrates that the creation of an artificial man by means of *Sefer Yeẓirah* was possible, this success being proof of the superiority of the Jewish mystical lore to the natural lore of the Gentiles. During the period when in Italy Jews were interested in the preparation of the elements which could become the body of an artificial man, in Turkey Ibn Gabbai was still immersed in a kind of speculation characteristic of thirteenth century Kabbalists.

Notes

1. See below, *Summary.*

2. Cf. Scholem, *Origins of the Kabbalah,* pp. 49–198. Compare, however, to another understanding of the sources of the *Bahir* as expressed in Idel, *Kabbalah: New Perspectives,* pp. 122-127 and especially in "The Problem of the Sources of the Bahir," *The Beginnings of the Jewish Mysticism in Medieval Europe,* ed. J. Dan (Jerusalem, Hebrew University in Jerusalem 1987), pp. 55–72 (Hebrew).

3. Isa. 59:2.

4. Gen. 2:7.

5. Ps. 2:6.

6. R. Margaliot, Ed., (Jerusalem, 1978), pp. 89–90. Gerhard Scholem, German trans., *Das Buch Bahir* (Darmstadt, 1970), p. 150. See also Scholem, *Origins of the Kabbalah,* pp. 102–103. He indicates that the views of the *Bahir* "are very close to the ideas of Eleazar of Worms regarding the creation of the Golem. All this can be easily explained etc." Unfortunately, Scholem did not explain how the views of the *Bahir* relate to those of R. Eleazar of Worms; despite the fact that Scholem considered such an explanation an easy matter, I do not know to which details he refers. See also ibid., pp. 121-122; idem, "The Idea of the Golem," pp. 192-193.

This passage was discussed by several Kabbalists, without, however, adding novel insights into the content of this text; see Ms. Moscow 347, fol. 151a; the commentary attributed to R. David Habillo, Ms. London, British Library, 10552, fol. 257a–b.

7. Ps. 103:1.

8. *Ẓurah be-tokh ẓurah.* The meaning is that God is able to introduce the inner parts of man and the soul notwithstanding the fact that the foetus is in the womb.

9. This is part of a fivefold comparison between God and the soul. On this comparison in the late twelfth century, see M. Idel, "A Speculative Fragment of R. Asher ben Meshullam of Lunel," *Qiryat Sefer,* vol. 50 (1975), pp. 149-153. (Hebrew)

10. *TB, Berakhot,* fol. 10a. Compare the discussion of this passage in R. Shimeon Lavi's commentary on the *Zohar, Ketem Paz* (Djerba, 1940), fol. 222c, where the Kabbalist uses the term Golem in order to point to a tridimensional creature.

11. See his commentary to *TB, Niddah,* fol. 6b.

12. On Kabbalistic theurgy in general and that of the book of the *Bahir* in particular see Idel, *Kabbalah: New Perspectives,* pp. 153–199, especially pp. 161–162.

13. See below our discussion of the view of R. Gershom Leiner, ch. 14, par. 9.

14. See below ch. 10.

15. See ch. 10, par. 1.

16. Literally *ruaḥ melalela* means a speaking spirit, but this phrase was understood by Naḥmanides as a reference to the intellective soul.

17. *Commentary on the Pentateuch,* ed. C. D. Chavel, vol. 1, (Jerusalem, 1959), pp. 33–34. See also below n. 22.

18. See the presentation of Scholem in *Origins of the Kabbalah,* p. 456.

19. *Commentary on the Pentateuch* ed. C. D. Chavel (Jerusalem, 1966), vol. 1, p. 63. See also the parallel passage in Baḥya's, *Kad ha-Qemaḥ,* ed. Chavel, vol. 4 (Jerusalem, 1969), p. 441. See Scholem, "The Idea of the Golem," p. 193.

20. See 2, ch. 28, fol. 46d–47a. This is the standard Kabbalistic psychology as proposed by the *Zohar*; see Tishby, *Mishnat ha-Zohar,* vol. 2, pp. 11–58. See also the analysis of this chapter of Ibn Gabbai in Roland Goetschel, *Meir Ibn Gabbay, Le discours de la Kabbale Espagnole* (Leuven, 1981), pp. 249–252.

21. Ibid., fol. 47a: "the *nefesh* and the *Ruaḥ* are the cause of the *ḥiyyut* and the *dibbur*". Compare to Naḥmanides' view in his Commentary to Gen. 1:20 that the vegetative soul has no *ḥiyyut.* However, it is obvious that Ibn Gabbai follows the way of R. Isaac the Blind with respect to the relationship between *ruaḥ* and *dibbur.* See below ch. 10, par. 1. In some medieval psychologies, like Abraham Ibn Ezra, the *ḥiyyut* was described as including the faculties of *nefesh, ruaḥ* and *neshamah;* see his *Yesod Mora'* ch. 7.

22. Compare to the view of Naḥmanides and its reverberation in R. Baḥya ben Asher, R. Meir Aldabi, *Shevilei 'Emunah,* (Warsau, 1887), fol. 71c, and the interpretation of R. Samuel Edeles on *Sanhedrin*, fol. 65b.

23. See *TB, Shabbat,* fol. 152b and Goetschel, *Meir ibn Gabbay,* (n. 20 above), pp. 249–250.

24. The *ḥiyyut* is conceived here as the result of an interaction between the descending *ruaḥ* and the *nefesh* still in the grave. It is not considered to be a bodily force. On this issue, see also below ch. 12, n. 5. Interestingly enough, Scholem argues that Ibn Gabbai differed on this point from Cordovero; see "The Idea of the Golem," p. 194. However, I see no basic differences between the two Kabbalists.

25. Ibn Gabbai attacks the allegorical interpretation of the 'Eiyn Dor episode, advocating, according to the above psychology, a literal understanding; thus the belief in the literal meaning of the Talmudic passage of the Golem serves as a support for the literal interpretation of the Bible.

26. See below ch. 11, n. 9.

10

Theosophical Interpretations of the Golem

The deep interest in the Golem techniques and practices, so characteristic of the Northern France and German Jewish masters conspicuously distinguishes them from their contemporaries in Southern France and Spain. The possible reasons for this divergence will preoccupy us later on. Here we shall analyze the discussions of those Kabbalists who dealt with the theosophical understandings of the Talmudic passage dealing with the Golem. The fact that most of the following passages are, basically, attempts to explain the Talmudic texts is an important characteristic of the theosophical-theurgical Kabbalah. The early Kabbalistic masters in Provence and Spain apparently did not inherit the techniques found among Northern European Jewry, and they simply had to deal with the implications of the *Sanhedrin* passage as the main source for their discussions on the Golem. Moreover, the basic interest which prompted the following discussions is not so much the possibility of imitating the achievement of the Talmudic masters, as the need of authentic Jewish material which may serve to explain Kabbalistic theosophy and some psychological views. It is not the bodily creations and their vicissitudes which are the foci of the early Kabbalists' analysis, but rather the possible theological implications of the artificial man.

Early Kabbalistic Theosophy of the Golem

I

R. Isaac ben Abraham, called Sagi-Nahor, (the Blind), the dean of the Provençal Kabbalah in the thirteenth century, and the teacher of two of the Geronese Kabbalists, refers to the Talmudic passage in a remarkable discussion in his *Commentary on Sefer Yeẓirah*:

> The half of the combination of letters of the wheel, which are the 231 gates, and the remaining half, which are 231 are above the wheel, since there are 462 alphabets and two of them are called a gate [*sha'ar*]. . . . And all the speech, if the formation [*yeẓirah*] does not speak, it is worthless, [*'einah kelum*] since the perfection of speech is [achieved] only by the spirit [*ruaḥ*].[1] And if Rava has created a man, he returned it to its dust since he did not know how to introduce the spirit so that [the creature] will speak and will be maintained by it [i.e., by the spirit].[2]

The main concern of the Kabbalist is the relationship between spirit and matter, and the total dependence of the latter on the former. The faculty of speech is conceived here only as a by-product of the infusion of the spirit. Though the Kabbalist resorts to the term *yeẓirah* in lieu of the original *yeẓur* in *Sefer Yeẓirah*, it seems that R. Isaac understood the affinity between the nature of the creature and the second topic mentioned in *Sefer Yeẓirah*, speech; from the relationship between them we may infer that he understood the term *yeẓur* as referring to an human being.[3]

From another text of R. Isaac we learn about a similar relationship between the body and the spirit; in this context the term Golem occurs, though its significance is different from the artificially created anthropoid. In the *Commentary on the Account of Creation* this Kabbalist writes:

> The spirit itself, when it enters the drop [that is the seed] it enters with [or by] its letters,[4] since according to the finesse of the spirit is the finesse of letters, and the spirit is engraved within the spirit, in an infinite manner. And the spirit is called, in the writings of the philosopher, form [*ẓurah*], since the sensuous body is called Golem, and the spirit that maintains the Golem is called *ẓurah.*[5]

Here, a polarity of letters, spirit and form versus drop, body and Golem is presented. In the first part of the discussion, the generative process is mentioned, implying the creation of the foetus; in the second part, the relationship between body and soul is dealt with. These two oppositions have the same structure, and the word Golem, meaning the human body, is included. Though this passage does not involve at all a magically created Golem, it includes the view that the seed is connected to the letters in the context of the word Golem.[6]

A similar stand can be found also in the formulation of R. Ezra of Gerona, a student of R. Isaac the Blind. After asserting that the souls are the fruits of the divine, implicitly assuming that they cannot be created by men, he indicates that: ". . . If Rava has created a man, he returned it to its dust since it has not the power of the [higher] soul [*neshamah*] . . ."[7]

Both the master and the disciple distinguish between the *amora,* who created the Golem, and the person who undid it, referring as they do solely to *Rava*: They were interested in the possibility of infusing the spiritual power into matter. It seems that even this concern can be understood against the background of their main theological topic, the structure of the ten *sefirot*. Considered as they were as a system of divine powers which can be conceived of and discussed in some details, though not drawn in a graphical anthropomorphical way, a better understanding of the inner structure of the supernal realm could be achieved by meditation on the human creation of an anthropoid. The Provençal Kabbalistic tradition, as represented by R. Isaac the Blind and his nephew R. Asher ben David, and also the writings of the Catalan R. Ezra, assume that there are two basic creative processes connected to the emanation of the *sefirotic* system. The first one is the constitutive emanation, namely the emergence of the ten divine powers conceived as vessel-like entities, parallel to the limbs which constitute the human body. Afterwards, another type of emanation is infused into these vessels, which, like the human spirit, sustain the anthropomorphical structure of the divine powers. Without the continuous outpour of the divine influx into the revealed deity, the *sefirotic* realm cannot continue to exist.[8] The conclusion that the creation of man reflects the emanation of the divine realm is corroborated by a discussion of R. Ezra regarding the nature of man, which is deeply influenced by a short formulation of his master, R. Isaac Sagi-Nahor.[9] In his *Commentary to the Song of Songs* we learn that:

> The [divine] name was not complete until man was created in the image of God, and [then] the seal [*ḥotam*] was complete . . . you were on the degree of Adam, who completed the ten *sefirot* . . . and He called a complete name on a complete world,[10] and the Lord was delighted by his creatures,[11] and the divine Spirit dwelled upon him, since he was comprised, crowned and adorned[12] by the ten *sefirot.*[13]

The description of man as comprising in his constitution all the ten *sefirot* is central for the anthropology of R. Ezra.[14] He repeats it several times in his works; here, however, it seems that this conception is related explicitly to the dwelling of the divine spirit on man. However, in the same context we learn that this constitution reflects the divine structure, and I assume that just as in the perfect man the affinity between the decad and the spirit is obvious, so also is the case with the divine pleroma which is completed by the creation of man. It seems that the reference to the seal is to be understood on two levels: indeed, it reflects the biblical notion of man as the perfection of the creation.[15] However, I assume that an additional issue is hinted at by using this metaphor. The seal stands for a structure that is formed out of ten components; apparently, R. Ezra points also to the fact that the perfected human form functions as a talisman which can attract the divine influx, in accordance to the parallelism between the supernal decad and the lower one. The ten *sefirot* are a seal because they capture the influx descending from the Infinite, whereas man is a seal which collects the influx coming down from the superior anthropomorphic structure.[16]

The status of the inanimated Golem is to be compared to the divine anthropos when the inner influx does not alimentate its limbs. The theosophical contexts of the two discussions quoted above allow the conclusion that the Talmudic Golem (more than pointing to the nature of the activity of men here below) was employed as a metaphor for the imperfect creation, which can reflect a supernal realm. This assumption seems to be fostered by the ancient views of the primeval man as a giant whose dimensions correspond to those of the universe, therefore allowing a cosmic interpretation of Adam as Golem.[17] In principle, it seems that the view of the Golem in *Sefer ha-Bahir,* which was concerned primarily with the possibilities inherent in the human activity, did not significantly influence the way R. Isaac and R. Ezra portrayed the Talmudic artificial man.[18]

R. Abraham Axelrod of Cologne.

II

An important development for the theosophical meaning of the term Golem can be detected in a short Kabbalistic treatise which combines Ashkenazi material with views occurring in the Geronese Kabbalah. In *Keter Shem Ṭov,* attributed to R. Abraham Axelrod of Cologne, or, according to other manuscripts, to R. Menaḥem, the disciple of R. Eleazar of Worms, we read:

> [The letter *vav*] is slightly corporeal . . . hinted at [the fact] that the body is secondary to the spirit, and the former is a vessel to receive the spirit, and when the spirit dwells in it, it becomes a building, [*binyan*] because at the beginning of its creation, before the coming of the spirit in it, it was like a Golem, and not a complete body. Therefore it, [the letter *vav*] is in the body, but only slightly, and it has no form, but is solely a Golem.[19]

The use of the term Golem in a context of a being which has no peculiar form, but is a half-corporeal entity ready to receive the spirit, is obviously reminiscent of the half-finished artificial man, who lacks the spirit and is called, roughly at the same time, Golem. Interesting from another point of view is the fact that a letter is described here as a Golem; later on a similar phenomenon will occur in the context of discussion of another letter of the Tetragrammaton, *Yod.*

R. Joseph ben Shalom Ashkenazi's Theosophy of the Golem

III

A major impact of this perception of the Talmudic passage as referring to the Golem in a microtheic manner is found in R. Joseph ben Shalom ha-'Arokh's *Commentary on Sefer Yeẓirah.* This Ashkenazi Kabbalist was interested also in the theological perception of the Golem creation as he was in the techniques to create it—as we have seen above—and his acceptance of this view contributed greatly to its diffusion in later Kabbalah. R. Joseph wrote:

> Since man was created in the image of God, in order to be His tabernacle, as it was said [But whilst I am still in my flesh] though it be after my skin is torn from my body I would see God.[20] Therefore you should understand that as the five fingers of the right [hand] and the five fingers of the left [one], all of them are bifurcating from the middle, which is the heart, (namely *tif'eret*) because it is the beginning of the formation [*yeẓirah*][21] . . . because it [the heart] is the root of all the entities which are dividing, so also in the ten *sefirot* . . . and since the mouth is in the image of the *yod,* which is engraved in it, and the twenty-two letters are linked to it, because they are especially related to the tongue, and by it [i.e. the mouth] the creature [*beri'ah*] is created, as our Sages, Blessed be their memory, said, "Rava created a man. So also in the case of the sign of circumcision, in the image of *yod,*[22] and by the means of it the foetus is formed, which is in the image of all the creatures."[23]

Man reflects in each and every important limb the whole spectrum of the creative powers of God, the ten *sefirot* and the twenty-two letters. This is why Rava was able to create a man using the sounds he pronounced by his mouth. In other words, the fact that each and every limb incorporates all the creative powers enables the mouth to become an instrument for the creation of the Golem. In a highly instructive passage, the same Kabbalist asserts that:

> [Abraham] combined [the letters] and was successful [in creating] a creature, as it is said,[24] "The souls they made in Ḥaran"; We learn that Abraham our ancestor occupied himself with the combination of letters of *Sefer Yeẓirah*, as our sages, blessed be their memory, said: Rava created a man . . . and they said, "And I shall fill him with the spirit of God",[25] Bezalel knew how to combine the letters by means of which heaven and earth were created. And when she emerged,[26] [*'aṭarah*], the Master [of the universe] revealed onto him [*yesod*] and He called him His beloved, because ten *sefirot* were engraved in his form.[27]

It seems that here, for the first time, the creation of the Golem, as it was exposed in the Talmud, and as it was hinted at the end of *Sefer Yeẓirah* was presented as dealing concomitantly with the human creation and the divine emanation. Abraham creating the souls in Haran, a conspicuous reference to the creation of the Golem in a series of Ashkenazi texts, and the revelation of God to him, was reinterpreted as symbolizing the emergence of the last sefirah, *'aṭarah,* and her relationship to the higher *sefirah, yesod.* At the same time Abraham himself becomes a perfect man, since he included in his form, apparently after his circumcision, the ten *sefirot.* Undoubtedly, this symbolical interpretation of the Golem in terms of a theosophical system is a strong exegesis, which attempts to enter in detailed symbolic explanations when dealing with a long series of texts, biblical, Midrashic or those belonging to the Heikhalot literature.[28] However, even if the details of this farfetched exegesis is characteristic of R. Joseph and his school, I assume that the principle of the relationship between the human-made anthropoid and the Sefirotic anthropoid was inherited from the earlier Kabbalistic traditions.

Highly interesting for our discussion is the interpretation of the Midrashic treatment of the creation of Adam, in another text of R. Joseph. In his *Commentary on the Genesis Rabbah* legends, we read:

> The plain sense [of the legend]:[29] When God mixed [*gibbel*] the dust [*'afar*] [*tif{'eret}*] out of earth [*min ha-'adamah*] [*'aṭ{arah}*] [with

> water] and He kneaded and arranged all his limbs in it, and He engraved them [i.e., the letters] and extracted them and combined them, and weighed them and changed their order, 248 limbs of man and 248 limbs of woman, and 365 veins of man and 365 veins of woman,[30] made out of this matter, forward and backward . . .[31]

In this case the creation of man is also reinterpreted theosophically, this theosophical interpretation of the Midrash being presented as the plain sense of the legend. The Midrashic view was combined with the view of *Sefer Yeẓirah* referring to the creation of the world by combination of letters. The matter out of which Adam was created is here referred to using the common biblical phrase, dust out of earth. However, later on, on the same page, when R. Joseph continues to comment on the same legend he writes:

> He created him as a Golem, it means that the creation of man was accomplished by means of the [*sefirah* of] *ḥokhmah,* because *ḥokhmah* is an entity [emerging] *ex nihilo,* namely a Golem without any visible form. And it means that just as the essences of the ten *sefirot,* the Golem was at the beginning, and [only] afterward He completed him.[32]

The comparison of the second *sefirah* to a Golem means here that it is the receptacle of the *havvayot,* or the essences, which are to be arranged later on in the structure of the ten *sefirot.* Just as Adam was a Golem, namely an unshaped matter,[33] in one of the early phases of his creation, so also during the process of emanation, the roots of the *sefirot* existed in an unordered state which was structured by the divine activity.[34] Moreover, it seems highly reasonable that the description of the creation of Adam, including the stage of the Golemic existence, is paralleled by the Sefirotic emanation, as is evidenced by the fact that R. Joseph mentions the creation of the Golemic man by the *sefirah* of *ḥokhmah.* This understanding will explain, at least partially, why this Kabbalist is so eager to transpose the creation of man or the Golem onto the theosophical realm: He deals with the same process which takes place on two levels at the same time.

Let me address another passage of the same author, where the term Golem is mentioned; dealing, again, with processes at the beginning of the emanation, R. Joseph indicates that the first *sefirah, keter,* is tantamount to *maḥshavah,* (Thought) and *hirhur,* (Rumination), which is the origin of man:

> Out of *hirhur,* the spirit [*ruaḥ*] arose and it operated its operation by the virtue of [the letters] *'amsh,*[35] until he discharged the Golem in his drop, in the form of the [letter] *yod*[36] and in it there is the spirit of life and from it all the parts [*ḥalaqav*] and structures [*sedarav*] were made.[37]

The *sefirotic* realm emerges just as the man's foetus does; the first *sefirah* corresponds to the initial thought of procreating; the ejection of the sperm is connected to this intention and is paralleled on the supernal level by the emanation of the second *sefirah,* which is, accordingly, including, in potentia, in the development of the fulfleged human body. In this highly influential treatise, we find to motifs related to the term Golem; one referring to the Golem as the hyle of everything, beginning with the *sefirot* which are included in the second *sefirah* in a chaotic manner, and ending with man whose hylic matter is also designated by the same term. The second type of understanding the emergence of the Golem is related to the conceptive process, and both the *sefirot* and man are mentioned in the same context with the Golem.

Another important passage from the introduction of the *Commentary to Sefer Yeẓirah*, is worthwhile of a detailed analysis:

> On that matter, which is neither in potentia nor in actu, but its existence is intermediary between what is in potentia and what is in actu, [it is said] that it is the principle and the arche of all the existing things, and all the existing things from *keter 'eliyon* downwards], came into existence from the essence of its existence . . . and it is called in the language of the prophets Golem, as it is said, "My Golem your eyes have seen" namely, Golem is *ḥokhmah,* [and] *yod,* because it is like a formless Golem,[38] but it is prepared to receive all the forms.[39] "Your eyes have seen, and on Your book [*sifrekha*] all will be written down", the meaning of *sefer* is [*ḥokhmah*] . . . because in *ḥokhmah,* which is *yod,* everything is written and inscribed,[40] the deeds of the supernal and the lower[41]

The philosophical background of this discussion is obvious; the *hyle* is an all comprehensive entity because it includes, in potentia, all the forms.[42] Golem therefore stands for that material stage of existence which is able to transform itself into any articulate form of existence. This philosophical presentation was propelled into the *sefirotic* realm, where the initial stage of emanation, the second *sefirah,* includes all the other ten *sefirot,* symbolized by the letter *Yod,* which means ten. The Aristotelian *hyle* and the quasi-Platonic realm of ideas meet together in this exposition of the Golem which unites the hylic and the ideal components of reality.[43] However, quoting the verse from Psalms, R. Joseph added the more human aspect to the two philosophical understandings of the Golem. Man, in his initial stage is a hylic being, capable of everything, but all his deeds are already inscribed in the divine wisdom.[44]

Creation of man begins, therefore, with the hylic state of *ḥokhmah,* where the substratum of the future limbs exists in potentia in the sperm; the further stages of the articulation of the Golem in the *sefirotic* realm, and of man on the human level, seem to be addressed in the following discussion found in the *Commentary to the Genesis Rabbah*:

> It is said "in the image of God he made him." The secret [meaning] is that the reception of the form [takes place] on the [level of the *sefirah*] *tif'eret.*[45] . . . but it [i.e., the form] is made on the [level of] *'aṭarah,* whereas the creation is on the [level of the *sefirah* of] *binah.*[46]

Thus, the descending *sefirotic* levels correspond to the progression of man from the sperm to the structured, namely "made", stage. The Golem when transformed in man reflects the evolution of the emanative process from *ḥokhmah* to *'aṭarah.* Creation, *beri'ah,* which is only the first act, takes place on the higher plane, in the *Sefirah* of *binah.* According to another passage of this work, the level of tif'eret is connected to the reception of the Image, *ẓelem,* whereas that of *'aṭarah* to the reception of the Likeness, *demut.* Consequently, the final touch of the humanizing process is the acquiring of the "lower" faculty of *demut.*[47] This view is reminiscient of another Kabbalistic discussion, to be elaborated below, concerning the relationship between the reception of the *demut* and the power of multiplying and being fruitful.[48]

I assume that the meditation on the meaning of the Golem might have influenced, also, the discussion of the development of the three terms, *qol,* (voice), *ruaḥ* (spirit) and *dibbur* (speech), occuring in *Sefer Yeẓirah.*[49] In his *Commentary on Sefer Yeẓirah*, this author describes the second *sefirah, ḥokhmah,* as a Golem, which receives the spirit from the higher *sefirah, keter,* apparently understood as symbolized by the voice, and the speech is acquired on the level of the *sefirah* of *tif'eret.*[50] In other words, when the second *sefirah* receives the spirit from the first it can develop the further stages of emanation. Or, we may formulate the above statement as the reception of the spirit by the Golem and the acquiring, at a later stage, of the faculty of speech. This formulation may reflect the observation that whereas the human creator can shape the row matter and infuse spirit into it, he cannot produce the later stage of speech, an achievement limited to God alone.

'Iyyun-Circle Conceptions and the Golem

IV

It seems that under the influence of the views of R. Joseph Ashkenazi, a certain development in the description of the relationship between the term Golem, the conceptive process and the *sefirotic* system, was elaborated not later than the beginning of the sixteenth-century. In a commentary on a pseudepigraphic epistle from the circle of Kabbalists who produced *Sefer ha-'Iyyun,* attributed to a certain R. Aharon,[51] we learn that the inner relationship between the three supernal lights, or *ẓaḥẓaḥot,* hidden as they are in the *'Ein sof,*[52] is similar to the relationship between the heart, the lung and the spleen, since these limbs come, according to a certain anatomical view, from the same root.[53] Notwithstanding the fact that those limbs develop later on as separate members, they come from the drop, where they exist in a potential way. This drop, or a certain part of it, is referred, exactly as in the case of R. Joseph by the term Golem. Therefore, also this unknown R. Aharon, posits the Golem, as the source of the later fulfledge human body, at the beginning of a process that comes to explain the inmost theosophical process. The importance of the occurrence of this theme in the writing of R. Aharon is that it was copied by R. Moses Cordovero, in his important compedium of Kabbalah, *Pardes Rimmonim,* and thus became well-known to all the Kabbalists. Moreover, Cordovero himself elaborated upon this text, concluding, on the basis of the occurrence of the terms Golem and *ẓurah,* in the pseudepigraphical epistle,[54] that the Golem refers to the instrumental facet of the *sefirot,* whereas the *ẓurah* stands for the essential aspect of the *sefirot.*[55] Therefore, Golem signifies, on the same page of an important Kabbalistic work, both the embryonic phase of the *sefirot* and the external, instrumental aspect of these entities. We may assume, that just as in the first case, the mention of the limbs and the drop, have explicit anthropomorphic significance, so also the external aspects of the *sefirot* may be understood as having an anthropomorphic shape. In another important discussion of the artificial man, Cordovero explicitly compares the body of the anthropoid, created by the sages, to the shape of the *sefirot,* in order to point out the significance of the absence of speech and intelligence, which correspond, according to his view, to *'Ein sof* or *'illat ha-'illot.*[56] Thus, the implicit comparison of the artificial creation below to the emanative creation above, consists in the parallelism between the structural components of the two entities.

Sefer ha-Peli'ah

V

Under the influence of R. Joseph Ashkenazi and his school, an anonymous Byzantine Kabbalist elaborated in his *Sefer ha-Peli'ah* upon the meaning of the *Sanhedrin* passage in an interesting way.[57] He copied the passage from the introduction to Ashkenazi's *Commentary to Sefer Yeẓirah*, but seems to have reproduced also views that are no more extant, which stem from writings originating from a circle of Kabbalists influenced by this author:

> The Emanation [*'aẓilut*] which precedes everything is the Emanation of *ḥokhmah* from *keter 'elyon,* and all the entities and letters were emanated together with *ḥokhmah* and from *ḥokhmah* to *binah* and so also all [things] . . . *bereshit,* which is *ḥokhmah,* created *'elohim,* which is *binah* and *beri'ah* and *yeẓirah* and *'asiyah* are all names of *'aẓilut,* and because the First Emanation, which is *keter,* [designated] by the B of *bereshit,* he called the half, *bara' Shit,*[58] meaning that [He] created the Emanation, since the Emanation is *'elohim.*[59] This is the meaning of *rava' bera' gavra',* he changed the order of the letters of his name and created [*bara'*]. From here you shall learn that everything is in the power of *'a*[*leph*], *bara', 'ever* [limb],[60] because all the limbs of man are in his power, and now, the emanation of *ḥokhmah* has all the limbs in itself, the right hand and the left one, the heart, the right leg and the left one, the [place of] circumcision and the *'aṭarah.* Then He said to the world, "Stop."[61 62]

As in the case of the Ashkenazi Kabbalist, here also the Talmudic text was interpreted theosophically; it stands for the emanative process. Here, however, the story is transformed in a more substantial way. I assume that *Rava'* is understood here as the Infinity, or perhaps *keter,* who creates *bera',* the second *sefirah, ḥokhmah,* apparently referred to here as *gavra'.* The letter is implicit in the mentioning of the limbs as part of *ḥokhmah.* However, the articulated man is not to be found there but only the limbs, 'ever, or *'avarim,* thus still remaining in the frame of R. Joseph's view of the potentiality of *ḥokhmah.* This whole story is presented as implied in the combination of the letters *BR'*: *Rava'*, the Master, *bara'*, created, *'ever,* limb. Conspicuously, the anonymous Kabbalist implies that the limbs are the whole man and woman, and at the same time, also the whole *sefirotic* realm.[63] Therefore, the *Sanhedrin* passage is understood here as a symbolical story pointing to the emanation of the divine anthropos. What is missing however is the connection between the emanative creation and the linguistic technique of combining the letters. Rava, the divine creator, is not presented as a combinator. The reason of this rejection of the combinatory technique is not clear, but it seems to be connected to the fact that the letters do not precede the *sefirot,* but are emanated only together with the second *sefirah.*

R. Isaac Luria Ashkenazi

VI

The writings of R. Joseph Ashkenazi analyzed above, and *Sefer ha-Peli'ah* were widely read texts, one of their greatest admirer being the famous R. Isaac Luria Ashkenazi, the most important Safedian Kabbalist. His disciple, R. Ḥayyim Vital, relates in his name that the author of the *Commentary on Sefer Yeẓirah* "was a great sage in matters of Kabbalah", an epitheton extremely rare in Luria's works in connection to medieval figures.[64] The *Commentary on Genesis Rabbah* also seems to have been under the eyes of Luria, since it was known to Luria's teacher, R. David ibn Zimra, and quoted by Luria's disciple, R. Ḥayyim Vital.[65] Therefore, the speculations about the status of the Golem and the story on Rava, as we have elaborated above, could have also easily been the result of the meticulous reading of the Kabbalistic source by Luria himself. In any case, it seems reasonable to assume that some points of the Lurianic view of the emergence of the *'Adam Qadmon,* the Primeval Man, are close to the material found in the writings of R. Joseph Ashkenazi.

However, the occurrence of the term Golem in the following quotation may be also the result of the influence of an important passage in the *Zohar,* where a difficult phrase "*'izqeta be-gulma'*" is mentioned in the context of the initial process of emanation.[66] It is incontestable that Luria was acquainted with and deeply interested in this text, as the commentary of Luria on this Zoharic passage testifies. However, even if this is obvious, it seems that there are good reasons to assume that the texts of R. Joseph were also influential in the formation of the Lurianic myth and terminology.

According to the Lurianic cosmogonic myth, the beginning of the creative process is an act of contraction of the divine light, or presence, from a circular space, which becomes the place for the creation of the world. However, in this sphere, named *ṭehiru,* some residue of divine light remained, which will constitute the matter of the worlds to emerge during the later processes. This residue, named *reshimu,* stems, according to some Lurianic texts, from the diluted roots of evil, which were in existence in the divinity before the process of contraction. During this cathartic process, the roots of evil become concentrated in one point, the *ṭehiru.* Out of this concentration of the roots of the evil, the divine anthropos, *'Adam Qadmon,* will appear. Evidently, there is here a process of creation, or emanation of an anthropoid out of matter, in a sphere[67] intended to serve this purpose. However, beyond this very vague similarity to the concept of the Golem prepared out of dust, or of the foetus in the placenta, it seems that there is one peculiarly interesting terminological affinity to the views exposed above. In a Lurianic version of the beginning of creation, printed only recently we read:

> The contraction of the light which lifted above and vacuous space [*maqom panui*] remained and all the fouls and the materiality [*'oviut*] of judgement which were in the light of the *'ein sof,* which are there like one [single] drop in the ocean,[68] it become separated and divided and it descended and collected to that vacuous space and a Golem appeared out of the fouls and the density of the powers of the judgement . . . and this Golem is enwrapped from above and below from the sides, by the light of *'ein sof,*[69] and out of this Golem emanated the four worlds: *'aẓilut, beri'ah, yeẓirah, 'asiyah.* . . . The Supernal Emanator, out of His simple will to actualize His intention, turned and caused some small part of the light which was contracted at the beginning, to descend into this Golem, but not the whole [light].[70]

There is no question that the Golem means here matter, which is the source of evil, but at the same time the material out of which the four worlds were created. These four worlds are, according to the Lurianic system, the Primeval Man, who comprises in himself these worlds.[71] Therefore, we may assume that the Golem is the matter of *'Adam Qadmon.* Moreover, it seems that the soulless Golem was animated by the descent of the divine light into it. I assume that this descent is tantamount to the infusion of the spirit into the Golem, on the human level,[72] and the entrance of the spirit in the *sefirot* according to the earlier Kabbalists. It is pertinent to remark that in the ancient Chaldean theurgy, the statues were considered as consecrated only when the divine light descended into the statue.[73]

According to another passage in the same treatise, the ten *sefirot* were formed in this Golem.[74] This assessment is peculiarly close to the view R. Joseph that the Golem parallels the essences of the ten *sefirot;*[75] as it was remarked recently, the status of the Golem in the texts brought above corresponds to the ten *ẓaḥẓaḥot,* the ten super-sefirot in Lurianic thought,[76] a view influenced by the circle of R. Joseph.[77] These *ẓaḥẓaḥot* are commonly portrayed in anthropomorphic shape.[78] Therefore, it seems that the correspondence of the Golem in the text of R. Joseph where the Golem is paralleled by the essences of the *sefirot* and the correspondence of the Lurianic Golem to the *ẓaḥẓaḥot,* point to a common view, which can be summarized as follows: the first stage of the theogonic process both in the school of R. Joseph Ashkenazi and in Luria contains an anthropomorphic figure, which precedes, in time and in degree, the regular *sefirotic* system; in both cases the term Golem is used in the context of this anthropomorphic structure.

In the other places where Luria mentions the term Golem, in his earlier writing, he tries to explain the Zoharic *gulma',* as pointing to a tool or vessel which is formless, without the anthropomorphical implications of the later Lurianic text.[79]

Before passing to the next development in the Lurianic theosophy and its affinity to the Golem concepts, I would like to suggest that Luria was concerned with the concept of creation in the context of the Golem concepts. In one of his Shabbat songs, composed in Aramaic and replete with Kabbalistic allusions we read:

> To beget souls and new spirits
> By the thirty-two paths[80] and three branches.[81]

This English rendition of the Aramaic original does not betray the subtle hints of Luria. The creation of the souls and spirits is described using the phrase "*leme'bad nishmatin*". The literal translation of this phrase, which is in my opinion also the correct one, is purely "to make souls", this phrase being an Aramaic parallel of the biblical verse dealing with the creation of the persons by Abraham and Sarah, "*ha-nefashot 'asher 'asu*", which was understood, as we have seen above, as dealing with the creation of the Golem.[82] The view that the spirits are new probably alludes to the surplus of soul which is bestown on the Jews at the entrance of Shabbat, and leaves them at the end of this day.[83] However, there is also another possibility to understand the nature of these spirits, which is corroborated by the context, which mentions the thirty-two paths. As we know, these paths were conceived of as consisting of ten *sefirot* and twenty-two letters, as the very beginning of *Sefer Yeẓirah* explicitly states. Thus, I assume that the creation of the souls and spirits which are new, a term already known in the context of creating a Golem[84], can be related to the use of the letters and *sefirot* as part of the creative process. Accordingly, the creation of the souls here is reminiscent of the creation of the Golem by means of the letters. The possible importance of this interpretation is that Luria was concerned with themes connected to the creation of the Golem also in the case of the creation of souls by God.

R. Israel Sarug and His Sources

VII

An important development in the Lurianic theosophy is found in the writings of R. Israel Sarug, a late sixteenth century and early seventeenth century Kabbalist, active mainly in Europe.[85] According to modern scholarship, Sarug proposed a Kabbalistic system where there are some theosophical innovations which constitute a major departure from the classical forms of Lurianic thought as they were presented by the main disciples of Luria. The crucial divergence between the Sarugian and the classical Lurianic theosophy is to be found, according to modern scholars, in the fact that Sarug interposed an important phase in the theogonic process, allegedly inexistent in Luria's version of Kabbalah.[86] This "innovation" consists in the theory of the *malbush,* the divine garment, which is woven of the combinations of the letters as combined in *Sefer Yeẓirah.* This texture of letters, named also the *torah,* to be explained later on, plays a similar role to that of the *ṭehiru* in Luria, being the space where the creation will take place. However, in order to enable this process, half of the combinations of letters were folded up and evacuated the place which will serve as the locus of the emanative process; only then the *'Adam Qadmon* emerged.[87] Obviously it is an important change in comparison to the classical version of Lurianism; in the version of Sarug, and its sources to be discussed below, the combinatory technique of *Sefer Yeẓirah* was placed above the emanative process concerning the ten *sefirot* or the various Lurianic configurations named *parẓufim.* The Kabbalists who generated this new stand of the combinations of letters above the emanations of an anthropomorphic entity, returned to the more comprehensive perception of the process of creating an anthropoid according to the technique of *Sefer Yeẓirah.*

A superficial inspection of the structure of this *malbush,* shows that it consists of combinations of letters that are based upon *Sefer Yeẓirah* and are identical to those combinations of two letters which are to be pronounced in order to create the Golem, namely the 231 gates, and of the 231 gates which serve to undo it.[88] The evacuation of the lower 231 gates can be reasonable explained as the evacuation of those combinations which may counteract the creation of the divine anthropos. The Sarugian texts specify, moreover, that the folding-up combinations of letters represent the attribute of judgement, whereas those combinations which remained in their place correspond to the attribute of grace. A similar view to the conception of 231 gates as related to judgement and, on the other side, to grace, was analyzed above in our discussion of the technique of R. Joseph Ashkenazi.[89] Therefore, we may well assume that the appearance of the figure of the *'Adam Qadmon,* after mentioning the combinations of letters, is a close parallel to the technique of creation a Golem, which was transposed on the theosophical level. As we have seen above, part of this transposition was already performed in the earlier Kabbalah, apparently accepted also be Luria himself, insofar as the divine anthropos emerges out of the Golem.[90] What remained for Sarug, who uses also the term Golem in the way some of the traditions attributed to Luria did, or for his sources in the circle of Luria or elsewhere,[91] was to transpose also the permutation of the letters by the creator of the Golem to the Creator of the *'Adam Qadmon.* Moreover, this transposition is even simpler if we are aware of the fact that the creation of the world was presented in a long series of pre-Kabbalistic and Kabbalistic texts as the result of the combination of letters done by God in *illo tempore.*[92] As we have already seen above, the creation of the Golem was conceived by some thirteenth century Kabbalists, and repeated in *Sefer ha-Peli'ah,* as competing with the divine creation, and therefore a forbidden act. Thus, the gap between the human person combining letters in order to create a Golem and the combinations of God in order to create the *'Adam Qadmon,* is substantially reduced, allowing a more simple transition between the classical Lurianism and the Sarugian one. In this later form of Luria's doctrine, a greater segment of the Golem traditions were ontologised, transforming it into the blueprint of a whole theosophy.

The Sources of Sarug

VIII

It is possible that the projection of the technique of creating a Golem on the theosophical plane was an innovation of Sarug or another Lurianic Kabbalist. This seems to be the consensus of modern scholarship. However, this is not a necessary conclusion and it is not even the most reasonable one. An analysis of some Kabbalistic traditions predating the emergence of Lurianism may allow another explanation. In a late thirteenth century collection of Kabbalistic traditions, combined with the Northern France mystical traditions stemming from the Circle of the Special Cherub,[93] we read:

> On[94] the river of *kevar* . . . The sages call [it] the Special Cherub, [*keruv ha-meyuḥad*] and this is [the meaning of] *kevar* [according to the] secret of *bekhor* [Firstborn] of his mouth; it is a hint at a wondrous issue. And because he said[95] "In the midst of the Golah," he said [spelled] *kevar* v using an [elliptic] spelling without the letter

of *V*[*av*], and this is sufficient for one who understands.[96] This is the meaning of the verse[97] "Big is our Lord and full of might," which are the 231 gates in the wheel, and all are confered upon him, and whosoever is acquainted with [the technique of] their pronunciation, and to combine them and to turn them together with five syllables,[98] will create a creature as Rava did.[99]

The verse mentioned here is the classical *locus probans* of the anthropomorphic speculations in the *Shi'ur Qomah* literature. There, and in some other few instances in early medieval Jewish literature, it serves as the starting point of the calculations of the measure of the divine stature; *verav koaḥ* is numerically equivalent to the number 236, the measure of the divine body in tens of thousands of parasangs.[100] There is no doubt that this topic is alluded to here, since the phrase, *Shi'ur Qomah* is mentioned twice on the same page. Thus, a certain relation between the creation of the Golem and the concept of the gigantic supernal anthropos of the ancient Jewish theology is intended here. It may be, that the gap between 231 gates and the 236 parasangs is bridged in some way not mentioned here but only in the later texts to be analyzed below; in any case, it seems that in Northern France, at the later part of the thirteenth century, in a speculative circle interested in the creation of the Golem,[101] there was an affinity between the concept of *Shi'ur Qomah* and the technique of creating an anthropoid. The short passage cited above seems to reflect some more detailed speculations, whose traces surface only later on, in a writing of R. Yehudah Ḥayyat in Italy at the end of the fifteenth century and in a special type of Kabbalah which flourished in Jerusalem in the middle of the sixteenth century. The Spanish Kabbalist writing in Italy attempts to neutralize the quantitative significance of the measures indicated in the book *Shi'ur Qomah.* He asserts that the meaning of the figures is not related to a size of the Infinity, the *'ein sof,* but to a certain aspect of the divine attributes, the *sefirot.* He goes on to say that all the parasangs occurring in the above book are:

letters, each of them called a piece [literally a parasang] because they were cut from the dough, like the stones from the mountain[102] . . . and they are [divine] names made out of the combination of the letters and the permutations of the alphabets of *Sefer Yeẓirah*, by means of which all the things were created.[103]

Here, the figures mentioned in the above quote are not mentioned at all. Nevertheless, it is obvious that this Kabbalist was acquainted with a basic relationship between the anthropomorphism of *Shi'ur Qomah* and *Sefer Yeẓirah.* The *sefirot qua shi'ur qomah* are viewed as another expression of the combination of letters in *Sefer Yeẓirah*—I assume the 231 gates—which alone are understood as those combinations that created the world. According to other passages in the same work, by the emanation of the letters, *behitpashṭut ha-'otiyyot,* everything was created. The meaning of this emanation is that the letters which were present in the divine thought, the highest plane preceding the realm of the *sefirot,* were imprinted in an inverse manner as part of the emanative process.[104]

According to a recurrent view of R. Joseph ibn Ẓayyaḥ, the emanations of the *sefirot* took place as a result of the combination of the letters of the alphabets, in accordance to the technique exposed in *Sefer Yeẓirah.* Several times is the relationship between the name Israel, decomposed into *ysh RL'A,*[105] as Abulafia had already done,[106] and the creation of the world pointed out. According to ibn Ẓayyaḥ, the name Israel alludes to the creation of the *yesh,* the existence, by the *RL'A,* the 231 gates of *Sefer Yeẓirah.* However, he goes beyond the theory of *Sefer Yeẓirah* when he assumes that the process of emanation is triggered by the process of the combination of letters:

> No part of the [world of] emanation was completed until all the parts emerged according to the secret of the creation ex nihilo [*meẓi'ut ha-yesh meha-'ayin*] by the virtue of the combination of letters, which allude to the sefirot, according to the 231 gates, which include 462 houses, one with all [of the letters] and all with one and so also all the letters as mentioned in *Sefer Yeẓirah* when you will take any part of the emanation, you will find there all the emanation . . . of the 231 gates by the means of which any existence emerged, and is created ex nihilo. This is the reason the emanation is called by the name Israel, whose secret is *yesh RL'A.*[107]

However, the anthropomorphic aspect of the emanation is found in another work of the same Kabbalist. In his voluminous *'Even ha-Shoham* he wrote:

> Know that the [processes of] emanation and creation appeared by the 231 gates, [constituted by] the letters of the alphabet mentioned in *Sefer Yeẓirah,* ' with each [letter] and each [letter] with ' . . . with the addition of the letter H, by which God created His world,[108] they become 236, whose secret is 236 tens of thousands of parasangs, the secret of *Sh'iur Qomah,* by the power of *Shekhinah.*[109]

The transition between the technique of combination of letters to the creation, namely emanation of the world is conspicuous; the emanation includes an anthropomorphical entity whose measure is that of *Shi'ur Qomah,* which, surprisingly enough, is deduced from the 231 gates of *Sefer Yeẓirah.* Why does ibn Ẓayyaḥ pass from the 231 gates to 236 is not clear, though the addition of the *H, 5,* has some congruence, as this letter was considered to be that sound which was pronounced by God in order to create the world, just as the combination of letters were done for the same purpose. However, it is obvious that ibn Ẓayyaḥ wanted to reach a certain fixed number 236 which is described here explicitly in anthropomorphic terms, as the mention of *Shi'ur Qomah* demonstrates. Before proceeding with the Sarugian texts, I would like to mention that the perusal of the context of the above text of ibn Ẓayyaḥ is reminiscent of the Ashkenazi Hasidic literature, for reasons which cannot be explained in the context of this work. It would be enough to mention that the figure 236 is used in order to point to the 236 times the name Abraham, but not Abram, is mentioned in the Bible.[110]

Other Sarugian Texts

IX

This sequel of the 231 gates and 236 tens of thousands of parasangs is found is some texts from the school of Sarug. Thus, for example, a Sarugian text mentions the 231 gates of *Sefer Yeẓirah*, which form the *malbush,* and the letters that form the supernal garment are described as follows:

> each of these letters has a measure of breadth like the measure of the whole garment, and the breadth of the garment is 236 tens of thousands of parasangs, and they correspond to the *kavod* that sits on the throne, as hinted at in the *Chapters of Heikhalot* composed by R. Ishmael ben 'Elisha', the Great Priest together with his master, R. Neḥunyah ben ha-Qanah and R. 'Aqivah and the companions of R. Ishmael, the breadth of the *kavod* sitting on the throne is 236 tens of thousands of parasangs.[111]

Again the affinity between the combinations of letters from *Sefer Yeẓirah*, which form the *malbush,* and the anthropomorphic structure of *Sh'iur Qomah* is manifest. Interestingly, the divine anthropos is described here as the Glory, the *kavod,* i.e., an entity which is not identical to the highest instance in the divine world. In this sense the term *kavod,* as the interpretation of the divine anthropos which is different from God, occurs in the theological literature of Ḥasidei Ashkenaz.[112] Again, we witness that the nexus between a certain aspect of theosophical speculation of the Golem and Ashkenazi views is conspicuous. It is in order to recall that in ancient Gnostic texts, whose affinity to the Jewish mythologomena is demonstrable, we have already a view that the combinations of two letters are related to the limbs of a gigantic anthropos.[113] May we assume also that the Hebrew medieval sources analyzed here reflect such an ancient tradition? This question cannot be answered here in a definitive way, though I am inclined to answer in the affirmative. Additional material will, hopefully, help us clarify this possibility; thus, for example, the relationship between the views of *Sefer Shi'ur Qomah* and *Sefer Yeẓirah*, either in ancient times or in the works of a medieval author, could supply a clue for a better understanding of the background of the affinity between the 231 gates and the 236 tens of thousands of parasangs.[114]

I assume that the existence of the two texts which predates Sarug's Kabbalah points to the fact that he was not the innovator of the linkage between the 231 gates and the gigantic anthropos that emerges from them in the supernal world. The most elaborate discussion of the relationship between the combinatory technique of *Sefer Yeẓirah* and the anthropomorphic figure on the divine plane is found in *Sefer 'Emeq ha-Melekh* of R. Naftali Bakharakh. There we find the correlation between the combinations of the 231 gates and each of the divine configurations, the *parẓufim,* which are so characteristic of the Lurianic Kabbalah.[115]

The awareness of the affinity between the Golem-technique and the structure of Sarug's theosophy does not occur in those writings which are attributed to Sarug; however, it was expressed in a rather clear way by a famous follower of the Sarugian Kabbalah, R. Naftali Bakharakh. In his *'Emeq ha-Melekh,* he mentions explicitly the technique of creating a Golem by the combinations of the letters as proposed in *Sefer Yeẓirah,* in the context of his explanation of the combinations of letters which form the *malbush.*[116] Though he does not elaborate upon the significance of this observation, it is obvious that he realized that there is a certain affinity between the two techniques of combining letters. It seems that the fact that Bakharakh has already noticed the affinity between the Sarugian theosophy and the technique for creating a Golem may help us understand the precise significance of an assertion of another author, influenced by Sarug and interested in the creation of the Golem. I refer to R. Joseph Shelomo del Medigo, who was presented by Bakharakh as one of his former disciples,[117] and at the same time one of the earliest persons to quote extensively from the writings of Sarug, considered by him to be authentic Lurianic texts. As we shall see below, he was also aware of several texts and legends connected to the Golem and Golem-like creatures. According to this author, the 231 gates of the *malbush* are already alluded to by *Sefer Yeẓirah*, which is quoted in the context of the Sarugian discussion of *malbush,* together with the commentary of R. Azriel, attributed by him to Naḥmanides, where the creation of the *yeẓur* and the *dibbur* by 231 gates is adduced.[118]

The theosophy of Sabbateanism, as it was formulated by Nathan of Azza, was influenced by some elements of the Sarugian view of the emanation, and the theory of the Golem as the prime-material for the following processes; Golem stands for the higher level of *ḥokhmah,* namely the still unpurified unformed matter, and for the lower matter which is identical to the *qelippot,* that are to be mended by the Messiah. As far as I am aware, the anthropomorphic aspect of the Golem and the relation between the combination of letters and the emergence of the Supernal anthropos is not central in this version of Kabbalistic theosophy.[119]

Notes

1. On the theological status of the spirit in early Kabbalah see Pedaya, "'Flaw' and 'Correction,'" pp. 179–180, n. 69.

2. *Commentary on Sefer Yeẓirah*, printed as an appendix to G. Scholem's lectures on the *Kabbalah in Provence,* ed. R. Shatz, (Jerusalem, 1963), p. 10, corrected according to Ms. Halberstam, 444, now New York, JTS, 1887, fol. 129b.

3. On *yeẓur* as human being see ch. 2, par. 3.

4. See ch. 5, par. 11.

5. Ms. New York, JTS, 1887, fol. 29a.

6. See ch. 5, par. 11.

7. See *Commentary on the Song of Songs,* in C. D. Chavel, *Kitvei Ramban,* vol. 2, p. 504. See also ch. 9, par. 1 on the occurrence of the term *neshamah* in *Sefer ha-Bahir.*

8. See Idel, *Kabbalah: New Perspectives,* pp. 181–191.

9. *Commentary on Sefer Yeẓirah*, p. 14. R. Isaac defines man as the great seal, *ḥotam gadol.* The same phrase occurs also in Heikhalot literature; see Scholem, *Jewish Gnosticism,* p. 69. Interestingly the term "great seal" refers there to a name of an archon. For our discussion it is pertinent to remark that in the Talmudic discussion in *Sanhedrin,* fol. 38a, the seal, *ḥotam,* by which all men were sealed, i.e., created, was either Adam or, according to another possible interpretation, the seal by which Adam was created. Compare also to the Ashkenazi view found in Ms Leiden-Warner 27, printed in Jacob Gellis, *Sefer Tosafot Hashalem,*

vol. 1 (Jerusalem, 1982), p. 98, where it is explicitly said that, "man is the seal of God".

See also Altmann, "The Delphic Maxim" p. 12, n. 83–84. For the influence of the mystical concept of man as a seal, see Ze'ev Harvey, "Kabbalistic Elements in R. Hasdai Crescas's, *'Or ha-Shem*", *JSJT,* vol. 2 (1983), pp. 97–98. (Hebrew) On man as the seal of creation in the text from *Hadrat Qodesh,* Ch. 5, par. 9, see Pedaya, "'Flaw' and 'Correction,'" p. 167 and n. 39, and p. 186. See also below n. 87.

10. See *Genesis Rabbah,* section 13: par. 3, p. 115; section 15: par. 1, p. 135.

11. See n. 1 above.

12. Cf. *Sefer ha-Bahir,* pars. 146, 190, 196.

13. *Commentary on the Song of Songs, Kitvei Ramban,* vol. 2, p. 510. See also Pedaya, "'Flaw' and 'Correction,'" pp. 185–186.

14. See Idel, *Kabbalah: New Perspectives,* pp. 118–119.

15. Ibid., p. 330, n. 37.

16. Compare the talismatic view of the Golem in *Sefer ha-Ḥayyim,* ch. 6, par. 2.

17. Idel, *Kabbalah: New Perspectives,* pp. 117–118.

18. On the divergences between the view of man in *Sefer ha-Bahir,* as reflecting the lower seven *sefirotic* entities, versus the view that man reflects the ten *sefirot,* see Altmann, "The Delphic Maxim," pp. 12–13.

19. See the version printed by Adolph Jellinek, *Auswahl Kabbalistischer Mystik* (Leipzig, 1853), Erstes Heft, pp. 38–39, corrected according to Ms. New York, JTS, 8128, fol. 50a.

20. Job. 19:26. This is the locus probans for the Kabbalistic views regarding human body as a reflection of, and a way to contemplate, God. See Altmann, "The Delphic Maxim," pp. 19–21, and Idel, *Studies in Ecstatic Kabbalah,* p. 163, n. 132.

21. It is a commonplace in medieval medicine that the foetus begins his growth from the heart.

22. See Elliot Wolfson, "Circumcision, Vision of God, and Textual Interpretation: From Midrashic Trope to Mystical Symbol," *History of Religions,* vol. 27 (1987), p. 205.

23. *Commentary on Sefer Yeẓirah*, fol. 22d.

24. Gen. 12:5.

25. Exod. 31:3.

26. *'Altah.* Literally it means when he succeded, she, the *'aṭarah* emerged, or ascended.

27. *Commentary on Sefer Yeẓirah*, fol. 60a.

28. R. Joseph commented also on some treatises belonging to the Heikhalot literature like *Ma'aseh Bereshit* and *Ma'aseh Merkavah.*

29. Theosophy is regarded here as the plain significance of the text. This is an outstanding example of the theosophical understanding of the creation of the Golem; for the Kabbalist is no more aware that he is propelling theosophical concepts into the Talmudic discussion, but rather regards theosophy as an integral part of the meaning of the original passage.

30. It is probable that the Kabbalist alludes to the creation of the Supernal Anthropos as an androgyne, a theory recurrent in this writing of R. Joseph Ashkenazi.

31. *Commentary on Genesis Rabbah,* p. 135.

32. Ibid., p. 135.

33. This understanding of the term Golem betrays the influence of Maimonides; see below Appendix B.

34. Compare the very close view of R. Ezra of Gerona, who describes the unordered *havvayot* at the beginning of the process of emanation. *Commentary on the Song of Songs,* p. 483 and in the introduction to the *Commentary on Sefer Yeẓirah*, fol. 2b–c.

35. On these letters as the formative principles, see *Commentary on Genesis Rabbah,* pp. 176–177 and in an important passage of the *Commentary on Sefer Yeẓirah*, fol. 21b–c.

36. Compare also the discussion of this author on Golem and *yod* in the *Commentary of Sefer Yeẓirah*, fols. 2c, to be discussed below, and 33a.

37. *Commentary on Sefer Yeẓirah*, fol. 28b. See also the very important parallel in the same work fol. 21c, where the sperm is compared to the Golem and the *yod,* which comprises the ten *sefirot.*

38. The book referred to here is related to *Sefer Yeẓirah* but also, indirectly, to the Torah as it was conceived by some medieval thinkers, philosophers and Kabbalists, as the intelligible world. See Idel, *Language, Torah and Hermeneutics,* pp. 29–38, 160–161. See also the *Commentary on Genesis Rabbah,* p. 183.

39. Again, it is obvious that the philosophical concept of matter and form influenced the Kabbalist.

40. See n. 33 above.

41. *Commentary on Sefer Yeẓirah*, fol. 2bc, *Sefer ha-Peli'ah* part 1 fol. 61a, and the text on the technique to create a Golem from Ms. Sasson 290, analyzed above and the important parallel in the *Commentary on Sefer Yeẓirah*, fol. 13a.

42. R. Joseph was, nevertheless, an anti-philosophical Kabbalist; see Georges Vajda, "Un Chapitre de l'Histoire du conflit entre la Kabbale et la philosophie. La polemique anti-intellectualiste de Joseph ben Shalom Ashkenazi de Catalogne", *AHDLMA,* vol. 23 (1956), pp. 45–127.

43. For the possible source of R. Joseph's view of the intelligible matter in the Kabbalah of R. Azriel of Gerona, see Vajda, ibid., pp. 136–142 especially p. 141 n. 3.

44. On free will and divine knowledge in R. Joseph's thought, see Vajda, ibid., pp. 79–86.

45. I assume that the Kabbalist refers to the act of formation of the embryo, since in a passage quoted above *tif'eret* was described as the place where the *yeẓirah,* or the division of the members from the heart, takes place. See n. 21 above.

46. *Commentary on Genesis Rabbah,* p. 58. Compare also Ibid., p. 149.

47. Ibid., p. 148. See also Vajda, "Un chapitre," p. 73.

48. See below ch. 5, par. 4.

49. *Sefer Yeẓirah*, Gruenwald, *SY,* par. 10, p. 144.

50. *Commentary on Sefer Yeẓirah*, fol. 30b. Compare to the statement of this author that the voice produces the speech both in the supernal man, *'Adam 'Elyon,* and in man; ibid., fol. 38b.

51. On the bibliographic questions related to this work, see Gottlieb, *Studies,* pp. 405–412.

52. See Scholem, *Origins of the Kabbalah,* pp. 347–354.

53. Cf. *Pardes Rimmonim* 1, fol. 63a.

54. Printed in ibid., fol. 61d.

55. Ibid., fol. 63b.

56. Ibid., Part 21, ch. 2, fol. 98a. See also ch. 12 below.

57. On this work see the dissertation of Michal Kushnir-Oron *The Sefer Ha-Peli'ah and Sefer Ha-Kanah: Their Kabbalistic Principles, Social and Religious Criticism and Literary Composition* (Ph. D. thesis, Hebrew University, 1980) (Hebrew) On the influence of the views of Ashkenazi Hasidism on *Sefer ha-Peli'ah* see pp. 187–193.

58. Apparently an allusion to the fact that the word *bereshit* will be divided in two parts. *Shit* means six in Aramaic, and below the author mentions six limbs.

59. The transformation of *'Elohim,* the subject of the first biblical verse

into an object, symbolizing the third *sefirah* is widespread in Kabbalah; see, Scholem, *Major Trends* p. 221.

60. The consonants *'BR* can allude, according to their various combinations and vocalizations, to *rava', bara', 'ever.*

61. See *TB, Ḥagigah,* fol. 12a and below ch. 13.

62. *Sefer ha-Peli'ah* 1, fol. 3b.

63. Ibid., fol. 11c, where each limb is conceived as a *sefirah,* and as including also all the other limbs.

64. See Idel, "Inquiries," p. 242.

65. See Idel, "The Image of Man above the Sefirot," *Da'at,* vol. 4 (1980), p. 48, n. 48. (Hebrew)

66. See *Zohar,* 1, fol. 16a.

67. Compre to the occurrence of the description of the Golem as *Ḥokhmah,* as a sphere, *Kadur,* in R. Joseph's *Commentary on Sefer Yeẓirah*, fol. 33a.

68. This simile appears, in a similar context, also in R. Joseph ibn Tabul's treatise found in Ms. Parma 77, fol. 1b, *Zohar ha-Raqi'a,* fol. 23c and in R. Samson Baqi; see Tishby, *Studies,* pp. 247–248; idem, *Torat ha-Ra',* pp. 24, 56–57.

69. Compare to the penetration of the light into the statues in order to animate them according to the Chaldean rituals. Cf. Lewy, *The Chaldean Oracles,* p. 247 and see Tishby, *Torat ha-Ra',* pp. 24–25; *Zohar ha-Raqi'a,* fol. 23c.

70. See the *Treatise on 'Olam ha-'Aẓilut,* that was given by R. Ḥayyim Vital to R. Shelomo Sagis, in ed. D. Touitou, *Liqquṭim Ḥadashim* (Jerusalem, 1985), p. 17.

71. See above, ch. 7, par. 5.

72. See above par. 1.

73. See n. 69 above.

74. *Liqquṭim Ḥadashim,* p. 18.

75. See above, par. 4.

76. See Ronit Meroz, *Redemption in the Lurianic Teaching,* (Ph. D. Thesis, Hebrew University, Jerusalem, 1988), p. 200 (Hebrew).

77. Idel, "The Image of Man," pp. 48–49; "Differing Conceptions of Kabbalah," p. 184, n. 223.

78. Ibid., pp. 54–55.

79. See *Perush le-Reish Hormenuta' de-Malka',* in G. Scholem, "The Authentic Writings of R. Isaac Luria," *Qiryat Sefer,* vol. 19 (1942/1943), pp. 198–199 (Hebrew) commenting on *Zohar,* 1, fol. 16a.

80. In the text, the term "path" has no correspondence. However, as both Scholem and Liebes have understood the text, the figure alludes to the paths of *Sefer Yeẓirah*. See the next note.

81. See the translation of Scholem, *On the Kabbalah,* p. 144, which was slightly changed, and the edition of Yehudah Liebes, "The Holy Ari's Songs for the Shabbat Meals" *Molad,* vol. 23, (233) (February, 1972), p. 544. (Hebrew)

82. See above ch. 2, par. 4.

83. See Liebes, (n. 81 above), p. 544, note 31. It is possible that the interpretation suggested here does not contradict that proposed by Liebes but only complements it.

84. See above ch. 1, par. 2; ch. 4, par. 2.

85. On this Kabbalist, see Gershom Scholem, *Abraham Cohen Herrera, the Author of Sha'ar ha-Shamayim* (Jerusalem, 1978), pp. 15–19, 36–37 (Hebrew).

86. See Scholem, *Kabbalah,* pp. 132–134, who offered a rather Neoplatonic interpretation of the Sarugian theory, not corroborated by the authentic Sarugian texts; cf. Alexander Altmann, "Lurianic Kabbalah in a Platonic Key: Abraham Cohen Herrera's *Puerta del Cielo,*" *HUCA,* vol. 53 (1982), p. 340. I expressed doubts as to the innovative nature of the *malbush* theory in my "Differing Conceptions of Kabbalah," pp. 192–193, n. 268, for reasons that differ from the point made here, which strengthen the possibility that the theory of *malbush* was not completely new with Sarug. Compare also to the Kabbalistic tradition quoted by R. Meir Poppers that Vital was acquainted with the concepts related to the processes taking place on the plane higher than the Supernal Man, but he concealed them; cf. *Zohar ha-Raqi'a,* fol. 23d.

87. Ibid. Compare to the Sarugian text printed in *Zohar ha-Raqi'a,* fol. 24b, where the Zoharic discussion of "*Gulma' be-'izqeta,*" is explicitly related to the lower part of the *malbush* and to the emergence of *'Adam Qadmon,* understood also as a seal, *ḥotam,* and related to the verse in the Psalms on the Golem. See also n. 9 above.

88. See above ch. 5, par. 2 and 3, n. 19.

89. In any case, the *Commentary on Sefer Yeẓirah* of R. Joseph Ashkenazi was well-known to some Sarugian Kabbalists, who quote both his view of the Golem (see *Novelot Ḥokhmah,* fol. 72b–73a) and his theory of the combinations of letters [see *Shever Yosef,* fol. 62a, where the author asserts that:

> the modes of combination [*'ofnei ha-ẓeruf*] of the 231 gates are to be studied from the *Commentaries to Sefer Yeẓirah* of Rabad and R. Eleazar, because it seems that their words contain the essence.

The commentary of R. Joseph Ashkenazi is also quoted several times in another book of del Medigo, *Mazref le-Ḥokhmah* (Warsaw, 1890), fol. 21b, 25a, 26a, and passim. Last but not least; mention should be made of Ms. Sasson 290, which includes two versions of R. Joseph's technique of creating a Golem, (see ch. 8 above) which was in the hands of Safedian Kabbalists and it influenced, as I tried to show in another place, the Lurianic view of *'Adam Qadmon;* see Idel, "Image of Man above the Sefirot," pp. 46–49 and n. 65 above.

90. It should be mentioned that the Sarugian texts also use the image of the drop containing in potentia the whole human structure as a metaphor for the existence of all the ten *sefirot* in the first point, which corresponds in a certain Sarugian source to the "spherical Golem". Compare, e.g., Sarug's, *Limmudei ha-'Azilut* (Muncacz 1897), fol. 3c; R. Menaḥem Azariyah of Fano's *Kanfei Yonah* (Lemberg, 1884), fol. 1bc and R. Joseph Shelomo del Medigo of Kandia's, *Novelot Ḥokhmah,* fol. 169a.

91. See below par. 7b.

92. See Idel, *Language, Torah and Hermeneutics,* p. 9.

93. The combination of these two types of esotericism is reminiscent of the texts of R. Moses ben Eleazar ha-Darshan, printed by Scholem, *Reshit ha-Kabbalah,* pp. 206–238. See especially ibid., pp. 218–219 where the anthropomorphic nature of the Cherub, connected to the figure 236, is mentioned.

94. See Ezek. 1:1.

95. Ibid.

96. The author alludes to the relationship between the spelling of the name of the river *Kevar,* which includes all the consonants of the words *bekhor,* Firstborn, and *keruv,* Cherub. I assume that the term *bekhor* refers to the special status of the Cherub as a high supernal instance. The name of the river is, according to this interpretation, written in an elliptic form since it does not include the sign of the vowel V; the explanation is, I assume, that the revelation in the Diaspora is defective.

97. Ps. 147:51.

98. *Ḥavarah.* Compare above ch. 6, par. 1, n. 6.

99. Ms. Moscow-Guensburg, 96, fol. 18b. I have no doubt that even the dating of the late thirteenth century for the material from this circle does not reflect the period when the linkage between the macranthropos and the combinations of the letters related to the creation of the Golem. See below Appendix C.

100. See Cohen, *The Shi'ur Qomah, Liturgy and Theurgy,* pp. 104–105.

101. See ch. 6, par. 1.

102. This is reminiscent of the view of *Sefer Yeẓirah*, where the letters are conceived of as hewn from the mountain. See Gruenwald, *SY*, par. 19, p. 148 and par. 20, p. 149.

103. See *Minḥat Yehudah,* printed in *Ma'arekhet ha-'Elohut* (Mantua, 1558), fol. 35b. See also R. Yoḥanan Alemanno's *Collectanaea,* Ms. Oxford, 2234, fol. 157b. On the possible affinity between this text of Ḥayyat and the theory of Sarug on the *malbush,* see Idel, "The Concept of the Torah" p. 39, n. 43.

104. *Ibid.,* fol. 21ab. Compare also to the view of R. Menaḥem Recanati in his *Commentary on the Torah,* fol. 1c and to *Minḥat Yehudah,* fol. 13b.

105. See above ch. 7, par. 1. On the possible influence of Abulafia on ibn Ẓayyaḥ, see Idel, *The Mystical Experience,* p. 195.

106. See *Ẓeror ha-Ḥayyim* the commentary of R. Joseph ibn Ẓayyaḥ on R. Todros ha-Levi Abulafia's *'Oẓar ha-Kavod,* Ms. Montefiore, 318, fol. 43b, 46a, 64b.

107. Ibid., fol. 71b.

108. See above ch. 2, par. 4.

109. *Sefer 'Even ha-Shoham,* Ms., Jerusalem, National and University Library, 8° 416, fol. 5a. See also below n. 111.

110. The influence of the Ashkenazi esotericism and that of the Cherub Circle can be easily demonstrated because in a Commentary on the prayer book in the possession of Ibn Ẓayyaḥ, those two schools are abundantly represented.

111. See Ms. Mantua 115, fol. 207b. On the origin and the development of this text see Joseph Avivi, "The Writings of Rabbi Isaac Luria in Italy before 1620," *Alei Sefer,* vol. 11 (1984), pp. 92–96. (Hebrew) See also Sarug's, *Limmudei ha-'Aẓilut* (printed together with *Sefer 'Adam Yashar,* Cracow, 1885), fol. 22b:

> And the impression of the half [of combinations of letters namely] 231 lower [gates] remained in the Primeval Air [*'avir qadmon*] and the light of the [other] half [the] higher 231 [gates] shined on it [on the 231 lower gates] according to the secret of H[eh, namely, 5] as it is written in the treatise, and thus 236 emerge.

This is a striking parallel to the thirteenth century text and especially to the view of R. Joseph ibn Ẓayyaḥ.

112. See Dan, *The Esoteric Theology,* pp. 104ff.

113. See above ch. 2, par. 3.

114. See, for the time being Appendix C below and Cohen, *The Shi'ur Qomah, Liturgy, and Theurgy,* pp. 179–181. On the anthropomorphism and *Sefer Yeẓirah* see our remarks above, chapter 2, par. 4, where the Creator is described as having a throne.

Recently, Professor S. Pines has advanced an hypothesis which is partially reminiscent of that proposed above; in his article on *Sefer Yeẓirah* [see above ch. 1 n. 16] he wrote as follows:

> There is not known connection between the Heikhalot literature, in which we find references to God's beauty, and the *Sefer yeẓira*, one of whose main tenets is the doctrine of the sefirot. *Homilies XVII,* on the other hand, presents a text in which the concept of God's Extensions, which parallels the notion of the sefirot in *Sefer yeẓira*, is joined with an affirmation of God's beauty. We should not, however, lose sight of the possibility, pointed out above, that each of these two doctrines in *Homilies XVII* was originally evolved by a different set of people and in a different milieu, and that their unification into a single coherent theory was affected at some later stage.

Here, we witness a phenomenon similar to that proposed by us above; An ancient non-Jewish text includes in a coherent manner, two different opinions which were expressed separately in apparently later Jewish texts. It should be mentioned that the combination of the theory of *Sefer Yeẓirah* on the Extensions with God's beauty implies a combination of the theory of this book with a certain type of anthropomorphic theology, a fact reminiscent of our proposal above.

115. *Sefer 'Emeq ha-Melekh,* (Amsterdam, 1648) fol. 4a–6a. I am not quite sure that the correlation between the tables of combinations of letters and the different divine configurations is totally new with this Kabbalist; a certain correlation between tables consisting of combinations of letters and the different *sefirot* is implicit already in the school of R. Joseph ben Shalom Ashkenazi and R. David ben Yehudah he-Ḥasid; see above ch. 8 and in R. David's *The Book of Mirrors: Sefer Mar'ot ha-Ẓove'ot,* ed. Daniel Ch. Matt (Scholars Press, 1982) pp. 247–248. (Hebrew)

116. Ibid., fols. 3d, 6c and 9c. See also R. Shelomo Rocco, *Sefer Kavvanot Shelomo* (Venise, 1670), fol. 46a.

117. Ibid., introduction of the author fol. 7d.

118. *Novelot Ḥokhmah,* fols. 163b–164a. See also fol. 165b.

119. See Gershom Scholem, *Sabbatai Ṣevi, The Mystical Messiah,* trans. R. J. Zwi Werblowsky (Princeton University Press, 1973) pp. 301, 305, 309, 311; Isaiah Tishby, *Paths of Faith and Heresy* (Ramat Gan, 1964), p. 36. (Hebrew)

PART THREE

Renaissance Period

11

Sixteenth and Seventeenth Century Discussions in the West

R. Abraham Bibago

I

A surge in the new interest in the creation of an anthropoid is conspicuous among Jewish and Christian authors during the period of the Renaissance. This phenomenon is evident in Italy, where the Jewish cultural center remained intact in the fifteenth and sixteenth centuries, in contrast to the destruction of Spanish Jewry. However, in Spain before the Expulsion, an influential text dealing with the Talmudic passage was composed as part of the sustained effort of the Jews to prove the superiority of their ancient lore over Greek science and philosophy. It was exactly during the period of an unprecedented effervescence of the Christian culture that some Jewish authors, most of them Kabbalists, introduced the theme of the artificial anthropoid as a proof of the unequaled achievement of the Jewish mystical lore. R. Abraham Bibago, a philosopher who flourished in Aragon in the middle of the fifteenth century[1] wrote:

The account of the Chariot is so perfect and fine, that it is impossible to say that it is the divine science [theology—*ḥokhmat ha-'elohut*] known by the philosophers. This is the reason, I think, that the wisdoms called the science of nature [*ḥokhmat ha-ṭeva'*] and the divine science can be understood in two ways: a) as the science of nature [it is] the knowledge of the generic things, and the causes which are shared by all the changing parts and the [entities] that are generated and corrupted; b) the comprehension of these causes, according to their qualities and quantities, so as to act, by the intellectual lore and the natural knowledge, natural operations, by mixing the elements according to the quality and quantity,[2] so that this expert will be able to make natural creatures according to individual mixtures, just as nature itself does. The divine lore too contains two aspects; the first one is the wisdom learned from the books of metaphysics, [in order to] know Being as being and its division into substance and accident, actuality and potentiality, one and many and the comprehension of the cause of the sensible substance. And the second [understanding] is [called] *hamshakhah* [mystical experience] and *devequt,* [union or communion][3] by which the essence of the intellectual and spiritual world is comprehended. *Hamshakhah* is the designation of the human intellect and *devequt* and prophecy is the designation of the theologians. Behold how we can comprehend the natural and divine [sciences] from the books of the intellectuals only some aspects of the first part, and it not impossible that one of the intellectuals of the Gentiles will comprehend them, but the other aspects [the second division] it is impossible [to be comprehended by them] except by those who fear God and meditate on His name, who are the sages of the true lore [*ḥokhmat ha-'emet*] and the masters of the Torah, for only by it and through it all these perfections emerge, and [also] the other [perfections]. And the proof is that none of the natural intellectuals of the gentiles did reach the level of creating a novel creature, [using] the natural order. But Rava created a calf and he created a man and sent it to R. Zeira and he spoke to it and it did not answer. He said, 'You are from the *ḥavraya*.' It seems that this sage [Rava] out of his knowledge in the topics of the Account of Creation and the natural science according to the second division, created a man, i.e., he made by the mixture and combination of the elements a form similar to the human form. R. Zeira had seen it and spoke to it, as he considered it to be a man. But, as it did not possess the perfect human form, that is, the intellectual form which is emanated from the world of the intellect, since this form will not come to it . . . it did not answer him at all, and this is the reason that he said: You are of the *ḥavraya*; namely [a result of] an operation done by [means of] the science of the *ḥaverim*, which is not the natural science at all. This [situation] concurs with what the philosopher has written in *Animalia*, chapter 15,[4] that the mouse born out of a father and a mother is of species different from that emerging from the putrification of the earth. This is the reason for his saying: "Return to your earth," namely, you do not possess but an image [*temunah*] which is of the same species like that [being] which is the natural cause [*Sibbah ṭiv'it*].[5]

Bibago distinguishes between the intellectual and the mystical cognitions. The first one is identical to Aristotelian epistemology as applied to Aristotelian physics and metaphysics; the second one is formulated in terms originating from both the mystical epistemology of Ibn Tufail and the Jewish religion. Nevertheless, the absence of the unique elements of *Sefer Yeẓirah* is conspicuous, even more so since Bibago was acquainted with, and positively oriented toward, Kabbalah.[6] The mentioning of the true lore as a designation of that knowledge which provided the superiority of the Jews may include an implicit interpretation of the meaning of Kabbalah as a practical lore rather than a theosophical knowledge. Bibago avoids the identification of the Account of Creation with *Sefer Yeẓirah*, which was already formulated by some authors before him.[7] The Talmudic passage is interpreted as pointing to a type of superior natural knowledge that is not linguistic, but rather includes the practical application of the theoretical science which was unique to the sages of Israel.

R. Yoḥanan ben Isaac Alemanno

II

At the end of the fifteenth century, some of the traditions on the Golem were quoted and discussed by R. Yoḥanan Alemanno (1435/8-c.—1510) in Northern Italy.[8] As we shall see below, this author was acquainted with an Ashkenazi tradition concerning the creation of the Golem, with Abulafia's views, with R. Joseph Ashkenazi's *Commentary on Sefer Yeẓirah*[9] and with views dealing with the artificial creation of a man stemming from non-Jewish sources. It seems that this combination of traditions, without precedent in any known author, betrays a deep interest in the question of the creation of a man in the Renaissance period. Let me begin with a passage that presents Abraham as an autodidact[10] who, at the beginning learned from himself the details included in *Sefer Yeẓirah*, and then achieved the power to create:

> . . . he combined [the letters] with each other and it [the combination] succeeded [to create] wondrous [things] and out of them [he created] wondrous [things], and he created new creatures [*beri'ot ḥadashot*],[11] which [possess] an animal soul, like the ancient sages, who created a calf and a likeness of a man [*demut 'adam*], though he did not possess the power of speech, and he understood that by these letters all the beings were created.[12]

It is only after this stage of creating "mute things" that Abraham advanced to an ecstatic experience in which he contemplated the supernal world of the *sefirot* which was revealed to him in a "sudden vision", *hashqafah pit'omit.*[13] However, this gradation of the creative moment as preceding the highest mystical experience seems to be a later development in Alemanno's thought. Earlier, in his *Collectanaea,* he wrote as follows:

> The Account of Creation[14] is the knowledge of the essences of things, such that he would know the forms [themselves] not only their actions, since the knowledge of actions is the wisdom of nature, which is known by speculation, and the knowledge of essences is the wisdom of prophecy,[15] achieved by the sudden vision. And from it the knowledge of the roots of the corruptible things is derived so that [he will] know the intermingling of those roots[16] in the sphere of the intellect, also named the sphere of the letters [*galgal ha-'otiyyot*][17], and he will know how to combine them according to the lore of *Sefer Yeẓirah*, so that from this knowledge he will know how to create a creature as Abaye and Rava[18] who created a three-year old calf, as it is said that he[19] was acquainted with the combination of the letters by which the world was created.[20]

Here, the gnosis is conceived not as part of a natural rational development but as the result of a revelation of the roots of the whole cosmos, a revelation that allows the practical application of this knowledge for the sake of the creation of beings. Alemanno attributes the creative possibilities inherent in the letters not only to their magical powers, the details of which are transmitted from one sage to another, but to the ascent of the mystic to a prophetic vision which enables him both to reach the archetypes appointed upon the lower world and to use this knowledge.[21] Mysticism is presented as the preceding stage for the apex of human achievement, which is the magical act. Such a conception is reminiscent of the location of *devequt* as a stage before the creation of the Golem, as we have already seen above.[22] This vision of the creative application of the highest knowledge is perfectly consonant with other stands of Alemanno, where magic is envisioned as the acme of human development.

However, it seems that a third occurrence of the discussion of creation by the combination of letters will elucidate the above passages, as well as another important issue in Renaissance magic. In the same *Collectanaea*[23] Alemanno quotes the technique of creating a Golem by R. Eleazar of Worms, with some slight changes. He did not comment upon the content of the quotation but, immediately after the passage on the Golem, on the same page, he copies an excerpt from Claudius Ptolemaeus' *Centiloqium,* with the *Commentary* of Ali ibn Ragel. The quotation from Ptolemaeus runs as follows:

> The forms in the world of composition[24] obey the forms of the spheres. This is why the masters of the talismans draw the forms of the spheres in order to receive the emanation of the stars in the object with which they intend to operate.

The Arab commentator explains, in the text copied by Alemanno, that there is a close correspondence between the supernal and the terrestrial forms, and this is the reason that the "masters of the idols [*ẓelamim*] bring [down] the efflux of the stars in those spherical forms and their ascent in the Orient, and they ornamented at that time their forms with the stones etc." On the margin of this Hermetical explanation of magic connected to the efflux of the stars into the idols, i.e., the statues prepared according to the special features of a certain star, Alemanno noted:

> This is the secret of the world of letters; they are forms and seals [made in order] to collect the supernal and spiritual emanation as the seals collect the emanations of the stars.

As against the alien type of magic, based upon constructions of the idols, or statues which correspond to the upper spherical world, Alemanno proposes a Jewish version of magic based upon the assumption that the higher world consists of the forms of the creatures. This world is further conceived as the world of the letters, and here below we may collect the emanation expanding from that world by using the Hebrew letters which function as seals and talismans. Since this view is written down immediately after the passage on the Golem of R. Eleazar of Worms, which deals with creation by means of the combination of letters, and since the term "world of letters" is closely related to the "sphere of the letters" mentioned above in a text of Alemanno dealing with creation by means of *Sefer Yeẓirah*, it is plausible to assume that Alemanno understood the text of the Ashkenazi author in terms of the astral magic disclosed at the bottom of the same page. Such a view is not completely new in Judaism, as the

Golem was already interpreted in astral terms in *Sefer ha-Ḥayyim,* and it occurs elsewhere in Alemanno, as we shall see immediately. I would like to emphasize that here the medieval technique of creating a Golem was understood as the Jewish counterpart to talismatic-astral magic. In other words, was the Golem understood by Alemanno as an instrument to collect the supernal efflux, after it was created by means of the letters conceived as talismatic entities? A positive answer seems to be supplied by Alemanno's views expressed in several instances when dealing with other issues. Thus, for example, he describes the activity of Moses as fully consonant with the attraction of the astral efflux here below using, as indicated above, linguistic techniques:

> Moses . . . had precise knowledge of the spiritual world which is called the world of the *sefirot,* and divine names, or the world of letters. Moses knew how to direct his thoughts and prayers, so as to improve the divine efflux. . . . By means of that efflux, he created anything he wished, just as God created the world by various emanations. Whenever he wanted to perform signs and wonders, Moses would pray and utter divine names, words and meditations. . . . The emanations then descended into the world and created new supernatural things.[25]

Moses acted, therefore, as a *sefirotic* magician, for he was able to direct his thought and recitations to the proper divine powers, so as to be able to create the required things. According to another text of Alemanno, Moses even "prepared the golden calf. The intention was only to cause the spiritual forces to descend by means of a form of a body."[26] Therefore, the preparation of the forms below is a licit way of acting from the religious point of view. Is the Golem conceived also as an acceptable way to capture the supernal emanation as the golden calf was? It seems that the answer is positive; according to another passage of Alemanno, the ancient wisdom:

> was so vast that they boasted of it in their books which they attributed to Enoch whom the Lord has taken,[27] and to Solomon who was wiser than any man, and to many perfect men who performed actions of intermingling various things and balancing [literally comparing] qualities in order to create new forms [*ẓurot ḥadashot*][28] in gold, silver, vegetable, mineral, and animals that had never before existed, and to create divine forms that foretell the future, laws, *nomoi,* and spirits of angels, of stars and of devils by the changes of their constitution which is the reason of the differences between men, be these [differences] great or small.[29]

The creation of the new forms is described in Hermetical terms as the combinations of the various regions demonstrate. Since the aim of this creation is to build up an entity that foretells the future, it is reasonable to assume that the forms are identical to the statues constructed by the Hermetical and Neoplatonic magicians, and consequently, have human form. If so, then the artificially created human form, like the calf, served to capture the emanation from above. There can be hardly any doubt as to the similarity between the Golem, an anthropoid, whose description is immediately followed by the passage of Ptolemaeus, dealing with the attraction of the emanation by combinations of letters, and the anthropoid as it appears here, which is also understood as a means to capture the higher emanation. If we are correct in the present juxtaposition of the two discussions of the anthropoid, the first created as a regular Golem, but implicitly understood according to the astral magic of Ptolemaeus, and the explicit creation of the statue and the calf for similar reasons, then we may describe Alemanno as proposing, implicitly, a combination of the classical Ashkenazi technique with the hermetical type of magic using astral concepts. Such an understanding is corroborated by an additional passage of the same author found in his commentary on the Song of the Songs, *Ḥesheq Shelomo.* According to Alemanno, only prophets can understand the words of other prophets because these were not addressed to the vulgus, but to those who are similar to the prophets in the degree of their:

> wisdom, understanding and knowledge of every operation. To combine the letters by which the world was created as the dictum of our sages, blessed be their memory, says[30], "Beẓalel was acquainted with the letters by means of which the world was created." This is a secret belonging to the secrets of prophecy[31] which has no equal, because by means of it, it is possible to the wise investigator to comprehend the quality of the material combination and the measures of the elements which enter this mixture and are blended in such a manner that it was possible to take from the four elements, parts which are measured in such a way that are on the degree of human semen. And he will provide for it a measured heat, similar to the heat provided by the womb of a woman so that it was possible to give birth to a man without [the need of] the male semen and the blood of the female, and without the [intervention of] masculinity and femininity. If this would [be achieved] it would be considered a wondrous wisdom according to the scientists, just as it would be wondrous according to the physicians, who are experts in the combination of opposite medicines. Thus is the thing according to the prophet who

knows the plain meaning of the spiritual forces,[32] which correspond to the level of the elements in relationship to the forms which dwell upon matters; [the prophet] would call them letters, as it is explained in *Sefer Yeẓirah*. And he knew, afterwards, how to permute them and combine them with each other, in such a manner that an animal form or a human one will emerge in actu. This is a wondrous wisdom, unsurpassed, out of which come all the mighty wonders. And in this [context] they said that Rava created a three-year calf, and he created a man when he studied *Sefer Yeẓirah*, and this is [the meaning of] the Account of Creation,[33] concerning which our sages said[34] it is forbidden to discuss the Account of Creation to [more] than two [persons].[35]

The combinations of the letters as disclosed in *Sefer Yeẓirah* are presented here as the clue for the understanding of the emergence of several issues. Though different from each other, these issues share a common characteristic; the precise knowledge of the science of combination of elemental ingredients is the key of the success. These issues are the creation of the world by means of letters, the attainment of prophecy, and the creation of the form of an artificial calf or man. This technique of combination is similar to the artificial creation of man when using the ingredients which enter in the composition of the human semen, provided the precise proportions of the components is known. However, even more sublime than the quasi-alchemical process which uses the material elements,[36] is the prophetic creation of the form of man by the knowledge of the combination of the spiritual, astral forces, which when combined in a proper way, serve as the material substratum for the emergence of the required forms that of a calf or of a man. Here the creation of the anthropoid is conceived of as purely astral, even more than in the passage quoted from the untitled work of Alemanno. I assume that the peculiar way of the creation includes, again, the view that the letters function as talismatic signs which can be combined in such a manner as to collect the supernal influx in a specific order that generates the emergence of a requested form.[37] This account of the creation of the Golem does not mention the dust and it seems that the substratum of the form is provided by the crystallization of the specific combination of the astral forces, upon which a form, apparently originating from the super-astral world, descends. Thus the anthropoid is constituted by letters, astral forces and superastral form. On the basis of other passages of Alemanno, it becomes clear that the superastral plane is the realm of the *sefirot,* which are conceived as the forms of the letters which function as their matters, exactly as in the above passage.[38]

In another interesting discussion of the Account of Creation the topic of the formation of creatures by means of combinations of letters occurs again:

> The Account of Creation, in its primary root meaning, refers to the ten *sefirot* that Abraham counted in his *Sefer Yezirah*, which was written down by Rabbi Akiva, and to the letters with which He formed all the creation, just as Bezalel, who dwells in the shadow of God, knew them and understood the letter combinations through which the world was created. And only the numbered remnants does He call forth in each and every generation, to teach them the letter-combinations with which were created creatures [*beri'ot*]. But for [the people of] flesh and blood it is almost impossible [to understand this]. Therefore Moses, our master, did hide it and he began with the revealed aspects of creation so as to let it be known by the masses.[39]

According to this discussion the creative power of the combinations of letters is part of the esoteric tradition hidden by Moses but still revealed to the select few. As part of understanding this linguistic technique, the creation of creatures is mentioned as part of the account of the creation. This view is apparently influenced by R. Abraham Abulafia's view of *Sefer Yezirah* as the Account of Creation.[40] In the above texts, Alemanno does not use the term Golem but he refers to the *Sanhedrin* passage or to *Sefer Yezirah*. This understanding of the creation of the anthropoid is reminiscent of a view to be analyzed below in detail regarding the relationship between the astral body, viewed as a *Zelem,* and the term Golem.[41]

III

The position of Alemanno is not articulated in detail, but it was important to elaborate upon it not only for the reason of unfolding his views on our subject, but also because of the possible impact such a stand might have had on a contemporary of Alemanno who, apparently, put an astrological interpretation of the Golem technique into practice.

It should be remarked that Alemanno differs from Bibago's explanation by his introduction of the Ashkenazi and Abulafian theory of the combination of letters and his adoption of an astral type of magic. However, despite these crucial divergences,[42] these two authors share an important feature in their concept of the Golem: the naturalistic element of the artificial man as produced also by the knowledge of the proportions between the various components of the human body. In order to be able to create an anthropoid, it is not sufficient to be acquainted with the science of *Sefer Yeẓirah*, in the case of Alemanno, but also with some medical and natural science dealing with the real human body from its biochemical aspect. With Alemanno's theory, the Jewish view of the Golem leaves the avenue opened by the ancient tradition focused as it was on linguistic gnosis, and it passes to a more complex approach, combining Arabic naturalism with ancient Jewish magic. Indeed, this synthesis can be expressed also in a more geographical manner; the Jewish Spanish philosophical tradition, influenced by Ibn Tufail's *Ḥayy ibn Yaqṭan* and the Arabic magical tradition based on astrology—also influential in Spain—combined with the Ashkenazi linguistic traditions in Northern Italy and the result was a more complex presentation of the Golem-concept. In other words, the Jewish magical-mystical tradition with which Alemanno was acquainted could be understood better by resorting to the discussions of the finest of the philosophers, as Alemanno considered Ibn Tufail to be. As part of Alemanno's broader endeavour to explain Kabbalah philosophically, we can locate the coalescence of the theory of creation by combination of letters to the assumption that even nature can produce such a combination of elements as to culminate in the reception of spiritual faculties.

In this context it is pertinent to suggest the possibility that Alemanno, who combined the naturalistic vision of the emergence of man as the result of a balanced proportions of the elements and the *Sefer Yeẓirah* combination of letters, had also introduced the use of a retort in this context. This is merely an hypothesis, based however upon the fact that Alemanno recommended in his ideal curriculum the study of alchemy and the science of the alembicum, which are followed by the recommendation to study medical and pharmaceutical matters as well.[43] Furthermore, the creation of the Golem was compared in one of the passages quoted above, to the science of medicine, though it was conceived as a higher one, namely, a prophetic lore.[44] If the hypothesis of the existence of such a combination of alchemical, magical and linguistic practice, on one hand, and the use of the alembicum, on the other, will be demonstrated from the writings of Alemanno, most of them still in manuscripts, then he could be regarded as a turning point between the magical approach of the medieval period and the more experimental attitude emerging in the Renaissance. In this context, we should recall that Alemanno was a physician by profession, and his interest in artificial creation might have been motivated not only by intellectual curiosity but also by more professional concerns.[45]

Let me address one detail of Alemanno's description of the creation of artificial anthropoids adduced above from his untitled writing; it includes the following sentence: "to create divine forms which tell the future, the laws and the *nomoi,* as well as (to create) spirits of angels, stars and devils".[46] The divine forms were created out of elements belonging to all the natural regions. As we suggested above, Alemanno seems to be influenced by views found in Hermetic magic; the compounded nature of the statues and the fact that they were conceived as a source of revelations suggest an influence of pagan magic. However, the assumption that the divine forms, i.e., the compounded forms, promulgate laws, *nomoi,* may indicate an additional type of influence. In the writings of the famous Muslim alchemist, Jabir ibn Ḥayyan, the most perfect artificial production was designated *asḥab al-nawamis,* the legislators or the prophets; their peculiar nature was also referred to as legislative, *namusi al-ṭiba'*.[47] Thus, the artificial construction is different in this author from the regular Golem in the Jewish tradition: it possesses both intelligence and speech. The fact that Alemanno bestows the divine forms with the faculty of prophesying, assumes the existence of these two faculties; it seems probable that a tradition stemming from medieval Arabic alchemy contributed to Alemanno's view of the artificial construction.

Before proceeding to discuss the Christian interest in the Jewish anthropoid, it would be pertinent to remark that there is at least one short discussion on anthropoids in Spain that does not stand in the classical tradition of Jewish mysticism. It appears in *'Iggeret ha-Teshuvah,* a treatise attributed to R. Isaac ibn Latif, but actually composed in the middle of the fourteenth century.[48] *'Iggeret ha-Teshuvah* mentions the view of Ibn Sina,[49] according to which it is possible that as a result of the influence of the celestial movement, the elements can produce, as part of their combinations,[50] a subtle and pure creature, *Beri'ah zakhah neqiyah.* This creature can receive the divine influx, *Shefa' 'Elohi,* and then cause its soul to cleave on high by its intellectual activity.[51] This extraordinary being, which can even reach the intellection of the First Cause, is comparable to the perfection of Adam. However, I would like to indicate that this anthropoid is created by nature, by a rare coincidence of facts, and not by man. Nevertheless, we can see that some interest in a discussion related to a non-human creation of an anthropoid can be found in a Spanish Jewish author.

Lodovico Lazarelli

IV

The relatively open relationship between Jewish and Christian intellectuals during the late fifteenth and early sixteenth centuries constitutes a rare case of spiritual exchange. One of the most impressive results of this exchange is the emergence of a new branch of Christian theology, Christian Kabbalah. The influence of Kabbalistic material in Christian circles became more prominent from the eighties of the fifteenth century, when the first substantial corpus of Kabbalistic writings was translated into Latin by Pico della Mirandola's teacher, the apostate Flavius Mitridathes. However, this large corpus of Kabbalistic writings, including translations of R. Eleazar of Worms' and Abulafia's treatises, does not contain any recipe for the creation of an anthropoid. Nevertheless, by other channels, at least two such recipes came to the attention of Christian intellectuals; it is obvious that Lodovico Lazarelli and Johannes Reuchlin were acquainted with medieval recipes. Lodovico Lazarelli,[52] an Italian intellectual at the end of the fifteenth century, wrote in his dialogue *Crater Hermetis*:

> Abraham who teaches . . . in the book named *Sepher Izira,* that is the book of formation,[53] how to form new men; go to a desert mountain where animals do not feed, and take from the middle of it Adama, which is a red and virgin earth, and out of it form the man, and arrange the limbs according to the letters.[54]

Scholem has already noted that this passage reflects the influence of R. Eleazar of Worms' recipe;[55] indeed, the details mentioned in the above text are closer to the recipe of R. Eleazar than to any other recipe. However, there is still place to ponder the possibility that another, yet unknown, probably Ashkenazi, recipe generated this Latin text. However, what is interesting is not so much the details of the recipe, but the allegorical interpretations offered by the Christian author. Lazarelli interprets the cattle as the corporeal senses and the red earth, identical to Adam, as the intellect of the sage. However, even more interesting is the fact that this creation is compared to the divine creation which is generated by the mystic's utterance of words made up of letters as elements.[56] Thus, the combinations of letters were conceived as the material substratum of the divine creation, whereas the material creation is vivified by the recitation of the sage. Moreover, the whole process was presented by Lazarelli as the new, spiritual birth of Ferdinand, the king of Aragon. This spiritualization of the "Golem-creation" seems to have been influenced by Yoḥanan Alemanno's implicit interpretation of the recipe of R. Eleazar of Worms, using astral magic, on one hand, and the spiritual understanding of the significance of the creation of the Golem as it appears in the ecstatic Kabbalah, on the other. In the same folio where Alemanno quoted the Ashkenazi recipe, he also added a quotation from Abulafia's *Ḥayyei ha-'Olam ha-Ba'.* Abulafia, like Lazarelli, understood the real creation as the generation of the intellect of the king, rather than the corporeal activity. Moreover, it seems that the inducing of the spiritual elements into the king has some affinity to the attraction of the spiritual elements by astral magic in Alemanno's understanding of the Golem as presented above. On the ground of these similarities, it seems plausible that the two Northern Italian intellectuals were in contact and the traces of Alemanno's complex vision of the Golem are visible in the discussion of Lazarelli.

Johannes Reuchlin

V

At the end of the fifteenth century, interest in the Golem is shared with Lazarelli by one of the most famous Christian Kabbalists, Johannes Reuchlin. In his famous *De Arte Cabalistica,* he copies some Hebrew sentences from the passage on the Golem from the text stemming from the so-called circle of the *Book of 'Iyyun,*[57] and he translates most of the text into Latin.[58] From this quotation several sixteenth and seventeenth century authors copied this recipe, thus propagating it in the European culture.[59] Let me analyze this rendering of the Golem creation in detail, since the translation of Reuchlin includes crucial variations in comparison to the known versions of the Hebrew original, and because of its being the most widespread description of this Kabbalistic topic in any European language. I reproduce here the Latin text of the 1517 printing of *De Arte Cabalistica,* and I shall comment upon the translation and the understanding of the texts. An English translation of the Hebrew original was already given above,[60] and an English translation of Reuchlin's rendering has recently been done by M. and S. Goodman. Here and there some improvements in their translation are offered, based both on the Latin original and on the Hebrew text as quoted by Reuchlin himself:

> These are the words of that excellent contemplative scholar Ḥamai in his book *On Speculation,* to which he usefully attaches the book on the *Fountain of Wisdom,*[61] though so fine and clear a man has no need of such a testimonial. Now I shall try to translate this passage into Latin without, if I can, affecting the quality of his thought: . . . the mixture [of letters] produced by permutation of the alphabet [*alphabetice revolutionis*][62] has information hidden from the uncouth and the unworthy that has been revealed, by combination of letters, [*ex alphabeticaria combinatione*] to holy men who lead a contemplative life. The revelation came through the agency of Jeremiah, for he often used to read the *Book of Creation,* according to a passage in the *Book on Hope* written by the author, R. Judah.[63] Jeremiah used to immerse himself in the *Book of Creation* a great deal

> and would often spend all night and all day with it in his hands. It is said that this was because there once came to him a *bat qol,* or voice from heaven, which ordered him to spend three years sweating over the one volume.[64] At the end of the three years, when he was sufficiently interested in the combining of letters and other such methods to be able to employ them, he soon managed to create for himself and his fellows a new man [*homo nouus*][65]. On the forehead of this newly created man was written *Yhvh 'elohim 'emet* i.e., "God the Tetragrammaton is true." The man felt[66] the writing on his forehead and without hesitation moved his hand and removed and destroyed the first letter in *'emet* which is *'alpeh.* There remained then these words *yhvh 'elohym mth,* meaning "God the Tetragrammaton is dead". Jeremiah was struck with indignation, tore his clothes and asked him: "Why do you take the *'aleph* from *'emet?*" He replied: "Because everywhere men have failed in faithfulness to the Creator who created you in his own image and likeness." Jeremiah asked, "So how are we to apprehend Him?" To which he replied: "Write the alphabets in the space where that dust was thrown in accordance with the understanding of your hearts." They did so, and the man became dust and ashes in their sight and disappeared. This is why Jeremiah used to say that he then received from God himself the virtues and powers of the alphabets and the commutations of the elements, [all this] because of the combinations of letters he had already known from the *Book of Creation.*[67] From that time on this alphabetical Kabbalah [*Cabala alphabeticaria*] or Receiving [*receptio*] has travelled to posterity and through it are laid open on the greatest secrets of the divine.[68]

There are several crucial changes that were introduced in the Latin translation of the original Hebrew version of this legend on the Golem. The first and most visible one is the description of Jeremiah as studying *Sefer Yeẓirah* alone, i.e., without Ben Sira as in the Hebrew version.[69] Jeremiah has also created the Golem alone, without the help of his son. Whatever the interest of Reuchlin might have been, his attempt to attribute the whole activity described in the Kabbalistic original to Jeremiah alone is conspicuous. Moreover, the particular way Jeremiah is conceived is unique to Reuchlin, and does not have any specific source in the legend. To Jeremiah alone was revealed the importance of the study of *Sefer Yeẓirah* and he is conceived as the source of the revelation of the alphabetical Kabbalah, a view unknown from other sources.[69] There is, no doubt, a renewed emphasis on the importance of revelation and contemplation. The real meaning of the whole operation is not so much the magical one as the contemplative-revelatory one. This is evident from the very beginning of the above quotation, R. Ḥamai is described as a contemplative scholar, and perfect sages lead a contemplative life. This vision of Kabbalah as basically a contemplative lore is characteristic of Reuchlin, who expressed such a view in other instances, as well.[71] I assume that this evaluation of Kabbalah has something to do with the fact that Reuchlin was acquainted with the Kabbalah of Abraham Abulafia and the great esteem he had for this brand of Kabbalah.[72]

Given the elevated status of Kabbalah, it was regarded as the patrimony of the elite, and the combination of letters is presented here as an esoteric device, intended to conceal the true meaning of the theologoumena from the eyes of the profane. Further, this view is, apparently, an innovation of Reuchlin, having no basis in the Hebrew version of the passage. On the other hand, the presentation of the act of the creation of the Golem stands apart from the Hebrew source; the creature is presented as if it were generated in order to serve the needs of its creator or of his companions. Thus a strong magical tone is highlighted in this version more than in the original.

Cornelius Agrippa of Nettesheim

VI

A younger contemporary of Alemanno, the notorious Cornelius Agrippa of Nettesheim (1486–1535), seems to have been also acquainted with the Jewish concept of creating an artificial man. When discussing the preparation of the talismans according to the celestial images, he writes:

> But who can give soul to an image, life to stone, metal, wood or wax? And who can make children of Abraham come out of stones? Truly this secret is not known to the thick-witted worker and someone cannot give what he has not. And no one has such powers but he who has cohabited with the elements, vanquished nature, mounted higher than the heavens, elevating himself above the angels to the archetype of himself, with whom he then becomes co-operator and can do all things.[73]

The mention of Abraham's children in this context seems to indicate that Agrippa was acquainted with a Jewish source which discussed the creation of the "souls" by Abraham and Sarah, as it appears in a series of texts. The mentioning of the coming out of the children from the stones may reflect the verb *ḥẓv*, to carve out from a stone, which occurs in connection with the operations of Abraham at the end of *Sefer Yeẓirah*. The need to rise to the archetype in order to be able to "give soul to an image" seems to point to Alemanno's description of Abraham who was able to create a Golem after he received a revelation, which directed him to investigate the composition of his body as a preparatory act to the highest revelation.[74] Moreover, the mentioning of the various regions in the context of infusing the soul in the image is reminiscent of Alemanno's expression that Abraham created an image of man, in the first text of his quoted above, and the list of the various realms in the other passage of Alemanno.[75]

The middle of the sixteenth century in Italy witnessed an epigonic interest in the artificial man as presented in the previous examples. With the major exception of Paracelsus, the Jewish and Christian authors limited themselves to repeating the discussions found in their sources. The printing of the Latin translation of *Sefer Yeẓirah* by Postel in 1552 includes a short discussion apparently based on Reuchlin's passage discussed above;[76] a decade later, the printing of the original Hebrew version of *Sefer Yeẓirah* together with some commentaries, that attributed to R. Eleazar of Worms, the Pseudo-Sa'adyan commentary and the commentary of R. Joseph ben Shalom Ashkenazi, attributed in print to R. Abraham ben David, contributed to the dissemination of the knowledge of the texts related to the Golem.[77] Since then unknown material related to the Golem surfaced only rarely.[78] R. Yehudah Muscato, an important preacher in the second half of the sixteenth century, copied the end of the commentary attributed to the Rabad and the Pseudo-Sa'adyan passage on the creation of the Golem in his *Qol Yehudah,* a commentary on *Sefer Kuzari.*[79] Other quotations from the 1562 edition, or perhaps from *Qol Yehudah,* influenced some other authors' treatment of this topic.[80]

Abraham Yagel

VIII

However, some more original observations regarding the Golem and its nature appeared after the absorption of the Renaissance view of *magia naturalis.* One of the followers of Alemanno, also a physician, continued his interest in the magical understanding of Kabbalah in the late sixteenth century and early seventeenth century; his name was R. Abraham Yagel.[81] Writing long after the establishment of the Renaissance view of natural magic as a leading concept, Yagel combines it with the classical Jewish type of magic as exposed in the previous discussions of the Golem. Commenting upon the passage from *Sanhedrin,* he asserts in his encyclopedia *Beit Ya'ar ha-Levanon,* that:

> Even if he will create a third-year old calf or another animal or [even] a man [it is permitted] as the scholars told us. For a man will be able to do this through the wisdom of nature;[82] he only will be unable to give him the spirit of life in his nostrils . . . as Giulio Camillo wrote in his book;[83] also the wise man, the author of *De occulta philosophia*;[84] and Roger Bacon[85] along with other scholars, both recent and ancient, who offer instruction among themselves and their disciples to people [so that they] can change their initial nature and produce things and new creatures,[86] removing and replacing forms according to the composition of the different kinds of substances.[87]

Yagel seems to have been influenced by the magical understanding of Alemanno as the use of the phrase, "*beri'ot ḥadashot*" in connection with the creation of the Golem indicates; moreover, the natural explanation of the changes in the composition, which is the basic theory of Yagel, seems to be also derived from Alemanno's discussions in Ms. Paris BN, 849, and we know for certain that Yagel cited this work of Alemanno.[88] As we stressed there, Alemanno does not include the combinations of letters as part of the creative process in that context as Yagel does not here as well. Indeed, Yagel presents the combination of letters and divine names, which are conceived by Rashi as the technique of creation of the calf and the artificial man, as a process basically different from the "preparation of the matter, according to the (proper) measure and weight, and this is called natural magic".[89] In another important discussion of the *Sanhedrin* passage, he differentiates between the various statements in the Talmudic text as follows: the creation of the worlds by the righteous is possible by the combinations of letters, whereas the fact that the *Gavra* created by Rava cannot speak is a convincing proof for the fact that this Rabbi did not use the technique of *Sefer Yeẓirah*, based on letter-combinations, but the natural magic whose range of possibilities is much more limited. Thus, the *ḥilkhot yeẓirah* mentioned in connection to the creation of the calf is not to be identified as the classical *Sefer Yeẓirah*, a stand that is unique among the medieval and Renaissance authors, but it comprises rather the technique of the natural magic. Rashi, Yagel indicates:

> was wrong since he did not distinguish between the *hilkhot yeẓirah* and *Sefer Yeẓirah*, thinking as he did that they are identical and explaining that they [the Talmudic masters] were practicing combinations of letters of the [divine] name by which the heaven and earth were created etc., since *Sefer Yeẓirah*, attributed [*ha-mekkuneh*] to Abraham our ancestor is, in principle following the way of combination of letters in 231 gates, known to the Kabbalists, by which they

> may create a man and a spirit and a soul in his nostrils, and other creatures . . . as the sages say there: "Rava said, If the righteous desired they could create the world."[90]

Therefore Yagel, wanting to integrate the natural magic of the Renaissance, does not identify it with the Kabbalistic technique, but rather with a hypothetical corpus of Jewish knowledge, the *hilkhot yeẓirah.* The latter corresponds to natural magic but is to be carefully distinguished, on the one hand, from *Sefer Yeẓirah* and, on the other hand, the Kabbalistic practice which is presented here as evidently superior to magic. Accordingly, the Kabbalists are able to create a perfect man, who will be infused also with spirit and soul. Yagel is, therefore, conferring to Kabbalah the status of supermagic, a higher lore than the regular natural magic; it seems that this gradation of the Kabbalistic magic as higher than the natural is completely in consonance with the classification of Kabbalah as the highest lore and as magic in Pico's *Theses.* Interestingly enough, the supreme part of the natural magic is, according to Pico, not Kabbalah in general nor even magical Kabbalah in particular, but a lore that is closely related to Raymundus Lull's science of combining letters;[91] accordingly, Kabbalah is, in the opinion of the Christian Kabbalist, a magical technique based on combining letters, just as in Yagel's case.

The difference between the man referred to in the *Sanhedrin* passage and the "ideal" man created by *Sefer Yeẓirah* is radical; the Talmudic sages function as natural magicians. Quoting the Talmudic text, Yagel asserts that:

> it is doubtless that he [the man] was also created by the natural science . . . and he possesses the sensual faculty and the animal soul, which are the operations of nature and [the effect of] the preparation of the matter and its refinement and perfection. However, the power of speech was absent as it is [the prerogative] of God alone and His divine names . . . and the deed of the righteous by the way of His names and letters.[92]

R. Meir ibn Gabbai

IX

The righteous individual is therefore tantamount to the Kabbalists, as he operates using the same technique of combining letters and names and creating men, and they surpass the natural magicians. Here, it seems that Yagel is indeed utilizing the categories of Pico, though regarding the relationship of the magician to the Kabbalists he illustrates the difference between them by the example of the artificial man. In this context, an important parallel to Yagel's discussion is to be adduced, though a partial one, where the Golem is brought in order to demonstrate the superiority of Jewish tradition over the alien, Greek science. R. Meir ibn Gabbai, a sixteenth century refugee from Spain, wrote in his classical *'Avodat ha-Qodesh* as follows:

> The natural science known to the sages of Israel is not [identical] to the natural science in which the Greek [i.e., Aristotle] and his companions were versed, following the way of investigation. The proof for this is that it is unheard of and unseen that they made natural creatures using the natural ways, [even] for a [short] time [*lesha'atam*], notwithstanding their expertise and the depth of their investigation [*haflagat ḥaqiratam*] as it is seen and heard with respect to the sages of Israel. This is the demonstration that the natural science transmitted to them is not [identical] to the Greek natural science: It is said in [chapter] "Four [types of] death" [i.e., chapter seven of the tractate *Sanhedrin*] Rava said that if the righteous desired they could create a world. . . . Behold, since he was acquainted with the science of the natural entity [*ḥokhmat ha-hawwayah ha-ṭiv'it*] according to that way, as it was generated at the inception of its creation, he [Rava] was operating and creating such a creature. But from the perspective that iniquities separate [one from God] he was not able to confer upon it a speaking soul. Thus it is evident that their science of nature is different from that of the Greeks, since it [the former] transcends the way of investigation. This science was in their possession insofar as they were experts and erudite in *Sefer Yeẓirah* of Abraham, our ancestor.[93]

This differentiation of the Greek from the Jewish natural science is intended to denigrate the achievement of the natural sciences of the philosophers who followed the Greek science. The presentation of the Kabbalah as the superior Jewish natural science is part of the antiphilosophical polemic waged by Spanish Kabbalists for two preceding centuries. In contrast to the later Italian Kabbalist, Ibn Gabbai envisions the science of *Sefer Yeẓirah* by which the man and the calf were created as reflecting a superior lore, unrelated to that of the Greek science. By doing so he attempted to elevate the creation of the Golem far above the level of natural science, as understood by the medieval philosophers, to a sphere unattainable by the alien scholars.[94] It is only due to iniquities that the ancient Jewish master was unable to complete his creation by conferring upon it speech. Yagel, on the contrary, posits the creation of the man as described in the Talmudic text on a lower level than Kabbalah, and by doing so he identifies it with the Renaissance *magia naturalis.* Notwithstanding the differences, Ibn Gabbai and Yagel agree on a point that seems to be essential regarding the status of the artificial man: a perfect man can be created. In the case of Ibn Gabbai it was only a matter of sins that prevented the infusion of the faculty of speech; with Yagel, on the other hand, it is indeed the prerogative of the Kabbalists to create an animated man. In both cases this perfect creation is a clear demonstration of the superiority of Kabbalah over the alien sciences.

X

A slightly different attitude can be found in a writing of a younger contemporary of Yagel, R. Joseph Shelomo del Medigo. In his *Mazref le-Ḥokhmah,* in a larger discussion to be analyzed in details below,[95] del Medigo refers to the achievements of the practical scientists as higher than that of the scholastic abstractions; preferring the former, he mentions alchemy, algebra, agriculture and the attainment of Archimedes as examples of the applied philosophy; then he asserts that these achievements are superior to those who indulge in philological intricasies. He then mentions the description of Abraham at the end of *Sefer Yeẓirah*, as one who uses the techniques referred to in this book, and he quotes the interpretation of R. Joseph ben Shalom Ashkenazi regarding the creation of a Golem by Abraham.[96] Earlier in this context he copied the passage of Bibago analyzed above.[97]

The assumption that the Jewish lore is a science higher than the Greek one was argued in connection to the creation of the anthropoid at the beginning of the eighteenth century. R. Joseph Ergas mentions in his *Shomer 'Emunim* that various Jewish philosophers had already rejected the Maimonidean identification between the Mishnaic concepts of *ma'aseh bereshit* and *ma'aseh merkavah* and the Aristotelian physics and metaphysics. Instead, he argues that the meaning of these concepts cannot be attained by means of the human intellect but only by way of the Kabbalah; this is demonstrated, according to Ergas, by the fact that none of the Gentile sages reached the level of creating a creature as Rava did.[98]

XI

Some broader conclusions regarding the interest in the Golem techniques are pertinent at this point. A survey of the authors who were interested in these ideas in Italy, show that they were persons inclined to philosophical thinking, two of them, Alemanno and Yagel, being also physicians. The third one, del Medigo, was deeply interested in scientific issues. Thus, the ancient Jewish magic and the medieval mysticism entered into their preoccupations not only as students of the Jewish tradition, or of medieval Islamic philosophy, but also as persons aware of the scientific turn of their age and as physicians concerned with the nature of the human being. The Golem was understood in a more natural way because of the philosophical bias of the intellectual ambiance of the Jews in Northern Italy.[99] I believe that the Golem discussions presented in this chapter serve as a good foil for the more theosophical understanding of this topic in the Orient, as we attempted to demonstrate in the preceding chapter;[100] a more scientific attitude characterizes the Italian Jews in comparison to their contemporary coreligionists outside Italy. Assuming this divergence in relationship to the Golem, we may speculate on the combination of magic, science and mysticism which is evident in our case, and the general syncretistic atmosphere of Renaissance Italy in general. The question of the contribution of this syncretistic thought to modern science was disputed hotly in the last generation. After Yates had presented her thesis, several critics pointed out the weakness of the evidence regarding the contribution of Hermetical and magical elements to the emergence of modern science.[101] As far as I am aware, the case of the Golem was not discussed in this context.

According to the current views, the Jewish concept of the Golem contributed to the emergence of the Paracelsian view of the homunculus.[102] Thus, a substantial link between ancient magic and the beginning of modern medicine could be established. However, an examination of the pertinent material in Jewish sources evinces that there is no substantial affinity between the basic views of the Golem and the homunculus material. I would like to end this chapter by pointing out the divergences between these two concepts. The homunculus was conceived by Paracelsus as a tiny anthropoid generated during the process of putrefaction of human semen and menstrual blood.[103] These two basic components do not appear in any of the devices discussed by Jews, where the Golem is formed solely from clay or dust and water; neither is the central theory of the combination of letters hinted at in the writings of Paracelsus. Even when authors like Alemanno attempted to explain the emergence of the Golem by preparation of matter to receive a human form, he does not mention the semen and blood. He followed the medieval theory, of Aristotelian extraction, that the proper preparation of matter will enable it to receive the requested form. Thus, the mineral matter will gradually change into an organic one; the mineral is the starting point of the natural process and not the organic one. Moreover, the possibility that Jewish authors used the retort in order to create an anthropoid, an hypothesis advocated by Scholem[104] and accepted by Pagel[105] as an evidence for the Jewish connection to the homunculus, is unfortunately based on weak evidence. It was the linguistic alchemy which interested the Jews, not the metalurgic or organic ones. I believe that the fact that none of the Jews mentioned Paracelsus in the context of creating a Golem is interesting evidence with respect to their awareness that different phenomena are represented by the Golem and the homunculus. Since Jewish authors, in our case Yagel, even resorted to the notorious Agrippa in order to point out the existence of parallel views to the magical Golem, there is no reason why a late Renaissance Jew would ignore the Paracelsian homunculus as a similar entity to the Golem. For the time being I am not aware of any quotation from Paracelsus in Hebrew Renaissance sources, nor does Paracelsus refer to any of the recipes discussed above, although at least that of Reuchlin was in print in his lifetime. Thus, the Golem recipes, as found in the known texts, seem to reflect a different paradigm than the homunculus does. On the basis of the extant material it seems that it is implausible to assume an organic link between ancient Jewish magic and Renaissance speculations regarding the emergence of the homunculus out of organic maters.

Notes

1. On this author see Allan Lazaroff, *The Theology of Abraham Bibago* (University, Alabama, 1981); Abraham Nuriel, *The Philosophy of Abraham Bibago* (Ph. D. Thesis, Hebrew University, Jerusalem, 1975). (Hebrew) These studies do not deal with the passage analyzed below.

2. *Be-'Eiruv ha-yesodot be-kamut u-va-'eikhut.* It is possible that the phrase *Be-kamut u-va-'eikhut,* betrays an influence of the formulation in *Sefer Kuzari* 4, 25 fol. 48b. See also above ch. 6, par. 4, n. 16 below.

Bibago's assumption is that the artificial creation is an endeavour to imitate nature, by attempting to find out the proper balance and proportion between the different elements which enter the composition of the anthropoid, rather than an emphasis on the knowledge of the combination of the letters, and thus imitating the divine creation of man. Compare also to the similar phrase of R. Berakhiel Qafman, a sixteenth century Italian Kabbalist, as quoted by R. Yehudah Muscato, who describes the effect of the combinations of letters as the preparation of the matters in the appropriate quantity and quality to receive the form which is emanated from the Creator. cf. *Qol Yehudah* on *Sefer Kuzari* 4, 25 fol. 48a. There is little doubt that here the naturalistic approach of Bibago was combined with the linguistic magic of *Sefer Yeẓirah*, in a way similar to Alemanno's combination to be discussed below. See also n. 79 below.

3. On the meaning of these terms and their sources see Nuriel, (n. 1 above), pp. 92–99.

4. I could not locate the precise passage of Aristotle dealing with this issue.

5. *Derekh 'Emunah* (Constantinople, 1522), fol. 11a–11b. This text influenced several authors: R. Meir ibn Gabbai, R. Joseph Shelomo of Kandia and R. Joseph Ergas. It is also possible, but this point cannot be clarified for the time being, that it influenced R. Yoḥanan Alemanno; see n. 15 below.

6. See Lazaroff (n. 1 above), p. 3. It should be noted that, although Bibago does not mention *Sefer Yeẓirah* in the context of creating an anthropoid, he nevertheless describes Abraham as acquainted with the highest form of theology, just before the aforecited passage.

7. See Idel, *Language, Torah and Hermeneutics* pp. 49–52; 174–175.

8. On this author and his relationship to magic, see Erwin I. J. Rosenthal, "Yoḥanan Alemanno and Occult Science," ed. Y. Maeyama – W. G. Saltzer, *Prismata: Naturwissenschaftsgeschichtliche Studien, Festschrift fuer Willy Hartner* (Wiesbaden, 1977), pp. 349–361; Idel, "The Magical and Neoplatonic Interpretation," and my article mentioned below n. 10.

9. See Alemanno's untitled work, Ms. Paris BN, 849, fol. 69a–70a.

10. Alemanno was deeply influenced by Ibn Ṭufail's *Ḥayy ibn Yaqṭan.* This issue deserves a special study; meanwhile, see M. Idel, "The Study Program of R. Yoḥanan Alemanno," *Tarbiẓ,* vol. 48 (1979), pp. 307, n. 36, p. 313 n. 78–79 (Hebrew). Alemanno appreciated Ibn Ṭufail to such a degree that he described the relationship between him and all the other sages as the relationship between Moses and all the other prophets. See *Ibid.,* p. 313, n. 79.

11. On this phrase see above ch. 1 beside n. 17 and below n. 28.

12. Ms. Paris BN, 849, fol. 79a.

13. This term stems from the Hebrew translation of Ibn Ṭufail's, *Ḥayy ibn Yaqṭan,* Ms. Oxford, 1337, fol. 102b.

14. *Ma'aseh bereshit.* This understanding of the Account of Creation is rare, differing from the accepted understanding of this concept as dealing with physics as conceived by Aristotle.

15. Compare below the text from *Ḥesheq Shelomo,* where the wisdom of creating an artificial anthropoid is also envisioned as a prophetic lore. Compare also above the text of R. Abraham Bibago. It is possible that Alemanno was acquainted with his work, at least from the chronological point of view, though it is also probable that they were influenced by common sources, like R. Moses Narboni's, *Commentary on ibn Ṭufail's Ḥayy ibn Yaqṭan.*

16. *Harkavat 'otam ha-shorashi(m).* For the understanding of the Account of the Chariot, which is in my opinion dealt with here, and the coalescence of the letters, see already Abraham Abulafia's view; cf. Idel, *Language, Torah and*

Hermeneutics, pp. 50–52 and the view of R. Yehudah ha-Levi mentioned ch. 6, par. 4, n. 2 above. Yehudah ha-Levi, though comparing the movement of the spheres with the combinations of letters and the preparation of the matter to receive form from God, does not mention the creation of an anthropoid.

17. On this term see Idel, *Language, Torah and Hermeneutics,* pp. 38–41.

18. Prima facie, it seems that Alemanno misquotes the names of the Amoraim involved in the act of the creation a man, according to the *TB Sanhedrin.* However, it is possible that he, or his source, interprets the Talmudic dictum that the Account of the Chariot is an exalted thing in comparison to the issues dealt with by Abaye and Rava. Alemanno probably understood the Account of the Chariot as the higher roots, in connection to which he uses the verb *rkb,* whereas the application of this lore by creating a calf is regarded by him as inferior. Such a tentative reading will detract from the importance of the practical versus theoretical knowledge. However, it may well be that the matter of the calf gave rise to a rather sarcastic attitude to this practice in comparison to the knowledge of Beẓalel, who knew the combination of letters by which the world was created.

It should be noted that, the possibility that there was in existence a source which attributed the creation of the calf to these two Amoraim and predated Alemanno's text, seems to be alluded to in a text of R. Moses ben Menaḥem Graff of Prague, a late seventeenth century Lurianic Kabbalist, who wrote:

> In those generations, when there were holy and pure men, and men of deeds [*'anshei ma'aseh*] like Abaye and Rava who made for themselves a three-year old calf each eve of Shabbat.

See *Va-Yaqhel Moshe* (Zalkow, 1741), fol. 6b. It seems improbable that the text of Alemanno was known to the Kabbalist in Prague and I assume that both used a common source which escapes me. It is possible, though this assumption does not answer the problem as a whole, that Graff was influenced by the remark of R. Naftali Bakharakh in *'Emeq ha-Melekh,* fol. 3d, 6c and 9c that these two Amoraim created a calf. In any case, I doubt whether it is reasonable to assume that Bakharakh was influenced by Alemanno.

19. Namely, Beẓalel, cf. *TB, Berakhot,* 55a. See also below in the quotation from *Ḥesheq Shelomo* where the same dictum recurs.

20. Ms. Oxford 2234, fol. 17a, on the margin of a citation from Abraham Abulafia's commentary on the *Guide of the Perplexed,* entitled *Sitrei Torah.*

21. Compare our discussion above of R. Isaac of Acre's understanding of the creation of the Golem as connected to the highest realm in the universe, *'Olam ha-'Aẓilut;* ch. 7, par. 5. Although there is only a slight chance that Alemanno could have been acquainted with the earlier Kabbalist's text, this possibility should not be completely excluded. See also below, par. 6, the text of Cornelius Agrippa of Nettesheim.

22. See above ch. 7, par. 4.

23. Ms. Oxford 2234, fol. 95b.

24. *'Olam ha-harkavah.*

25. Ms. Oxford 2234, fol. 17a.

26. Ibid., fol. 22b. For the context of this view and its possible influence on Bruno, see Idel, "The Magical and Neoplatonic Interpretations," pp. 203–204.

27. Gen. 6:4.

28. Compare this attribute of the creatures as new to the quotation from the same untitled work adduced above, n. 11, and the quotations from the *Collectanaea.* See below the discussions on Reuchlin (beside n. 65) and Abraham Yagel (below n. 86.)

29. Untitled work in Ms. Paris BN 849, fol. 25b. See also Idel, "Hermeticism and Judaism," pp. 66–67.

30. *TB, Berakhot,* fol. 55b.

31. The relationship between combinations of letters and prophecy is characteristic of the prophetic—ecstatic Kabbalah of R. Abraham Abulafia, whose influence on the views of Alemanno was mentioned already above; see n. 16–17.

32. *Peshuṭei ha-koḥot ha-ruḥaniyot.* The spiritual forces are part of those forces manipulated in the intellectual medieval magic, among Arabs and Jews; see Idel, "The Magical and Neoplatonic Interpretations," pp. 201–202.

33. This view too seems to be influenced by Abraham Abulafia's view of *Sefer Yeẓirah*, understood on its exoteric level as dealing with the creation of the world; see Idel, *Language, Torah and Hermeneutics,* p. 52.

34. *TB, Ḥagigah,* fol. 11b. The mention of the necessity to study the Account of Creation by two persons may have something to do with the fact that *Sefer Yeẓirah* was supposed to be studied by two persons, not by one alone. See above chapter 2, par. 6 and above ch. 15, n. 16.

35. Ms. Moscow-Guensburg, 140, fol. 251b. On the possible relationship between medicine and the creation of the Golem, see also below in this chapter.

36. In another important discussion, in Ms. Paris BN 849, fol. 25a, Alemanno describes the possibility that a fulfledged human being may emerge in a natural manner in certain atmospheric conditions, by the manner of *generatio aequivoca.* See below par. 3.

37. See the quotations above in n. 23 and 25.

38. See the untitled writing, Ms. Paris, BN 849, fol. 77a, 124b.

39. Ibid., fol. 17b.

40. See Idel, *Language, Torah and Hermeneutics,* p. 175.

41. See below Appendix A.

42. Abulafia's Kabbalah and these Ashkenazi traditions were almost totally unknown in Spain since the end of the thirteenth century, whereas they were well-known in Italy.

43. See Idel, "The Study Program," (n. 10 above), pp. 307–308.

44. See the passage indicated by n. 35 above.

45. On Alemanno as a physician, see Daniel Carpi, "R. Yehudah Messer Leon's Activity as a Physician," *Michael,* vol. 1 (1973), pp. 290–291, 295–296. (Hebrew) See also below n. 89.

46. See above the passage referred in n. 35.

47. See Paul Krauss, "Jabir ibn Hayyan et la science grecque," *Memoires presentées a l'Institute d'Egypte,* vol. 45 (1942), pp. 104–105, 133.

48. See "The Idea of the Golem," pp. 191–192.

49. See *Qoveẓ 'Al Yad,* vol. 1 (1885), p. 48. In the printed text, the version is Ben Sira, and not ben Sina. However, this version was conceived as incorrect already by the editor of *'Iggeret ha-Teshuvah,* ibid., p. 68 who pointed out to the correct version. (See also Scholem, "The Idea of the Golem," pp. 191–192, n. 3, who also corrects the printed name to Ben Sina, apparently unaware of the learned remark on p. 68). The editor also mentioned the fact that the phrase used to refer to the artificial man, "*Yeḥiel ben 'Uri'el,*" was coined under the influence of the Arabic *Ḥayy ibn Yaqṭan.* Since there is no reference to this work of Avicenna, or to a possible parallel by Ibn Tufail, in the thirteenth century Hebrew literature, I assume that they were coined by R. Moses Narboni, or the unknown translator of Ibn Tufail's *Ḥayy ibn Yaqtan,* which served as the text of Narboni's *Commentary.* Thus, I propose to date the composition of *'Iggeret ha-Teshuvah* to the middle of the fourteenth century. On the natural generation of man in the Arabic medieval sources, see Sami S. Hawi, *Islamic Naturalism and Mysticism* (Leiden, 1974), pp. 14, 103–120.

50. The noun used in order to point to the coalescence of the elements is derived from the root *mzg,* in two forms: *himazgut* and *hitmazgut.*

51. Compare *'Iggeret ha-Teshuvah, Ibid.,* p. 64 where the terms *shefa' 'elohi* and *devequt 'elyyon* stand for the summum bonum. See also Hawi, (n. 44 above), pp. 231–239.

52. On this author, see Paul O. Kristeller, *Studies in Renaissance Thought and Letters* (Rome, 1956), pp. 236–242; Daniel P. Walker, *Spiritual and Demonic Magic: From Ficino to Campanella* (London, 1958), pp. 64–72.

53. Lazarelli mistook a commentary on *Sefer Yeẓirah* for *Sefer Yeẓirah* it-

self. This mistake confused the scholars who attempted to locate the passage in the known versions of *Sefer Yeẓirah*. See below n. 55.

54. E. Garin, M. Brini, C. Vasoli, P. Zambelli, eds., *Testi Umanistici su l'Ermetismo* (Roma: 1955), p. 68.

> Item asserunt hebraeorum magistri, Enoch in quodam suo libro de superiori et inferiori rege mentionem fecisse, et qui ambos uniret quotidie sibi disponi laetitiam desuper. Quod nihil aliud est mea sententia quam huius archanum misterij. Haabraam quoque in libro qui Sepher Izira, id est liber formationis, appelatur, docet sic novos formari homines: adeundum videlicet esse in desertum montem ubi iumenta non depascant, e cuius medio Adamam, id est terram rubram et virgineam esse eruendam, deinceps ex ea formandum esse hominem, et per membra rite litterarum elementa fore disponenda. Quod sic mea sententia est intelligendum: monti deserta sunt divini sapienties, qui ideo deserti, nam vulgo despiciuntur, iuxta illud sapientiae: nos insensati vitam illorum extimabamus insaniam.

55. "The Image of the Golem," pp. 405-406, n. 62.

56. Walker, *Spiritual,* (n. 52 above), p. 68, See also Idel, *The Mystical Experience,* pp. 202-203 and "Hermeticism and Judaism," pp. 68-70.

57. See Scholem, *Origins of the Kabbalah,* pp. 309-364.

58. Reuchlin does not quote the long parable, discussed by Scholem, "The Idea of the Golem," p. 180. I wonder if this change is to be explained by the fact that Reuchlin himself decided to exclude the parable, or that his source has already done it. It is remarkable that in the version of the legend as quoted at the beginning of the Pseudo-Sa'adyan *Commentary on Sefer Yeẓirah*, found in manuscript, the appearance of the artificial man is described in a manner that is very similar to the discussion in Reuchlin's view. See the edition of this version by Moritz Steinschneider, "Pseudo-Saadia's Commentar zum Buche Jezira", *Magazin fuer die Wissenschaft des Judentums,* vol. 19 (1892), p. 83. See also Scholem, "The Idea of the Golem," pp. 178-179. Thus, though I considered this assumption as an improbable one, it is still possible that in Reuchlin's hands there was a version of the *Commentary on the Tetragrammaton* from the circle of the *Book of 'Iyyun,* different from the extant ones. See ch. 5, n. 85.

59. See the sources collected by François Secret, *Johann Reuchlin, La Kabbale [De Arte Cabbalistica]* (Paris, 1973), p. 289, n. 197.

60. Ch. 5, par. 10.

61. On this extant Kabbalistic work, see Scholem, *Origins of the Kabbalah,* p. 321.

62. This term was influenced by Pico della Mirandola's identical phrase; See *Opera Omnia* (Basle, 1572), pp. 108, 181. On the source of this concept of Pico,

see M. Idel, "Ramon Lull and Ecstatic Kabbalah, A Preliminary Observation," *JWCI,* vol. 51 (1988), pp. 170–174.

63. That is, R. Yehudah ben Bateirah.

64. Reuchlin's version differs substantially from the Hebrew parallel; there the *bat qol* insisted on the need to study *Sefer Yeẓirah* together with another person, and not simply to study *Sefer Yeẓirah.*

65. See above n. 11 and 28, and below n. 86.

66. *Sentiens*; nothing similar is to be found in the Hebrew sources.

67. This sentence has no parallel in Hebrew; compare the text translated after n. 84 in ch. 5.

68. *De Arte Cabalistica* (Stuttgart-Bad Cannstatt 1964), fol. 73b–74a (258–259). In the original Latin some Hebrew phrases were included and they permit a better understanding of the significance of the text. I have transliterated the pertinent Hebrew words. For the English version, see Martin and Sarah Goodman, *Johann Reuchlin, On the Art of the Kabbalah* (New York, 1983), pp. 333, 335.

69. See above ch. 5, par. 10.

70. The single significant topic which apparently has something to do with this tradition is the view that Jeremiah handed down an esoteric tradition to Plato in Egypt. See Idel, "Kabbalah and Ancient Philosophy," pp. 82–83, 104–105.

71. See especially the lengthy discussion of the nature of Kabbalah in *De Arte Cabalistica,* fol. 6b (124), "Est enim Cabala divinem revelationis, ad alutiferam dei & formarum separatarum contemplationem traditae, symbolica receptio, . . . Cabalici dicuntur." See also Ibid., fol. 7a (125).

72. Ibid., fol. 13a (139). Reuchlin's view, expressed already in his *De Verbo Mirifico,* regarding the divine name as both a means of union between man and God, and as a magical instrument, seems to reflect the influence of Abulafia. See Charles Zika, "Reuchlin's *De Verbo Mirifico* and the Magic Debate of the Late Fifteenth Century," *JWCI,* vol. 39 (1976), pp. 104–138 especially pp. 106, 111.

73. *De Occulta Philosophia* II, ch. 50; cf. F. A. Yates, *Giordano Bruno and the Hermetic Tradition* (Chicago and London, 1964), p. 136; see also Ruderman, *Kabbalah, Magic and Science* p. 209, n. 59 where he pointed out the similarity between this passage of Alemanno and the second text of his from the untitled Ms. in Paris 849.

74. Yates, ibid., p. 137, n. 6 indicates that the source of the ascension in this text is a Hermetic one; however, the reference she gave there (above pp. 24–5) does not include an explicit passage on the necessity to ascend in order to be a magician.

75. See above beside n. 35.

76. See Secret (n. 59 above), p. 289, n. 197.

77. Mantua, 1562.

78. See however, the material quoted by R. Abraham Galante discussed above ch. 5, par. 11.

79. See his *Commentary on Kuzari* 4, 25 (Warshau, 1880), fol. 47d–48a. See also n. 2 above.

80. See e.g. the discussion of R. Joseph del Medigo in his *Mazref le-Ḥokhmah,* fol. 25a, where he quotes both the Commentary attributed to the Rabad and the Pseudo-Sa'adyan one. On the context of these quotations, see below ch. 15, par. 2. See also R. Jacob Barukh's gloss to Alemanno's *Sha'ar ha-Ḥesheq,* fol. 31ab.

81. On this author see Ruderman, *Kabbalah, Magic and Science.*

82. See above par. 3 on the relation between creation of an anthropoid and natural science in Yoḥanan Alemanno.

83. See Ruderman, *Kabbalah, Magic and Science,* p. 113.

84. See above par. 6 and Ruderman, ibid., p. 113.

85. Ruderman, ibid., pp. 113–114.

86. On the new creatures, see n. 11, 28 and 65 above.

87. Ms. Oxford 1304, fol. 243b–244a, following the translation of Ruderman, *Kabbalah, Magic and Science,* p. 112.

88. Compare, e.g., Yagel, *Beit Ya'ar ha-Levanon,* Ms. Oxford 1303, fol. 41a refers to *Sefer Petaḥ Tiqvah,* the name which appears on the first page of Alemanno's untitled writing.

89. *Bat Sheva'* Ms. Oxford 1306, fol. 85b. Compare also to the emphatical tone of Yagel in another passage where he defends the conception of *Sefer Yeẓirah* as including natural lore rather than a demonic one, as maintained by some masters; see *Beit Ya'ar ha-Levanon,* Ms. Oxford 1303, fol. 45a, and the discussion of Ruderman, *Kabbalah, Magic and Science,* pp. 114–117.

In this context it is important to mention the view of Yagel that the natural magus, namely, someone wise in the science of nature, is also a doctor. See Ruderman, Ibid., pp. 110 and 120. It seems that one of the sources of this view is Marsilio Ficino; see Yates, *Giordano Bruno,* pp. 150–151 and Pagel, *Paracelsus,* p. 218.

90. Ms. Oxford 1301, fol. 47a.

91. On this issue, see Yates, *Giordano Bruno* pp. 96–99, (n. 73 above), and Idel, "Ramon Lull" (n. 62 above), pp. 170–174 and Zika, "Reuchlin's" (n. 72 above), p. 125.

92. Ms. Oxford, 1303, fol. 47b.

93. Part III, ch. 67, ed., Jerusalem, 1973, fol. 110a. Strangely enough, this important passage escaped the attention of the scholars dealing with the Golem. See Roland Goetschel, *Meir Ibn Gabbai, Le discours de la Kabbale Espagnole* (Leuven, 1981), p. 95. For another discussion of the *Sanhedrin* passage see Ibid., fol. 47a, discussed above ch. 9.

94. A similar view was expressed by R. Jacob Emden in his *Miṭpaḥat Sefarim* (Lvov, 1871), p. 69:

> The natural science of the gentiles [*'anshei ha-'olam*] is a coarse and thick garment to the account of the creation [*ma'aseh Bereshit*] that is the hidden fruit and the very essence of its issue. The natural science of the philosophers deal with the external shells that are thrown away, [because] they are not pleasant to be eaten by the intelligent [persons]. Since they [the philosophers] do perceive only the accidents. . . . But God posited the true divine wisdom, which deals only with the inner part and the essence, and this is the reason why it is called the practical [wisdom], because in its power is [the power] to innovate new creatures in actu . . . like Rava who created a man, and R. Ḥ[ananiyah] and R. O[shayah] who created for themselves a three-year old calf and ate it, and the least of them is able to resurrect the dead, in addition to all the other miracles they performed.

See also Emden's *Birat Migdal 'Oz* (Jitomir, 1874), fol. 25ab.

95. See below ch. 15, par. 2.

96. Chapter 7, fol. 24b–25b.

97. Ibid., fol. 24ab.

98. *Shomer 'Emunim,* (Jerusalem, 1965), p. 9.

99. See Idel, "The Magical and Neoplatonic Interpretation" and "Major Currents in Italian Kabbalah between 1560–1660," in *Italia Judaica* (Roma, 1986), pp. 243–262; idem, "Differing Conceptions of Kabbalah in the Early 17th Century" eds. I. Twersky and B. D. Septimus, *Jewish Thought in the Seventeenth Century,* (Cambridge, Mass. 1987), pp. 155–200.

100. See also M. Idel, "Universalism and Particularism in Kabbalah: 1480–1650" (forthcoming); idem, "Jewish Magic from the Renaissance Period to Early Hasidism", in *Religion, Science and Magic,* eds. J. Neusner, P. Flecher, E. Frerichs (New York, Oxford University Press, 1989), pp. 82–117.

101. See *Hermeticism and the Scientific Revolution,* papers by R. S. Westman and J. E. McGuire (Los Angeles, 1977); Brian Vickers, ed., *Occult & Scientific Mentalities in the Renaissance* (Cambridge U. P. 1986) and Charles Schmitt, "Reappraisals in Renaissance Science", *History of Science,* vol. 16 (1978), pp. 200–214.

102. See Scholem, "The Idea of the Golem" p. 197; W. A. Schulze, "Der Einfluss die Kabbala auf die Cambridger Platoniker Cudworth und More" *Judaica,*

vol. 23 (1967), p. 88: "Der Homunculus des Paracelsus ist eine Variante dieses Golem"; Pagel, *Paracelsus,* p. 215: "It is a Jewish-Gnostic idea that seems to have inspired Paracelsus' speculations on the 'Homunculus'—the idea of the 'Golem'".

103. Pagel, *Paracelsus,* p. 117. See also Scholem, "The Idea of the Golem," p. 197 where he pointed out the difference between the homunculus and the Golem in this matter.

104. Scholem, "The Idea of the Golem," p. 197, where he refers to R. Nissim Gerondi's *Ḥiddushim* to *Sanhedrin,* fol. 65d as if the text deals with the creation of an anthropoid in a retort. However, the reference is mistaken and the correct folio is 67b where no anthropoid is mentioned. Scholem was apparently aware of this mistake as his more cautious formulation in the Hebrew version of the article evinces; see "The Image of the Golem," pp. 417–418. There, Scholem indicates fol. 67b as the place of R. Nissim's discussion. However, he did not change his mind as to the possibility of understanding the text as related to the creation in a retort. However, a perusal of the context demonstrates that the term *keli,* understood by Scholem as retort, means simply instrument, particularly a tool used in a magic operation. This is the meaning of the term in the Talmudic discussion and also in the text of R. Nissim Gerondi. Thus, the whole theory regarding the use of the retort is based on an interpretation that has no support. Compare R. Nissim's explanation there to the responsum attributed to Naḥmanides, n. 283, quoted also by R. Shelomo ibn Adret in his responsum, vol. II n. 413, which is a possible source for R. Nissim's tradition. For the hypothesis that Alemanno could, in principle, have proposed the use of the alembicum in connection to the creation of the Golem, see our discussion above.

105. *Paracelsus,* p. 216, n. 52. The evidence adduced by Pagel in his paragraph on the influence of Kabbalah on Paracelsus, pp. 213–217, may reflect a vague knowledge of Kabbalah by Paracelsus, but there is not even one solid evidence with respect to his acquaintance with the Golem devices.

12

R. Moses ben Jacob Cordovero's View

I

If the position of R. Isaac of Acre is the most radical view among the Kabbalists concerning the possibility of creating a perfect artificial man,[1] the opposite extreme is that of the Safedian Kabbalist, R. Moses Cordovero. For him, it is impossible to draw down even the lower soul, called *nefesh, a fortiori* the spirit and the high soul.[2] Therefore, he had to account for those features of Rava's creature that went beyond the normal, i.e., the very fact that the artificial man was able to walk. Since Cordovero believed that the Talmudic master could not provide even the lowest faculty, what element in the constitution of that man insured his commutation? This quandary of Cordovero was understood by Scholem as follows: since no spiritual powers came from above, there are tellurian forces, inherent in the elements that constitute the man, which are able to put in motion this aggregatum. Apud Scholem, Cordovero's theory implies "a truly tellurian creature" which "remains within the realm of elemental forces". As such, Scholem argues, this conception of the Golem could pave:

> the way for, or run parallel to, the development in which, reverting from the purely mystical realm to that of Kabbalistic legend, the

golem once again becomes the repository of enormous tellurian forces which can, on occasion erupt.[3]

The most important implication of this observation is that Cordovero's theory could explicate the later development of the Golem-legend, including the uncontrolled growth of the creature that will ultimately compel the creator to annihilate it. If Scholem's interpretation of Cordovero is correct, then the discussion of this Kabbalist would represent a crucial stage in the crystallization of the later conception of the Golem. In principle, Scholem could be right; Cordovero's *Pardes Rimmonim* was a highly influential compendium of Kabbalah, widespread all over Europe. De facto, however, the situation seems to be much more complicated. A perusal of Cordovero's passage dealing with the *Sanhedrin* statement, as well as other Cordoverian texts, will demonstrate that his theory differs substantially from the description proposed by Scholem. Let us, therefore, analyze anew Cordovero's original contribution to the concept of the Golem.

The basic assumption of Cordovero is that upon everything in this lower world a certain "spirituality and vitality", *ruḥaniyut* and *ḥiyyut,* dwells, in accordance with the distance of the respective entity from the source of spirituality and vitality. There is, accordingly, a hierarchy of beings, each one reflecting the "quantity of the light of the supernal vitality which emanates upon it."[4] Consequently, the active powers in the material world are not tellurian, i.e., forces that reside uniquely in the elementary world and crystallize with the structuring of the matter in a peculiar way; on the contrary, these powers are reflections of the supernal light that is continuously captured in this lower realm. Such a view, which contradicts Scholem's concept of tellurism, is part of a larger concept of Cordovero which was summarized in the statement of one of his followers, R. Abraham Azulai: "There is no vitality to a lower being but [what stems] from the supernal influx."[5]

The terrestrial elements can be combined in various forms, each of the forms being also part of a great chain of being.[6] According to Cordovero, no being, with the exception of man, possesses supernal crystallized powers, similar to the human soul, spirit or higher soul. Only these crystallizations of the divine emanation can confer to a certain material composition the status of man. In distinction from the light of vitality, which is reflected upon entities all over the universe, the spiritual faculties of man originate from specific *sefirot,* and function in very specific ways. They are additions to the diffused light mentioned above. In Cordovero's opinion, even the motion of the animals is not the result of the existence of a lower, animal soul, but of the reflection of divine light in accordance with the degree of the structure of a given piece of matter.[7] The more complex the structure of a certain being is, the more elevated it is on the chain of being and closer to the source of the light; consequently, more light will be reflected on this being. Therefore, a certain structuring of matter also elevates the elements entering in this structure to a higher status, closer to the *sefirotic* sources. I should like to stress that this comprehensive reflection is to be understood in sharp distinction from the substantial descent of articulated spiritual nuclei which enter or are immersed in man.[8] The artificially created man will, therefore, reflect more light, i.e., he will be able to collect more energy from the upper world, and therefore will be able to surpass the performance of animals. The vitality reflected upon an anthropoid will be greater than that dwelling upon an animal since the human structure is closer to the supernal source, an assumption easily understandable for a Kabbalist who envisions the *sefirotic* realm as symbolized by the human shape.[9]

Let me address another discussion of the creation of the anthropoid in Cordovero: at the end of his *Commentary on Sefer Yeẓirah*, we learn that Abraham

> . . . combined [letters] . . . in order to create a certain being, and he formed, as in the case of Rava who created a man [as reported] in *Sanhedrin,* and he was successful and he actualized the science of formation [*ḥokhmat ha-yeẓirah*] because by this [operation] the issue of formation was proven to him, and the transformation of nature [*hippukh ha-ṭeva'*], which contradicts the opinion of [philosophic] speculation . . . and the Lord revealed to him etc. . . . then, when he was convinced and he became stable in [his] belief in true belief . . . the Lord was revealed to him by the way of prophecy.[10]

The creation of man by means of the permutations of letters in *Sefer Yeẓirah* is limited, according to Cordovero, to the formation of a material body; this act cannot induce the spiritual forces into this being. As he formulates it elsewhere, the drawing down of the spirituality by means of the letters is the secret of prophecy.[11] Otherwise, as Cordovero argues in *Pardes Rimmonim,*[12] what would be the difference or the superiority of a being created by God, in comparison to that created by man? The Kabbalist compares the human shape to that of the ten *sefirot,* and asserts that speech and intelligence reflect the *'eyn sof,* the highest divine level. This is the reason, continues Cordovero, why the sages were capable of creating the body of the artificial man but not his spiritual capacities.[13] The emphasis in Cordovero's explanation is on the technical achievement of the scholar studying in the *Sefer Yeẓirah,* but not on the spiritual attainment that must precede the act of creation, as R. Nathan, the commentator on the *Bahir* and the Maharal conceived the perfect creation of man.[14] I assume that Cordovero focuses on the formal, or structural, similarity between the artificial man and the structure of the *sefirot,* much more than on the affinity between their spiritual components. For him, the prophetic experience of Abraham was not an integral part of the creation of a creature, as it was in the case of Abulafia, but an event that follows the establishment of the correct beliefs, which Abraham achieved by the experience of creating a creature. In contrast to the statement of R. Isaac of Acre that Jeremiah and Ben Sira were able to cause the descent of the intellectual soul, Cordovero vehemently protests against this demiurgic claim indicating that it is a bizarre view. This reduction of the creation of an artificial man to a merely technical achievement may be one of the reasons for the relative decline of interest in this subject in post-Cordoverian Jewish mysticism. According to the views of Cordovero, this creature was considered no more than an animal in the form of man which can be killed as an animal is, since it possesses no spiritual faculty.[15] In his discussions of the artificial creation Cordovero does not enter into the details of the differences between the human structure as it was formed according to the natural course and the artificial anthropoid: why does the same external form become ensouled in one case and not in the other? Some possible answers can be found in an elaboration on the discussion of Cordovero by R. Samuel Gallico in his compendium of *Pardes Rimmonim,* named *'Asis Rimmonim.*[16] The following explanation of Gallico seems to stem from the writings of Cordovero himself, as I found a similar passage in Azulai's *Ḥesed le-Avraham,* and it is reasonable to assume that, notwithstanding the fact that Azulai's work was composed later on, the two authors drew upon a common source.[17] Gallico implies that there are two main reasons for the difference: in the case of the natural man, the four elements were previously refined and organized in the human image, apparently in contrast to the preponderance of the element of dust in the case of the artificial man. The second reason, and the more important one, seems to be the view, that the perfect human image itself is able to draw down, talismatically, the spiritual forces which are the soul and spirit of man. In addition to these reasons we may assume that the basic approach of Cordovero is that the sublime status of the theories concerning the combinations of letters will be revealed in its entirety only after the resurrection of the dead. Thus, given the relative ignorance of this sublime topic[18], we may assume that it is impossible to create a perfect Golem.

II

Cordovero's view was copied in, and thereby disseminated by, a widespread treatise, *Ḥesed le-Avraham* of R. Abraham Azulai (c. 1570–1643)[19]. It became part of most of the later discussions of the nature of the Golem because of the acceptance of Azulai's view in writings of both Ashkenazi and Sefardi authors dealing with the Golem. As we shall see below, it was quoted by R. Jacob Emden as part of his attempt to establish the pure animality of the Golem.[20] On the Sefardi side, it was repeatedly cited by the famous descendant of R. Abraham, R. Ḥayyim Yoseph David Azulai, known as the Ḥ.Y.D.A.' (1724–1806). His encyclopedic interests and literary creation contributed greatly to the reverberation of the views of Cordovero in broader circles, especially because he treated these issues in a variety of works of different literary genres: the *Commentary on the Pentateuch,*[21] as well as bibliographical[22] encyclopedical[23] and Halakhical writings.[24] In most of these discussions he quotes his ancestor's *Ḥesed le-Avraham.* Let me attempt to extract what seems to be the more original aspects of the discussions of Ḥ.Y.D.A.' In his *Ẓavarei Shalal,* as he will rather strangely argue in a later text,[25] he was not yet aware of the passage dealing with the Golem in *Ḥesed le-Avraham.*[26] Nevertheless, his main point there does not basically differ from the theory of Cordovero: Ḥ.Y.D.A.' indicates that he reports the views of some ancient authorities, with some additions of his own, and he presents two stages in the creative process connected to the emergence of man: the material and the spiritual. The first one can be accomplished by means of the combination of letters as described in *Sefer Yeẓirah.* Thus only the "first formation," *ha-yeẓirah harishonah,* is in the reach of the righteous, whereas the spiritual one is beyond the capacity of human activity. The clear-cut distinction between the two types of creation is intended to distinguish between the human creator, the righteous, and the divine one, God. God alone is able to perform the two stages of creation. Azulai starts his discussion by attempting to explain the meaning of the biblical verse, "To whom then will you liken me, that I should be his equal, says the Holy One" (Isa. 40:25). Conspicuously, the main concern of the author is theological, i.e., he is interested in emphasizing the gap between the divine and human acts by pointing out the limitation of the human creation, which can reach only the first stage of the process. This conclusion is derived from the above verse by a hermeneutical device. The phrase, "says the Holy One" is, in the biblical context, conceived as related to the sentence stated earlier by God. However, according to Ḥ.Y.D.A.', the Hebrew phrase, *yomar qadosh,* is the sequel of the preceding sentence, its meaning being, "who will say, *qadosh*".[27] This change transforms the indicative form into an interrogative one, in the vein of the previous sentences. The underlying assumption of Ḥ.Y.D.A.' is that just as it is impossible to find a being who will equal God, so even in the case of man's creating an anthropoid, that anthropoid will not be able to say, "*qadosh,*" i.e., it cannot speak; This is the classical Golem. In other words even if it is possible to compare the divine and human creations up to a certain point, the second stage of creating a speaking being is not the prerogative of the righteous. This interpretation is immediately translated into legalistic terms; the inability of the creature to pronounce the term *qadosh* disqualifies it from participating in a liturgical performance, where the recitation of *qadosh* is required, namely in the prayer of the eighteen benedictions, which requires the presence of ten Jews. Thus, the creature was not conceived as a fulfledged man and, consequently, it cannot participate in a Jewish ritual.[28]

What is characteristic in most of Ḥ.Y.D.A.'s discussions is the combination of the tradition of the Azulai family, which stems from Cordovero, with the tradition of the descendants of the family of R. Eliyahu of Helm, the master of the name. The two traditions share a common assumption, which will shape most of the subsequent treatments: the Golem is a completely nonhuman being and has no Halakhic status as a man who may participate, in any manner, in the Jewish rituals which require the presence of a quorum of ten mature Jews.[29] The Azulai family followed the assumption of Cordovero that the Golem is no more than an automaton; the tradition of the family of R. Eliyahu had to account for the annihilation of the Golem by their ancestor after it became dangerous. In the latter case, the attitude is more nuanced, a fact that concerned Ḥ.Y.D.A.' for he could not understand how can a first-class Halakhist, like he-Ḥakham Ẓevi, hesitated with regard to the status of a being that is no more than an animal, in relation to the quorum.

Let me return to the basic concepts which govern the previous discussions, and others influenced by them; the Golem possesses a certain amount of vitality, *ḥiyyut,* which is the source of its acts. This vitality does not stem from the earth of dust which constitute the body of the Golem, as Scholem implied, but the supernal light. The focus on the *ḥiyyut,* so conspicuous in Cordovero and his followers, can explain the later view on the growth of the Golem. Precisely because of the rejection of any possible spiritual aspect of the Golem, the uncontrolled growth came to the fore, as the processes of growth are connected to the concept of *ḥiyyut.*[30]

Notes

1. See ch. 7, par 5.
2. *Pardes Rimmonim* I, fol. 50b–c, Gate 24, ch. 10.

3. "The Idea of the Golem", p. 195. See also idem, *Kabbalah,* p. 353.

4. *Pardes Rimmonim,* Gate 24, ch. 10. See also Joseph Ben-Shlomo, *The Mystical Theology of Moses Cordovero* (Jerusalem, 1965), pp. 288–289. (Hebrew)

5. See *'Or ha-Ḥamah* vol. 1, fol. 63d. Compare Cordovero's own statement in *Pardes Rimmonim,* Ibid., fol. 50c; "there is no thing in this world concerning which an emanation is not emanated upon it from above". See also above ch. 9, n. 23.

6. On the great chain of being in some Jewish sources, see David Blumenthal, "Lovejoy's Great Chain of Being and the Medieval Jewish Tradition," eds. P. & M. Kuntz, *Jacob's Ladder and the Tree of Life* (New York, 1986), pp. 179–190.

7. See Cordovero, *Pardes Rimmonim,* fol. 50c, where he writes that even the elements are graded in accordance to the "light of the supernal vitality which descends upon them."

8. See our discussion below in Appendix A of the *ẓelem,* the lowest spiritual faculty, as it is found in Cordovero.

9. It should be mentioned that Cordovero accepts the view that man is created by the twenty-two letters and the 231 combinations, and can be destroyed by the inverse combinations, without however specifying if this is connected to the artificial man. See the quotation in the name of Cordovero in Azulai's *'Or ha-Ḥamah* I, fol. 62c. On the drawing down of the spirituality on the embryo by his father at the moment of the inception, see *Pardes Rimmonim,* 20:1 fol. 89c.

10. Ms. Jerusalem, National and University Library, 8° 2646, fol. 42a and ibid., 4° 10, fol. 45a.

11. Ms. Jerusalem, 4° 10, fol. 40b. This view ostensibly reflects the similar concept of Abraham Abulafia. The descent of the letters from the intellectual level to the spiritual, namely astral, level and from there to the terrestrial level is the blueprint of the emanation, and the letters permit us to understand how from a simple light a plurality of lights emerges. In this context he mentions the possibility that man will be created from dust, in opposition to the views of those who believe that man can be created only out of man; then, he refers to the passage in *Sanhedrin.* It should be mentioned that, according to Cordovero, it is the secret of the vowels which may insure the perfect creation, because they alone point to the supernal sources from which the influx descends upon the creature that someone wants to create. See *Commentary on Sefer Yeẓirah*, Ms. Jerusalem, 8° 2646, fol. 11b. The source of this view is the *Zohar,* I, fol. 15b; see also Wolfson, "The Anthropomorphic Image," n. 125.

12. *Pardes Rimmonim,* Ibid., fol. 50c.

13. Ibid., Part 21:ch. 2, fol. 98a. Compare to our discussion in chapter 10 par. 4.

14. See above ch. 7, par. 4.

15. *Pardes Rimmonim,* fol. 50c.

16. *'Asis Rimmonim,* fol. 63b.

17. See *Ḥesed le-Avraham,* (Lvov, 1863), fol. 26b.

18. See the text from *Pardes Rimmonim* analyzed in Idel, *Studies in Ecstatic Kabbalah,* pp. 139–140.

19. *Ḥesed le-Avraham,* fol. 26ab. See also the important discussion on the Golem in Azulai's, *Commentary on the Zohar, 'Or ha-Ḥamah,* analyzed above ch. 5, par. 11.

20. See below ch. 13.

21. See *Ẓavarei Shalal,* printed together with *Penei David* (Jerusalem, 1965), fols. 120d–121b.

22. *Shem ha-Gedolim,* see below ch. 17, n. 1, and 24.

23. See n. 25 below.

24. See *Birkhei Yoseph,* on *Shulḥan 'Arukh, 'Oraḥ Ḥayyim,* par. 55, and his *Novellae, Mar'it 'Ayin* (Jerusalem, 1960), fol. 77b.

25. See *Medabber Qedemot* letter Y, par. 27.

26. Nevertheless he quoted *Ḥesed le-Avraham* in *Ẓavarei Shalal* on the same page!

27. This interpretation of this verse occurs in an identical context in R. Jacob Barukh's additions to Yoḥanan Alemanno's *Sha'ar ha-Ḥesheq,* fol. 31b.

28. *Ẓavarei Shalal,* fols. 120d–121b.

29. See ch. 13 below.

30. See below ch. 13 and Appendix C.

PART FOUR

Early-Modern and Modern Reverberations

13

R. Eliyahu, the Master of the Name, of Helm

The earliest known legend of the creation of a Golem by an historical figure living during the second part of the sixteenth century, stems from Christian sources, as late as 1674. Their authors, Johann Wuelfer and Christoph Arnold reported the story as a tradition connected to the Rabbi of Helm, R. Eliyahu Ba'al Shem.[1] This tradition, in one form or another, is the blueprint of the later legend of the creation of the Golem by R. Eliyahu's famous contemporary, R. Yehudah Loew of Prague.[2] This story can, however, be predated by approximately two generations, on the basis of a manuscript report of the legend whose hero is R. Eliyahu of Helm, a fact which apparently has escaped the scrutiny of scholars. Let me first translate the manuscript version and then deal with some details of its content:

> It is known that whoever is an expert in *Sefer Yezirah*, is able to perform operations by the holy names, and out of the elements, dust of a virgin soil and water, a matter [Go{lem}] and form will emerge, which has a vitality;[3] even so it is called dead [met], since he cannot confer upon it knowledge . . . and speech, since knowledge and speech are [the prerogative of] the Life of the Worlds.[4] The Holy,

> Blessed be He, has sealed man, [by the sign of] *'emet* [truth], which is alluded to in the verse,[5] "And He breathed into his nostrils the breath of life," the end letters of these words being *ḥotam* [seal][6] since man was the seal of the formation in the Account of Creation, and His seal is the creation of man. And this is said in the verse "God has created and performed". . .[7] And we have found in the Gemara . . .[8] And I have heard, in a certain and explicit way, from several respectable persons that one man, [living] close to our time, in the holy community of Helm, whose name is R. Eliyahu, the master of the name, who made a creature out of matter [*Golem*] and form [*ẓurah*] and it performed hard work for him, for a long period, and the name of *'emet* was hanging upon his neck, until he finally removed for a certain reason, the name from his neck and it turned to dust.[9]

The person who related this story was a Polish Kabbalist writing, I assume, on the basis of the analysis of the material included in his voluminous work, between the thirties and fifties of the seventeenth century.[10] This evaluation is corroborated by the sentence included in the above passage, that R. Eliyahu flourished close to his period, and indeed this Rabbi passed away in 1583. Thus, even if we date the composition of the Kabbalistic work quoted above to the fifties, it is the earliest evidence for the legend of the Golem as a famulus in Central Europe. Moreover, according to this Kabbalist, the legend was known to several persons, thus allowing us to speculate that the legend indeed circulated for some time before it was submitted to writing and, consequently, we may assume that its origins are to be traced to the generation immediately following the death of R. Eliyahu, if not earlier. The present version includes some crucial parallels to the story told by the Christian and Jewish sources one or two generations later, though some colorful details are still missing here.

Let us elaborate upon the above quotation. The Kabbalist seems to be the only source that relates the legend in the continuation of the *Sanhedrin* passage and the Ashkenazi Ḥasidic recipe for creating an artificial man.[11] Therefore we can witness a continuum of stories from the Talmud, through the Middle Ages and into the seventeenth century. With the exception of the first source, all the others stem from Ashkenazi sources. The Kabbalist is completely convinced that the whole magical operation is possible, including the legend he reports concerning R. Eliyahu. Interestingly, he uses the term Golem not, however, as the designation of the creature, but rather in line with standard medieval terminology—as an equivalent for matter. This is obvious here, as well as in some other instances in the book.[12] Therefore, we learn that the term Golem was, apparently, not so widespread among the Polish Jews as we are told by the sources in the second part of the seventeenth century. However, in line with the evidence of the Christian sources, it seems that the legend was indeed well-known in the middle of the seventeenth century though it may be that this Rabbi was not the single hero of the Golem creation.[13]

Apart from these influences, the usage of the term *ḥiyyut,* vitality, together with the emphasis on the conception of the creature as dead, seem to reflect the influence of the Cordoverian view of the nature of the creature as totally nonhuman.[14] The dangers related in the later version of this Golem story and R. Eliyahu, did not appear at least not in explicit manner, in this version; the Rabbi took away the name *'emet,* without indicating the precise reason for this act. It should be noted that according to this version, this being was considered as a dead thing from the very beginning, an issue that seems to have a certain relationship to the fact that its creator undid it, for a mysterious reason. This point, connected to the annihilation of an human-like being, was elaborated upon in the writings of the descendants of R. Eliyahu, as we shall see it below.

"Tellurian" powers of the creature are not mentioned at this early stage of the development of the legend, nor is the magician explicitly described as being worried on account of his creature. If the extant sources are indeed representative of the earliest historical development of the legend, then it seems evident that the dramatization of the legend is to be dated not earlier than the middle of the seventeenth century or even slightly later. Interestingly enough, the letters *'emet* are neither written on the forehead, nor on a parchment attached to his forehead:[15] It seems to be an amulet hanging on the neck.

Let us inspect now the details of the same legend as it was transmitted by the descendants of R. Eliyahu. The descendant of this Rabbi, R. Ẓevi Ashkenazi, better known as he-Ḥakham Ẓevi, himself a famous figure, indicates that R. Eliyahu created a Golem, without supplying details. From the formulation of the sentence it is obvious that he was acquainted with this tradition from persons who were not part of his family, but, rather it is something he heard from other sources.[16] However, it seems that he-Ḥakham Ẓevi transmitted some details to his son, R: Jacob Emden, an even more famous Rabbi, who writes in his autobiography that his father told him that the creature created by R. Eliyahu:

> was without speech, and he was serving him as a servant. And when the Rabbi saw that the creature of his hands[17] grew stronger and greater, because of the divine name written on a paper stuck to his forehead, R. Eliyahu, the master of the name, was afraid that he would be harmful and destructive. He quickly overcame him and he

> tore the folio on which the name was written and separated it from the forehead, and he fell as a lump of dust, as he was [in the beginning], but he harmed his master scratching him when he took up the writing [*ha-ketav*] and separated the name from him.[18]

Some of these details occur also in a *Responsum* of Emden, to be discussed later on, where the formulation is even more dramatic; the Rabbi was afraid that the ever-growing Golem would destroy the world.[19] This reference to the cosmic danger involved in the uncontrolled expansion of the creature is to be compared to a similar situation connected, according to the Midrash, to the expansion of the world at the moment of its creation. This expansion was stopped by God, according to some sources, by the use of the divine name or by the pronunciation of the word *dai*, which was understood as the etymology of the divine name *Shaddai*, interpreted as the divine power who said to the world *dai*.[20] In these two cases the creator enters into a quandary because his creation is growing in such a way that he cannot control the process any more, and he is thus compelled to stop this process. In both cases the divine name is involved, though in different ways. The motif of the uncontrolled expansion apparently points also to a possible influence of the motif of the "Sorcerer's apprentice" which was added to the Midrashic view on the expansion of the universe.[21] It is also possible, as Scholem has already noted, that the growth of the Golem is somehow connected to a process that is the inverted event of Adam, who was primarily a gigantic being reduced by God to his present stature.[22] However, this possible interpretation does not account for the dangerous factor in the story.

The fact that the sixteenth century Kabbalist was conceived as a creator of a Golem, and especially its annihilator had, I assume, an important impact on the attitude of his offspring toward the nature of the Golem. It is possible that the traditions that their ancestor had annihilated the creature was apparently influential on their decisions concerning the non-human status of this being, an attitude already formulated by some earlier Kabbalists, but not formulated by Halakhists and not so prominent among the Ashkenazi authors. As we shall see below, from the point of view of the Halakhah, it was also possible to reach different conclusions than those of the two Halakhists,[23] who seem to have been conditioned by family traditions.[24]

One last observation on the implicit importance of the mid-eighteenth century text dealing with the Golem of R. Eliyahu. If the two members of the family of R. Eliyahu were preoccupied by the concept of the Golem as a legal issue and referred to the "actual" creation of their ancestor alone, there was no reason to neglect other traditions regarding the creation of the Golem by important figures in Jewish life. The fact that a Golem created by the Maharal was not mentioned by R. Jacob Emden, and even not later on by Ḥ.Y.D.A' is indirect evidence for the absence of traditions on the Golem of the Maharal. Therefore, the most famous version of the creation of the Golem is the product of the early nineteenth century at the earliest.

Notes

1. See Scholem, "The Idea of the Golem", pp. 200–203. On this figure as a magician see R. Ḥayyim Joseph David Azulai's, *Shem ha-Gedolim,* letter A, n. 163, and n. 24 below.

2. Scholem, ibid., pp. 202–203.

3. See above ch. 13.

4. See above ch. 5, par. 8, n. 58.

5. Gen. 2:7.

6. See ch. 5, par. 9, n. 66.

7. Gen. 2:3.

8. The author quotes here the passage from *TB, Sanhedrin,* fol. 65b.

9. Ms. Oxford 1309, fols. 90b–91a.

10. I hope to devote a separate study on this voluminous treatise, totally ignored by modern scholarship.

11. See above ch. 5, par. 9, n. 68.

12. See e.g. Ms. Oxford 1309, fol. 67a: "He forms light and creates darkness, light by the form (*ba-ẓurah*) and darkness by the matter (*ba-golem*)."

13. See Scholem, "The Image of the Golem", pp. 419–420.

14. See idem, "The Idea of the Golem", p. 196.

15. According to an addition on the margin of the folio translated above, added by the author himself beside the discussion of the name hanging on the neck: "There are persons who said that it (*'emet*) was written on his forehead and at the end he (R. Eliyahu) erased *'A(leph)* from his forehead and there remained met". Therefore, later on, another tradition came to the attention of the author, which is similar to the later version of the legend on R. Eliyahu.

16. *Responsa,* (Fuerst, 1767), vol. I, fol. 39b, n. 93. On this text see also ch. 14 below and n. 23 here.

17. This phrase is reminiscent of the Midrashic description of Adam as the creature of God's hands; see *Pesiqta Rabbati* (Wien, 1880), fol. 190a and ch. 14, n. 26. See also ch. 2, n. 11.

18. See *Megillat Sefer,* ed. D. Kahana (Warsau, 1897), p. 4. See Scholem "The Idea of the Golem," p. 201.

19. *She'elot Ya'aveẓ* (Lemberg, 1884), part 2, fol. 28a, n. 82.

20. On this mythologumenon see the Talmudic discussion in *TB, Ḥagigah,* fol. 12a. See also above ch. 10, par. 3.

21. Scholem, "The Idea of the Golem," p. 202, n. 1.

22. Ibid., p. 202. Scholem emphasized the role of the tellurian powers that are awakened by the "earth magic". However, it is not clear how these powers were stirred while the divine name was checking them, and disappear precisely when it is removed from the Golem. I assume that the expansion is connected to the divine name, or alternatively to the word *'emet.* See below Appendix C.

23. See below ch. 14, pars 7–9. See also our discussions of R. Ẓadoq ha-Kohen and R. Gershom Leiner.

24. See also the evidence of Azulai in his *Shem ha-Gedolim* A, 163, who quotes the son of R. Ephraim Katz, a seventeenth century descendant of R. Eliyahu of Helm, and an ancestor of R. Ẓevi Ashkenazi, who related traditions on the master of the name.

14

Golem in the Halakhah

I

Halakhah is a legal system that intends to clarify the minutiae of the behaviour of the Jews, as they were disclosed in general lines in the earlier strata of Judaism: Bible and Mishnah.[1] Though dealing with details related to real entities and events, Halakhah does not totally refrain from addressing situations that are hypothetical; these types of events, however, only rarely include, to the extent that I am acquainted with this type of literature, categories and entities conceived of as inexistent or phantastic.[2] Exceptions are dealt with, as in the case of the androgyne or of the *'Adnei ha-Sadeh,* the latter to be mentioned below, but even they are still considered to be real entities. In the following pages we shall analyze a series of discussions which, in my view, are rare from the Halakhic point of view, as they have as a major subject an entity that was believed to have been real, though it was not encountered by any of the authors dealing with this subject. The Golem is a sui generis category, which provoked different reactions from the various Halakhists, though none of them ever explicitly questioned the reality of this subject. This fact is worthy of a more elaborate reflection. It seems that in this case, Jewish mysticism was able to introduce an issue that, originally, had no immediate Halakhic implications, but subsequently assumed such, and provoked a series of new discussions in the Halakhic literature. For those Halakhic authors who were not interested in mysticism, or even opposed it, like Maimonides, the status of the artificially created anthropoid is not discussed at all or it was reduced to the status of an illusion.[3] Being merely an illusion, there is no need to account for its Halakhic status; thus the Golem did not enter the halakhic categories of rationalistic authors.

The existence of the ambiguous category of the Golem as a fact in the classical and medieval Jewish bodies of literature, enabled some Jewish authors to apply this category in order to solve some legalistic quandaries. As we shall see below, in the seventeenth century R. Isaiah Horwitz made use of a view on the female-Golem in order to explain how to "properly" understand a difficult biblical passage. The new category of a man, or woman, who nevertheless is not a human being, allowed solutions that were otherwise impossible.[4] The fact that the Golem was considered to be a mixed entity enriched Jewish thought and permitted a more subtle definition of the significance of the human phenomenon. The existence of an entity externally similar to man, enabled a deepening of the discussions on the essence of human activity, mostly from the Halakhic point of view. Let me now survey some other discussions, found in later sources, where the emergence of the new category of the nonhuman anthropoid, allowed smoother solutions to legal questions.

It should be remarked from the very beginning that most of the following authors were not only Halakhists, though some of them were important figures even in this domain, but also people involved in Kabbalah or Hasidism, and thus people whose concern with mysticism is obvious.

II

The *Sanhedrin* passages dealing with the artificial creature appears in the context of a discussion on the variety of the forbidden magical practices. This is especially obvious in the case of the discussion on fol. 67b. However, subsequent Jewish authorities only rarely addressed the question of to what extent were the deeds of the Amoraim a transgression from the Halakhic point of view.[5] The very fact that Rava and R. Zeira were mentioned in this context legitimized this operation in the eyes of Halakhic authorities. It seems, moreover, that in those surroundings where magic was considered an illicit activity, the creation of an anthropoid was, implicitly, regarded as totally different from the practices of the magicians and thus discussions regarding the problems related to the creation of the anthropoid were avoided. It seems that the emergence of Halakhic discussions was motivated by external factors; as we shall suggest below, the descendants of R. Eliyahu of Helm addressed the problem in the context of their ancestor's deed. However, at the outset I would like to point out another external element which triggered an elaborate discussion based on a Halakhic distinction: the novel discrimination between different types of magic and the partial legitimization of magic in Christian and Jewish circles in the Renaissance period in Italy.

Since the last third of the fifteenth century a new evaluation of magic was gradually exposed in larger circles of intellectuals; initially it is obvious in Italy, but within time in Europe generally. The beginnings of this phenomenon are to be found in the writings of Marsilio Ficino, Pico della Mirandola and Johannes Reuchlin among the Christians[6] and in the writings of Yoḥanan Alemanno among the Jews.[7] These authors were attacked on this ground by the more conservative figures in their respective religions. Pico had to leave Italy for awhile; Alemanno's evaluation of Judaism as a ritual of attracting the supernal powers downwards was criticized by R. Eliyahu del Medigo.[8] However, their novel and positive attitude to magic was accepted in larger audiences, and soon much more audacious formulations on the status of magic were expressed in an open way. Cornelius Agrippa of Nettesheim can be regarded as the most outspoken ideologue of this new trend in the sixteenth century. Though he openly retracted his exposition of magic later on, the avenue opened by him in his *De Occulta Philosophia* remained a vital alternative for intellectuals in the late European Renaissance.[9] In the Jewish camp, magic was presented by Alemanno as the culmination of the ideal curriculum; it was placed even higher than the sacrosanct Kabbalah.[10] Thus, for Renaissance Jewish figures, the halakhic status of magic was deeply different from that usually formulated by medieval authors. For Alemanno, the problem was simple; Judaism in general is a large corpus of directives on how to attract by punctilious behaviour the influxes from "above." Thus, when magic was understood in a similar way, the differences were blurred.[11] However, Alemanno, and even more his Christian contemporaries, were anxious to distinguish their monotheistic practice from the polytheistic theologies of the classical sources for their astral magic. Basically, the assumption was that magic is a natural phenomenon and thus it should not be condemned. Especially the Christian authors carefully discriminated their practices from the demonic magic condemned by the Church.[12] It is this "natural" attitude to magic that prompted a halakhic discussion of the Golem technique at the beginning of seventeenth century Italy. Abraham Yagel, whose discussions on the Golem were already analyzed above,[13] was heir to both the thought of Alemanno among the Jews and Ficino, Pico and Agrippa among the Christians.[14] His deep interest in *magia naturalis*, mentioned above in our analysis of the creation of the Golem, is a key concept in his attempt to reveal his approach. Let me paraphrase here, from the peculiar angle of the *Halakhic* perspective, some passages which were already adduced and analyzed above.

A controversy regarding the understanding of the significance of the creative activity in the Talmud between major *halakhic* figures, served as the starting point of Yagel's discussion. The term *hilkhot yeẓirah* mentioned once in *Sanhedrin* was understood by R. Yeruḥam as identical to demonic operation, *ma'aseh shedim,* a term occurring also in the Talmud.[15] However, R. Joseph Qaro, the outstanding mystic and *halakhist,* could not accept that the *hilkhot yeẓirah,* identified by another authoritative figure like Rashi, as related to operations done by the divine names[16], could be identified with demonic operations. Qaro argued that the intention in the Talmud is that, despite the fact that the status of *hilkhot yeẓirah* and *ma'aseh shedim* is legally similar, these two disciplines are different in their essence.[17] Yagel did not accept the opinion of Qaro regarding the difference between them. He proposes another distinction: *Sefer Yeẓirah* is not to be identified with the demonic operation because it is simply not mentioned in the Talmudic discussions of the matter. The fact that the term *hilkhot yeẓirah* occurs therein is to be understood as a reference to a discipline totally different from the content of *Sefer Yeẓirah.* Yagel argues that Rashi offered a faulty interpretation when he identified the Talmudic term with the content of *Sefer Yeẓirah.*[18] In fact, Yagel continues, *hilkhot yeẓirah* are to be understood as natural magic, defined by him as the preparation of matter to receive the primary human faculties. In principle, it is possible that Yagel was acquainted with the opinion of Bibago, who did not mention *Sefer Yeẓirah* when he discussed the Talmudic passage, but introduced the naturalistic explanation stemming from ibn Tufail's work.[19] However, Yagel continues, the Talmudic masters were not able to induce the higher faculties, an achievement possible only for the righteous, by their use of the combinations of letters and divine names, as in *Sefer Yeẓirah.* In other words, the Kabbalistic operation known by the interpreters of *Sefer Yeẓirah* is superior to the natural magic. Thus Yagel solved the quandary of Qaro while remaining, at the same time, faithful to the Talmudic formulation. Implicitly, Yagel admitted that the possibility of creating a perfect anthropoid depends upon the knowledge of the lore of *Sefer Yeẓirah.* Thus, this Renaissance figure is to be counted among those Jewish authors who admitted that it is possible to artificially create a perfect anthropoid.

I believe that one of the reasons for embarking on the entire discussion and disputing the argument of Qaro was the concept of the superiority of Kabbalistic magic to natural magic. As David Ruderman has already remarked, Yagel used the categories of preceding Christian Renaissance figures.[20] These concepts were applied here in order to elucidate a controversy between Halakhic authorities. This Renaissance author was ready to oppose the opinion of two of the most admired figures in Jewish culture, Rashi and Qaro, while preferring the opinion of a relatively obscure Halakhist, R. Yeruḥam, which facilitated the introduction of his distinction between higher and lower magic.

III

The first to discuss the status of the Golem as a Halakhic topic was R. Ẓevi Hirsch ben Ya'aqov Ashkenazi, better known as he-Ḥakham Ẓevi (1660–1718). He was appropriately described as the "First who discussed (Halakhically) the issue of the man formed by *Sefer Yeẓirah*" by a foremost Halakhic authority.[21] The text of his responsum states as follows:

> I became doubtful [as to the relationship] of a man created by *Sefer Yeẓirah* to that [mentioned] in *Sanhedrin, Rava' bera' gavra'.* Likewise, there were [persons] who testified against my grandfather,[22] the Gaon, our teacher and master, Eliahu, the president of the [Rabbinic] court of the holy community of Helm: Who is counted in the ten [persons] for things that require a quorum like *qadish* and *qedushah*? Those on whom it is written, "I will be sanctified amidst the sons of Israel."[23] Is [an artificial anthropoid] not counted or is it [counted], because it is taught in *Sanhedrin*: "He who raises the orphan in his home, Scripture considered it as if he had begotten him?" Because it is written, "Five sons of Michal. . . .[24] Did not Merav bear them? Yes, but Mikhal raised them."[25] Likewise in this case the deeds of the hands of the righteous are involved; it [the anthropoid] is counted in the category of the sons of Israel since the deeds of the righteous are [considered as] their progeny.[26] And it seems to me that since it is found that "R. Zeira said you are from the pious, return to your dust" he killed him. And if you consider that there was a benefit to count it among the ten in the case of a holy performance [*davar she-bi-qedushah*], R. Zeira would not have cast him from the world. Though there is no interdiction to spill its blood [since it is written—though there are also other interpretations (to this verse)—"Whosoever sheds a man's blood, by man shall his blood be shed,"[27] it is only in the case of a man who is formed within a man, namely, a foetus formed within his mother's womb, that someone is responsible for shedding his blood, and this was not the case with the man created by Rava, which was not formed in the womb of a woman] were it of any benefit, R. Zeira would have been prohibited to cast it from the world. But it cannot be counted among the ten for a holy performance. This seems to me [to be the solution].[28]

It is not quite clear what the role is of R. Eliyahu of Helm in this passage; was he also in a quandary regarding the status of the Golem, or is he mentioned in order to count him together with those who created a Golem? In other words, does the form "Likewise" refer to the creation of Rava, or does it refer to the beginning of the passage concerning the doubts of he-Ḥakham Ẓevi? From the testimony of his son, we know that he-Ḥakham Ẓevi was in the possession of traditions concerning not only the creation of a Golem but also of his undoing of this creature. Thus, a reference to the legal status of the undoing is, in our context, as pertinent as the assumption that Ẓevi was simply mentioning the fact that one of his ancestors had created such a creature. Moreover, the tradition which was in the hand of the he-Ḥakham Ẓevi stated that R. Eliyahu had to undo the Golem since it was prone to destroy the world. Therefore, the decision to undo it was not due to the view that it was a nonhuman being, or at least not exclusively, but rather on account of the fact that it was a terribly dangerous creature. In other words, the fact that the Golem began to change and actually went out of control, i.e., it acquired the status of an independently acting creature, was the reason for its undoing. Doubts with respect to the problem of this undoing may have caused the formulation of this halakhic responsum which seems to have been initiated by he-Ḥakham Ẓevi himself, as the name of a person who asked him the question, or the question itself, is not mentioned in the text. Thus it was the unexpected metamorphosis of the Golem, which was accepted by the descendants of R. Eliyahu as a fact, that may have had an impact on the preoccupation of the two Halakhic authorities with the status of the artificial man. Their interest in the possibility of counting the Golem in the quorum is a novelty in the domain of Halakhic discussions and could have been motivated by the feeling that their ancestor undid the Golem, whose precise Halakhic nature was not established up to their time. By their attempt to decree the Halakhic status of the Golem as ritualistically irrelevant, Ẓevi and his son endeavored to retroactively absolve their ancestor from a dubious act.[29]

IV

The hesitating voice of he-Ḥakham Ẓevi impressed his son, R. Jacob Emden, a renown Halakhic figure himself. He addressed the issue of the artificial anthropoid in a responsum of his own, attempting to finalize the issue left open by the end of he-Ḥakham Ẓevi's text. He compares the Golem to the minor, the stupid and the deaf, who are excluded from the quorum, though they are considered to have a small amount of intelligence [*da'ata' qalishata'*].[30] However, according to the Halakhah, it is forbidden to kill them. Since the Golem was killed without mentioning any problem in this context, Emden concludes that it is inferior to them, as it even did not answer to R. Zeira, and thus it is to be excluded from the quorum. Nevertheless, it seems that even after this decision, some doubts still remained; discussing the case of the man in *Sanhedrin,* he writes:

> However, we must examine [the question] in a detailed way. Prima facie, it seems that it heard since it was sent to R. Zeira. Consequently, it may be that it was a deaf man who does not speak, whose legal status is like that of an intelligent man in every respect. However, it does not seem to be true since if it possessed the [faculty of] hearing, it was surely worthy also of the [faculty of] speaking. And it seems reasonable that it understood [the mission] by hints and allusions, just as a dog is trained to go to a certain mission, to bring something from someone or to return it to him. Afterwards [the training] it was sent to him [to R. Zeira] and he went [thither]. And it is written in the book *Ḥ[esed] L[e-Avraham]*[31] that its vitality is like the vitality of the animal, and hence there is no transgression in its being killed. Thus it is obvious that it is just like an animal in the form of man and like the three-year old calf that was created for R. Ḥ[anina] and R. O[shayah]. En passant I shall mention here what happened to that formation of R. Eliyahu[32]. . . .[33]

V

The question of the qualification of a Golem to complete the quorum recurs in the *Responsa* of R. Yehudah Asud, a late nineteenth century Hungarian Halakhic authority. He inspects the question, already discussed by earlier sources, regarding the status of a sleeping person, whether or not he should be counted among the ten qualified Jews to form a quorum.[34] He rejects this possibility on the basis that those authorities who disqualified the sleeping man emphasized that his soul does not dwell upon him during sleep but ascends on the high; a fortiori, as R. Yehudah argues, the artificial man who is devoid of any soul and possesses only an animal spirit, as he found in the books.[35]

VI

In order to understand better the type of consciousness that underlies the discussions on the artificial man created by means of *Sefer Yeẓirah*, let me adduce two discussions on the artificial calf, produced in the last hundred years. As we can easily see, there was no doubt regarding the reality of this artificial creation, and the discussions of these Rabbis were guided by their confidence with respect to the powers inherent in *Sefer Yeẓirah*. R. Meir Leibush, better known as the Malbim, a late nineteenth century Romanian Rabbi, explains the verse in Gen. 18:7–8 as follows: Abraham ran after the calf that escaped and he created another one as a surrogate; this second calf was created by means of *Sefer Yeẓirah.* On this basis one can explain how it was possible for Abraham to offer the angels both butter and milk together with the meat of the calf. In this case the construction of an artificial calf solves the quandary of a discrepancy between the biblical story and the biblical interdiction against consuming milk and meat together.[36] This discussion seems to be reflected in a modern Halakhist treatment of the above theme; R. Moses Sternbuch assumes that there was not even a problem of an appearance of transgression by serving milk and meat together since it was well-known that Abraham, the author of *Sefer Yeẓirah*, had created an artificial animal![37]

VII

Now, we shall present a unique discussion of the Golem, which is part of the Rabbinic concern for its special nature and an attempt to ponder its legal status from the Halakhic point of view. The uniqueness of the following presentation is that it seems to be the single extant case of a treatment of the Golem in a dream. Below, a literary translation in extenso of the passage of R. Ẓadoq ha-Kohen of Lublin will be offered, with some footnotes regarding sources and clarifications of details; afterwards the meaning of the passage will be partially analyzed:

> The night of Monday, [of the week of] the pericope *Bo*, the second day of [the month of] *shevat.* A dream was dreamt[38] concerning what it is written in *Sanhedrin* fol. 65b. He [R. Zeira] said to him: Return to your dust. This [formulation of] he-Ḥakham Ẓevi, was examined minutely in his responsum (n. 93) [concluding] that there is no benefit in joining him to any issue connected to a holy performance. [*davar she-bi-qedushah*] [This conclusion] is not necessary, since it is possible to say that he [R. Ẓevi] was worried that it [the Golem] may become harmful to people when it will become slightly greater, and then even its maker will take pains in order to return it to its dust, as it will be able to harm him also, as it was told in the responsum of Yaveẓ, part 2 (no. 82) about that [creature] formed by his grandfather, our Rabbi Eliyahu, the master of the Divine Name. This is the reason why it is forbidden to let such a creature remain [in existence] but rather he should create it for the sake of the purpose for which it was necessary, [it seems that it was sent to R. Zeira for a certain hidden purpose, which was not explicated in the Talmud; it was strictly necessary to send such a creature for this pur-

pose], and return it immediately afterward to its dust. This is the reason why it was placed after [the story of] R. Ḥanina and R. Oshayah who created a three-year calf. If it was in the eve of Shabbat, and in the *Responsum* of Rashba (n. 413) he scrupulously examined this question and wrote an explanation.[39] And this also seems to be part of the miraculous deeds, of which it is forbidden to benefit, as it is written in *Ta'anit* (fol. 24b) but [it is performed] for the sake of the commandment alone and so it is permitted. And they were poor, since they, R. Ḥanina and R. Oshayah, who are mentioned in 'A[*rvei*] P[*esaḥim*] [*TB, Pesaḥim*] (fol. 113b) were shoemakers . . . and they lacked the necessary things for Shabbat, and they ate it [the calf] [as part of] the meal of Shabbat. This is the reason why they made it on the eve of Shabbat . . . because if they would have done it beforehand, it would have grown until [the time of] Shabbat and would have become harmful, and they would have been compelled to return it to its dust. And it seems to me that it was also necessary to blemish it beforehand, so that it will not be fitting for a sacrifice, for otherwise it could not be returned to dust since there is a profit from it, as it is worthy to be sacrificed. (So it occurred to me in the dream, plainly, that if it is worthy to be sacrificed, then at the time of the Temple, when it could be sacrificed, it would be forbidden to return it to its dust, because of the interdiction not to destroy something that is fitting for a certain purpose, as it was plain to me in the dream. If so, its blemish would be forbidden, it [the grown calf] being appropriate to be sacrificed. However, the truth as it seems to me now is simple, that this [discussion] is part of the futile things concerning which it is impossible to dream. For it is certainly disqualified to be sacrificed, as it is written, "If it will be born"[40], and we conclude that the exception is excluded. A fortiori this [case] that was not born from the belly of a mother at all; and *a fortiori* what is written in the *Shelah,* pericope *Va-Yeshev,* that it does not require ritual slaughter[41]; and see there that the interdiction of fat and blood is not applied it; thus, it cannot be brought to the altar. And the principle of the decision of he-Ḥakham Ẓevi is . . .[42] and in my dream it plainly appeared to me that it is not as he decided and it is fitting for [participating in] a holy performance. And it seems that it is possible to sustain this and what it is written in the *Responsum* of Yaveẓ, ad. loc., that it is not better than a deaf man who does not hear and does not speak; and likewise [is the ruling] in *Birkhei Yosef, 'Oraḥ Ḥayyim,* par. 55. It is not necessary that a deaf man has no reason like a small child, because man is formed without reason and he acquires it only when he grows; and this [person] who does not hear and does not speak, if it is an innate [defect], and he does not learn from men, or if he became deaf later on [he is unqualified] since there is a defect in his brain and [thus] he has no reason. But this one who is formed in his [full] stature, as a mature man, we ought to assume that he also has reason [just] as a mature man, notwithstanding the fact that he does not hear and does not speak. It can be assumed that this [defect] is not connected to a defect in the brain and his reason and that he will no acquire reason [in the future]. This [view] contradicts what it is written in *Ḥesed Le-Avraham, 'Ein Ya'aqov, Nahar L[amed],* that he has no [higher] soul on a speaking spirit, only [possessing] an animal spirit; thus it can be killed as an animal is; see there.[43] And this is also the view of R. Shemuel Edeles in part 1 of *Sanhedrin,* ad loc.[44] [However], we ought to say that he is not like an animal possessing a human form, because he was formed by means of *Sefer Yeẓirah*, by the way a man is formed, not in the way an animal is formed. But the [higher] soul of life [emerged as it is written in the verse Gen. 2:7] "and He breathed into his nostrils the breath of life," that is, the speaking spirit; it is impossible to confer it upon him because it is a portion of God from above.[45] Yet, in any case, he is not worse than the idolator, who also does not have the portion of God from above, though he can speak, i.e., in his language, which is not regarded as speech. This is the reason why it is said (in *Midrash Rabbah,* pericope *balaq*)[46] that the idolater who speaks the holy language, his speech is corrupt, because he does not possess the authentic speaking spirit but something similar to the chirping of birds, and like the serpent before the sin, which was able to speak though it did not possess the [higher] soul of life. And he [the idolater who speaks Hebrew] is from the aspect of the Other Side, and the stature of *Adam Beli'al.* But this one formed in a holy way by means of *Sefer Yeẓirah*, it is impossible to induce in him speech from the aspect of the Other Side and equally impossible a speaking spirit from the aspect of holiness; this is the reason why he cannot speak. (Thus it is possible to assume that he does hear and not as it seems to them). Consequently, it is similar to the idolater and not to an animal. Even if someone will argue that one is permitted to kill it without [the sanction of] being killed [as punishment] for this act, it is possible to say that it is an inference from the biblical verse,[47] "[Whoever kills] a man by man [he will be killed], as it is written in the *Responsum* of he-Ḥakham Ẓevi. . . . However, in any case, as regards reason, it is better to assume that he has reason, [just] as the idolater is called a reasonable man . . . And you shall not say that reason completely depends on speech, but [in the case of] the idolator, the speech is from the side of the *qelippah,* just as his reason is . . . and his reason is not accountable in the case of divorce or matters pertaining to a *mizvah.* [Just so] the Golem has no speech because of the reason we mentioned, and just so he has no reason. . . . Moreover, reason does not depend upon speech alone[48] because a mute possesses reason, even if he is mute by birth, it is possible that he hears; and thus it is possible that he be considered one who possesses reason. However, it is possible to say that because of another reason it is not under the category of the man who must perform the commandments; he-Ḥakham Ẓevi concluded that if it is possible to count him among the [quorum of] ten, it is because it is the deed of a righteous, [but] in any case it is not [adviceable] to impose on it the imperative of the commandments because of this reason [its being the deed of a righteous]. What it is written in the Torah [cannot be applied to him]: "Speak to the sons of Israel",[49] because it is not in [their] category since it does not have the [high] soul of life and the eternity of the soul in the next world, [following the principle of] retribution or punishment. If so, how can it be added to a holy performance since it is not requested [to fulfill] the commandments? In any case, it is possible to say that when the issue of [the quorum of] the ten [men] required for grace after the meal is concerned, if it can eat it may be added just as a small child may be counted; and it is possible that it is even aware who is blessed[50]. This is an issue that requires [futher] investigation and there is no place to elaborate here [on this issue.])[51]

The author's intention is only clear in very general terms. As we shall see below, the contents of this text were considered a strange discourse even in the eyes of an accomplished Halakhist, who applies to R. Ẓadoq the epitheton of *gaon.* The author himself was aware of the bizarre facets of his dream. What is obvious is the fact that R. Ẓadoq was not satisfied with the attitude of he-Ḥakham Ẓevi and his son. Against their decision that the Golem cannot be counted in a ritual, he indicates that the Golem enjoys, at least, the status of an idolater and it can be counted, as a minor is counted, in a blessing after the meal which requires a quorum. It seems that for the first time, the Golem was conceived as an entity that transcends the nonhuman status to which it was reduced by the two eighteenth century Halakhists. It should be emphasized that R. Ẓadoq insists that the Golem is not, in any case, to be considered worse than the idolaters. R. Ẓadoq stated earlier that the Talmudic master should not have killed the artificial man. His decision, which overtly disagrees which the responsa of his predecessors, testifies that an Halakhic authority could reach a conclusion which contradicts the Halakhic rationale offered by the descendants of R. Eliyahu of Helm. Even if R. Ẓadoq's opinion is debatable, as we shall see in a moment, his view helps us to place the decisions of R. Eliyahu's offspring in a broader perspective.

VIII

The above passage underwent sharp criticism by another Hasidic leader, R. Ḥayyim Eleazar Shapira, the Ẓaddiq of Munkacs, in the early twentieth century. He explicitly refers to the fact that the whole legal discussion of R. Ẓadoq took place in a dream, but he, nevertheless, undertook a survey of the questions involved in his discussion since it was written by such a great authority who decided to commit it to writing.[52] The formulation of the criticism is very strange; it includes attributions to R. Ẓadoq, which can hardly be sustained by the extant text, and repetitions of the same issues, without any visible reason. Basically, the criticism focuses upon the problem of the blemish proposed by R. Ẓadoq, in order to disqualify the calf from a sacrifice. Strangely enough, R. Ḥayyim Eleazar understands the view of R. Ẓadoq as if he proposed the issue of the blemish in the context of the artificial anthropoid, who could have been, in principle, considered to be qualified for a sacrifice. This possibility indeed surprised the later Hasidic master, who points out that this is inconceivable. He continues to say that even if R. Ẓadoq intended to relate it only to the calf, this is also meaningless inasmuch as the creators lived after the destruction of the Temple, a point which was made explicitly also by R. Ẓadoq himself. Moreover, argues R. Ḥayyim Eleazar, a calf created by *Sefer Yeẓirah* cannot be considered a first-born calf, which, as such, must be sacrificed. He concludes that "the words of the Gaon (R. Ẓadoq) are strange, and cannot be understood at all," and "that there is no meaning to the above words."[53]

IX

The dream of R. Ẓadoq is interesting for yet another reason; the concern about the humanity of the Golem, which so fascinated this Hasidic master, may reflect a wider interest in the status of the Golem in the milieu of this author. R. Ẓadoq was attracted to Hasidism by R. Mordekhai Joseph, the founder of a new Hasidic dynasty of Iszbiza; his grandson, R. Gershom Ḥanokh Leiner, the founder of the Hasidic dynasty of Radzyn, a contemporary of R. Ẓadoq, also produced an interesting approach to the Golem. In his controversial Halakhic writing, *Sidrei Ṭehorot,* he opens a new avenue regarding the nature of the Golem from the perspective of the Halakhah, as he addresses the question whether or not the corpse of the Golem causes impurity as the corpse of a regular man does.[54] He decides that, according to "reason", it seems that indeed it causes impurity. He reaches this conclusion by an a fortiori argument: if, according to R. Joseph, a Tannaitic master, *'adnei ha-sadeh*[55] a[n] [anthropoid?] being which was considered to be an animal from the Halakhic point of view, causes impurity, even more so does a being created by means of *Sefer Yeẓirah*. He mentions the view, already adduced by earlier Halakhists, that the deeds of the hands of the righteous are considered to be a man; this is considered also as an argument for the human-like status of the Golem.

However, the fact that the anthropoid was killed by R. Zeira, complicates his argumentation. Since he was aware of the previous Halakhic discussions from the family of R. Eliyahu of Helm, he could not overlook such a strong argument against the approach of humanizing the Golem. After adducing the view of he-Ḥakham Ẓevi, he argues that it is surprising that a being which is fraught with vitality and is formed in an anthropomorphic shape, should be permitted to be killed. His main argument is that, given the fact that the shape is human, and it is an animated creature, it is hard to distinguish it from a real man. He rejects also the distinction proposed by he-Ḥakham Ẓevi that the prohibition of homicide refers only to those anthropoids who were born "in man," i.e., in the belly of a woman. According to this criterion, continues Leiner, Adam could have "legally" been murdered: this view is absurd for Adam was the creation of God. The Rabbi returns to the source of all the subsequent discussions, the *Sanhedrin* passage, and submits it to an incisive inquiry. If R. Zeira was not aware that the creator of the anthropoid was Rava, how could he have killed it? Given the fact that the anthropoid did not answer, he could have easily confused it with a mute person. On the other hand, if he was aware that Rava created it, why did R. Zeira undo it because it did not answer his questions? These quandaries require, according to Leiner, a novel approach.

Leiner's main contribution consists of an endeavour to read the whole *Sanhedrin* passage as one organic continuum. The reference to the righteous who could create a world is understood to be part of the discussion on the creation of the anthropoid. The world referred to in the text is understood to be a man, apparently because of the Rabbinic view that man is the entire universe.[56] It follows that there are two cases in the Talmudic text; the perfectly righteous would be able to create a perfect man, the "world", whereas the less perfectly righteous, like Rava was conceived to be, are able to create an imperfect man. Leiner emphasizes that, in principle, according to the Talmudic text there is no difference between the man created by the righteous and that created by God. This assumption may explain the situation as portrayed in the Talmud; R. Zeira attempted to check if the man created by Rava was a perfect one who was able to speak; when he discerns that the anthropoid does not answer, he understands that it is similar to the creation of the imperfect righteous, and thus not a perfect man, and he kills it. However, continues Leiner, a perfectly righteous man would create an anthropoid who could be admitted in the quorum. The main texts adduced by Leiner in order to substantiate his approach are Rashi's commentary on *Sanhedrin* and *Sefer ha-Bahir,* where the possibility of creating a perfect Golem is implied though it was not explicated in a clear manner.[57] Thus, although the actual Golem in *Sanhedrin* was not a perfect creation, such a creation is possible in principle and from the theoretical point of view the Golem created by means of *Sefer Yeẓirah* could become a being who will be counted among the sons of Israel in a ritual performance. As to the initial concern of the author, if the corpse of the Golem does cause impurity, it seems that the answer would be positive, as the introductory remarks of his discussion indicate; in any case, Leiner did not change his mind. If this is the case, then the discussion of Leiner may indicate that at the beginning of the last third of the nineteenth century, the view that the remnants of the Golem created, and undone, by Maharal were extant in the attic of the synagogue in Prague, was not known in Poland, where Leiner flourished.

The fact that two persons who had personal relations and corresponded for a certain time,[58] approached the topic of the Golem from the Halakhic point of view, and were inclined to attribute to this being a more humane status than other Halakhists did before, at least in principle, shows that the Golem might have served as a topic of discussion in the circle of R. Mordekhai Joseph of Iszbiza. The fact that Leiner's view concurs with that of R. Ẓadoq, though for different reasons, demonstrates that the decision of the eighteenth century Halakhists discussed above was motivated by reasons which could be easily rejected by an outstanding Halakhist as Leiner was.

X

Interestingly enough, the question of the impurity of the corpse of the Golem is aborted in the version of the Golem legend of R. Judel Rosenberg. According to this version "the Golem does not cause impurity after his death, because its body was not born but made, and an animal that was created in virtue of this, does not require a ritual slaughter, and is not considered as *'ever min ha-ḥay.*"[59] The author combined here two themes which were already in existence: The first is the impurity of the Golem, which apparently reflects the problem posed by Leiner for the first time. The fact that Leiner, who rejected all the opinions which did not conform to his views, does not refer to a treatment similar to the conclusion of the last text, points to the probability that he was not acquainted with our text or the opinion expressed in it. Thus, it seems reasonable to assume that the version of Rosenberg reflects, though it does not agree with, the discussion of Leiner. The second theme, dealing with the status of the animal created by means of *Sefer Yeẓirah* as not requiring a ritual slaughter, is reminiscent of the discussion found in Horwitz's *Shelah.*[60]

XI

A Sefardi contemporary of the two Hasidic masters, R. Abraham Anaqawa, discussed the question of whether the creation of the Golem by means of *Sefer Yeẓirah* on Shabbat is permissible.[61] His objections against such a practice are drawn from two sources: the two Amoraim who created the calf accomplished their operation on the eve of Shabbat, this being an oblique indication that it is not permissible to do this act on Shabbat itself. The other argument is the fact that the creation of the anthropoid was accomplished by the divine name, which was used in the creation of the world. However, because the creation of the world was finished before the time of Shabbat, the divine name is not to be used on Shabbat for creative purposes. In principle, the creation of the Golem is understood, in contrast to the great majority of the texts dealt with above, as achievable by the combinations of the letters alone, without the need of dust and the other operations related to the material part of the Golem. For this reason the preparation of the body of the Golem would be ostensibly forbidden from the Halakhic point of view; moreover, the act of creation is compared to that of study, which is conspicuously not forbidden on Shabbat. Thus, we may conclude that the thrust of the activity referred to by Anaqawa was the activation of letters since their recitation is shared by the two practices: loud study and incantation of the combination of letters. According to the Kabbalistic understanding, the significance of study, as referred to explicitly by this Halakhist, is to create new worlds or firmaments.[62] Thus, the linguistic creation of the Golem has a basic parallel in creative study: the effects are new entities emerging from human activation of letters. It should be mentioned that a leitmotif of Anaqawa's discussion is the affinity between the creation of the Golem and the creation of the world, a topic which was already hinted at in the Talmud, as we have attempted to demonstrate above.[63]

Notes

1. E. E. Urbach, *Ha-Halakhah* (Givatayyim, 1989). (Hebrew)

2. Moshe Silberg, *Principia Talmudica,* (Jerusalem, 1964), pp. 24–25. (Hebrew)

3. See above, ch. 4.

4. See below ch. 15, par. 3.

5. See e.g. the *Ḥiddushim* of R. Nissim Gerondi on *Sanhedrin,* fol. 67b and n. 15 below.

6. See Yates, *Giordano Bruno,* pp. 62–129; idem, *The Occult Philosophy in the Elizabethan Age* (London, Boston, Henley, 1979), pp. 23–28.

7. Cf. Idel, "The Magical and Neoplatonic Interpretation," pp. 197–215.

8. Ibid., p. 201, and idem, "Differing Conceptions", p. 175, n. 178.

9. See Yates, *Giordano Bruno,* pp. 130–143; idem, *The Occult Philosophy in the Elizabethan Age* (note 6 above), pp. 37–47.

10. Idel, "The Study Program of R. Yoḥanan Alemanno," pp. 321–330.

11. Idel, "The Magical and the Neoplatonic Interpretation," pp. 202–210.

12. Yates, *Giordano Bruno,* pp. 156–168, and D. P. Walker, *Spiritual and Demonic Magic from Ficino to Campanella,* and Ioan P. Couliano, *Eros and Magic in the Renaissance,* trans. M. Cook (Chicago, London, 1987), pp. 144–175.

13. See ch. 11, par. 8.

14. Ruderman, *Kabbalah, Magic and Science,* pp. 110–114, 117.

15. See R. Yeruḥam ben Meshullam of Provence, *Sefer 'Adam ve-ḥavah* (Venice, 1553), Path 17, par. 5, fol. 159cd. R. Yeruḥam simply identifies the discipline dealing with demonic operations with the operations made by means of *Sefer Yeẓirah,* following some authorities whose names he did not mention; see *Ibid.,* fol. 159d. It seems that he refers to the discussion in the *Ṭur, Yoreh De'ah,* par. 179. This author considers the use of the demons in order to attain certain effects as totally licit. This is not exceptional in Jewish Halakhah; see e. g. Naḥmanides', *Responsum,* n. 183; R. Shelomo ibn Adret's, *Responsum* n. 413 and the *Ḥiddushim* of R. Nissim Gerondi on *Sanhedrin,* fol. 67d. Some of the sources mention the Ashkenazi masters who used demons in their practices. It seems that the above Halakhists regarded the operation during which demons were employed as a natural activity, similar to the natural powers inherent in the letters according to *Sefer Yeẓirah.* Aware of this concept of magic, Yagel could more easily conceive the relationship between magia naturalis and demonic magic. However, the negative and pernicious aspects of this demonic magic seem to be remote from the

strong infernal conception related to the demons in medieval Christian culture. Compare, however, the more infernal view of the *Zohar* where magic is regarded as Satanic worship. Scholem is correct when he distinguished between the magic as inherent in *Sefer Yeẓirah* and the view of the *Zohar* on this matter; See "The Idea of the Golem," pp. 174–175.

16. See Rashi to *Sanhedrin,* fol. 65b and 67b.

17. See *Beit Yoseph,* on the *Ṭur, Yoreh De'ah,* par. 179. Interestingly enough, the *Tur* himself, at the beginning of the fourteenth century, rejects the use of demonic operations; Qaro, in the middle of the sixteenth century in the Orient, adopts partially the view of R. Yeruḥam, that the demonic operations are licit. This occurred during the beginning of the persecution of magic in Europe.

18. See above ch. 11, the text indicated by n. 90.

19. See above ch. 11, par. 1.

20. Ruderman, *Kabbalah, Magic and Science,* p. 118 and above ch. 11, par. 8.

21. See R. Ẓevi Hirsh Shapira of Munkacs, *Darkhei Teshuvah* (Vilna, 1892), fol. 38a.

22. The Hebrew form is *ziqni,* which is commonly translated as grandfather. However, given the fact that Ẓevi was born in 1660, it is rather doubtful if R. Eliyahu, who died in 1583, was his grandfather, but rather the father of his grandfather.

23. Lev. 22:32.

24. II Sam., 21:8.

25. *TB, Sanhedrin,* fol. 19a.

26. See Rashi to Gen. 6:9 based on *Genesis Rabbah* section 30, par. 6; cf. the note of Sherwin in *The Golem Legend* p. 21 and ch. 13, n. 17.

27. Gen. 9:6. See also below, n. 48.

28. *Responsa* (Fuerth, 1767) part I, n. 93, fol. 39b. Another English translation, which was consulted for the preparation of this version, is found in Sherwin, *The Golem Legend,* pp. 21–22.

29. For the time being I am not aware of any alternative explanation of the fact that these two Halakhists were the first who indulged in Halakhic discussions on our issues.

30. Compare *TB, Yebbamot,* fol. 113a.

31. On this passage see ch. 12, par. 2.

32. On the following passage see ch. 13.

33. *She'eilat Yaveẓ* (Lemberg, 1884), part 2, fol. 28a n. 82.

34. I did not find the Rabbinic proof text of this assertion.

35. *Yehudah Ya'aleh* (Lemberg, 1893) part I, fol. 10b, n. 26. The books referred to by Asud may have included R. Abraham Azulai's *Ḥesed le-Avraham,* quoted earlier, ibid., fol. 5a, n. 8.

36. *Sefer ha-Torah ve-ha-Miẓvah* (Jerusalem, ND), vol. I, fol. 36c.

37. *Mo'adim u-Zemanim* (Jerusalem, 1971), vol. 4, p. 139, n. 319. Sternbuch remarks that the verb *'SH,*—in the text meaning "prepare" and literally "make"—used in the biblical verse, is pointing to the creation by *Sefer Yeẓirah.* See above ch. 2, n. 55.

38. *Ḥalam li.* Literally, He caused me to dream a dream. This is an irregular form, apparently pointing to the authors's intent to confer to his dream a greater credibility, by relating it to an objective entity which caused the dream.

39. I assume that there is a mistake here and R. Ẓadoq intended another responsum. See the *Responsa* of R. Shelomo ben Abraham ibn Adret, vol. I, n. 410. This responsum deals with the creation of the calf on the eve of Shabbat. This passage was quoted several times in connection with the creation of the Golem; see, e.g., in R. Yehudah Muscato's *Qol Yehudah* and in R. Joseph del Medigo's *Maẓref le-Ḥokhmah* referred to in ch. 11, par. 7. However, in Responsum 413 there are also several references to discussions in *Sanhedrin* related to magic.

40. Lev. 22:27.

41. See below ch. 15, par. 3.

42. Here, there is an abbreviated word that is unclear to me.

43. See above ch. 12, par. 2.

44. See his *Commentary on Sanhedrin,* fol. 65b.

45. *Ḥeleq 'eloah mi-ma'al.* Cf. Job. 31:2. This verse is a *locus probans* of the view that the soul of the Jews emanates from the divine pleroma. See also below ch. 17, n. 10.

46. See *Tanḥuma,* Balaq, par. 9.

47. Gen., 9:6. See above, beside n. 27.

48. See above ch. 9, par. 4.

49. Ex. 14:2 etc.

50. The Golem is conceived here as able, in principle, to have a certain awareness of the existence of the Creator, just as a small child is sometimes capable of perceiving; cf. *TB, Berakhot,* fol. 48a. This description concerning a pos-

sible religious awareness might have been reflected in the assumption of the version of R. Judel Rosenberg, that the Golem has a level of lower spiritual comprehensions. See *Nifla'ot ha-Maharal* p. 21, n. 4.

51. *Quntres Divrei Ḥalomot,* the last part of the treatise, *Resisei Laylah* (Lublin, 1903), fol. 91d–92c.

52. Compare, for example, his own discussion of issues revealed to him in a dream; *Divrei Torah* (Munkacs, 1930), Third version fol. 48c.

53. *Divrei Torah* (Munkacs, 1930), Fourth version fol. 75cd.

54. *Sidrei Ṭehorot, Ohalot* (Josefow, 1873), fol. 5a.

55. See *Mishnah, Kilayyim* 8:5. Some commentators explain the form *'Adnei* as a plural of the form *'Adam,* man. On this phrase see Daniel Sperber, "Varia Midrashica", *REJ,* vol. 129 (1970) pp. 89–92.

56. The view that man is a whole world is found already in the ancient Jewish literature; see, e.g., *'Avot de-R. Nathan,* version A, ch. 31, ed. S. Schechter, fol. 46a.

57. See ch. 9, par. 1 above.

58. See R. Ẓadoq ha-Kohen's responsum to R. Gershom at the end of the former's *Taqqanat ha-Shavin* (Benei Beraq, 1967), fol. 85–87.

59. See *Nifla'ot ha-Maharal,* p. 73, n. 13.

60. See ch. 15, par. 3 below.

61. *Kerem Ḥemed, Responsa,* on *'Oraḥ Ḥayyim,* par. 3. (Livorno, 1869), fol. 4d–5a. This volume of responsa was printed in the printing-house of Eliyahu ben Amozegh whose positive attitude to the creation of the Golem by means of *Sefer Yeẓirah* was discussed above, ch. 4.

62. See e.g., *Zohar* 3, fol. 216b and in a long series of Cordoverian sources like *Sefer Shi'ur Qomah* (Warshau, 1883), fol. 18a–b.

63. See above ch. 3, par. 2.

15

Golem and Sex

I

The Aramaic term for an anthropoid used by the editors of the *Sanhedrin* passage is *gavra',* literally, a man, and, more specifically, a male person.[1] In Hebrew, on the other hand, an unmarried woman was considered to be, like an unmarried man, an imperfect being, and she was referred to in classical texts as a Golem. This designation implies her being an imperfect, hylic entity, prior to her becoming a vessel (*keli*) for her husband, so that she will attain her essential perfection as woman.[2] In light of our previous explanations of the meaning of the Golem, it seems that in this case as well the term stands for a human body that did not receive its ultimate perfection. Moreover, the relationship between the woman, conceived of as a Golem, and the process of her becoming a vessel, *keli,* namely her reaching her "natural" goal, is reminiscent of other Talmudic discussion where Golem stands for the unfinished form of a certain vessel, which becomes that vessel when it is given the final touch[3]. The penetration of the needle is paralleled by the Talmudic view of the husband as the maker of his spouse: *bo'alaikh- 'osaikh.*[4]

II

However, the question of the artificial creature was not discussed by medieval Jewish authors and it seems that they were indifferent as to the

Golem Woman

precise interpretation of the *Sanhedrin* text regarding this issue. Discussions concerning the question of the gender occur only in the first third of the seventeenth century in works written by persons who inhabited Central European lands: v.z. in a book of R. Joseph Shelomo del Medigo, originally from Candia, Crete, but living in Poland,[5] and in the classic of the Kabbalistic ethical literature, R. Isaiah ben Abraham ha-Levi Horwitz's *Shenei Luḥot ha-Berit.*[6] The former work was written in 1625, the latter in the thirties or early forties of the seventeenth century. Given the temporal proximity and the geographical vicinity of the only two books which indulged, for the first time in a written document, in a discussion on the female Golem, the question may be raised if there is indeed any affinity between the two passages. A scrutiny of the details included in those texts, to be analyzed below, reveals that there is no literary dependence of one of these texts on the other. However, the hypothesis that a third text preceding these two texts, which included both the details of the female of R. Shelomo ibn Gabirol and the Golem of the sons of Jacob, was in existence is worthwhile to mention as a probable explanation for the concomitant interest in this neglected problem.[7] In any case, it is clear that the two authors dealing with this issue explicitly mention the fact that they gave expression to an already existing tradition.

Let me begin with the quotation of R. Joseph Shelomo del Medigo. In his *Maẓref le-Ḥokhmah,*[8] he quotes the discussions on the creation of the Golem from the Pseudo-Rabad *Commentary on Sefer Yeẓirah* and the Pseudo-Sa'adyah *Commentary*; afterwards he indicates that:

> They said about R. S[helomo] ben Gabirol, that he created a woman, and she waited on him. When he was denounced to the authorities, he showed them that she was not a perfect creature, and [then] he turned her to her original [state], to the pieces and hinges of wood, out of which she was built up. And similar traditions [*shemu'ot*] [or rumors] are numerous in the mouth of everyone, especially in the land of Ashkenaz.[9]

The context of the quotation demonstrates that the source of del Medigo regarded the creature of Ibn Gabirol as belonging to the same category of beings as the Golem created by the techniques of *Sefer Yeẓirah.* However, all the details of the legend are new in comparison to all the previously known versions. Obviously, the presentation of Ibn Gabirol as the hero of a legend related to an artificial man was motivated by the fact that del Medigo quoted just before this legend the description of Ibn Ezra as a creator of a Golem according to the *Commentary on Sefer Yeẓirah* of Pseudo-Sa'adyah. Nevertheless, it seems that, notwithstanding the context, the source which was before del Medigo hinted to a mechanical creature rather than a creation out of dust and water, and one that was animated by the recitation of letters. If this suggestion will prove correct by additional material, then there is no particular reason to infer from the present text that Ibn Gabirol was interested in the magical aspects of *Sefer Yeẓirah*,[10] a book that otherwise influenced him in a substantial way.[11] We witness here the first clear example of a female famulus[12] that bears evidence, according to the legend, to the mechanical achievement of Ibn Gabirol, and not to his indulgence in magic. The fact that he was able to reduce the creature to its components, apparently in order to escape the punishment of the authorities, demonstrates that he may have been suspected as being a magician, whereas in reality he was only a technician. Furthermore, the speculations on the possible romantic, Pygmalionian, overtones of this legend seem to be an overemphasis on implications which are not substantiated by any exact term in the text.[13]

III

On the other hand, the sexual implications of a female Golem were exploited in the source quoted by R. Isaiah Horwitz. In his famous *Shenei Luḥot ha-Berit,* the author addressed a serious quandary concerning the denounciation of the sons of Jacob by their brother Joseph. According to the verse in Genesis 37:3, "Joseph brought to his father an evil report." The precise nature of this report was not specified in the Bible; according to some Midrashic sources, there were three main topics which were reported by Joseph to his father: that his brothers used to eat limbs of an animal before its death, *'Ever min ha-ḥai,* that they had some type of relations with maiden of the country, namely with Canaanite females, and finally that some of the brothers behaved contemptuously toward those other brothers who were the sons of the servants.[14] According to Rashi ad locum, the sexual relations are much more specific, and more grave. Joseph accused his brothers of having incestuous relationships with unspecified females.[15] The occurrence of such an accusation against Joseph as a denouncer, raised serious questions about the veracity of the report; was it possible that Joseph, the symbol of the righteous in Jewish tradition, was a liar? And if not, did the sons of Jacob actually transgress these grave transgressions? In order to solve the quandary, Horwitz adduced a tradition, presented as something that he heard was written in an ancient manuscript, which seems to solve the whole problem. Let me translate in extenso the text of this tradition, a unique document for the history of the Golem legends:

> I heard that in an ancient codex [*qoveẓ yashan*] there is [a solution for] the issue: Abraham our ancestor wrote *Sefer Yeẓirah* and gave

> it to Isaac, and Isaac gave it to Jacob, and Jacob gave it to the most noble of his sons, since it is forbidden to transmit these secrets of the Torah but to the modest persons and to the noble one of the people of Israel in each and every generation.[16] This is why it was not transmitted except to the sons of the lady but not to those of the maid servants. And it is written in the *Gemara* that a three-year old calf was created on each and every eve of Shabbat, by the study of *Sefer Yeẓirah* and by the combination of [divine] names.[17] It is certain that that [calf] created by the names, and not by [the process of] procreation, does not require a ritual slaughter [*Sheḥiṭah*] and it is allowed to be eaten while it is [still] alive[18], as was done by the tribes [i.e., the brothers]. Joseph, however, was not aware of it, thinking as he did that it [the calf] was a creature of a father and a mother; he brought the evil report to his father, namely, that they ate a living animal, though they were right, doing [what they did] according to the law. It is also written in the Gemara that Rava created a man and he sent him to R. Zeira etc., and Rashi commented that by the names of *Sefer Yeẓirah* [he did it]. Behold that there are names out of whose combinations a male is created and there are names out of whose combinations a female is created.[19] And it is possible that the tribes [i.e., the brothers] have created a female using the combination of letters from *Sefer Yeẓirah*.[20] They were walking with her. But Joseph, who was not aware of it [the fact that she was created by *Sefer Yeẓirah*], thought that she was a woman born from a father and mother, and he thus came and announced to his father that they were suspect of committing incest. When the tribes were studying the combinations of these secrets, the sons of the maid-servants wanted to be in their company; the tribes said to them: You are the sons of servants! And their intention was for the sake of heaven since those topics were not transmitted except to the noble one in this generation. But Joseph was not aware of it and he thought that they disregarded the honor of their brothers, and he came and told it to his father. Look how the tribes were righteous and Joseph was righteous too, being the foundation of the world and righteous in all his ways.[21]

The above passage is an ingenious tour de force in solving a quandary which seems to be completely unsolvable; how to preserve the honor of Joseph while mitigating the grave accusations against the brothers, mentioned in authoritative sources. The common denominator between two of the alleged sins is the fact that only an organic creature, an animal in the context of the eating and a real person in connection with the act of sex, involved in the acts denounced by Joseph, will change that act into a blatant transgression, from the legalistic point of view. The Talmudic legend supplied a way of explaining the quandary. According to the halakhic ruling, it is forbidden for close relatives, brothers, sons and fathers, to have intercourse with the same female. This interdiction was allegedly transgressed by the brothers, who "walked", *hayyu meṭayyilim,*[22] an euphemism for having intercourse, with the same woman. However, provided it is not a human being, but merely an artificially created entity, the Halakhic interdiction does not hold in such a case. Implicitly, the assumption of the source quoted by Horwitz, or of Horwitz himself, is that the Golem cannot be considered a human being from the halakhic point of view. On the basis of this discussion of Horwitz, the female Golem was denied any human quality in a detailed halakhic treatment of R. Ẓevi Hirsh of Munkacs.[23]

An interesting version of the passage of Horwitz is found in R. Ḥayyim Joseph David Azulai's *Midbar Qedemot.*[24] He refers explicitly to his source but nevertheless offers a slightly different version. The secrets of *Sefer Yeẓirah* were transmitted to the sons of Leah, and they created maidens [*ne'arot*] and they walked with them. The form of the plural was inserted in order to facilitate the presentation of the situation; while the sexual relationship of the brothers with one woman is explicitly forbidden as incestuous, the "existence" of several maiden attenuated the religious problem.

IV

Last but not least: What is the legal status of the Golem in comparison to a woman? In the version of Rosenberg, the spurious letter of R. Isaac ben Samson Katz ends as follows:

> [The Maharal] did not agree in any way to count it in the quorum so as to complete the figure of ten.[25] He said that even in accordance with those who say that the woman is counted in the quorum, even they do not count the Golem. In this issue it is less than the woman is, because it does not conform to the verse that "I shall be sanctified amidst the sons of Israel"[26], whereas the daughters are counted sometimes among the sons of Israel. Moreover, the daughters [of Israel] are required to conform to all the legal prohibitions, but the Golem is not.[27]

It seems that the use of the verse related to the sanctification of God by Israel alone in the latter legend does reflect the impact of the responsum of *he-Ḥakham Ẓevi.* This is not only my guess, for in a footnote to the above passage, Rosenberg mentioned a certain Ḥasid who had drawn to his attention the responsum of the above mentioned Halakhist. The superiority of the woman in comparison to the Golem is also visible in the first answer attributed to the Maharal, where it is removed from all the imperatives, including those required of women and servants.[28]

In another context, the version of Rosenberg indicates that the Golem did not have any sexual desire, otherwise it could have been dangerous as his power would have overcome everyone. In this context, the fallen angels are mentioned, obviously in order to compare the sexual liberties of these mighty angels with the possible danger of the Golem.[29]

V

As we have seen above, there are opposing attitudes regarding the possibility of conferring a rational power to thc Golem.[30] However, as far as another faculty is concerned, the generative one, it seems that there is a unanimous opinion, namely, that the operator is unable to bestow such a faculty. This stand occurs already in the thirteenth century in a text adduced by Scholem; there the anonymous Kabbalist argues that:

> When the sages say, whoever has no sons is like a dead man, they mean that he is like a Golem, without form. Therefore the images that someone depicts on the wall are Golems without form, since notwithstanding the fact that all the forms are there it will not be called but an image.[31] This is [the meaning of] [Rava] created a man, he created, by the power of combinations of the letters, an image in the form of man, but he was unable to confer upon him the demut; it is possible that, using wondrous powers, someone will make a man who speaks, but he cannot [confer the faculty] of procreation nor that of intellect, for this is unattainable for any creature to accomplish except God, May He be blessed.[32]

This is, as Scholem correctly pointed out[33], a unique reference to the problem of the procreative power of the Golem, and he wondered how it recurred later on, in the famous legend of R. Judel Rosenberg.[34] A possible intermediary text can be suggested. At the end of the eighteenth century, R. Pinḥas Eliyahu Horwitz, composed his widely read *Sefer ha-Berit,* an encyclopaedic work that combines Kabbalah and science. Two editions of the work were printed in the author's lifetime and it immediately became a classic of Jewish enlightenment literature. Already in his first version R. Pinḥas Eliyahu wrote that:

> As long as the power of the intellect does not illuminate the infant, he is mute, being unable to speak. And if a man will create a crea-

ture, a Golem, by the [divine] names and the holy letters mentioned in *Sefer Yeẓirah*, that Golem will have a figure with the appearance of a man shaped out of matter[35] having [even] a soul with all the powers and senses, but without [the power of] speech[36], since he has no reason and his soul lacks the power of intellection, for man is unable to infuse an intellective soul and the power of procreation [*koaḥ ha-molid*] but God alone, as we have explained in the book *Beit ha-Yoẓer*, which I have composed on *Sefer Yeẓirah*. And this was perceived by R. Zeira, concerning that man, that he is a Golem, as it is said in *Sanhedrin*: Rava created a man.[37]

Unfortunately, most of the Kabblistic works of this author, including *Beit ha-Yoẓer* are lost; consequently, lost also is the discussion of the nature of the Golem that could have provided interesting material concerning this topic. However, even from this short passage we may infer that the anonymous text quoted above could have influenced R. Pinḥas Eliyahu. However, the formulation of the eighteenth century author regarding the absence of the generative power of the Golem is identical to that of Judel Rosenberg, using the same expression *koaḥ ha-molid*[38], and it may serve as a possible indication with respect to the sources of the twentieth century understanding of the Golem.

Notes

1. See Marcus Jastrow, *A Dictionary of the Targumim, the Talmud Babli and Yerushalmi and the Midrashic Literature* (1986), vol. 1, pp. 208–209.

2. *Sanhedrin,* fol. 22b. The affinity between Golem and *keli* occurs also in the later theosophical speculations on the Golem as connected to the Supernal Man as the vessel of the divine influx; see chap. 10.

3. See e.g. *TB, Ḥullin,* fol. 25a–b.

4. Cf. Isa. 54:5; *Sanhedrin,* fol. 22b.

5. On this author, see Isaac E. Barzilai, *Yoseph Shlomo Delmedigo, Yashar of Kandia* (Leiden, 1974).

6. N. 21 below.

7. The single significant similarity between the two texts seems to be the fact that in both stories the element of denounciation appears.

8. Odessa, 1865, fol. 10a, ch. 7.

9. Nota bene: this author refers explicitly to Ashkenaz as the locus of the Golem practices and traditions.

10. See Yehudah Liebes, "Rabbi Solomon 'Ibn Gabirol's Use of Sefer Yeṣira and a Commentary on the Poem "I Love Thee" in ed., J. Dan, *The Beginnings of the Jewish Mysticism in Medieval Europe, JSJT,* vol. 6 (Jerusalem, 1988), pp. 104–105 (Hebrew) who envisions the creature of Ibn Gabirol as "*Golem mamash.*" The mechanical nature of the creature attributed to ibn Gabirol was recognized already by Leopold Dukes, *Literaturhistorische Mittheilungen ueber die Aeltesten Hebraeischen Exegeten, Grammatiker und Lexicographen* (Stuttgart, 1844), p. 177, who correctly compares the servant of Ibn Gabirol to the legendary famulus of Albertus Magnus, and by Solomon Rubin, *Ma'aseh Ta'atu'im* (Wien, 1887), p. 118 [Hebrew].

11. Compare Liebes, ibid.

12. I am not aware of female parallels to the famulus of Ibn Gabirol in the earlier literature.

13. Liebes, ibid., p. 105. For a romantic turn of del Medigo's text see S. Y. Agnon's story *'Ido ve-'Einam* (mentioned by Liebes, *ibid.,* p. 104) where the Hebrew *malkhut,* authorities, was transformed into a *Melekh,* a king who fell in love with the automaton of Ibn Gabirol.

14. See the pertinent material collected in R. Menaḥem Kasher's, *Torah Shelemah,* vol. 6 (New York, 1948), pp. 1394–1396. (Hebrew)

15. The problem of the sexual relation of Joseph's brothers is much more complicated than I can elaborate here. Already the Midrash adduces the tradition that a twin sister was born with each and every brother, and they did marry them, all this in order to supply a proper spouse in lieu of the Canaanite alternatives. This is an explicit transgression on the interdiction of incest, promulgated later on in the Pentateuch, and it contradicts the plain meaning of the story of the Bible in the case of Yehudah who married a Canaanite woman.

16. This story was shaped by the Talmudic tradition that Abraham transmitted the pure divine names to the sons of his wives, whereas to the sons of his concubines he gave the names of impurity. See *Sanhedrin,* fol. 91a. See also Idel, "The Concept of the Torah," p. 28 n. 20, and the text of an anonymous disciple of Abraham Abulafia, the author of *Sefer Sha'arei Ẓedeq,* discussed in Idel, *Language, Torah and Hermeneutics,* p. 17.

Compare also the view of R. Yehudah ha-Levi in his *Sefer ha-Kuzari* IV, 25 that the study of *Sefer Yeẓirah* is to be done in limited circles, in accordance with some, unspecified, peculiar conditions, *bitena'im,* related, I assume, to esoteric restrictions. See above ch. 9, n. 34.

17. *Nota bene*: there are two different acts related to the artificial creation of the calf: use of *Sefer Yeẓirah,* apparently the combination of letters of the alphabets, and, secondly, the combinations of the divine names; this distinction corroborates the existence of two phases connected to the creation of the Golem, as discussed above in the cases of R. Eleazar of Worms and R. Abraham Abulafia.

18. This special status of the calf is reminiscent of the description of the calf as not having the quality of meat, as envisioned by the Malbim; see above ch. 14, par. 6.

19. See R. Eleazar of Worms', *Commentary on Sefer Yeẓirah*, fol. 5d.

20. When discussing the creation of the female, in contrast to that of the calf, the distinction between the two technical stages, one related to the letters and the second to the divine names, vanished; see n. 17 above.

21. *Shenei Luḥot ha-Berit, Torah Shebikhtav,* Pericope *Va-Yeshev,* vol. 3, (Jerusalem, 1969), fol. 65a. This passage seems to be the source of the remark of R. Joseph Barukh, the printer of Yoḥanan Alemanno's *Sha'ar ha-Ḥesheq,* who writes that there is evidence for the knowledge of the technique of combination of letters by the tribes, as it is written in "books". Since this remark occurs immediately after the mentioning of the preparation and consumation of the calf, as it occurs at the end of the *Commentary on Sefer Yeẓirah* of R. Joseph ben Shalom Ashkenazi, I assume that the books are a reference to the *Shelah.* See *Sha'ar ha-Ḥesheq,* fol. 31b.

22. This significance of the root *ṭyl* deserves a separate study.

23. See *Darkhei Teshuvah,* (Wilna, 1892), fol. 38a analyzed above ch. 14.

24. Letter H, n. 17, par. 12, (Jerusalem 1962), fol. 21d.

25. I am not acquainted with an earlier discussion which related Woman to Golem. See also beside n. 12 above.

26. Lev. 22:32.

27. See *Nifla'ot ha-Maharal,* p. 74, par. 19.

28. Ibid., p. 71, par. 1.

29. Ibid., p. 72, par. 9. See also ch. 3, par. 3.

30. See also Scholem, "The Image of the Golem," pp. 197–198.

31. The Kabbalist distinguishes between *ẓelem,* here conceived as a lower spiritual faculty, and *demut,* presented as the quintessence of the human entity.

32. Ms. New York, JTS, 838, fol. 35b; Scholem, "The Idea of the Golem," p. 194.

33. Scholem, ibid.

34. See n. 37 below.

36. Cf. Job. 33:6.

36. On this point R. Pinḥas Eliyahu differs from the medieval source quoted above. It is to be remarked that R. Pinḥas Eliyahu was well acquainted with Kab-

balistic material, even those in manuscripts, as his roundnotes found in manuscripts, testify.

37. *Sefer ha-Berit* (Bruen, 1799), fol. 95b; second edition (Wilna, 1897), fol. 89b.

38. *Nifla'ot ha-Maharal,* p. 72, no. 9.

16

Vicissitudes of the Golem Techniques

The explicit assumption that *Sefer Yeẓirah* includes the technique to create a man was widespread in Judaism since the Middle Ages. Though there were several versions regarding the precise manner to create the Golem by means of combinations of letters, there is no evidence for views that considered these techniques to be fruitless attempts; even sceptical attitudes with respect to the effectiveness of these techniques are not extant. One of the reasons for this respectful silence concerning the problems involved in the linguistic technique to achieve a material goal seems to be the assumption that the precise formulas of the combinations of the letters are not extant. This sort of argument is very close to an ancient treatment of the order of the letters of the Torah. According to R. Eleazar ben Pedat in the third century, "The various sections of the Torah were not given in their correct order. For if they have been given in their correct order, anyone who read them would be able to wake the dead and perform miracles. For this reason the correct order and arrangement of the Torah were hidden and are known only to the Holy One, Blessed be He, concerning whom it was said,[1] 'And who. as I, shall call, and shall declare it, and set it in order for me.'"[2]

Thus, the magical potentialities of the Torah were intentionally concealed by God in order to allow the common path of life not to be disturbed by the transmission of the code for extraordinary operations. A similar attitude seems to be reflected also in a widespread medieval text, the preface of Naḥmanides to his *Commentary of the Torah*; according to the view expressed there, the reading of the Torah in accordance to the path of the names was hidden, and instead we were given only the reading according to the commandments.[3] Thus, it was the sublimity of the hidden order that explained its absence, thus preserving the allegedly magical powers present in the letters of the Torah on a pedestal.

This attitude was also adopted, in principle, with respect to the technique of combining letters in order to achieve an extraordinary effect. According to R. Moses Cordovero, only the rudimentaries of the higher type of studying the Torah, the Kabbalah of letters and their combinations, are in our hands, whereas the entire corpus of this Kabbalah will be revealed after the resurrection from death; he indicates that this lore requires a complete purification of the human person, which is possible only in the messianic future.[4] When this Kabbalist commenced his discussion of the combination of letters, he warns that the ancients knew the relationship between letters and their spirituality and the combination of letters, but they did not use them; their knowledge permitted them to fathom the power of the Creator. However, because of the vicissitudes of the dispersion, the eyes of the sages closed and there was a decline of the knowledge of the theoretical Kabbalah, a fortiori of the practical Kabbalah.[5] Moreover, even the views of those who exposed this practical Kabbalah is not understood nowadays by the Kabbalists, and Cordovero enumerates those of the Kabbalists who used the names either in a positive manner or in a negative one.[6] Thus, it seems that according to Cordovero, it is difficult to assume that the ultimate techniques of combining letters and exploiting the potentialities inherent in them, are available.[7] However, it seems that until the time of Cordovero, no one expressed an explicitly doubtful opinion regarding the nature of the techniques extant in *Sefer Yeẓirah*.

At the end of a manuscript copy of Cordovero's *Commentary on Sefer Yeẓirah*, an anonymous person added the following remark: "Do not believe . . . that, nowadays, there is a power to operate by means of this book. Not (at all), because the (supernal?) sources of the practices are closed and the Kabbalah disappeared and there are no (more) faithful [Kabbalists]."[8]

This sceptical attitude is slightly different from that of Cordovero expressed above; in this case the most exalted Kabbalah was not yet in the possession of men, whereas a lower type of magical Kabbalah was disclosed, but not understood; in the case of the anonymous passage, it was once in their hands but it disappeared. The result is, however, similar. In any case, in the middle of the seventeenth century, the precise arrangement of the 231 combinations of letters was considered an important Kabbalistic achievement, attained in a revelatory experience, and whose printing without the name of the Kabbalist who compiled it was considered to be a plagiary. R. Naftali Bakharakh, whose interest in the topic of the Golem was profound, complains that his former disciple, R. Yoseph Shelomo del Medigo, had printed the 231 gates, which were revealed to him in a night vision.[9] These gates are "a wondrous thing" based on the views of Luria.[10] He claims that all his students in Poland and Germany know that he is the real innovator of these 231 combinations. Undoubtedly, the author does not intend the mere list of the combinations of two letters, but the much more complex arrangements of combinations which are the source of each of the anthropomorphic configurations, the *parẓufim,* characteristic of the Lurianic theosophy stemming, according to Sarug, from the combinations of letters. These combinations were printed in *'Emeq ha-Melekh* and were copied time and again by a long series of Kabbalists.[11]

According to R. Jacob Barukh, the printer of *Sha'ar ha-Ḥesheq,* he was told by Ḥ.Y.D.A.' that he had seen several persons who performed miracles by means of the combination of letters; however, this is a very dangerous performance as the fate of those who did it demonstrated. Then Ḥ.Y.D.A.' asserted that it is not sufficient to know the "material combination," *ha-Ẓeruf ha-gashmi*[12] mentioned in these books.[13] Unfortunately, Ḥ.Y.D.A.' did not disclose what exactly is missing in the books so that we remain in complete darkness regarding the additional elements required, according to this Kabbalist, in order to perform the magical operations by means of the combination of letters.

In Lurianic Kabbalah, the interest in the magical implications of the combination of letters seems to be even more problematic. It is an outstanding fact that the creation of an anthropoid by man was not mentioned in the classical writings of this brand of Kabbalah. Luria is even reported to have forbidden the use of the various linguistic techniques which yield extraordinary results. R. Moses ben Menaḥem Graff of Prague writes that the various magical books and techniques were handed down in a distorted way by the ancient authors in order to prevent the use of them; in this context the creation of the calf by "Abaye and Rava" is mentioned. Luria asserted that he could improve the texts but he did not want to do it, lest people will take advantage of the powers inherent in these books.[14]

This is the background of a discussion between R. Ḥayyim of Volohzin and his master, R. Eliyahu, the Gaon of Vilna. The major topic of this conversation was the extraordinary ability of the Gaon to correct the mistakes which crept into important Kabbalistic texts, a sort of activity which was indeed characteristic of the literary production of this figure. When asked about the text of *Sefer Yeẓirah*, he answered:

> Concerning *Sefer Yeẓirah*, his view was definite already from the years of his youth, [having] a correct version and a wondrous depth; I proposed to him ten different variants of the versions of *Sefer Yeẓirah*, and he told me his correct version, [just] as the version of Ari's text, but for one mistake that had crept into the printed editions of the Ari's text. When I [R. Ḥayyim] said to him that in that case it should now be easy to create a Golem, he answered, "Once indeed I started to create a Golem, but while I was engaged in making it I saw an apparition [*temunah*] above my head and desisted from continuing, saying to myself that Heaven apparently wanted to prevent me on account of my youth." When I asked him how old he was at that time, he answered that he had not yet reached his thirteenth year.[15]

Thus we learn that in the second part of the eighteenth century the assumption of a highly respected Halakhist and Kabbalist was that all the printed versions of the combination of letters in *Sefer Yeẓirah* were mistaken including that of Luria. Such an approach seems to be reflected in the version of R. Judel Rosenberg as well. In the text attributed to the Maharal, we learn that:

> It is not pertinent to study the combinations of letters in *Sefer Yeẓirah* as they are printed, and create by their means a man or an animal. The person who will study the combinations solely from the book has no power to create anything. First, because there are many mistakes and they are deficient in a great degree. Moreover, the most important fact is the comprehension of the person, who has to know from the very beginning which light alludes to each and every letter.[16]

The question of the defective printing of the combinations seems to reflect the view of R. Ḥayyim of Volohzin more than anything attributable to the Maharal. As in the case of the comparison of other themes of the text attributed to the Maharal to similar materials, also in this point it seems easier to assume that the last discussion of a certain topic related to the Golem is reflected, by acceptance or by opposition, in the version of R. Judel Rosenberg.

Notes

1. Isa. 44:7.

2. See *Midrash Tehillim,* ed., S. Buber, p. 37; see Scholem, *On the Kabbalah,* p. 37.

3. On this issue, see Idel, "The Concept of the Torah," pp. 52–56.

4. Idel, *Studies in Ecstatic Kabbalah,* p. 140; (above ch. 12).

5. *Pardes Rimmonim* XXI, 1, fols. 96d–97a. See also the introduction of R. Naftali Bakharakh to his *'Emeq ha-Melekh,* fol. 5d.

6. See Idel, "R. Shelomo Molkho as a Magician", pp. 199–202.

7. See *Pardes Rimmonim* part 21: ch. 2, fol. 97a, where Cordovero is confused about the correct way to pronounce the letters connected to the creation of a man; he quoted the scheme of Abulafia, based on combinations of five vowels, and that of R. Joseph Ashkenazi, based on combinations of six vowels, and he cannot decide which of them is better. He concludes that only in the messianic era will this quandary find its solution.

8. Copied from an apparently lost manuscript in the description of the manuscript of Isaac Hirschenson, printed in the literary supplement of *ha-Ẓevi,* vol. 2, (1886) n. 31; Ms. n. 27. According to the description of Hirschenson, this manuscript included also two other pieces of great interest for our subject: a tract including the words of the ancients on creation, seemingly the magical creation, of man and a *Commentary on Sefer Yeẓirah* by R. David Ḥabbillo. Unfortunately, I could not trace the fate of this manuscript and it seems that no other manuscript including the same material is extant.

9. *'Emeq ha-Melekh,* fol. 7d of the introduction of the author.

10. Ibid.

11. See e.g., R. Moses Prager's *Va-Yaqhel Moshe,* R. Shelomo Eliashov's *Leshem, Shevo' ve-'Aḥlemah,* and R. Jacob Meir Spielmann's *Ṭal 'Orot.*

12. This phrase occurs already in R. Joseph Ashkenazi's, *Commentary on Sefer Yeẓirah*, fol. 18c; there the context deals with the combination of letters in the Torah.

13. *Sha'ar ha-Ḥesheq,* fol. 32a.

14. *Va-Yaqhel Moshe* (Zalkow, 1841), fol. 6b. See also above chapter 11, n. 18.

15. The introduction to R. Eliyahu of Vilna's *Commentary on Sifra' de-Zeni'uta* (Jerusalem, 1986), pp. 8–9. The bulk of this passage was translated into English by R. J. Zwi Werblowsky, *Joseph Karo, Lawyer and Mystic* (Philadelphia, 1977), p. 313, where the reader can find also the larger context of this quotation.

16. *Nifla'ot ha-Maharal,* pp. 73–74, par. 17.

17

Golem and Ḥasidic Mysticism

The early Ḥasidic literature is surprisingly impoverished in discussions on the nature of the Golem or in the descriptions of techniques of creating such a being. Even the legends regarding this extraordinary being are very rare.[1] Outstanding exceptions are the discussions found in the writings of famous Hasidic masters who flourished at the end of the nineteenth century, the famous R. Ẓadoq ben Jacob ha-Kohen of Lublin and R. Gershom Ḥanokh Leiner.[2] As we have already seen, the discussions of the latter are focused upon the nature of the Golem. Another passage of R. Ẓadoq ha-Kohen, to be analyzed here, deals with the explanation of the creation of this artificial man. What appears to be new in this exposition of the creation is a peculiar combination of the classical technique of creating an artificial man and the Ḥasidic linguistic theory, which together create a daring explanation, that contributes a special flavor to the preceding views.

In his *Liqquṭei 'Amarim,*[3] the author proposes a view that the lore as expressed in *Sefer Yeẓirah* exists on three levels; on the level of the thought, *maḥshavah,* there is no difference between the content of this book as understood by Jews or Gentiles. Thus it was possible for this book to be translated into foreign languages, together with other Kabbalistic treatises, and the Gentiles were able to understand something of this level of meaning.[4] However, there seems to be a difference; since only the people of Israel ascended to divine thought, according to a well-known Midrashic dictum,[5] they alone can ascend to this supreme level, which consists of fathoming the divine unity. This limit of the gentiles is connected, I assume, to the fact that the mentioning of the sefirot may be understood as compromising the divine unity because of the trinitarian propensities. Since the major assumption of this book is the doctrine of the complete unity, the discussions of this book are meaningful only for those who are able to transcend the plurality; for whomever this transcending movement is impossible, the words of *Sefer Yeẓirah* are conceived of as futile things; this is the attitude of the Gentiles.

The second level of *Sefer Yeẓirah* consists of the existence of the letters in the heart, namely topics which cannot be expressed in a written form but are transmitted orally, from the mouth of the master to the disciple, and this is the reason why this level is regarded as the *mysterion* of Israel, an expression used in a Rabbinic source in order to designate the Oral Law as a unique prerogative of Israel.[6] This level is totally unattainable by the Gentiles. Even if all of them will come together in order to create any creature, they will not be capable of doing it in the way that Rava was capable, according to the *Sanhedrin* passage quoted by R. Ẓadoq.[7] The basic assumption is that the vitality, *ḥiyyut,*[8] dwelling in the heart of the righteous of Israel, is the energy which enables the creation by combination of letters, as proposed in the *Sefer Yeẓirah.*

The last level is the natural realm, which is revealed to the Gentiles, as they contemplate the deeds of God. What is unique to the sages of Israel is the understanding of, and the operation by means of, the second level of *Sefer Yeẓirah*. Neither its abstract message, which can be approximated in translation even by those who are not Jews, nor the third level, namely the natural realm which is open to everyone, is the unique aspect of the book. The second level, therefore, is that which is limited to an esoteric oral transmission and it alone enables the creative processes by the activation of the vitality of the operator.[9]

The vitality dwelling in the heart of the operator is, according to Hasidic theory, part of the divine pneuma, or a limited aspect of the divine present in the individual.[10] Therefore, R. Ẓadoq writes, when someone recites the combinations of the letters of *Sefer Yeẓirah*, he uses his vitality and thereby activates the divine realm.[11] The basic assumption is that human activity is ultimately an activation of the divine, this being the clue for the creativity of the combinations of letters. R. Ẓadoq uses a view, widespread in both Kabbalah and Hasidism, that asserts that the relationship between the divine and human is tantamount to the relationship between the shadow and its source, the hand. When man moves his hand, the divine is automatically responding to this movement.[12]

This daring explanation is easily understood against the background of the pantheistic views of Hasidic masters and it permitted an attenuation of the magical implications of the creation of an artificial man, or animal, according to the Talmudic passage. R. Ẓadoq, like R. Yehudah Barceloni beforehand,[13] was interested in purifying the eccentric expressions of magical activity of the Talmudic masters. Whereas the twelfth century commentator transforms the Amoraic figures into scholars who are able to achieve a perfect status by their immersion in their study, the creation being only a retribution for their efforts; the nineteenth century master portrayed Rava as a mystic in the Hasidic manner, who is successful not because of the peculiar knowledge or powers inherent in the letters but because he activates the divine power present in him. In the two cases the magical aspect is subdued by the assumption that God alone is the real operator, as in the case of the transcedental theology of Barceloni or the pantheistic view of R. Ẓadoq ha-Kohen.

However, the assumption of the divine "indwelling" does not exhaust the creative aspect of the vision of R. Ẓadoq; after all, the capability to manipulate divine powers inherent in man may easily become a more powerful version of magic than the assumption that the powers are immanent in the letters. These magical implications are attenuated by the assumption that there is a certain personal contact between man and the divine. The contact takes place on the level of the heart; there the divine vitality is found and there man is able to encounter "the divine heart".[14] God contracts Himself in the heart of the mystic, and when such a contact is established, the possibility of influence on the divine requires a mystical encounter between the two hearts before an influence is able to take place.

Finally, it should be mentioned that R. Ẓadoq ha-Kohen does not refer here either to the creation of the Golem out of dust, or its return to dust. It seems that the act of creation is basically the structuring of the divine vitality, as found in man, by the recitation of the combination of letters. Is the creation of man, according to the Talmud, understood as merely a shaping of energy, without any material substratum? The discussions in *Liqqutei 'Amarim* would allow, in principle, the possibility of such an explanation though no explicit statement in this direction can be found. However, the other discussion of the same author, regarding the status of the created artificial man demonstrates that he believed in a fulfledged Golem, formed out of dust.[15]

Notes

1. See Israel Ta'-Shma', "The Golem and His Status in Halakhah," *Maḥanayyim,* vol. 84 (1984), p. 130; (Hebrew) and ch. 18 below.

2. See ch. 14, par. 7–9.

3. In *Divrei Soferim,* (Benei Beraq, 1973), fol. 57d–58a.

4. This is an extraordinarily rare case when the awareness of the existence of Christian Kabbalah is mentioned with an attempt to counteract it by a Hasidic master. Compare the views of R. Jacob Ẓemaḥ as analyzed in Idel, "Perceptions of Kabbalah," pp. 197–199.

5. R. Ẓadoq uses the principle of the joint vessels in order to explain why only the people of Israel are able to fathom the divine thought; only they ascended to this high point, and therefore are able to return to it.

6. See e.g., *Midrash Tanḥuma,* pericope *ki tissa',* par. 34.

7. *Divrei Soferim,* fol. 58a.

8. The concept of *ḥiyyut* is understood in the Hasidic texts in a different way than the Cordoverian *ḥiyyut* was. In the former's discussions it is the divine presence as energy, in the latter it is the lower form of energy which is described by this term.

9. The emphasis on the importance of direct contact for the attainment of religious perfection in matters of Kabbalah has a Hasidic flavor, since Kabbalah has lost the importance of direct contacts as a meaningful channel of transmission. It is through the Hasidic movement that the importance of the oral teaching and direct contact was restored. See Idel, "The Reification of Language".

10. See Louis Jacobs, "The Doctrine of the Divine Spark in Man in Jewish Sources," in *Rationalism, Judaism, Universalism: Studies in Memory of Leon Roth* (New York, 1966), pp. 87–114.

11. See *Divrei Soferim,* fol. 58a and the discussion ibid., fol. 63c–64b.

12. On the history of this view see Idel, *Kabbalah: New Perspectives,* pp. 173–179.

13. See ch. 4 above.

14. *Divrei Soferim,* fol. 58a. On God as the heart of Israel see R. Ẓadoq's, *Resisei Laylah* (Benei Beraq, 1967), fol. 21ab.

15. See ch. 14 above.

18

Modern Reverberations

In the preceding discussions we have avoided the treatment of the most widespread tradition on the creation of the Golem: that attributed to the Maharal, R. Yehudah Loew ben Beẓalel of Prague. It is the specific attribution of the creation of a Golem to this outstanding figure that became the classical form of legends related to the Golem since the nineteenth century. These legends seem to confirm the suggestion proposed above concerning sociological function of the Golem materials and legends in Jewish culture: they endowed some spiritual leaders of the Jews with the aura of the archmagician which originates from the recognition of the profound acquaintance of some masters with Jewish lore, whether magical or mystical. I would not like to enter here into further speculations on why the creation of the Golem was attributed to this particular figure and not to another one, contemporary with the Maharal, as for instance R. Isaac Luria. I am not able to suggest any credible explanation for this attribution; however, it is obvious that an examination of the voluminous writings of the Maharal shows that there is no plausible reason for the linkage between him and the legend. His attitude to magic reflects the "normative" view of the Jewish elite of his period. As scholars have pointed out, the attribution of the legend to the Maharal does not do justice to his spiritual profile as it can be reconstructed from his authentic opus. Moreover, the historical sources written in the circle of the Maharal and immediately after his death, among them reliable documents of his disciples, do not mention the legend.[1]

Nevertheless, since the end of the first third of the nineteenth century, the name of the Maharal is connected in written sources with the creation of an anthropoid. That this connection may be plausible is supported in an important Hasidic treatise, whose precise date cannot be determined, but it seems to have been written circa 1835. In his *Benei Isaskhar,* R. Ẓevi Elimelekh Shapira of Dinov says of the Maharal that his words were written under the inspiration of the holy spirit and "he was [magically] using (*hayah mishtamesh*) *Sefer Yeẓirah.*"[2] Though the Golem is not explicitly mentioned, I assume that there is no real possibility to doubt the necessity to understand this sentence as referring to the creating of a Golem by means of *Sefer Yeẓirah.* For the time being any other alternative interpretation seems to be less plausible. In the middle of the nineteenth century, legends related to this figure as the creator of the Golem are documented in Prague.[3] I should not like to elaborate upon the content of these legends as they belong to another domain of study: Jewish folklore; here we were concerned with the documentation and analysis of the magical and mystical views of the Golem. I doubt whether the folkloristic material can contribute to a better understanding of the magical and mystical facets of this theme analyzed above. However, there can be no doubt that the spread of the legend in Prague has to be related to the appearance of the theme of the artificial anthropoid in the works of authors who visited Prague or lived there, as the examples of Goethe and Hašek may testify.[4]

The most important literary outcome of the legend related to the Maharal in the domain of Jewish mysticism is the document published under the name of *Nifla'ot Maharal.* In 1909, a Polish Rabbi, Judel Rosenberg, printed material describing, inter alia, the creation of the Golem by the Maharal and his two assistants, one of them being his alleged son-in-law, R. Isaac ben Shimshon Katz, the second a certain Rabbi Abraham Ḥayyim. The part concerning the Golem includes two segments: "conversations" on the Golem, *Siḥot Maharal on the Golem,* written by R. Isaac Katz, which consists of nineteen statements describing the nature of the Golem, and a legend on the creation on the Golem itself, named here, perhaps for the first time by a proper name, Yosele Golem. The material was presented as being copied from a manuscript from the library of Metz, which was destroyed. However, for the time being, no manuscript containing the printed material is extant. As several authors have already suspected, there are good reasons to doubt the authenticity of the story and it is plausible that it is a forgery of the printer, Judel Rosenberg of Warshau.[5] Notwithstanding this conclusion, corroborated by the disclosure of the fictitious nature of other material presented by Rosenberg as stemming from the same library, it is obvious that the author was well acquainted with material related to the Golem from the printed, and perhaps even manuscript material, which is now lost. His attempt to elaborate upon this topic testifies to the eagerness of the Ghetto Jews to believe in the authenticity of such type of stories.

Combining Kabbalistic material describing the Golem, together with Hasidic terminology and themes,[6] Rosenberg was able to provide an elaborate description, which seems to be the first systematic discussion of this topic; it is also the most influential one. It was printed in the 1909 edition; yet, the other editions, and translations done by Hayyim Bloch, differing from the version of Rosenberg only in details, ensured the dissemination of this legend beyond the limited circle of the Hebrew readers in Poland.[7] Bloch presented his version as an original letter written by the Maharal himself, addressed to a certain R. Jacob Ginzburg of Friedburg. This substantially pseudepigraphic document is based upon the innovation of Rosenberg. It is the creative literary genius of Rosenberg and Bloch, together with the propagative efforts of Bloch that contributed to the spread of the Maharal legend in wider audiences. We may characterize the dissemination of the Golem legend as part of the diffusion of a greater series of Jewish mystical mythologoumena in wider segments of Jewry at the beginning of the twentieth century, as the interest in the *dibbuk* and the astonishing success of S. An-Ski's play dealing with this topic illustrate.

The belief in Maharal's Golem became part of the Jewish patrimony to such an extent that contemporary orthodox Jews have vehemently argued against an attempt to deny the historicity of the legend. In 1987, in a newspaper of the ultraorthodox community in Jerusalem, the veracity of the Maharal legend was discussed. In an article entitled "The Metamorphosis of a Golem" the author, Israel Holand, adduced some already known arguments against the authenticity of the version of Rosenberg, but the tradition in the *Benei Isaskhar,* discussed above, caused some hesitation to overtly deny the creation of the Golem by the Maharal.[8] At the end of his article, he ingeniously, though hesitantly, proposes that it is possible that, despite the fact that the Maharal did create a Golem, this was not recorded in Jewish sources because of the witch hunt in Europe during the period of the Maharal. It seems that the hesitant tone had provoked some strong negative and critical reactions from some readers, which triggered in turn the publication of another article;[9] this time the author examined in detail the arguments against the authenticity of Rosenberg's version, but ultimately its historicity was not openly denied. This article ends with the statement that the whole issue remains a mystery.

Orthodox readers interested in the matter of the Golem were not confined to the readers of *Yated ha-Ne'eman.* This newspaper, an organ of the nonmystical ultraorthodoxy current, was not the only one which discussed the matter of the Golem. Shortly after the publication of the two above-mentioned articles, another newspaper, *Kefar Ḥabad,* representing the views of the Hasidic sect of Ḥabad, devoted a lengthy discussion to the authenticity of the tradition which attributes the creation of the Golem to the Maharal.[10] In a later issue, an interesting reaction from a reader was also printed.[11] This time the veracity of the attribution is explicitly defended and the emphasis on the need to accept the content of tradition is obvious. The question is why did two newspapers decide to allocate lengthy columns to such an academic topic as the attribution of the legend to the Maharal? I assume that beyond the silent controversy we can discern a polemic on the source of authority. Those who tend to negate the authenticity of the legend do at the same time negate the authority of tradition and they question the miraculous endeavours of the Maharal. A defence of the authenticity of the legend is, at the same time, also a defence of the wondrous Maharal. Beyond such a defence stands the Hasidic establishment, which was interested in preserving the legitimacy of the Renaissance Rabbi in order to ensure the extraordinary claims concerning the present Rabbi, R. Menaḥem Mendel Shneursohn of Lubavitch. The fact that the latter is constantly attacked by the Lithuanian nonmystical Rabbis corroborates our assumption that under a dispute on the veracity of the Maharal legend, contemporary Jews were waging a religious war regarding the nature of spiritual leadership. The Golem therefore is emblematic of the possibility of a supernaturalistic leadership, whereas the denial of the attribution of the story to the Maharal serves as an allusion to the fact that the religious leadership has to be based upon Halakhic erudition rather than claims of supernatural achievements. This analysis of the significance of the Golem episode in recent religious newspapers corroborates our hypothesis on the sociological function of the Golem in the earlier phases of Jewish culture. To what extent such a discussion is influential on the religious configuration of modern orthodoxy and even beyond it, we can only guess from the participation of most of the orthodox groups, following the calls of the respective leaders, in political issues in the recent times.

However, I would not say that the belief in the authenticity of the legend is totally restricted to ultraorthodox circles. Even as Western an author as André Neher has changed his mind, and in one of his recent works he is inclined to retract his rejection of the authenticity of the version of the legend as presented by Rosenberg. Not that Neher would assume that the Maharal indeed created a Golem; he is merely inclined to assume, at least, that the attribution of the legend to this figure is much earlier; this is in order to build up an historiosophical parallelism between the Golem and the Maharal, on one hand, and the Faust legend on the other.[12]

An astonishing credulity is manifest in the psychoanalytical analysis of the Maharal in connection to his "creation" of the Golem, as proposed by Bettina Knapp.[13] Apparently accepting the historicity of the Bloch version of the legend as printed in English, she regards the Maharal as the archetype of the wise old man, whereas his Golem is "an archaic aspect of the 'savior type'." The two figures are conceived respectively in terms of spirit and matter, both of them inspiring "psychic energy in believers to enable them to survive."[14] The Golem is conceived by Knapp as a response to a collective need. Though this theory may indeed have some degree of truth, the description of the Praguean background as the explanation for the act of the Maharal renders this explanation very doubtful.[15] In principle, this collective need of ensurance is implicit also in Scholem's analysis of Rosenberg's version on the background of a late nineteenth century pogrom.[16] What is indeed strange is the psychoanalytical analysis of Knapp is the fact that she elaborates on the legend of Bloch in order to construct a psychological portrait of the Maharal, neglecting the authentic writings of this master. Moreover, the coalescence of different traditions related to the Golem, which were exposed in the study of Scholem, contributed to a strange mixture of unrelated elements in an allegedly unified conception of the Maharalian Golem. Conspicuously prominent is Knapp's attribution of elements stemming from the ecstatic Kabbalah, probably unknown by Rosenberg, to his description of the Golem, in an otherwise fascinating Jungian elaboration.[17] In predictable Jungian hermeneutics, Knapp even mentions the "parallels" between the creation of the Golem and an alchemical process.[18] Though this view is not totally devoid of interest, the fact that the author mentions in this context the Praguean concern in alchemy complicates the credibility of this suggestion. It seems that the material on the Golem does not fit comfortably on the psychoanalytical sofa.

Let me elaborate a little more on this "response theory" hinted at by Scholem and elaborated by Knapp, though she related it to another period. Both of them attribute a profound influence of a certain historical constellation for the emergence of a certain mythical theme. For Knapp, it is the "dire crisis" in Prague that helped the surfacing of a Jungian archetype, the "savior type".[19] For Scholem, it is the response to an historical crisis, a pogrom, that shaped the version of Rosenberg.[20] However, what complicates this hypothesis, without however rendering it completely implausible, is the fact that the savior archetype does not occur in the Ashkenazi discussions of the Golem in the Middle Ages, in a period when the memory of the 1096 pogroms, caused by the crusades, was still fresh. All the central European versions of the Golem in the Middle Ages discussed above ignore any salvific allusions. This is also clear in those discussions of the Golem penned by Sefardic figures, like Moses Cordovero, in the generation following the Expulsion from Spain.

Thus, it would be advisable to understand the emergence of the Golem theme not only as a reaction to an historical crisis, but more as the result of the accumulation of the treatment of this theme which could be exposed in a fuller and more organic manner later on in the development of the theme than was possible earlier. I propose to allow a greater place for the immanent development of a certain theme, which continues to evolve in the same area, rather than resort to history as the crucial clue for understanding a certain literary or religious phenomenon.[20] In other words, the two twentieth century Ashkenazi authors who contributed to the dissemination of the Golem legend continued the earlier traditions and concerns which characterized the geographical area within which they were active.[21]

Let me conclude this short survey of the perception of the Golem in those circles where there was an attempt to continue the speculations upon the Golem, with a still unprinted legend on this topic. It is found in the Archives of Jewish folklore in Haifa. The following story was told by a survivor of the holocaust, born in Prague, to a Jewish soldier in Bologna in 1945.[22] As the soldier remarked, the teller of the story appeared to be a free-thinker, *ḥofshi be-de'otav*:

> The Golem did not disappear and even in the time of the war it went out of his hiding-place in order to safeguard its synagogue. When the Germans occupied Prague, they decided to destroy the Altneuschul. They came to do it; suddenly, in the silence of the synagogue, the steps of a giant walking on the roof, began to be heard. They saw a shadow of a giant hand falling from the window onto the floor. . . . The Germans were terrified and they threw away their tools and fleed away in panic.
>
> I know that there is a rational explanation for everything; the synagogue is ancient and each and every slight knock generates an echo that reverberates many times, like steps or thunder. Also the glasses of the windows are old, the window-panes are crooked and they distort the shadows, forming strange shades on the floor. A bird's leg generates a shade of a giant hand on the floor . . . and nevertheless . . . there is something.

Notes

1. See especially A. Gottesdiener, "Ha-'Ari she-be-ḥakhmei Prag", ed., Yehudah Leib Fishman, *'Azkara le-nishmat Abraham Izḥaq ha-Kohen Qooq* (Jeru-

salem, 1937), vol. 4, pp. 307, 348–350, (Hebrew); Vladimir Sadek, "Stories of the Golem and their Relation to the Work of Rabbi Löw of Prague, *Judaica Bohemiae,* vol. 23 (1987) pp. 85–91, n. 2.

2. Benei Beraq, N. D., part II, fol. 44d.

3. See Schlomo Yehudah ha-Kohen Rappaport, Koppelmann Lieben, *Gal-Ed* (Prag, 1856), p. 6. (German part) Interestingly, on this same page a descendant of the Maharal is quoted as presenting the Maharal as using the holy spirit, exactly as in the above statement of the Hasidic master. However, the magical use of *Sefer Yeẓirah* is not mentioned here; yet, the creation of a "homunculum", [*sic*] conceived as a Golem, is referred to briefly. See also Gottesdiener, ibid., p. 307.

4. See already the discussion of Mueller, "Die Golemsage," pp. 24–40; especially the monographs of Beate Rosenfeld, *Die Golemsage und ihre Verwertung in der deutschen Literatur,* (Breslau, 1934), and Sigfrid Mayer, "Golem: Die literarische Rezepzion eines Stoffes", *Utah Studies in Literature and Linguistics* (Bern, 1975).

5. See, e.g., Immanuel Eckstein, *Sefer Yeẓirah* (Siget, 1910), (Hebrew), Gershom Scholem, the review of Bloch's edition of the collection of epistles, *Qiriat Sefer,* vol. 1 (1924), pp. 105–106. (Hebrew) Scholem pointed out the use of late Kabbalistic terminology.

6. See above ch. 6, par. 2 and ch. 14, par. 10 and ch. 15, par. 4.

7. See Ḥayyim Bloch, *Qoveẓ Mikhtavim Meqoriim me-ha-Besht* (Wien-Berlin, 1924), pp. 86–94. The Hebrew version of this letter of the Maharal was printed again by Bloch himself in R. Joseph Meir of Spinka, *Sefer 'Imrei Yoseph* (Vranov, 1931) vol. 2, fol. 2b–4b. Bloch served as proofreader for the printing of the voluminous writings of the Rabbi of Spinka. A German treatment of the Golem was published by Bloch as *Der Prager Golem* (Berlin, 1920), and an English version *The Golem. Legends of the Ghetto of Prague,* trans. Harry Schneidermann (Vienna, 1925).

8. Supplement to *Yated Ne'eman,* 'Elul 5747, pp. 6–7. (Hebrew)

9. Supplement to *Yated Ne'eman* 18 of Sivan, 5748, p. 12. (Hebrew)

10. *Kefer Ḥabad,* is a weekly publication of the youth of the Ḥabad movement in Israel. See the issue of August 23, 1988, no. 348, pp. 10–13. (Hebrew) The article is penned by Rabbi B. Schemuel.

11. Ibid., Sept., 22, 1988, no. 351, p. 51. (Hebrew) The short letter of R. Pinḥas-Abraham Meiers from Amsterdam contains some reference to the treatment of the Golem in modern Halakhic responsa. The articles from *Kefar Ḥabad* were drawn to my attention by Professor Sid Z. Leiman.

12. See above, *Introduction.*

13. Bettina L. Knapp, *The Prometheus Syndrome* (New York, Troy, 1979), pp. 97–131.

14. Ibid., pp. 110–111.

15. Ibid., pp. 106–110.

16. See Scholem, "The Idea of the Golem," p. 189, n. 1.

17. *The Prometheus Syndrome,* pp. 104, 122.

18. Ibid., p. 129, n. 50; p. 131, n. 60, 61, 64.

19. Ibid., pp. 97, 104, 110, 122–123.

20. This difference between Scholem's view of the history of Jewish mysticism and mine is evident also in other instances as, for example, the explanation of the emergence of the Lurianic Kabbalah. See Idel, *Kabbalah: New Perspectives,* pp. 264–266.

21. See also the quotation from Bruno Schultz's short story at the beginning of our Introduction. Concerning another story on the Golem in Poland, see in *Biographical Sketches and Selected Verses,* by Rev. Rabbi Samuel Marcus Gollancz, translated and Edited from the original German by Hermann Gollanz (London, 1930), pp. 50, 54. The memories of Gollancz refer to his childhood in Posen. Thanks are due to Professor Sid Z. Leiman who mentioned this discussion to me.

22. No. 11383 in the Archive. The story was originally told in Yiddish, but in the Archive it is extant only in the Hebrew translation. Thanks are due to Mrs. Edna Heikhal, the director of the Archives, who has kindly put at my disposal all the material concerning the Golem collected by the Archive. Out of the many legends on this topic, I preferred to mention only this one.

19

Golem: Imaginaire, Anomian, and Silent

I

After describing in detail the most important forms of the Golem phenomena, it would be pertinent to attempt to locate the various views in the larger field of the medieval "wonder-phenomena." In the last generation, a whole scholarly literature has been dedicated to imaginative literary and theological motifs, mostly as they occur in Christian literature. The works of Le Goff,[1] Schmitt[2] and Kappler,[3] to mention only some of the most important names who have investigated the phenomena of the imaginary in the last generation, have contributed substantially to a better understanding of a neglected area of medieval culture. To the contributions of these French scholars, mostly interested in literature as the main source for their analysis, we may add some works of their important colleague, Henry Corbin, who focused his attention on the manifestations of the imaginative in Eastern mysticism, analyzing the important concept of the imaginative world, *mundus imaginalis,* in Sufism.[4]

Unfortunately, Jewish forms of the wonderful and imaginative have remained outside the scope of those analyses and classifications; on the other hand, Jewish scholars who might have illuminated this topic, neglected it almost completely.[5] These facts complicate a proper location of the Golem discussions in a larger spectrum of Jewish imaginative production. Nevertheless, an attempt will be made here to point out the peculiar features of the Golem concepts, as discussed above, in the broader range of medieval phenomena.

In his essay on the imaginaire, Le Goff distinguishes between three major categories that constitute the larger domain of the medieval, in fact only the Western Christian, *imaginaire*: the wonderful or *mirabilis,* the magical or *magicus,* and the miraculous or *miraculosus.*[6] The first category deals mainly with the pre-Christian views which penetrated the medieval *Weltanschauung,* and covers a series of phenomena generated by supernatural beings. The Magical includes mainly maleficient phenomena, whereas the miraculous is close, if not identical, to the classical Christian view of miracles as they were performed by the saints or God.

According to this classification, the Talmudic Golem is closer to the last of the three categories, since it involves the special knowledge of a religious classical figure, an Amora. However, the Golem, the product of the act of this master is closer to beings which fit, in a very vague way, in the first category of the imaginaire, as it deals with an extraordinary entity. Most of the above discussions do not fit, even in a general way, into the categorization proposed by Le Goff, for at least two main reasons. By and large, the earliest Jewish version of the Golem, the *Sanhedrin* passage, includes, as we have attempted to suggest, a polemical component.[7] As against the more organic view of the animated statues in pagan rituals, the Talmudic discussion deals with a failure, or at least a deficiency of human ability to create an anthropoid. This reactive nature of the story is fraught with theological implications, for it criticizes a certain practice rather than present it in an unbiased way.

In the medieval versions of Ashkenazi and Northern French extraction, the attitude is much more positive, though the assumption still remains that the major possible achievement, the infusing of a rational soul and the bestowal of speech, is beyond the reach of human possibilities. Though trying to express the magical powers inherent in the combinations of the Hebrew language, and the acquaintance of the medieval masters with those powers, the message as it emerges from most of the versions reveals an unwillingness to allow too large of a range of creative acts even to the most admired masters. This is because of the feeling that the creation of a fulfledged man will be perceived as competing with the uniquely divine prerogative, that of creating man. Although the hagiographical elements are conspicuous in several versions of the Golem, the anonymous authors who attributed the creation of a Golem to historical figures were reluctant to attribute to them a God-like accomplishment. Moreover, the positive features of the Golem itself are presented, if at all, only in a very succinct way, and they are secondary, if not marginal, to the content of extant passages. The absence of a substantial use of the Golem for practical goals is obvious in the overwhelming majority of the discussed passages, thus eliminating the possibility of developing a more complicated plot in order to expose imaginaire situations. Though the details of the various versions of creating the Golem include obvious magical components, the Golem texts basically differ from Le Goff's *Magicus* category, because this category is conceived by him as connected to maleficient goals, which seem to be totally absent in the medieval Hebrew texts; the Golem never became demonic; at most, it may escape the control of the human creator, and then it may become, according to the latter versions of the Golem, dangerous. Therefore, despite the peculiar imaginative nature of these stories in the medieval texts, the imaginaire components of the discussions are weak.

It remained for the later stages of the Golem stories to introduce the more imaginaire motifs and to develop them into forms of literature which correspond better to the categories of the imaginaire as proposed by Le Goff. These stories related to R. Eliyahu of Helm and the later "Maharal" versions of the Golem represent the most important transformation of a magical technique, with important theological facets, into literature of the imaginaire genre. In other words, the imaginaire substantially invades the Golem stories only in the post-medieval period. However, even then the persona of the Golem remains in the shadow. In the classical versions of the Golem, as they were preserved up to the nineteenth century, there are no detailed descriptions of this creature, nor was his inner spiritual universe addressed. No elaborate aesthetic or psychology of this bizarre creature emerges, even from the latest traditional versions of the Golem. It still remains an abstract idea, which serves to put in relief some other topics rather than structuring a Golemic universe in itself. It stands as a proof of the order, rather than of disorder or exceptional creatures, as the gentile discussions and descriptions of the monsters do. Indeed, if the profound interest of medieval man in monsters refers first and foremost to the irregular external features of these creatures,[8] in the Hebrew texts on the Golem what seems to be exceptional is the fact that, despite the perfection of the bodily creation,[9] the inner constitution of the creature is unique. It is not the result of the playful activities of nature, as Kappler put it, "La nature s'amuse;" it is not even a display of the powers of nature, "la preuve de sa puissance,"[10] but a joint project of the divine powers inherent in the spiritual letters and the accomplished master. It is neither a part of nature nor a mishape of biology, as the monsters may be, but an unnatural exception which is a transitory being whose emergence or annihilation are premeditated.

II

On the other hand, the Golem stories differ from the classical versions of the Wonder-type of imaginaire, because the latter implies, as Le Goff remarked,[11] a certain resistance to the classical form of religion, Christianity, by allowing the interaction of para-monotheistic forces. The only possible conflict which can emerge in the medieval Golem texts is not between God and other supernatural powers, but between God and the accomplished master, the righteous. However, provided the fact that the figure presented as creating a Golem, or those who disclosed the principles or the techniques of such a creation, were either representatives of the certain types of religious medieval Jewish consensus, or mystics, like Abulafia and his followers, who considered this practice as the culmination of the ideal religious experience, a basic conflict between the Golem practice and the various common types of Judaism is improbable, though not impossible. In other words, the Golem is far from being a protest against classical Judaism, because it served as a confirmation of the peculiar power of the Hebrew language or of the important Jewish religious leaders. It is the firm belief in the unique character of this language, which enabled the ancient and medieval Jews to approach this topic not as an imaginary issue, but rather as an existing category as possible and probable as any other rare phenomenon. It was not considered to be imaginary because the powerful nature of Hebrew was a presupposition of most of the important Jewish figures, excluding Jewish philosophers, and the confidence that it is possible to fabricate an artificial anthropoid was as indisputable as any other miraculous story told in the canonical writings. The realm of language, the home of Jewish spirituality and the field of its natural growth, was considered as real as that of the material reality;[12] sometimes language was conceived as even more inspiring, and no Jewish mystic would negate the possibilities inherent in the activation of language or would dispute the content of the stories included in the sacrosanct literature.

A general characteristic of all the texts dealing with the creation of the Golem is their anomian nature. Like some other types of mystical and magical practices in Judaism, the Golem-techniques ignore any ritualistic elements similar to the rites described in the Jewish legalistic codexes.[13] The achievements of creating of an anthropoid are not described as an attainment of masters who have already reached the summit of religious perfection, nor are they conditioned by the accomplishment of strict purificatory or cathartic rites. The various rituals connected to the Golem are a separate domain that does not necessarily involve the partnership of the operator in a larger religious group. This feature of the Golem practices reflects the deep impact of the combinatory practices derived from *Sefer*

Yeẓirah. The peculiar separatist nature of this book has been duly recognized by scholars,[14] and their observation with respect to the unique nature of this book can be expanded to the Golem-techniques. However, the cautious formulations of the goal of *Sefer Yeẓirah*, where the magical elements were presented in a rather veiled manner, permitted a rather smooth acceptance of this book as a classic of the Jewish mystical and magical literature, an achievement unique to this ancient text.[15] It seems that no other ancient Jewish text, whose main concerns are not Halakhic or Aggadic, succeeded in entering the main line of Jewish creativity and imagination as this book did. Despite its anomian nature, the attribution of leading Jewish figures, Abraham and R. Aqivah, as well as the fact that it served theological purposes which were not supplied by other types of classical Jewish literature, opened the way to a smooth acceptance. The opening of the Geonic version of Judaism to a phenomenon which served, according to the above interpretation, theological purposes, is not difficult to understand if the emphasis was on the cosmological and cosmogonical aspects of the book. In this period, the "scientific", rather than the practical, aspects of the theories revealed in *Sefer Yeẓirah* were important. The nexus between cosmogony and magical ritual, which is apparently crucial for the understanding of *Sefer Yeẓirah*, was untied by the first commentators of this book.[16] I assume that they surpressed the experiential and practical facets in favor of a more scientifical approach. Since the end of the twelfth century, when other types of thought ascended to the front of Jewish thought, the ancient affinity between cosmogony and ritual was renewed and emphasized even more than in the formulations of *Sefer Yeẓirah* itself. Thus another type of ritual activity, neutral from the Halakhic point of view, but nevertheless never conflicting with the religious ritual of the community, was open to the demiurgic proclivities of some masters, who could express their synthesis between *homo religiosus* and *homo faber.*

In this context, the significance of two discussions concerning the techniques of creating a Golem must be addressed; the awareness of the relationship between the recitation of the powerful letters and their effects opened the way also to the awareness of the dangers involved in faults occurring during this recitation. Given the fact that the Golem can be undone by inversing a certain process, the assumption that these techniques may be also dangerous becomes inescapable. In the Pseudo-Sa'adyan *Commentary on Sefer Yeẓirah*, the creator may sink into the earth; in the case of Abulafia, a mistaken recitation may incur bodily harms to a limb of a recitator. I assume that this preoccupation with dangers can be better understood against the background of anomian techniques in general. Nomian practices in Judaism are invariably an imperative which do not involve any dangers in themselves. The halakhic requirements are understood as necessary to conduct one to life, not to danger. Not so in the anomian practices. They were only rarely exposed as an imperative for the masses, and commonly they were conceived as the enterprise of an exceptional individual, who deliberately chooses to confront a dangerous situation in order to attain a higher religious experience. This is so in the Heikhalot literature and in ecstatic Kabbalah.[17] Greater the spiritual achievement and stronger the means to attain it, greater are the dangers the mystic has to confront. On this point, the Golem techniques mentioned above do concur with the other anomian practices.

III

An examination of the overwhelming majority of the texts related to the Golem reveals that, although the techniques proposed to create an anthropoid are substantially linguistic, the result—namely, the artificial man—is considered to be a speechless being. The disonance between the linguistic techniques involved in the creation of the various Golems and their effects deserves a more detailed examination. A survey of similar techniques, like the mystical devices of Abraham Abulafia,[18] reveals that there is an obvious affinity between the technique and its final goal. Using linguistic devices, very similar to that appearing in the Golem-techniques, Abulafia describes visions which include elements that previously served as components of his technique. This is the case with respect to the apparition of the circle, or sphere, which recalls the technical use of the circles in his *Ḥayyei ha-'Olam ha-Ba',* or the vision of the letters of the seventy-two lettered name, in the same book, reflecting the use of this name in this work.[19]

In the case of the Golem, the disonance between the nature of the technique and that of its result requires an explanation. The silent Golem is, prima facie, a foil to the recitations involved in the process of his creation. There is no way, according to most of the Golem-texts, to communicate with the creature, notwithstanding the fact that linguistic factors are paramount for its emergence. However, upon reflection, the problem is less serious than it seems to be. Though the elements of language are employed as part of the creative process, they are recited in such a way that they do not form a communicative language. It is not the regular Hebrew that is intonated by the creator of the Golem in order to animate him, but mathematical combinations, which only accidently mean something, and even then the context is meaningless. Consequently, it is a metalinguistic "language," or if you want, a sublinguistic language, which is operative in the Golem, as well as in Abulafia's, techniques. It is the transcendence of the common, standard role of language which will be active in the Golem technique. Similar to some gibberish linguistics of ancient and medieval magics,[20] the above techniques assume that regular, significative language is less powerful than the combination of letters which are part of their techniques. Furthermore, it is not an attempt to communicate with a higher being by means of another language, since it is obvious that there is no possible grammar inherent in the combinations of letters as described above. Letters were conceived as sources of energies which can structure directly the inchoate matter, though they do not assume meaningful form. The role that the linguistic elements play in the Golem-techniques is not so much to communicate directly some order to the matter which is to be shaped, but rather to demonstrate the powerful effects of the letters of the Hebrew alphabet and the knowledge of their proper combination, which renders them alone creative. Disclosing this view of language practically is a direct demonstration of the way *Sefer Yeẓirah* conceived the creation of the world, i.e., by means of the Hebrew alphabet, and hence an indirect demonstration of the superiority of Jewish mystical knowledge. However, pushing this type of demonstration too far, by the creation of a perfect artificial man, would endanger the main purpose of the whole exercise, creating thereby a situation that challenged the utmost superiority of the Supreme Creator. This seems to be the reason for the discrepancy between the usage of language as part of the technique and the silent nature of the artificial men.

The importance of the theological implications of the Golem contributed to the neglect of the discussion of the peculiar nature of this being, as it is reflected in the absence of any personal data of the Golem in the mystical literature. This being is not a person having any importance in itself, to be described in its idiosyncracy. It has no particular name, its disappearance does not matter even to its human creator. It is an entity that serves the role of a silent witness of the creativity inherent in the tools which served God and men in their creative endeavours. It helps certain men to externalize their acquaintance with the divine way of creating; it is merely the result of an experiment without any intrinsic value.

This survey seems to be more adequate for the assumption of *Sefer Yeẓirah* and the Talmudic passage, rather than the medieval authors. In ancient Judaism, it seems that speech was an important medium for communication and study, which were conducted in a verbal way, the oral aspect being much more important than in the medieval period. Further, the highest type of worship, prayer, had to be performed in a verbal way, the inner prayer, without words, being considered inadequate from the Halakhic point of view. This is also true with the last phase of Jewish mysticism, Hasidism, which emphasized the importance of loud prayer and study of the Torah. However, in the medieval period, the absence of speech is related to what was conceived then to be the highest human faculty: reason, according to some writers, or the highest spirit, *Neshamah,* according to others. The silence of the Golem was now explained not as the result of the inability to create a speaking being, but rather as the inability to create a rational being. The new ideal, influenced by Greek philosophy, absorbed the problematics of speech as the characteristic of a human being. According to some medieval texts, the faculty of speaking stands between the animal faculty and the rational one.[21]

IV

The role of the various discussions on the Golem in the economy of Jewish theology is worthy of a closer examination. As I have already suggested, the effectiveness of the esoteric linguistic knowledge served a theological role; to combat the polytheism and pagan magic in favor of strengthening the veracity of Jewish monotheism. By the ability to create a being in an artificial manner, be it a man or an animal, the masters achieved something else: Hebrew language, the tradent of the whole spectrum of Jewish lore, came to the forefront as the effective language, bestowing on the expert a knowledge which transcends the magical operation. He shares with the Creator the cosmological secrets; he becomes a demiurge when he creates a world.[22] Judaism, a religion which developed during great parts of its formative stages in contact and conflict with other dominant religions, felt the need to assure itself of its superiority not only by the reliance on the statements of its canonical book regarding its uniqueness, but by competing with the alternative religions in the arena of technology and magic as well.[23] This self-affirmation was necessary, so I assume, for the masters themselves, but in the later stages of the development of the Golem legend, it becomes evident that the masses drew confidence from the fact that in the hostile environment of the Christian populations, the pogroms and blood-libels could be effectively met by the magical achievement of the religious leadership.[24] Strangely enough, a religion that in some of its early stages denigrated magic, managed to absorb this type of activity as part of a legal and effective type of religious activity. It seems that we witness here a phenomenon similar to the emergence of Jewish philosophy in ancient time and in the Middle Ages; when pressed by external forces, which compete with the existent forms of Judaism, some of the masters are ready to accept the patterns of the competing phenomena in order to show that Judaism is consonant with the standards of this peculiar type of thought.[25] The apologetical approach may in a short time evolve into an organic phenomenon which serves not only the polemical purposes but also enriches this type of religion by its gradual transformation into an aspect which is accepted by audiences who are no more aware of the apologetical motivations which generated the magical, mythical or philosophical interests. This type of explanation does not assume a pure type of Judaism which is transformed into a mythical, magical or philosophical one only as a result of the external pressures or influences. Mythical, magical or philosophical elements in Judaism may well predate the more elaborate Jewish formulations which articulate, in a more emphatical manner, these elements. However, it seems that those elements surfaced and came to the forefront either as part of inner theological developments or in apologetical-polemical contexts.

These two processes may be considered as basically different manners to elaborate upon already existing material, but it may also happen that polemical goals functioned as catalysts for more detailed discussions which ensured the exploitation of the potentialities immanent in the embryonic status of some of these motifs. This seems to be the fact in the case of the emergence of Kabbalah in general,[26] and this also is apparently the situation which explains the formulation of the theology of the Ashkenazi Hasidism and the writings of the Special Cherub circle in North France.[27]

Notes

1. Jacques Le Goff, *L'Imaginaire medieval* (Gallimard, Paris, 1985), pp. 17–39.

2. See Jean-Claude Schmitt, "Introduccio a una historia de l'imaginari medieval," in *El mon imaginari i el mon meravellos a l'edat mitjana,* (Barcelona, 1986), pp. 15–33.

3. Claude Kappler, *Monstres, demons et merveilles a la fin du Moyen Ages,* (Paris, Payot, 1982).

4. See Henry Corbin, "Mundus imaginalis ou l'imaginaire et l'imaginal" *Cahiers internationaux de Symbolisme,* vol. 6 (1964), pp. 3–26. For the repercussions of the Sufic view of the "imaginal world," see Idel, *Studies in Ecstatic Kabbalah,* pp. 73–89.

5. The studies of the legendary medieval material in Judaism suffer from descriptivist inclinations, whereas conceptualization of the questions related to this material is a rare exception. See Alexander Scheiber, "Elements fabuleux dans l'*Eshkol Hakofer* de Juda Hadasi" *REJ,* vol. 108 (1968) pp. 41–62.

6. *L'Imaginaire medieval,* pp. 22–23. The distinction between *mirabilia*

and *miracula* has been accepted by several scholars who analyzed the medieval imaginaire; see, e.g., D. Bouthillier—M. P. Torrell, "Miraculum, une cathegorie fondamentale chez Pierre le Venerable," *Revue Thomiste,* vol. 80 (1980), pp. 549, 566, and Schmitt, "Les traditions folkloriques dans la culture medieval. Quelques reflections de methode" *Archives de sciences sociales des religions,* vol. 52 (1981), pp. 14–15.

7. Above ch. 3.

8. Kappler, *Monstres,* passim.

9. See above ch. 11 the view stemming from the school of Cordovero that the Golem is an animal having a human form.

10. *Monstres,* p. 21.

11. *L'Imaginaire medieval,* pp. 24–25.

12. Idel, *Language, Torah and Hermeneutics,* ch. 1 and "Reification of Language in Jewish Mysticism".

13. See Idel, *Kabbalah: New Perspectives,* pp. 74–75.

14. See Ithamar Gruenwald, "Some Critical Notes on the First Part of *Sefer Yeẓirah,*" *REJ,* vol. 132 (1973), p. 477; Hayman "Some Observations" pp. 168, 182.

15. See Hyman, ibid.

16. See above ch. 16.

17. See Idel, *The Mystical Experience,* pp. 121–123.

18. Ibid., pp. 13–52.

19. Ibid., pp. 100–116.

20. See Patricia C. Miller, "In Praise of Nonsense," ed. A. H. Amstrong, *The Classical Mediterranean Spirituality* (New York, 1986), pp. 482–499.

21. See Idel, *Abraham Abulafia,* pp. 98–100.

22. See above ch. 3, par. 1.

23. See above ch. 11.

24. See Scholem, "The Image of the Golem," p. 410, n. 72.

25. See M. Idel, "Jewish Magic from the Renaissance Period to Early Hasidism," pp. 82–117.

26. See Idel, *Kabbalah: New Perspectives,* pp. 251–252.

27. This issue is worthy of a separate treatment; see, for the time being, Joseph Dan, "The Emergence of Mystical Prayer," eds. J. Dan and F. Talmage, *Studies in Jewish Mysticism* (Cambridge, Mass. 1982), pp. 85–120.

20

Summary

The findings of the above analyses may indicate more than unrelated descriptions of a certain subject recurrent in Jewish magical and mystical literature. A close reading of the material concerning a very specific topic as the Golem may also allow more general conclusions with respect to some points regarding the picture of the history of Jewish mysticism in general. Some of these conclusions were already pointed out in their proper places, as part of the detailed presentation of the pertinent material. However, I would like to return here to some of them in a more general context, where some previous statements will be integrated in a more comprehensive picture.

I

First and foremost, our discussions on the *yeẓur in Sefer Yeẓirah* and the late sixteenth century views presented in an elaborate manner in R. Israel Sarug's description of the emergence of *'Adam Qadmon.* The more that Jewish mysticism developed, as we can learn from the detailed theosophies which flourished beginning with the emergence of Kabbalah on the historical scene at the end of the twelfth century, the more it returned to a certain basic concept as it was found in the ancient Jewish and non-Jewish texts (the latter also presumably influenced by Jewish antecedents). The affinity between the technique used by God to create the world and the *yezur,* i.e., Man, in *Sefer Yezirah* and in the later Kabbalistic writings is obvious: combinations of letters in an identical fashion. On the other hand, the similarity of the ancient view of the supernal angels, presented as meganthropoi in various sources, as in Marcos for example,[1] and the supernal Man in the Sarugian version of Lurianism demand a basically different approach than the simplistic evolutionism adopted by modern scholarship of Kabbalah. The assumption that later layers of Kabbalistic writings invariably contributed to the Kabbalistic literature novel insights seems to be the regnant approach accepted by almost all scholars.[2] Thus, for example, elements in Lurianic Kabbalah were described as part of the reaction to the quandaries posed by an historical crisis. The Kabbalists themselves argued that they were disclosing issues already in existence beforehand, and this is one of the major perceptions of Luria's Kabbalah in the eyes of his disciples.[3] In the case of the description of the emergence of the *malbush,* I hope it is now evident that the regular view of scholars that Sarug invented this concept cannot be upheld and it would be more plausible to assume, on the basis of the earlier sources presented above, that the paradigm of the Kabbalists is more feasible and reliable than that of modern scholars.[4] It is therefore advisable to take seriously into consideration the possibility that the "novelty" of some elements in certain Kabbalistic texts may be the result of the disclosure of older traditions rather than the innovation of later Kabbalists. Only the constant awareness of the possibility that scholars today miss important segments of Jewish esotericism will contribute to more balanced conclusions, which will attenuate the overemphasis on the explanation of the evolution of Jewish mysticism as decisively related to historical crises and external influences.[5] It may be that a basic category for the understanding of the development of Kabbalah is not only the innovation of Kabbalists, a category obvious to any scholar of Kabbalah, but also the problem of disclosure and its vicissitudes. As I have attempted to show in several other instances, it is the later material, as preserved in Kabbalistic sources, which may preserve themes and structures that permit a reconstruction of more comprehensive theological structures out of disparate elements in ancient texts that today seem to be unrelated to each other.[6] In our case, the possible affinity between the *shi'ur qomah* view and *Sefer Yezirah,* obvious in the medieval texts presented above, may alert us to a more sensitive approach to the relationship between the linguistic elements in the ancient texts and the anthropomorphical one.

II

At least insofar as the issue of the Golem is concerned, the esoteric traditions appeared at the same time in different centers, in a rather diversified form. If our proposal to understand the plain sense of *Sefer Yeẓirah* as dealing with the creation of man, the *yeẓur,* by combinations of letters is correct, then we must allow for a long underground development from the ancient traditions in *Sefer Yeẓirah* itself to the variety of formulas expressed since the end of the twelfth century. This diversification of traditions does not automatically betray a simultaneous surge of medieval inventiveness, but rather the ramification of one hypothetical unified tradition in its ancient phase over lengthy periods of occultation and gestation. The basic differences between the French and Ashkenazi techniques are to be explained more easily as the result of complex changes continuing over a lengthy period of time. In particular, it is important to stress the fact, evident from the above discussions, that even among the Hasidic masters there were different traditions already in the time of R. Eleazar of Worms. Thus, the assumption of a vast historical period for the development of the Golem techniques will better do justice to the understanding of their development than an hypothesis of a medieval innovation. The assumption that certain mystical or theosophical views are ancient, as the Kabbalists often maintain, may facilitate an historical understanding of the process of diversification which generates the variety of medieval versions.

III

The inspection of the sources dealing with the Golem unmistakably demonstrates the centrality of the Northern European traditions, which obviously influenced treatments of this topic beyond this area. This finding may reflect a much larger phenomenon, which will allow to the Ashkenazi and French esoteric traditions a much greater role in the general picture of Jewish mysticism than scholars regularly allocate. I believe that this view on the centrality of North European traditions can be elaborated through the examination of other issues, especially related to mystical techniques. A confirmation of this crucial role of the esotericism descending from the North is supported by some traditions related by the Kabbalists themselves. If this view is correct, then the need for a deep restructuring of the modern concept of the history of medieval mysticism will become an imperative of future research. The Sefardi-mystique myth will, subsequently, have to be presented in a much more moderate manner.[7]

IV

The fact that there was in existence a variety of techniques to create a Golem demonstrates that the possibility to conceive the Golem as exhausted by one "idea" or "image" is a simplistic assumption. Indeed the

Golem changed forms in accordance to the metaphysical systems serving as the background of the discussion: In *Sefer ha-Ḥayyim,* it was conceived in astrological terms, as this book is permeated with a deep convinction in astrology. According to the circle of the Special Cherub, there is a certain relationship between its anthropomorphic theology and the relationship between the 231 gates and 236 tens of thousands of parasangs originating from the *Shi'ur Qomah.* In Abulafia, such an anthropomorphic concept is meaningless as he was concerned more with ecstatic experiences than ancient Jewish theology. The theosophical Kabbalists translated the Talmudic text and the views of *Sefer Yeẓirah* into an anthropomorphical theosophy which transformed the Golem into a supernal man, constituted by the *sefirot.*

V

As we have already pointed out, one of the major arguments of Scholem is that the creation of the Golem was intended to achieve a mystical experience.[8] This inference from the texts dealing with this topic is not sustained by any explicit statement of the sources, with the exception of the texts belonging to ecstatic Kabbalah, which were influenced, as we have attempted to show above, by the medieval Aristotelian epistemology and hermeneutics of the prophetic experience. Even in the case of this literature, it is only as the result of a more detailed analysis that we can ascertain the ecstatic nature of the Golem. The mystical interpretation of the Golem can be explained as the superimposition of a set of concepts on another, that may well be indifferent to this type of interpretation.[9] Scholem's assumption that the pursuit of mystical experience is to be inferred from the Ashkenazi texts is, therefore, more a matter of scholarly evaluation than an explanation of the content of the sources. Is such an argument plausible? Before making any attempt to answer the question, some methodological observations are appropriate.

It is possible that a certain magical practice, intended to obtain material purposes, will involve such a sort of devices that changes the consciousness of the operator, who may undergo what academic research will consider to be a mystical experience. However, such an event may happen also under other circumstances, and the atmosphere of the magic practices may contribute to the emergence of altered states of consciousness only unintentionally and marginally. The nature of the experience during a magical session may, or may not, be similar or identical to an experiment cultivated by mystics; unfortunately, it is rather difficult to examine and compare them in a responsible way. Consequently, Scholem may indeed be right when he pointed out that:

> We can gather indirectly from such instructions that the ritual culminates in ecstasy. The recitation of rhythmic sequences with their modulations of vowel sounds would naturally induce a modified state of consciousness.[10]

So far, his suggestion seems to me an interesting insight, which may, or may not, be supported by texts that may be unearthed by future scholarship; for the time being, as Scholem put it, it is only an indirect inference, which is not corroborated by any evidence of mystical experience during a Golem-creation session. However, Scholem continues, that the creation of the Golem "seems to have been designed for this purpose," namely, for the purpose of inducing a modified state of consciousness. This is an inference based upon another inference, the latter being as unproven as the former. This observation is even more indirect than the first one. I assume that this statement is an imposition of the Abulafian views of the Golem, which were not explicitly understood by Scholem as Abulafian, upon the Ashkenazi material. As far as the material bears evidence of the intention of the operators, the Ashkenazi texts testify that Scholem's insight regarding the mystical purpose of the practice is hardly probable. Scholem presents the Golem traditions as if they were practices standing in themselves and dedicated solely to the creation of the artificial man. However, this seems not to be the case. From the very beginning, the creation of a man is presented together with the creation of a calf, as we see in the *Sanhedrin* passage. This nexus is found also in early versions of the Golem creation as that of *Sefer ha-Ḥayyim.*[11] If this nexus remains in the early Ashkenazi texts, when using the same technique as in the case of the creation of man, then the "mystical" interpretation of the Golem creation entails a similar interpretation of the calf creation, an argument that is possible, but highly improbable. Therefore, if we cannot prove a mystical understanding of the creation of the man or the calf in the ancient texts, then the "mystical" hypothesis represents a radical change in the understanding of this issue among the Ashkenazi masters in comparison to the Talmudic version. In order to sustain such an extreme shift, we must supply more than indirect inferences. However, it seems that medieval sources may enable us to consider the Ashkenazi practices as magical ones, without the need to project a mystical interpretation. Our reading of the Ashkenazi texts as basically magical allows an organic continuation of the conception found in the ancient texts on one side, and some of the treatments of the post-medieval versions of the Golem on the other side.[12]

The major objections against Scholem's hypothesis are found in some of the above-mentioned texts. As we attempted to show, it is obvious that the same technique of collecting special dust and kneading it with pure water and using some recitations of incantations, were used in other contexts, purely magical: the ordeal of the *soṭah* and the practice of unfolding the name of the thieves. These practices were in use also in Ashkenazi milieux. Even the manner of the presentation of some of the Golem techniques compels us to conceive them as particular cases of a broad magical practice, as is obvious from the version preserved by R. Abraham Galante.[13] Moreover, according to some other texts, the practice is to be accomplished by two or three persons together, a requirement that complicates the mystical understanding of this ritual. This point was already recognized by Scholem himself,[14] who nevertheless was not impressed by the weight of the implications of an hypothesis that assumes a collective vision of the Golem. However, it seems that even explicit statements complicate the proposed experiential approach to the Golem.

VI

According to three statements, written in the thirteenth century, the creation of the man follows the same pattern as that of the calf, or a cow, with at least the latter being consumed as food. These statements testify that the practical purpose of the practice was not attenuated in the medieval period in Northern Europe, and consequently it does not allow an indirect reading of the Golem devices as designed for mystical goals. In some manuscripts including the Ashkenazi devices the combinations of letters of the divine name and the letters of the alphabets vocalized according to the pattern of the *notariqon,* which is the quintessence of the second stage of the creation, these combinations are considered as proper also for the creation of the calf.[15] A similar stand is found in a work of R. Eleazar of Worms: beside the technique of the combinations of the letters of the alphabet, identical to those of the Golem, it is written that "in the case of the creators of the calves they have shortened."[16] The very fact that the phrase *"ha-bore'im 'agalim"* was in existence in connection to the combinations of letters is important evidence that the technique employed for the Golem is a magical one. Therefore, the special technique that is elaborated by the Ashkenazi masters can, in principle, be applied also for ends other than an allegedly mystical creation of the Golem. Furthermore, a statement of R. Abraham of Esquira,[17] at the end of the thirteenth century, indicates that "in France (*Ẓarfat*) there was someone who was acquainted with this[18] and he was engraving the form of a cow on a wall, and it changed into a cow, and they [ritually] slaughtered it and ate it like Rav Ḥanina and Rav Hoshayah." Therefore, even a highly cultivated Spanish Kabbalist, with a certain knowledge of Arabic philosophy, did not doubt for a moment that the episode of R. Yehudah ben Bateirah was not only part of the glorious past but that these devices were still in the possession of the French masters, who did not hesitate to exploit the possibilities inherent in this magical gnosis. En passant, this mention of France may indicate that there were traditions related to the use of *Sefer Yeẓirah* in this area, thus strengthening our assumption that the Pseudo-Sa'adyan *Commentary on Sefer Yeẓirah* was composed in Northern France.

VII

After presenting the major texts concerning the creation of the artificial man in Franco-Ashkenazi and Sefardi mysticism, some general observations on differences between their treatments of this topic are in order. One major difference seems to be the attitude on the very act of creation: the Franco-Ashkenazi descriptions of the techniques of creation do not include a basic reticence regarding the performance of the ritual of creating a Golem. Indeed, they require certain conditions of purity, but that is basically all. In the case of Ashkenazi texts which include a warning against the creation, it is obvious that these are parts of an earlier text, which were influential on the Franco-Ashkenazi authors. I would like to emphasize that even then the warning does not occur together with the technique to create the man. On the other hand, those Sefardi texts which elaborate on the issue of the Golem end with a warning, as in the case of Abulafia, or the act of material creation is presented as an inferior activity to be transcended by the intellectual creation. In the most extreme case, that of Cordovero, the creation of the Golem is presented as a totally meaningless activity from the spiritual point of view. This last motif is totally absent from the Franco-Ashkenazi texts. This basic divergence is to be understood, as we have already remarked, by the influence of philosophical speculations which preferred the intellectual over the material, thought over matter, intellection over action. This fundamental divergence is carried down to the later centuries, when the Golem is discussed in a favorable light by Ashkenazi authors, as almost a human being, in comparison to the continuation of the line of Cordovero, so evident in the Sefardi milieux.

Each of the important types of thought in the Franco-Ashkenazi provinces developed, in the thirteenth century, a certain view on the technique of the creation of the Golem. The differences between these techniques are obvious, and the common interest in this topic in the different circles may be important evidence that the deep concern with the Golem predates the period when the above texts were committed to writing. This situation stands in sharp opposition to the indifference toward this topic among the Sefardi mystics who, with the exception of Abraham Abulafia did not pay much attention to this tradition. Let us ponder the implications of the above distribution of the interest in the Golem. The early Kabbalists, Provençal and Catalan, deliberately minimize the interest in this topic in comparison to the Ashkenazi Hasidim. The attitude of the theosophical-theurgical Kabbalists in Castile during the last third of the thirteenth century is even more reticent. It is highly significant that the luxuriant Kabbalistic production, which is unpreceded in Jewish mysticism, including the works of R. Joseph Gikatilla, R. Moses de Leon, R. Joseph of Hamadan and the literature which constitute the *Zohar* itself, are indifferent to the practice of creating a Golem. This is the case also in Safedian Kabbalah. As we have seen, R. Moses Cordovero, the single important Safedian Kabbalist who has something new to contribute to the idea of the Golem, is rather reticent in attributing any spiritual degree to the Golem, assuming as he does that no real spiritual faculty can be infused in the artificial being. The great Kabbalistic corpus of literature named Lurianic Kabbalah seems to totally ignore the issue of the Golem.[19] Therefore, the two main bodies of Kabbalistic literature, the Castilian and the Safedian, were reticent in including this topic in their spiritual agenda. On the other hand, the Ashkenazi Hasidism and the ecstatic Kabbalah seem to be the only types of medieval Jewish mysticism which developed this idea, presenting it either as a mystical or as a magical technique. The most important influence of their interest in the artificial creation of man are the texts of the Renaissance authors, whose affinity to the texts of R. Eleazar of Worms and Abulafia is conspicuous. Therefore, using the distribution of the discussion of the topic related to the Golem, we may design two lines of medieval mysticism: the theosophical and theurgical Kabbalah running from Provence through Catalonia and Castile to Safed, indifferent to the problem of the artificially created man; the ecstatic one, flourishing in Germany, appearing momentarily also in Spain, but resurfacing basically in medieval and Renaissance Italy, and the East, namely, the Land of Israel.

VIII

I would now like to suggest an explanation for the different attitudes to the Golem in Jewish mysticism. J. Dan has already remarked that there is a certain inverse correlation between speculation on the *sefirot* and interest in the Golem.[20] Those Kabbalists whose interest is focused on the ten *sefirot* seem to be indifferent to the Golem, whereas the Ashkenazi masters, less interested in the doctrine of ten *sefirot,* are more interested in the Golem. Nevertheless, Dan did not offer an explanation for his important observation. This distinction is indeed interesting, though there are at least two major exceptions, that of R. Joseph Ashkenazi and R. Isaac of Acre who combined an elaborate *sefirotic* system with a deep interest in the Golem. Dan, who was not acquainted with these manuscript texts, could not discuss this point. Let me attempt to suggest another possible explanation for the differences in attitude on this topic, which will both complement Dan's suggestion and elucidate the religious backgrounds of these two lines.

The theory concerning the *sefirot* as divine powers involves, in a substantial number of Kabbalistic systems, the possibility of influencing the divine realm; this influence will be referred to below as the theurgical operation, which is to be defined as the operation that can possibly change the dynamic processes taking place in the divine world.[21] This influence is basically achieved as part of the mystical awareness regarding the impact of the ritual on the higher world. This theosophical-theurgical theory was central for the Provençal, Catalan and Castilian Kabbalah, but only marginal for the Ashkenazi and French theologies and ecstatic Kabbalah. The Spanish Kabbalists invested their mystical efforts in the elaboration of the theurgical meaning of human activities, as formulated by the halakhah. Inter alia, we can find several interesting discussions among the Spanish Kabbalists related to the structuring of human activity in accord with the structures of the divine anthropos; the ten *sefirot,* arranged as a divine anthropos, are the object of human activity, which may sustain the *sefirotic* system in its harmonious state, repair it, or negatively affect the relationship between the divine powers.[22] According to some Castilian texts, the Kabbalists are not only safeguarding the divine harmony; they maintain that the Kabbalistic activity even "makes" the divine, and they use exactly the same term used in connection to the creation of Adam as Golem, *'asa'o.*[23] It may well be that the identical use of the same grammatical form is a sheer coincidence; however, even if this is so, we may use it in order to reflect on the differing foci of medieval Jewish mysticism. On the one hand, the magical activity, anomian ex definitio, is accepted by a theological system where the structure of the canon is divinely designed and Hebrew is conceived as the uniquely influential tool, as the theory of *Sefer Yeẓirah* indicates. Language is creative when used by man just as it was creative at the moment of creation when the world was generated by language. On the other hand, the Spanish Kabbalists proposed a theurgical understanding of the ritual, which was designed in such a way as to be in close affinity to the divine anthropomorphical structure so as to be able to affect it.

Two anthropoids seem to have fascinated the imagination and motivated the activity of both the Franco-Ashkenazi and Spanish Kabbalah: a microanthropos, completely material, in the case of the Northern European Jews, and a meganthropos, utterly spiritual, in the case of the Spanish Kabbalists. Both types of anthropoi depend upon human acts and bear evidence to the spiritual powers and mystical knowledge of the master. In the case of the magical creation, the knowledge is that of *Sefer Yeẓirah* which includes the gnosis of magic, consisting basically in the combinations of letters and divine names; in the other case, it is another part of the same book that is formative for the Spanish Kabbalah, that which deals with the ten sefirot that are conceived as the constitutive elements of divine anthropos. This divine structure is the key for the understanding of the ritual. In both cases the creation of an anthropoid is a way to imitate the divine activity; in the case of the Northern European masters, the creation of the Golem includes, as we have attempted to demonstrate, clear evidence of the influence of the midrashic description of the creation of Adam. When dealing with maintaining the structure of the ten *sefirot,* Spanish Kabbalists attempted to safeguard the status quo of the dynamic system designed to mediate between the infinite and the finite.

IX

The difference between the two religious emphases is duc, I assume, to the influence of the alien philosophical theologies on the respective Jewish theologies. The Ashkenazi and French masters were immersed in the ancient Jewish mystical theology of the Heikhalot literature with its magical and anthropomorphical proclivities. The influence of the Sa'adyan thought, great as it is considered to be, did not totally erase the importance of the older forms of thought and practices. On the other hand, Spanish Jewish authors of the eleventh and twelfth centuries were already under the impact of Neoplatonic and Aristotelian philosophies, without betraying a significant stratum of older Jewish theology, formulated under the influence of the Heikhalot literature. The impact of philosophy in Spain was earlier, greater and more profound than it was in Germany and France. The Franco-Ashkenazi elite was much more closed to external influence and even the influence of philosophy was already mediated by Eastern or Spanish Judaism. In comparison to the fine knowledge of Islamic philosophy found in the Spanish elite, the Northern European Jewish masters seem to be much more isolated and even reticent toward the alien lore. Even when the Spanish Kabbalists did refer to the Golem, it is as part of a more speculative discussion in the context of arguments on the nature of the soul; these discussions are conspicuously consonant with their general philosophical concerns.

It seems that the obvious absence of the Golem legend and technique in the last important form of Jewish mysticism, the East-European Hasidism, is a highly significant fact. Hasidism, flowering in close vicinity to Helm and Prague, emerged less than one century after the legend on the creation of the Golem was articulated among Jews and Christians. Hasidic literature, rich in legends in a way that no other prior Jewish mystical literature was, ignored this peculiar type of legend. Between the first formulations of the legend in the middle of the seventeenth century and the late nineteenth and early twentieth century, when the legend was revitalized in Hasidic and non-Hasidic circles, lies the whole creation of the Hasidim who deliberately, I assume, excluded this legend from their spiritual patrimony. Though no definitive answers for this absence can be supplied, it seems that the basic attitude of ecstatic Kabbalah on the meaning of the mystical life, affected also the Hasidic attitude to this topic. Based upon the assumption that the spiritual achievement of man is the most important aim in religion, in the vein of ecstatic Kabbalah, and maintaining, following the theosophical-theurgical Kabbalah, that this achievement is attainable solely through the mystical performance of the commandments, an anomian technique as that of the Golem practice remained beyond the scope of Hasidic mysticism. Or, to use the formulation of R. Menaḥem Mendel of Kotzsk when someone told him about the wondrous powers of a wonder-maker: "Can he also make a Hasid?"[24]

Notes

1. See Idel, "The World of the Angels," pp. 2–5.

2. Compare, however, the views of Yehudah Liebes especially as they appear in his article in the *Pines Jubilee Volume.* (See below, Appendix C n. 10.)

3. See, for example, the Lurianic text printed in M. Idel, "More on R. David ben Yehudah he-Ḥasid and R. Isaac Luria," *Da'at,* vol. 7 (1981), pp. 69–70. (Hebrew)

4. See above ch. 10, pars. 7a–7c.

5. See Idel, *Kabbalah: New Perspectives,* pp. 20–22, 32–34.

6. See e.g. Idel, "Enoch is Metatron," pp. 159–161.

7. Idel, *Kabbalah: New Perspectives,* pp. 96, 100–103, Asi Farber-Ginat, *The Concept of the Merkavah in the Thirteenth-Century Jewish Esotericism—"Sod ha-'Egoz" and Its Development* [Ph. D. Thesis, Hebrew University, Jerusalem, 1986] pp. 128–129 [Hebrew] and Ivan Marcus, "Beyond the Sefardi Mystic", *Orim,* vol. 1 (1985), pp. 35–53.

A clear-cut evidence of the descent of the Northern European traditions concerning the Golem to the South, more exactly Italy, is extant in one of the most important manuscripts that includes several versions of the Golem recipes: Ms. Cambridge, Add. 647, fol. 19a:

> All these matters were found in codexes [*quntresim*] which were brought by the sage R. Reuven, when he came from the land of Ashkenaz. And this [another device to create a Golem] he found in another codex".

On fol. 19b the copyist mentions another book, lent to him by "the Ashkenazim [living] in Venise".

8. "The Idea of the Golem," p. 187 and above, *Introduction.*

9. See above ch. 7, end par. 1.

10. "The Idea of the Golem," p. 187. See also the next footnote. Scholem's characterization of the Golem ritual as culminating in an ecstatic experience, has been accepted enthusiastically by B. N. Knapp in her psychoanalytical, Jungian interpretation of the Golem; see *The Prometheus Syndrome* (New York, 1979), pp. 100–102. I shall not elaborate here on the misunderstandings in her analysis that result from the unqualified acceptance of Scholem's thesis.

11. Compare the description of the avatars in the concept of the Golem in Scholem's, "The Idea of the Golem," p. 174, where he asserts that:

> The Golem . . . starts out as a legendary figure. Then it is transformed into an object of a mystical ritual of initiation, which seems actually to have been performed, designed to confirm the adept in his mastery over secret knowledge. Then in the whisperings of the profane it degenerates into a figure of legend, or one might even say, tellurian myth.

I would rather say that the whispering of the profane mystic transformed the ancient magical practice into a mystical initiation.

12. This approach is part of my broader attitude to the organic development of Jewish mysticism; see Idel, *Kabbalah: New Perspectives,* pp. 30–32, 156–172.

13. See Scholem, "The Idea of the Golem," p. 196. n. 1; ch. 5, par. 11.

14. Scholem, ibid., pp. 185–186, 190.

15. Ms. Firenze-Laurentiana, 44, 16, fol. 4b: "These are the *'Alefim* for creation of the calf."

16. Ms. Oxford, 1566, fol. 44b. Such a statement regarding the creation of calf by the means of *Sefer Yeẓirah* could have infuriated the anonymous kabbalist who penned the ecstatic Kabbalistic work, *Ner 'Elohim.* See above ch. 7, par. 3 and n. 44. Compare also to the version of R. Eleazar's recipe as quoted by R. Naftali Bakharakh, *'Emeq ha-Melekh,* fol. 6c, 9c where a calf is mentioned in connection to the technique used to create a Golem.

17. Ms. Moscow-Guenzburg, 607, fol. 53a. See also the list of the animals

that can be created by the combinations of letters of *Sefer Yeẓirah* in R. Yoḥanan Alemanno's untitled work, Ms. Paris, BN, 849, fol. 6b: an ox, a sheep and a calf.

18. On the transformation of the magical Golem into a theosophical view, but not into an actual ritual, in some pre-Lurianic and Lurianic texts, see above ch. 10.

19. *Ḥuggei ha-Mekubbalim ha-Rishonim* (Jerusalem, 1973), pp. 59–60 [Hebrew].

21. See Idel, *Kabbalah: New Perspectives,* chaps. 7–8.

22. Ibid., pp. 170–181.

23. Ibid., pp. 185–188.

24. See the version of Martin Buber, who freely inserted into this story the concept of the robot, apparently alluding to the Golem, which however is absent in the original; see *Tales of the Hasidim: Later Masters* (New York, 1948), vol. 2, p. 285.

PART FIVE

Appendixes

A

Golem and Ẓelem

I

In the liturgical piece, *'Eleh 'Ezkerah,* consisting of the recitation of the martyrology of the ten ancient sages killed by the Romans in the second century C. E., the death of R. Ḥananiyah (or, according to another version, R. Ḥanina ben Teradyon) is described as follows: "They burned his body [*Golemo*] using bunches of branches."[1] The translation of the word *Golemo* as referring to the body of the Rabbi seems to be a reasonable possibility and apparently no other specific denotations are involved in its use. However, another tradition connected to the death of R. Ḥananiyah, or according to some manuscript versions, the death of R. Neḥuniyah ben ha-Qanah,[2] assumes an end which differs substantially from that apparent in the above version. According to the ancient mystical tract entitled *Heikhalot Rabbati,* one of the archangels of this literature, Surya, exchanged this Rabbi with Lupinus Caesar, who is executed in his place, while the Rabbi played the role of Caesar until his identity was revealed. He was about to be executed when again his form was changed to that of Lupinus, who was in the meanwhile vivified, and the latter died in lieu of the Rabbi.[3] In the version of *Heikhalot Rabbati,* the term Golem does not occur. However, the assumption that there was a bodily substitute for the Rabbi was interpreted later on, in medieval sources, by using the term Golem, which occurs in order to indicate the death of the real Rabbi. In this context it should be mentioned that in the Heikhalot literature, the concomitant presence of the same person in two places seems to be a crucial issue. Thus, for example, R. Neḥuniyah ben ha-Qanah is described as sitting in the special posture of Elijah in the lower world, surrounded by his disciples, apparently in a lethargical state, whereas he is also described as sitting and gazing upon the divine chariot at the same time.[4] I would like to emphasize the use of the verb sit, *yoshev*;[5] this Rabbi is represented as sitting in two different places at the same time. This observation on the double-presence of the mystic in the Heikhalot literature may provide a clue for the proper understanding of the whole phenomenon of the ascent to the Merkavah; it was not simply the ascent of the soul, or a corporeal ascent; it combined both of them by assuming that the spiritual body of the mystic is the entity which undertakes the celestial journey, while the corporeal body remains in the special posture in the terrestrial world. I cannot elaborate here on the possible implication of such a proposal for the understanding of the Heikhalot literature, and I hope to be able to do it elsewhere; however, for the time being, it is sufficient to remark that the assumption of a double-presence in a context connected to the term Golem may have something to do with the concept of a spiritual or astral body.

II

Before examining the views of the later Kabbalists, it is important to deal with the occurrence of the term Golem in *Sefer ha-Ḥayyim,* at the turn of the thirteenth century:[6]

> Each man has a part [stemming] from the seven planets [*meshartim*] and the twelves constellations, [*mazzalot*] in accordance with the position in the moment [literally, the hour] of the descent of the Golem or in the moment of birth, and the two are always identical.[7] This is the reason for the impurity of the seven days [connected to the corpse of man]. But the [corpse of] reptiles and that of an animal . . . the spirit they receive in the moment of their birth and their departure, and that moisture which descends from the nature of the planet is linked [to it], and the impurity [connected to the contact with it] is of one day. And this Golem defiles those who touch it and take it out, and whatever emerges out of it. Because this Golem is separate and differentiated from the light of the supernal entities, from the fountains of wisdom, from the wells of understanding,[8] there is only loathing and abhorrence in it, and in the power of its air there is no purity, and the supernal glory[9] does not dwell on it, and it is more abhorrent than any other being is.[10]

This text uses the term Golem as related both to a certain aspect of the human corpse, on the one hand, and to the astral influences descending in the moment of his birth, on the other. Because of the separation between the supernal sources and the lower crystallization of these influences, the astral powers become, in the moment of the death of a human being, impure and they defile to whoever touches them. According to the first part of the above quotation, the astrological connotation is conspicuous. We may therefore assume that here there is a special version of the Neoplatonic conception of astral body,[11] though it is also possible that the peculiar form of our discussion absorbed also connotations of the medical spirit,[12] as we learn from other discussions in *Sefer ha-Ḥayyim.*[13] Accordingly, it seems obvious that the term Golem absorbed here at least two different connotations, astral body and medical spirit, a phenomenon known also in Renaissance literature.[14]

III

In a late thirteenth century Kabbalistic passage discussed above, the similar meaning of the terms Golem and *ẓelem* is conspicuous.[15] The figures of man designed on the wall are considered as *ẓelamim* which are, at the same time, *Gelamim* without form. The fact that the ultimate significance of both these terms is a purely external structure is conspicuous; it stands for the static, soulless form. Thus, this affinity of the meanings of Golem and *ẓelem* points to an understanding of the Golem different from that found in *Sefer ha-Ḥayyim.* Moreover, the affinity between these terms is interesting because it will recur later on in different contexts in other Kabbalistic discussions.

The term Golem occurs in a highly interesting passage of R. Moses Cordovero, where it stands for the form of the body of man which collects in it the three other spiritual parts of man: *nefesh, ruaḥ, neshamah.* Actually, the Golem is the *ẓelem,* the statue which is also the stature of man. This form, which emerges in the air of Paradise in the moment of conception, is referred to by Cordovero as *Golem ha-'Avir.*[16] Apparently, Cordovero combined the view of the *Zohar* on the nature of the *ẓelem* with views on the same topic expressed in R. Shem Tov ben Shem Tov's *Sefer ha-'Emunot.* Just as the Golem in *Sefer ha-Ḥayyim,* the *ẓelem* in the *Zohar* appears at the moment of conception. It is a semispiritual entity which has the form of the future body, though smaller; the growth of the body extends also the size of the *ẓelem.*[17] In the fifteenth century *Sefer ha-'Emunot,* the Zoharic doctrine was combined with a view, whose sources are not clear, regarding the "spiritual body" of man, whose significance is very similar to the *ẓelem.*[18] It may be too simple to suggest that it describes the meaning of the term spiritual body in this context; the term used is *geviyah ruḥanit.* Literally, *ruḥanit* stands in medieval Hebrew for spiritual, but it is possible that in our context this term refers to a special form of spirituality, that of the stars, descending below. This understanding of the term *ruḥanit* bridges the gap between the view of *Sefer ha-Ḥayyim* and the Spanish Kabbalah, by the substitution of the Golem by the *geviyah.* Moreover, in *Sefer ha-'Emunot* there is a theory, whose history is crucial for the understanding of the development of the term Golem, which seems to appear here for the first time. According to R. Shem Tov, it was not the physical body of the ten ancient Jewish martyrs, one of them being R. Ḥananiyah ben Teradiyon who was mentioned above, that underwent martyrdom, but rather their astral body:

> The ancients received [a tradition] that the ten martyrs were the sons of Jacob, according to the secret of impregnation, [*sod ha-'ibbur*].[19] There is an [esoteric] tradition in the hands of the sages that when the second Temple was destroyed all the light was stored away, the divine light emanated from the holy light and they clothed themselves into one form [*ziyyur*] [and] a lower one was the other spiritual body which is that [body] which is worthy to receive the punishment.[20]

Thus, following the ancient tradition regarding the substitution of the body of the martyrs by other bodies, the medieval Kabbalist saves the honor of the ancient sages. He did not however accept the more popular solution of substituting the persecutor for the persecuted, but rather the lower body, named here the spiritual body, was exchanged for the real body of the sage. In other words, the classical astral body was inserted in the ancient tradition on order to provide a more "logical" explanation concerning the fate of the prominent ancient figures.

Cordovero was obviously acquainted with *Sefer ha-'Emunot,* but I am not aware of him using the term *geviyah ruḥanit.* Instead, he uses the term Golem in a very similar way. Likewise, I am not aware of Cordovero's explanation of the martyrdom as a substitution of one body for another astral body. However, such an explanation seems to have existed in some writings of Cordovero, because his disciple, Menaḥem 'Azaryah of Fano, combines the explanation of the martyrdom proposed by R. Shem Tov ben Shem Tov with the term Golem as used by Cordovero. To return to Cordovero himself; the Golem is the formal blueprint of the future man, which apparently corresponds to the embryonic form of the material component of an infant, also referred to by the term Golem in this context.[21] According to this Kabbalist, the *ẓelem,* being less spiritual than the soul, *Nefesh*—the lowest spiritual part of man—is visible to the eyes of the pious men.[22] If there is a possibility to envisage the *ẓelem,* which is identical to the Golem, then the pious men are able to see their Golem, which is their *forma individualis.* An important historical question as to the affinity between the similar view of *Sefer ha-Ḥayyim* and the concept of Cordovero cannot be answered here in a definitive way. There may be an intermediary source which elaborated upon the concept of the Golem as found in *Sefer ha-Ḥayyim* and served as a source for Cordovero.

This transfer of meaning from Golem as material entity to a *terminus technicum* for the lowest spiritual form of man is manifest in a Kabbalistic treatise of R. Menaḥem 'Azaryah of Fano, at the beginning of the seventeenth century. This Kabbalist was a disciple of Cordoverian Kabbalah at the beginning of his Kabbalistic career; in the following discussion R. Menaḥem 'Azaryah conspicuously followed the avenue opened by the Safedian Kabbalist.[23] When dealing with the quandary of the authorship of the last verses in the Pentateuch, written after the death of Moses, and the assumption that Moses penned the whole Pentateuch, the Kabbalist offers a solution which can be summarized as follows: the death of Moses means the departure of his lower image and likeness [*demut ve-ẓelem taḥton*], whereas the higher image and likeness remained for some days in order to write down the remaining verses.[24] The stay of the higher likeness and image [*demut ve-ẓelem 'elyon*][25] was made possible by the occurrence of a Golem, apparently a visible body which serves as the vehicle of the higher spiritual qualities. Supported by the Golem, the higher image and likeness wrote down the final verses of the Pentateuch. This solution is compared by the Kabbalist to the three men, namely the angels, which were seen by Abraham and to the death of R. Neḥuniyah ben ha-Qanah and the other martyrs. In the case of the latter, the likeness of their archetype [*demut diyoqanam*] descended and underwent the martyrdom, whereas the martyrs themselves were saved.[26]

The Golem mentioned in the case of Moses is apparently paralleled by the likeness of the archetype in the case of the martyrs, an assumption endorsed also by the existence of the theory of rescue by substitution and the mentioning of the Golem in the ancient texts. It is far from clear how the Golem, standing as a refined body,[27] means also the archetype. It is possible that the mentioning of the likeness, *demut,* points to a lower status of the archetype, and thus it may serve as a term for the astral body. However, it seems that the emergence of the Golem at the time of the departure of the soul, constitutes a bizarre version of the astral body, which commonly is acquired at the time of procreation. It is important to note that R. Menaḥem 'Azaryah of Fano refers to the principle of enclothing, *hitlabshut,* as an explanation for the nature of the substitute. He has in mind the important Kabbalistic view, occurring already in early Kabbalah, that explains the emergence of the angelic or spiritual revelations as the result of descent of the spiritual entities, enclothed in a mystical garment, *malbush*.[28]

IV

The stand of R. Menaḥem 'Azaryah of Fano influenced a Kabbalistic preacher in the middle of the seventeenth century, R. Berakhiah Berakh. He applies the principle of substitution of a body in the moment of its death with the higher image, on the one hand, and a Golem, on the other. This principle is used in the explanation of the death of Jacob. According to a famous Midrashic dictum, Jacob did not die.[29] This view ostensibly contradicts the Biblical description of the death of the patriarch and his burial. Berakh asserts that the departure of Jacob is tantamount to the departure of the lower image, whereas the higher image, visible to the eyes, apparently identical to a Golem, was mumified.[30] The process of mumification had as its object the image or the air (*'avir*)[31] but not the real body of the patriarch.[32] The preacher applies the earlier explanation related to Moses in order to explain the discrepancy between the Biblical and Midrashic versions of the death of Jacob. These passages imply that the bodily death is mainly relevant to the lower spiritual faculties, whereas the higher one, together with its substratum, the Golem, is still acting in the lower world. This extraordinary conception concerns only the fate of the few elite and is not the lot of the common people.

V

In the nineteenth century, a certain Oriental Kabbalist, R. Israel Basu, devoted in his encyclopedic *Tif'eret Yisra'el* a whole entry to the Golem, covering an entire folio.[33] However, he never mentions the artificial creation of man, or any pertinent technique, or even the Talmudic text. Golem was understood as related to (1) the celestial body built up by the performance of the commandments, *ḥaluqa' de-rabbanan*,[34] (2) the vision of one's own form during a mystical experience,[35] or (3) the explanation of the magical transport of the magician from one place to another.[36] This entry is convincing evidence of the disinterest in the topic of an anthropoid in the Sefardi Jewish culture.

VI

It is worth noting that this view of the term Golem as standing for a certain type of double, seems to be reflected in the remark adduced by Ḥayyim Bloch in the name of some persons, who considered the Golem to be the "ghost of R. Yehudah Loew."[37] Though it is rather complicated to account exactly for the source of this remark, the above discussion seems to require a qualification of the implicit approach of Scholem on the possible innovation of this view by Bloch, because it is not found in the Hebrew version of the Golem of the Maharal.[38] It may well be possible that the modern interpretation of the Golem as a double contains a greater "authentic" basis in the earlier sources than Scholem was ready to recognize. In principle, even a Kabbalist who would deny the higher spiritual forces of the Golem, would be able to assume that the lower soul, the *nefesh,* standing for the animal soul, needs a *ẓelem* in order to be able to dwell in the body.

Finally, it is remarkable that the term Golem as a reference to the astral body has some affinity to the significance of the same term in the Talmudic-Midrashic literature. In both cases this word stands for a human body which has some inferior spiritual characteristics, whereas the higher intellectual or linguistic qualities are absent. The use of Golem in relation to the astral body is an indirect proof for the fact that this word had explicit anthropomorphic implications, unrelated to the magical ritual as presented in the medieval texts.

Notes

1. *Maḥzor Le-Yamim Nora'im,* ed. D. Goldschmidt (Jerusalem, 1970), vol. 2, p. 572. Compare this legend to that regarding R. Yehudah ben Yaqar, as preserved in a late, perhaps seventeenth-century manuscript. Cf. C. B. Chavel, *Rabbi Moshe Ben Nachman: His Life, Times and Works* (Jerusalem, Mossad Harav Kook, 1973) pp. 159–160 n. 49. [Hebrew]

2. See Schaefer, *Synopse* p. 59, par. 120.

3. See Schafer, *Synopse,* pp. 59–60, par. 119–121. Gottfried Reeg, *Die Geschichte von den Zehn Martyrern* (Tuebingen, 1985), p. 90, par. 40. This passage is translated into German, ibid. pp. 82–83. In most of the manuscripts of this text, the passage on the miraculous exchange between the Rabbi and the Caesar is missing. On the question of the exchange between the images of two persons in the ancient period, see Gruenwald, *Apocalyptic and Merkavah Mysticism,* p. 157, n. 28, and now Peter Schaefer, *Uebersetzung der Heikhalot-Literatur* (Tuebingen, 1987), vol. 2, pp. 43–51.

4. *Heikhalot Rabbati,* ch. 20; Schaefer, *Synopse,* p. 98, par. 225–228; Idel, *Kabbalah: New Perspectives,* p. 318, n. 99.

5. On this posture, see Idel, *Kabbalah: New Perspectives,* p. 89. See also *Heikhalot Rabbati,* ch. 22; Schaefer, *Synopse,* p. 104, par. 236 and Ithamar Gruenwald, "New Passages from Heikhalot Literature," *Tarbiẓ,* vol. 38 (1969), p. 359. [Hebrew]

6. On this book, see above ch. 6, part B.

7. Compare also to the similar view stated on p. 37 where the relation of the body, soul and spirit to the seven planets is mentioned.

8. These terms occur again ibid., p. 37; on their possible significance, see Scholem, *Origins of the Kabbalah,* pp. 181–183.

9. *Kavod 'elyon.* The whole context is conspicuously influenced by R. Abraham ibn Ezra. See the occurrence of a similar phrase, *Mar'eh kevod ha-Shem ha-'Elyon* in ibn Ezra's, *Commentary on Daniel,* 10:21.

10. J. Dan, Ed., p. 31; Ms. Oxford, 1569, fol. 72a.

11. See *Proclus, The Elements of Theology,* ed. E. R. Dodds (Oxford, 1971), pp. 313–321; Lewy, *Chaldean Oracles,* pp. 178–184.

12. W. W. Jaeger, "Das Pneuma im Lykeion," *Hermes,* vol. 48 (1913), pp. 29ff. On the transmission of the *pneuma* at the time of procreation see Dodds, *ibid.* p. 316.

13. Dan, Ed., p. 30 where the moisture of the heart and brain is mentioned. For the view of the Ashkenazi Ḥasidism on the astral body, designated as *re'aḥ ha-guf* or *re'aḥ ha-demut,* and their theory of the *Ẓelem,* which means an archetype, see Dan, *The Esoteric Theology,* pp. 224–229, 247–248. Already Rashi was acquainted with a view that the soul, "*Neshamah*" or "*Ruaḥ*" is formed in the image of the body: see his commentary to *BT, Ḥagigah,* fol. 12b and R. Eleazar of Worms', *Ḥokhmat ha-Nefesh,* fol. 2c.

14. See D. P. Walker, "The Astral Body in the Renaissance Medicine," *Journal of the Warburg and the Courtauld Institutes,* vol. 21 (1958), pp. 119–133.

15. See ch. 15, par. 2.

16. The relationship between the root *glm,* the air of the world, the air of Paradise, and revelation in this world is conspicuous in various passages of the *Zohar,* which served as the main source for Cordovero. See e.g., *Zohar* I, fol. 101a, 144a, and Cohen-Alloro, *The Secret of the Garment,* pp. 26–44. Cordovero himself uses several times, in the same manner as the *Zohar* does, the verb *'itgalim,* in order to point to the materialization of a spiritual being in the air of the world. See *Shi'ur Qomah,* passim.

17. See *Zohar* III, fol. 104b, and Scholem, "Ẓelem," pp. 372–374; Tishby, *Mishnat ha-Zohar,* vol. 2, pp. 90–93. Attention is to be drawn to the remark of Tishby (p. 92) that the theory of the astral body was already known by a medieval Jewish author, who composed the Arabic treatise on the soul, erroneously attributed to R. Baḥya ibn Paqudah. However, since there was no Hebrew medieval translation of this treatise, it seems that the *Zohar* drew its view of the astral body from other sources. It is significant that there is no relationship between the *ẓelem* and the air as far as the *Zohar* is concerned. Interestingly, the view of the astral

body was presented by a follower of the *Zohar,* R. Joseph Angelino, in his *Livnat ha-Sappir* (Jerusalem, 1915), fol. 6d, as the "second garment," namely, that spiritual body which was created by God for the souls of the righteous after their death. Angelino does not use the Zoharic term *ẓelem* as astral body in his discussion. See already Franz Cumont, *Lux Perpetua* (Paris, 1949) pp. 429–430, who has pointed out the affinity between the garment of the souls in the lower Paradise, according to the *Zohar,* and the Neoplatonic views he discussed there (*ibid.* pp. 293, 355, 358).

18. See *Sefer ha-'Emunot,* (Ferrara, 1556) fol. 40b, 62a, 68b, 73b, 77b and n. 19 below. The views on the "spiritual body" were very influential at the end of the fifteenth and beginning of the sixteenth centuries, as the writings of R. Joseph Alqastil, (see n. 19 below) R. Meir ibn Gabbai and R. 'Ovadiyah Hamon demonstrate. See also Roland Goetschel, *Meir Ibn Gabbai, La Discours de la Kabbale Espagnole* (Leuven, 1981), pp. 212–213.

19. It is certain that some form of metempsychosis is involved here; according to the Kabbalists, the ten martyrs underwent their ordeal in order to expiate the sin of the ten brothers of Joseph, who sold their brother. For another discussion on metempsychosis in relation to the spiritual body, see R. Joseph Alqastil's view in Gershom Scholem, "On the Knowledge of the Kabbalah in the Generation of Expulsion from Spain," *Tarbiẓ,* vol. 24 (1955), p. 196. (Hebrew) This author uses the term *geviyah ruḥanit* several times; see Ibid., pp. 189, 190, 194 and p. 201 and Scholem's footnote 170.

20. *Sefer ha-'Emunot,* fol. 83d. See also the discussion on fol. 85a.

21. *Pardes Rimmonim* part 31, ch. 4, fol. 73cd. In another book Cordovero hints also to a certain affinity between the *ẓelem* and the Golem; he quotes the verse in Ps. which includes the term Golem, though this term itself is not explicitly mentioned by Cordovero, and a verse which deals with the *Ẓelem.* See *Shi'ur Qomah* (Warsaw, 1883), fol. 60a.

22. Ibid., fol. 73c. Compare to the view of the *Zohar* 3, fol. 43a, that the magicians can see their *ẓolmin,* namely their astral bodies, as part of a magical practice when demonic powers take possession of these bodies; see Cohen-Alloro, *The Secret of the Garment,* pp. 82–88. On the revelation of the "second garment," another term for the astral body, or the *ẓelem,* see in the writing of the student of Cordovero, R. Ḥayyim Vital's, *Sefer Ha-Gilgulim;* Cf. Scholem, "Ẓelem," p. 374.

23. Menaḥem 'Azaryah of Fano summarized the discussion of Cordovero in his commentary on *Pardes Rimmonim, Pelaḥ ha-Rimmon.*

24. The view that the ẓelem of Moses left at the end of the writing of the Torah, whereas Moses still continued to write down its last verses, is found in a glossa quoted in R. Abraham Azulai's *'Or ha-Ḥamah,* vol. 3, fol. 80d. Thus we may infer that also this view of R. Menaḥem 'Azaryah was already in existence independently of his view of the Golem of Moses. See also Meir Poppers, *Sefer ha-*

Liqquṭim (Jerusalem, 1981), p. 334, where the death of Moses is presented as his awareness that the *ẓelem* had departed his body. Ultimately, this view stems from the Zoharic theory that the *ẓelem* leaves the body thirty days before the actual death of the person. See *Zohar* I, fol. 117b.

25. For the nature of these four spiritual faculties see the lengthy discussion of the author in *'Asarah Ma'amarot,* Ma'amar 'Olam Qaṭan, which is dedicated to this topic. On the other hand, it is obvious that the main line of the interpretation of the martyrdom of the ten sages understood in Lurianic Kabbalah, which was accepted by this Kabbalist in this work as the more significant form of Kabbalah, implicitly rejected the substitution-explanation in favour of a sacrifice type of interpretation of the tragic death of the sages. The real sacrifice, which means the voluntary death, was understood by Lurianic Kabbalah as a theurgical endeavour.

26. See *'Asarah Ma'amarot,* Ma'amar Haqor Din, part II, ch. 13, (Frankfurt A/M, 1658), fol. 53a. The view that the *diyoqan* is higher than the source of *Ẓelem* is found in the *Zohar* III, fol. 104b.

27. The term used by R. Menaḥem 'Azaryah is *nizdakhekh 'eleiah golem.*

28. On this concept in the *Zohar* see Cohen-Aloro, *The Secret of the Garment,* passim.

29. *Ta'anit,* fol. 5b. Indeed, the verb *mwt* does not occur in the context of Jacob's death in the Bible, where the verbs *va-ygva'* and *va-ye'assef* occur. The explanation offered by this Kabbalist differs from the regular Kabbalistic reading of this episode, where the assumption is that another body, a subtle one enveloped the soul, and enables the visible revelation of the souls of the righteous. See e.g., R. Baḥya ben Asher's, *Commentary on the Pentateuch* to Gen., 49: 33. There, the continued existence of the bodily form of the patriarch is safeguarded by the assumption of the astral body, whereas in our case, the existence of the Golem enables the assumption that Jacob remained as a visible entity here below.

30. See *Zera' Berakh* (Cracaw, 1646), fol. 5, 2d. In the same context, the author mentions that the ten martyrs were saved by the transposition of their bodies with *golemei gufot,* perhaps meaning forms of bodies.

31. On "air" in the context of this problem, see the quotations above from *Sefer ha-Ḥayyim* and *Pardes Rimmonim.* See also the term *malbush 'aviri,* the aetherian or aerian garment, occurring since the late thirteenth century Kabbalah; Cf. Gershom Scholem, "Levush ha-Neshamot ve-Ḥaluqa' de-Rabbanan," *Tarbiẓ,* vol. 24 (1956), pp. 294–296. [Hebrew] For the source of the concept see Dodds, (note 11 above), p. 318. It is interesting that the possibility of the creation of a man out of air by means of magic was already the patrimony of ancient magic, as proposed by Simon Magus. See ch. I above.

32. Compare the view that there is a second garment, used after death in order to reveal oneself, also in connection to Jacob; cf. Scholem, ibid., pp. 296–297.

33. See Ms. New York, JTS Mic. 9274, fol. 3b. Thanks are due to Professor Joseph Hacker who kindly drew my attention to this material.

34. See above n. 31.

35. See above ch. 7, n. 23–24 and Scholem, "Ẓelem," pp. 359–367.

36. The author combines the magical flight of R. Eleazar of Worms, as presented in R. Isaac ben Jacob ha-Kohen's, *ha-'Aẓilut ha-Semalit,* ed., Gershom Scholem, *Madda'ei ha-Yahadut* vol. 2 (1927), p. 254. (Hebrew); with a legend related to the study of Kabbalah by Naḥmanides with R. Eleazar, who decided to fly in order to initiate him in this lore. Interestingly enough, it is possible that the Kabbalist was aware of the Ashkenazi theory of the *ẓelem* as a supernal double, as proposed in the works of R. Eleazar; see Scholem, "Ẓelem," pp. 367–368. However, according to the Ashkenazi author, the magical use of the *ẓelem* is not possible apparently because either the nature of the *ẓelem* is not known to the person or the technique to magically conjure it is not known.

37. *Gespenst der Golem,* p. 95.

38. Scholem, "The Idea of the Golem," p. 189, n. 1.

B

Golem: Some Semantic Remarks

I

The following reflections on the semantics of the Golem were prompted by a statement of Scholem, who categorically denied one of the meanings attributed to the Golem: the embryonic one. Scholem knew that in Psalms:

> probably, and certainly in the later sources, 'golem' means the unformed, amorphous. There is no evidence to the effect that it meant 'embryo', as has sometimes been claimed.[1]

The attribution of the significance of "unformed" to the term Golem is not novel with Scholem; it is shared by all the Hebrew dictionaries which possibly follow the Greek and Latin translations of this term[2] but even more, as we shall see below, the medieval philosophical one; however, Scholem's acceptance of this meaning opened the question of the period when the amorphous Golem turned into a designation for the artificial man. This question was answered by him in a very conclusive way; it is in the circle of the Ashkenazi Hasidim, at the beginning of the thirteenth century, that the Golem began to signify the artificial man.[3] In order to substantiate his assessment, Scholem quotes passages from the *Commentary on Sefer Yeẓirah* of R. Eleazar of Worms and Pseudo-Sa'adyah's commentary of the same work. Scholem's assumption is that the two commentaries were written in the same circle[4] and thus they reflect an innovation of this circle. However, as we have seen above, it is plausible that the two commentaries were composed in two distinct circles which were unrelated to each other, and it seems that they were even composed in different countries.[5] Thus, the question is opened with respect to the common source of their usage of this term.

Apparently, such an answer was supplied already by Isaiah Tishby in his rejoinder to Scholem's remark. According to Tishby, the possible source of the Ashkenazi use of the Golem is the Hebrew translation of R. Yehudah ha-Levi's *Kuzari* done by R. Yehudah Qardinal.[6] However, the common assumption of both Scholem and Tishby is that there is a novelty in the manner in which this term is used among the Ashkenazi authors. Thus, they do not check earlier sources; they agree that the "magical" use is still to be found among the medieval authors living in the Rhinelands[7]. In this appendix I shall attempt to show that these assumptions are erroneous, both because the way the term Golem was used in the commentaries on *Sefer Yeẓirah* was misunderstood and because this word was used in the same way in texts written before the end of the twelfth century.

II

The word Golem is a biblical *hapax legomenon.* As such, its significance was the subject of a long array of speculations, including several suggestions to abandon the traditional reading.[8] I will not here add new speculation on the meaning of this term as far as the biblical usage is concerned, but will ponder rather upon some of the uses that this word exhibits in post-Biblical Jewish texts. Whether our different understanding of the word Golem in the Talmudic and Midrashic texts reflects also the biblical meaning is an open matter; in any case, I see no reason not to envision the later Jewish understanding of the Golem as human body, as pertinent, in principle, also to biblical Hebrew. If the *Golemi* in the biblical verse is understood in contrast to *'Aẓmi,* my bone, then we may conceive the former as pointing to the external form and the later to an inner entity.

The verse in Psalm 139:15 was translated into Aramaic using the term *gashmi* for *golmi.* The meaning of *gashmi* can be easily deduced from the Biblical Aramaic where is stands for the body of man. In Daniel 4:30 this word occurs in the following context: Nabuchadnezzar "was driven from men, and did eat grass as oxen, and his body was wet with the dew of heaven". The term for the phrase "his body" is *gishmeih.* Thus, the Aramaic translation is one of the earliest testimonies with respect to the meaning of Golem as the body of a human being.

III

As we have seen above in our discussion of the Midrashic text,[9] it seems plausible that the word stands there for a formed status of the embryo. Let me elaborate further on another well-known Midrashic passage, recurring in several instances.[10] Adam is described as laying before God as a Golem; in some versions of this legend, Adam was shown all the generations which will originate from him. The locus probans for this view is the verse in Psalm 139, in the words, "for in thy book all things were written". Thus, the Golem in the verse is Adam, his descendants being described as inscribed in a book shown to Adam. In some versions, an addition is found which mentions that not only was Adam shown the future generations but also the peculiar limbs of his body out of which each man will emerge.[11] Thus, at least according to these versions, Adam was a Golem, but also a formed entity. Thus it seems that this passage as well does not convey the idea of the unformed or amorphous status of the Golem. Though it will be more cautious not to impose this meaning on all the versions of the above legend where the term Golem indeed occurs, I assume that it will be more plausible to suppose that there was no semantic change between the different versions insofar as the significance of the Golem is concerned. My assumption is based on the fact that I could not detect an ancient usage of the Golem as amorphous and thus I do not see an alternative for our suggestion, even though we do not have a sufficient context to conclusively determine the precise meaning of the term.

Before proceeding with our discussion of the Golem, it is significant to remark that the ontological status of the Golem in this legend—he is a giant that fills the whole world—was combined with the concept of a book mentioned in the biblical verse and in the Midrashic material, as well as in the Kabbalistic[12] and later on the Sarugian discussions of the *Malbush.* As it was pointed out above, the *Malbush* was conceived to be at the same time the combinations of letters à la *Sefer Yeẓirah,* and the primordial Torah, that is a book. In several instances, the relationship between speculations on the *Malbush* and Golem was motivated by the occurrence of the terms Golem and *sefer* in the verse from Psalms.[13]

IV

The term Golem occurs in an interesting context in the versions of *Sefer Yosippon.* Alexander Macedon is said there to have requested the creation of a statue of his, made out of gold, to put in the Temple in Jerusalem. The formulation of this request is as follows: "And they will build up an image of mine [*ẓalmi*]. . . . My Golem will be a remembrance in the House of the Lord".[14] As the editor of the text has remarked, the term *ẓelem* was conceived of as being of female gender and thus it apparently reflects the word *statua;*[15] such an understanding of the *ẓelem* is congruent with our interpretation of the meaning of the Golem in earlier sources, as a term pointing to the silouhette of the human body. However, for the present discussion, it is even more important to remark that the parallelism between Golem and *ẓelem,* both of them meaning a statue, demonstrates that these two terms were related to each other already before the time of the discussions that we referred to above.[16] According to a recent remark of Shelomo Pines, it is possible that this use of the term Golem reflects the influence of the Greek word *agalmata,* meaning statue; moreover, as he pointed out, the magical statues of the Greeks could have influenced the later, medieval Hebrew understanding of the term Golem as a magically animated body.[17]

For our discussion, it is pertinent to point out that already in a Hebrew text, *Megillat 'Aḥima'aẓ,* contemporary with *Josippon,* the use of the term Golem already includes important elements characteristic of the later understanding of this word in magic. A dead child, animated in a magical way by the insertion of the divine name into his body, reveals the place where the divine name is found; then a Rabbi, "Took out the divine name—and the body [*ve-ha-guf*] remained breathless, [*Be-lo' Neshem*]. . . . And the Golem had fallen rotten as if decayed for many years and the flesh returned to its dust."[18]

It is probable that the Golem is a synonym for the body, *guf;* however, it is a body animated by means of the divine name. Though it is obvious that here there is no artificial creation, the connection between the Golem and the divine name is conspicuous. A similar event is related also latter on in the same book, where the divine name was inserted into the mouth of a dead body;[19] also in this case, the phrases, "*Nafal golemo,*" and "*Ve-ha-Golem shav le-'afarah,*" reflect a similar formulation to that occurring in the first example. Thus the term Golem and the divine name were associated in a context including magical linguistic operations. Scholem was well aware of these texts, and even assumed that they influenced the Ashkenazi traditions on the Golem, an assumption that seems very plausible.[20] However, strangely enough, in the same article wherein he affirms that the Italian works influenced the Ashkenazi use of the term, he still maintains that the magical understanding of Golem emerged only in the thirteenth century.[21]

It should be mentioned that despite the fact that the term Golem is used in *Megillat 'Aḥima'aẓ* in connection with the divine name, it basically retains the same meaning as that of its usage in the Midrashic literature: a human body. This is also evident in R. Shabbatai Donnolo's *Commentary on Sefer Yeẓirah,* composed in the same area and period as the *Megillat 'Aḥima'aẓ*; there Golem is explicitly identified as a human body.[22] However, the meaning of body is not the only one occurring in Southern Italy. Under the influence of the *Piyyuṭ*, which also seems to follow earlier views, it meant as well embryo; so, for example we read in a verse of R. 'Amitai ben Shefatiyah, a poet related to the 'Aḥima'aẓ family: "The texture of the limbs of the Golem in the vagina, when it was formed."[23] Here the embryonic significance is obvious; it is not an unformed entity which is described but one which already possesses limbs.

V

The identity of meaning of Golem and *Geshem* is reflected as well in medieval sources where the Golem occurs as a synonym for *Goshem.* In a translation of R. Sa'adyah, *Goshem* and *Golem* are perfect synonyms; according to the twelfth century translator, R. Berakhiyah ha-Naqedan, man was created "with a small body [*gufo qaṭan*] and a minuscule and subtle Golem. Why was he not created with a great body and a grand Golem".[24]

According to an eleventh century author, R. Isaac ibn Ghiyyat, Golem stands for the body of the creature. In one of his poems we read: "The bodies of his creatures He sealed by the means of one seal".[25] The phrase translated as "bodies of his creature" is *golemei yeẓurav.* Without question the word *yeẓurav* alludes not to creatures in general but rather to human creatures, as can be deduced from the context. *Golemei* therefore stands for the bodies which were stamped by the form of man, referred to by the act of sealing.[26]

VI

At a later stage the meaning of the Golem as the form of the body was transposed to the form of the letter. So, for example, we learn from the *Commentary on Sefer Yeẓirah* of R. Eleazar of Worms: "The [term] *sefer* is the writing of the Golem of the letter, so that they may be taught [reading of] a book."[27] Likewise we find in a late fifteenth century discussion that "when the corporeal part of the letters is separated from the Golem, what remains is a hollow Golem as the form of the letter inscribed."[28] Since the occurrence of the term Golem in the above text of the *Commentary on Sefer Yeẓirah* points to the body of the letter, and in any case there is no magical connotation related to it, let me inspect another quotation from this writing adduced by Scholem in order to prove his statement regarding the origin of the new meaning of this term: "He shall knead the dust with the living water and he shall make a body [Golem] and he shall begin to permutate the alphabets."[29] The term Golem stands here not for the magically created anthropoid but for the simple kneading of dust and water, i.e., for the human body which has nothing magical in it. It is only after the kneading of the dust that the recitation of the letters began and only at the end of the whole process does the magical anthropoid emerge. Hence, it is more plausible to assume that here the term is used with the regular meaning of the body or form of the body. I cannot find anything unique in this passage in comparison to the earlier sources. This seems to be true also in the case of the Pseudo-Sa'adyan commentary, though there the context is less conclusive. In any case, the third example brought by Scholem from the *Commentary on Sefer ha-Bahir* attributed to R. Meir ibn Sahulah does not prove that the Golem is the final living creature. There the "dead Golem" is mentioned as a being into which the Talmudic master was not able to infuse the higher soul. In addition, the example brought by Tishby can be simply understood as reflecting the usual meaning, namely the bodies of man. It seems that only in the last passage quoted by Scholem, from the seventeenth century work of R. Naftali Bakharakh, *'Emeq ha-Melekh,* does the term Golem stand for a magically created anthropoid as it was understood in the later periods.[30]

VII

In all the texts surveyed above there are only a few where Golem can be reasonably understood as amorphous. So, why after all, was this meaning accepted and why did it become so widespread? It seems that the answer can be found in a remark of Scholem, coming immediately after his rejection of the embryo meaning. He writes that, "In the philosophical literature of the Middle Ages it is used as a Hebrew term for matter, formless *hyle,* and this more suggestive significance will appear in the following discussion."[31] Then Scholem adduces a Talmudic text parallel to that of *Leviticus Rabba* analyzed above.[32] As to why the philosophical significance is more suggestive than the embryonic one, Scholem does not tell us. However, his own statement is indeed suggestive; I think, that the medieval philosophical usage of the term Golem as hyle, which is an innovation in comparison to the basic use of the term in the earlier layers of Hebrew, was projected on the pre-medieval use of the term. This philosophical use of Golem as hyle is obvious since the twelfth century Hebrew as employed in Maimonides's *Mishneh Torah.*[33] It seems that our discussion revealed a unique instance in which the acceptance of the priority of a philosophical concept distorted the understanding of a topic related to Jewish magic and mysticism. Scholem, generally critical of the role of Jewish philosophy as a departure from organic Judaism,[34] was himself the victim of such a departure because of the influence of Jewish philosophy. He was not alone; several Kabbalists can be listed who accepted the philosophical understanding of the term Golem, since the end of the thirteenth century.

Notes

1. "The Idea of the Golem," p. 161.

2. *Septuaginta, akatergaston*; Symmachus, *amorphoton*; *Vulgata,* imperfectum. The Vulgata follows the significance of the Septuaginta.

3. See Gershom Scholem, "'Golem' and 'Dibbuq' in the Hebrew Dictionary," *Leshonenu,* vol. 6 (1934), pp. 40–41. (Hebrew)

4. Ibid., p. 40 and idem, "The Idea of the Golem," p. 174, n. 1.

5. See above ch. 6, par. 1.

6. "On the Emergence of the Term 'Golem'," *Leshonenu,* vol. 13 (1943/1944), pp. 50–51. (Hebrew)

7. Ibid., p. 51. Scholem himself was not convinced by Tishby's proposal; see "The Idea of the Golem," p. 174, n. 1.

8. See e.g. Mueller, "Die Golemsage," pp. 12–13; Naftali Tur-Sinai, *Lashon va-Sefer,* vol. 2 (Jerusalem, 1960), p. 144. (Hebrew)

9. See above ch. 3, par. 4.

10. See *Bereshit Rabbah,* section 24 par. 2, pp. 230–231. The earliest Rabbinic occurrence of the term *Golem, Mishnah, Kelim,* XII, 6, *golemei kelei matakhot,* can be translated as the bodies of the tools made of metal. Thus the significance of this phrase will conform to the regular understanding of the term as we have attempted to propose here: the body of a being before it reached its perfection, or sometimes the initial phase of the development of a certain entity, but not the amorphous stage. Compare the view of R. Abraham Azulai in his *Commentary on 'Avot* (Jerusalem, 1986) fol. 44a:

> Golem is the person who has intellectual faculties and ethical virtues, which nevertheless are not perfect and there is a certain mixture and [some] confusions [in them]. It is called golem in order to compare him to a vessel which production was not finished by the artisan.

Compare also to the use of the term *Golem* in *'Avot,* V, 7 where it stands for a fully human being, who is not endowed with wisdom. In this context, the view of *Golem* as the spiritual body discussed in the preceding Appendix concurs with our understanding of the word. See also above ch. 15 par. 1.

11. *Tanḥuma,* pericope *ki tisa',* par. 12.

12. A lengthy interpretation of this Midrashic text is found in R. Shime'on Lavi's, *Ketem Paz,* (Djerba, 1940), fol. 135cd. There the Golem is related to the *Sefer Yeẓirah* phrase of, "*Kol ha-yeẓur ve-khol he-'Atid laẓur,*" on the one hand, and with the idea of the book, on the other. Thus in this case it is clear that the Kabbalist understood the term *yeẓur* as refering to man, since the context of his discussion is the dependence of the later generations on the various limbs of Adam qua Golem. Compare to ch. 2, par. 3 above. See also Ibid., fol. 136a, where the view of Adam in Paradise as a book is developed.

13. See e.g., R. Moses Graff's, *Va-Yaqhel Moshe,* fol. 6a.

14. *The Josippon,* ed. D. Flusser (Jerusalem, 1981), p. 56.

15. Ibid., n. to line 38. See also *ibid.,* p. 22 n. to line 29.

16. See Appendix A.

17. "On the Term *ruḥaniyut* and Its Sources and the Doctrine of Yehudah ha-Levi" [forthcoming] in *Tarbiẓ,* vol. 57 (1988), p. 523, n. 48. (Hebrew) According to the proposal of Pines, the magical meaning of the Golem entered Judaism in Southern Italy.

18. *Megillat 'Aḥima'aẓ,* ed., Ze'ev ben Ḥayyim, (Jerusalem, 1965), p. 4.

19. Ibid., p. 10.

20. See "The Idea of the Golem", pp. 182–183. The affinity between the use of the term Golem in a magical context that mentions the use of the divine name, and the later creation of the Golem by the use of linguistic techniques in Ashkenazi Hasidism is reminiscent of a famous issue concerning the emergence of Ashkenazi esotericism. According to the indications of R. Eleazar of Worms, he received the secrets of the prayers, together with other secrets, as a tradition stemming from Italy, where they were brought by Abu Aharon of Baghdad. Does the semantic affinity between the use of the term Golem in the two centers of Jewish esotericism allude to the dependence of the Hasidic discussions on the Golem on the earlier Italian center? On the controversy related to the possibility that the Ashkenazi masters preserved esoteric material stemming from Abu Aharon, see Israel Weinstock, "The Discovery of Abu Aharon of Baghdad's Legacy of Secrets" *Tarbiẓ,* vol. 32 (1963), pp. 153–159. (Hebrew); and the rejoinder of G. Scholem, "Has Abu Aharon's legacy of Secrets Been Discovered?," Ibid., pp. 252–265. (Hebrew); and the rejoinder of Weinstock, "The Treasury of 'Secrets' of Abu Aharon — Imagination or Reality?" *Sinai,* vol. 54 (1964), pp. 226–259. (Hebrew) In our context it is perhaps pertinent to mention that in a manuscript which includes, according to Weinstock, material related to Abu Aharon, there is a concise mention of the creation

of a Golem out of earth, by the combination of the letters of the divine name of forty-two letters; see Scholem, *ibid.,* p. 257 n. 13 and above ch. 3, par. 2.

21. Ibid., 174, n. 1. Compare ibid., p. 191, n. 1 where the very fact that the term Golem was used in a manner different from the philosophical meaning is sufficient in order to betray, according to Scholem, an Ashkenazi influence.

22. Fol. 65a. Already Flusser, *The Josippon,* p. 26 n. referring to line 29, has pointed out that Golem means "body" in several instances in the early medieval Jewish literature in Italy.

23. See *Sirei 'Amitai,* ed. Yonah David (Jerusalem, 1975), p. 16. The affinity between the verse of 'Amitai and that of Yannai (discussed above ch. 3, par. 5) was already noted by Ẓvi M. Rabinovitz, ed. *The Liturgical Poems of Rabbi Yannai* (Jerusalem, 1985), p. 78. On the influence of this formulation on *Josippon,* and not that of Sabbatai Donnolo, see Reuven Bonfil, "Between Eretz Israel and Babylonia," *Shalem,* vol. 5, ed., J. Hacker (Jerusalem, 1987), p. 30. (Hebrew)

24. Hermann Gollancz, *The Ethical Treatises of Berachya,* (London, 1902), p. 23 (Hebrew part). See the English part, p. 44 where the term Golem is not translated. Compare also to R. Menaḥem Recanati, *Be'ur ha-Torah* (Jerusalem, 1961), fol. 68ab.

25. See Yonah David, ed., *The Poems of Rabbi Isaac ibn Giyyat* (Jerusalem, 1987), p. 103. In this edition this is a typographical error and instead of *golemei* it is printed *gomelei;* after inspecting the sources it is obvious, however, that there is no ground for this form. On *yeẓur,* see above ch. 2, par. 3.

26. *Mishnah, Sanhedrin* ch. 4 par. 5. Interestingly enough, the Mishnaic statement on the sealing of man with the divine signet is reminiscent of the sealing of the world by the combination of the letters of the divine name in *Sefer Yeẓirah.* Cf. above ch. 2, par. 2. On the divine name as the seal, *ḥotam*, of God, see above ch. 10, par. 9.

See also the twelfth century poem written by R. Benjamin bar Samuel; the Hebrew original says: "*Ṭerem hinshim bo neshem, Golem muṭba' demuto.*" The Latin translation of this verse, stemming from the thirteenth century is: *ante quam insuflaret animam, in forma erat impressa similitudo ipsius.* Golem is translated as in forma, namely in the form. Thus the *similitudo* is conceived as being added to the formed body. Since in the preceding verse the creation of man out of blood and water, and his shape, *tavnito,* were mentioned, there is no reason to assume that Golem stands for the body in an unshaped state. See Ch. Merḥavia, "Some Poems of Rabbi Benjamin bar Samuel in a Latin Translation" in eds., Sh. Abrahamson—A. Mirsky, *Ḥayyim (Jefim) Schirmann Jubilee Volume* (Jerusalem, 1980), p. 202. (Hebrew)

27. *Commentary on Sefer Yeẓirah,* fol. 15d.

28. *Minḥat Yehudah,* fol. 20a.

29. *Commentary on Sefer Yeẓirah,* fol. 2b.

30. See Scholem," 'Golem'," (n. 3 above), pp. 40–41.

31. "The Idea of the Golem," p. 161.

32. Ch. 3, par. 4.

33. *Hilkhot Yesodei Torah* 2:3 etc. It is possible that R. Abraham bar Ḥiyya's use of the term Golem as body in general, and not human body in particular, may have influenced, together with the Talmudic use, Maimonides' preference of this term in order to allude to matter. See Israel Efrat, *Mediaeval Jewish Philosophy, Terms and Concepts,* vol. 2 (Tel Aviv, 1969), p. 129. (Hebrew). See also ibid., p. 128, sub voce *guf.*

34. *Major Trends,* pp. 28–29.

C

Was There a Macranthropos Named 'Emet?

As we have seen in several passages above, the Golem appears to its creators with the inscription *'emet,* truth, on his forehead. On the other hand, we have seen in the tenth chapter that Kabbalists developed a theory concerning the macranthropic nature of the technique of creating a Golem. I would like to speculate here on the possibility that in antiquity there was an hypothetical conception which combined these two themes. It is appropriate to emphasize from the very beginning the speculative nature of the following suggestion; all the material adduced below only hints at the possibility of the existence of a concept related to a macranthropic entity called *'emet*; I cannot consider the accumulation of the following suggestions as conclusive, but I would like to expose this speculation in order to invite further material from scholars who may, otherwise, not pay attention to such a possibility.

As the starting points for our speculations, let me translate an Ashkenazi Hasidic passage, authored by R. Eleazar of Worms. Though the creation of an artificial man is not mentioned at all, it seems that this passage may reflect a tradition related to a macranthropos, described in such a manner that it may point to a certain affinity to the *'emet* theme connected to the Golem:

> At all the sides of the *shekhinah* there are crowns of royalty,[1] and the size of it is two hundred and thirty six myriads of parasangs, and on it David has said: "Great is the Lord, and of great power",[2] in the *gemaṭria* two hundred thirty and six "and his understanding is infinite". Jeremiah said on it: "And the tetragrammaton *'elohim 'emet* [he] is the living God and the king of the world";[3] in *gemaṭria* [it is equivalent to] two hundred and thirty six, she is ruling the world according to her,[4] and she is called the angel of the Lord, on the name of the mission,[5] but there is no separation in her.[6]

The shekhinah is conceived here as a feminine supernal entity, ruling over the whole world. Conspicuously, the medieval author refers to the huge dimensions of the ancient *Shi'ur Qomah* as pointing to the size of the divine presence. This relationship between the huge size and the entity name *shekhinah* is not new with the medieval source; it is found already in the mystical Midrash *'Otiyyot de-Rabbi 'Aqiva',* where the body of the *shekhinah* is described as having gigantic dimensions.[7] What seems to be novel in the above text is the use of the verse from Jeremiah in order to refer to the mentioned size; in all the earlier sources dealing with the macranthropos, only the verse of the Psalms functions as locus probans for extracting the figure 236. It is only in a later anonymous Ashkenazi treatise, *Sefer ha-Navon,* that the end of the verse occurs, as we shall see below, in exactly the same context. Our text hints at the figure by means of the numerical equivalent of the phrase *melekh 'olam,* the King of the world. Thus, there is a corelation between the size, 236 myriads of parasangs, and the function of this entity, as ruler of the world.

However, the above passage may reflect more than the description of a gigantic angel that rules the world. The very fact that the verse from Jeremiah was quoted may imply more than the calculation of the dimension of the *shekhinah* from the phrase *melekh 'olam.* Its opening words are exactly the same words written on the forehead of the Golem in accordance with the version preserved in the *Commentary on the Tetragrammaton* from the circle of the *Book of Speculation* discussed above.[8] Does this citation reflect also the possibility that the *shekhinah* in the above text has something to do with the creation of a macranthropos similar to the Golem? This is a tenuous suggestion and I cannot provide, for the time being, a conclusive answer to this question, but I would like nevertheless to present some evidence, in addition to the occurrence of the verse from Jeremiah, for the probability of such a reading.

I

A macranthropos, related to the creation of the Golem, is explicit in the text originating from the circle of the Special Cherub, discussed above.[9] There, in the very technique of creating the Golem, the combinations of letters were linked to the size of the macranthropos. A similar case, found in a recipe for creating a Golem, in the circle of R. Eleazar himself, will be adduced here below. In the case of the above passage, the connection between the macranthropos and the anthropoid may be hinted at by the word *'emet.*

II

An attribute of God named *'Emet* and *Aletheia* is already known in the classical Midrash,[10] so that the possibility that the angel of God, identical to the *Shekhinah,* mentioned in our text, is related to this Midrashic theme. Interestingly enough, several commentators on this Midrash introduced the term *ḥotam,* seal, in order to explain the significance of the term Aletheia.[11] Apparently, the introduction of the term "seal" in the commentaries is the result of the association of truth with a seal, because of the Talmudic dictum, "Truth is the seal of God". Below, we shall return to this statement. Is it possible that the seal of God was originally a divine, or angelic, hypostasis?

III

A female angel, apparently of gigantic size, named *Aletheia,* i.e., Truth, was described already in the second century, reflecting the influence of ancient Jewish mythologoumena.[12] Moreover, in the passage describing the *Aletheia,* the Gnostic source mentions the speculations on the letters of the divine name, and what seems to be more specific the *plene* spelling of the letters. Thus, the possible similarity between the angelic *Shekhinah,* gigantic in proportions and related to *'Emet,* and the ancient Gnostic view, points to an affinity between Jewish ancient sources dealing with a hypothetical, angelic *'Emet* of gigantic size and the medieval passage.

IV

Our next suggestion is a rather complicated one: let me quote a sentence from a version of the creation of the Golem from the circle of R. Eleazar of Worms:

> All the combinations of letters have thirty-six syllables,[13] equivalent to the number of the hidden [letters] of the [divine] name: How is

> it? IVD-VD, HY-Y, VV-V, HY-Y,[14] this is [the meaning] of the [verse] "Serafim stood above Him".[15] And so also is the courtyard of the Holy One, Blessed be He, in accordance with the appearance of the visible Glory,[16] [namely] thirty six thousands parasangs of His.[17]

Here the thirty-six syllables, characteristic of the pronunciation of the combinations of letters related to the creation of the Golem, are emblematic of the gigantic size of the visible Glory; this entity apparently has an anthropomorphic shape, as the reference to the huge dimensions, reminiscent of the *Shi'ur Qomah,* implies. However, in addition to the gematria *LV* ("to Him" in the verse) which is equivalent to thirty-six, another method is used: the *plene* writing of the letters of the divine name, minus the letters themselves [this being the meaning of the hidden part of the name] are equivalent to thirty-six.

In another text, closely related to the Ḥasidei Ashkenaz, *Sefer ha-Navon,* we read:

> In the *Book Hekhalei Qodesh*[18] in the *Book of Qomah* [it is written] YHVH when written in the *plene* form[19] . . . is equivalent in gemaṭria to *Ve-rav Koaḥ* and this is the gemaṭria of *Melekh 'Olam* . . . this is the courtyard of it [the Glory], the body of the *Shekhinah.*[20 21]

This text is close to that of the version of the creation of the Golem because of the occurrence of the term "courtyard" in a context dealing with the gigantic size of the Glory, and because of the use of the plene spelling of the divine name. On the other hand, the last text is reminiscent of the text authored by R. Eleazar of Worms, because of the use of the verse from Jeremiah in order to calculate the size of the Glory. I assume that beyond those similarities, there was a tradition dealing with the relationship between the dimension of the Glory, conceived as an anthropoid, and the technique of creating an anthropoid here below. The occurrence of the term *'emet* in the first text may be the only vestige of the technique of creating a huge anthropoid, in the supernal world, just as the term *'emet* occurs in some instances in techniques of creating an anthropoid here below.

V

In ancient Jewish literature, there is a conception that the name of God was engraved on a tablet on the heart of the angels.[22] What exactly this divine name was the ancient authors did not mention. Thus we may contemplate the possibility that the three words tetragrammaton, *'elohim, 'emet* could have been written on those mythical tablets. Moreover, the assumption that the word *'emet* was included on this inscription is corroborated by an ancient view, expressed in the *Odes of Solomon,* where it is said that the Archangels are clad with the seal of God.[23] Again, it is not clear as to what this seal exactly is. However, as the Talmud mentions several times, the seal of God is truth.[24] Thus we may surmise again that there was a probable conceptual relation between *'emet* and an angel. This possibility is to be considered especially in a Midrashic discussion of the above dictum, where angels are also mentioned in connection to the verse in Daniel 10:1 whose Hebrew version is *'Emet ha-davar ve-ẓava' gadol.*[25] A literal translation of this phrase is "The thing is true and the army," i.e., according to the Rabbinic interpretation of this term, the family of angels, "is great." Thus a possibility is open to conceive the parallelism between angels and *'emet.* However, the whole context is complicated, and the above suggestion must be corroborated by further material.

VI

In one of the Ashkenazi texts related to the Golem we learn that after three years of studying *Sefer Yeẓirah* "a man was created before them and on his forehead it was written *'emet,* as on the forehead of Adam".[26] The danger involved in this inscription is that "people shall not err concerning him, as it happened in the generation of Enosh." When discussing this sentence, Scholem referred to the idolatry in the generation of Enosh in general.[27] However, in our passage the idolatry seems to be of a very peculiar nature: it is related to a worship of Adam. This idea is not an innovation of the medieval source; according to *'Otiyyot de-Rabbi 'Aqiba'*:

> At the beginning, Adam was created [of such a size] from earth to heaven. When the servant angels had seen him they were shocked and afraid of him. Then all of them stood before the Holy One, Blessed be He, and said to Him: Lord of the world, are there two powers in the world, one in heaven and one on earth? What did the Holy One, Blessed be He, do? He put His palm on him and He diminished him to [the size of] thousand yards.[28]

Thus the gigantic size of Adam was the reason for the error of the angels. As to the error in the generation of Enosh it seems that it can be related also to the idolatry connected to the gigantic size of the construction done by the men of that generation, as we analyzed it above.[29] If so, in the medieval Ashkenazi text there may be a hint to the huge size of the Golem, in addition to the inscription of the divine name, as the reason for the error of men.

VII

Last but not least: in a Qumran text the phrase *malakh 'amito,* the angel of His truth, occurs.[30] Does it reflect the earliest documented phase of the conception of the relation between an angel and *'emet*?

Let me summarize the above discussions. A passage on a female angel, apparently of huge dimension, designated as *aletheia,* can be dated as early as the second century C.E. in Gnostic sources, probably influenced by Jewish material. A divine attribute named *'emet* appears in an early Jewish Midrash. The *shekhinah* is presented as the angel of God of a gigantic size, and described with the verse in Jeremiah related to the Golem. The techniques of creating a Golem mention the gigantic entities related to the *shekhinah.* All these assessments together make the assumption of the existence of an ancient concept of the macranthropic *'emet* plausible.

If the above speculations on the existence of a conception of a macranthropos named *'emet* are correct, this may explain the theme of the uncontrolled growth of the Golem on whose forehead the word *'emet* is written: the Golem strives to return to its original state as an macranthropos.[31]

Notes

1. On the possible meaning of these crowns see later on in the text; and cf. Dan, *The Esoteric Theology,* p. 122.

2. Ps. 147:5.

3. Jer. 10:10. It should be mentioned that *'emet* occurs in the vicinity of the Tetragrammaton also in other instances in the Bible. See e.g. Ps. 31:6. It is wellknown that Truth is a name of God in several religions, Samaritean and Islam. Accordingly it is possible that this word was considered also in Judaism as a divine name not only as a name of a divine attribute.

4. I do not understand why there are two feminine entities mentioned here.

5. This is a Midrashic principle that the angels are named in accordance with their mission. See *Genesis Rabbah* section 50 par. 2, pp. 516–517 and the footnotes ad loc.

6. See the text from *Sefer ha-Ḥokhmah,* as printed by Dan, *The Esoteric Theology,* p. 121, slightly corrected according to the manuscript, and the translation of Scholem, *Origins of the Kabbalah,* pp. 184–185, who has skipped some of the words dealt with here.

7. See Cohen, *The Shi'ur Qomah, Texts and Recensions,* p. 228. See also the text referred to in n. 20 below.

8. See above ch. 5, par. 10.

9. Ch. 10, par. 7b.

10. See *Genesis Rabbah,* section 8 par. 5, p. 60. In this context it is pertinent to mention a Talmudic passage occurring in *BT, Sanhedrin,* fol. 111a, where Moses is described as being able to contemplate one of the thirteen divine attributes named *'Emet.* It is very plausible that the Talmud implies an hypostatic entity which embodies the divine attribute named *'Emet* and thus *'Emet* would be very similar to the Gnostic *Aletheia,* which will be mentioned below.

It seems possible that in the above text *'Emet* is to be conceived as the pair of another divine attribute, *'Erekh 'Appayim,* mentioned immediately after *'Emet.* A comparison between this pair and the pair of angels in the Gnostic text of Marcos may indeed be compelling, as the manifestation of God is, related in both cases, to a couple one of its members being designated as Truth.

On the myth connected to *'Erekh 'Appayim* in ancient Judaism, late Orphism and the *Zohar* see the important article of Yehudah Liebes, "The Kabbalistic Myth of Orpheus" in eds. M. Idel, Z. Harvey, E. Schweid, *Shlomo Pines Jubilee Volume* [Jerusalem, 1988] pp. 425–459, especially p. 457. [Hebrew]

11. See the comments of the editors, ibid., on line 9.

12. See Idel, "The World of the Angels," pp. 2–7, and above ch. 2, par. 3.

13. See above ch. 5, par. 3.

14. VD+Y+VV+Y = 36.

15. Isa. 6:2.

16. The *Kavod nir'eh* is a rather exceptional term, though it seems quite plausible because of the existence of the theory of the Invisible Glory, *Kavod ha-nistar.*

17. See Ms. Oxford, 1638, fol. 59a, Ms. Firenze-Laurentiana, Plut. 44, 16, fol. 4a. On this text see above ch. 5, par. 3.

18. This title is characteristic of the quotations from the Heikhalot literature in *Sefer ha-Navon.* Interestingly enough, the same title appears also in the fragments of the text from which the text of R. Eleazar of Worms was quoted above. I am not aware of any attempt to relate *Sefer ha-Navon* to these interesting texts: see, for the time being, Idel, *Kabbalah: New Perspectives,* pp. 193–195.

19. The calculation of the plene writing of the Tetragrammaton is rather complex, but it is possible to supply at least one way to reach the gematria of 236. However, it is not here the place to enter the complexities of this calculation. In any case the technique of reaching the figure of the size of the macranthropic man is very similar to that used in the above passage from the recipe for creating a Golem. Moreover, a gloss inserted in the first text of R. Eleazar of Worms, whose author is not known, introduces immediately after the passage quoted above, a calculation of the figure 236 from the plene writing of the Tetragrammaton; see

Dan, *The Esoteric Theology,* p. 121. This is further evidence for the affinity between the texts treated above. Compare also to the calculation offered by the same author elsewhere in *Sefer ha-Ḥokhmah,* as printed by Konyevsky, p. 21.

20. See n. 7 above.

21. Dan, Ed., *Studies,* p. 126.

22. See Scholem, *Jewish Gnosticism,* p. 71, n. 21.

23. Ibid., p. 133 who mentions the *Odes of Solomon* 4:8. See also Gruenwald, *Apocalyptic and Merkavah Mysticism,* pp. 53–54.

24. *TB, Shabbat,* fol. 55a; *Yoma,* fol. 79b; *Sanhedrin,* fol. 64a. For our discussion in general the details of the passage in *Shabbat* seem to reflect the concept that people studying Torah, and the righteous in general, are sealed with the letter *T*[*av*], presented as the endletter of *'emet,* and it is possible even to understand that the seal on the forehead of the righteous was *'emet.* If this suggestion will be corroborated by further material, we may consider the Talmudic text as one of the sources of the theme of *'emet* as inscribed on the forehead of the Golem. It should be mentioned that a series of Ashkenazi texts refer to the fact that the endletters of the words *bara' 'elohim 'et,* form the consonants of the word *'emet.* In one of these texts, this fact is related to the verse from Jer. and to the statement that the seal of God is *'emet.* See R. Eleazar of Worms' *Sefer ha-Ḥokhmah,* p. 22; see also ibid., p. 26 where these endletters are mentioned together with those of the Hebrew phrase *Va-yipaḥ be-'appav nishmat ḥayyim,* (Gen. 2:7; and He {God} breathed into his nostrils the breath of life) which form the word *ḥotam.* Thus the relation between the creation of man, the seal and *'emet* is at least implicitly hinted at in an Ashkenazi text. It is possible that the author of this second discussion is the anonymous person who glossed R. Eleazar's *Sefer ha-Ḥokhmah.*

25. *Song of Songs Rabbah* on 1:9, ed. S. Dunski (Jerusalem, 1980), pp. 37–38. On truth as the seal of God in general, and the possible implications of this Midrash in particular, see Liebes, "Christian Influences", pp. 59–60.

26. See above ch. 5, par. 8.

27. "The Idea of the Golem," p. 179, n. 3. It should be mentioned that the fear of idolatry in the Ashkenazi text, as we have interpreted it here, differs from the similar opposition to the creation of the Golem in the text from the circle of the *Book of Speculation.* There, in the parable, which was not quoted in our translation, the danger is that the operators will be conceived as divine because of their knowledge of the secret of creating an anthropoid, and not because of the theological mistake related to the anthropoid itself.

28. See S. Wertheimer, *Battei Midrashot,* vol. 2, p. 412. See also Idel, "Enoch is Metatron," p. 153, p. 164, n. 19.

29. See above ch. 3, par. 3.

30. See the *Manual of Discipline 3,* 25.

31. See above ch. 13, n. 22.

Subject Index

Abraham, xxiii, 10, 14, 15, 16, 17, 18, 19, 20, 21, 22, 23, 24, 33, 41, 50–51, 62, 102, 106, 108, 109, 112, 113, 118, 139, 147, 152, 167, 173, 176, 179–80, 181, 183, 184, 187, 198, 220, 234, 239, 263

Adam, 5, 6, 12, 18, 28, 34–37, 41, 57, 61, 64–65, 70, 72, 73, 75, 110, 123, 130, 136, 137, 139, 140, 154, 175, 176, 210, 212, 225, 277, 298, 303, 310

Adam Qadmon, 111, 145–46, 148, 149, 159, 160, 269

'Adnei ha-Sadeh, 213, 225, 231

Air, 5, 6, 8, 10, 90, 95, 161, 287, 292, 294

Alchemy, 174, 175, 184

Alembicum, 174, 195

Androginy, 156

Angels, 34, 88, 117, 170, 174, 179, 237, 285, 306–13. *See also* Meṭaṭron; Sandalfon

Anthropomorphism, 13, 14, 48, 123, 137, 146, 151, 160, 161, 162, 272, 291

Arabs, xvii, 88, 90, 174, 189

Aristotelianism, xxii, 103, 130, 141, 183, 184, 185, 187–90, 272, 278

Ashkenazi Ḥasidism, xix, xxvii, xxix, xxx, 32, 38, 64, 66, 72–73, 93, 116, 119, 152, 153, 157, 267, 276, 292, 296, 303, 309. *See also* Eleazar of Worms

Astral body, 33, 173, 286–95

Astrology, xvii, xxii, 20, 72, 86–89, 90, 91, 94, 95, 169, 172, 174, 177, 202, 286–87

Automata, xx, 3, 233–34, 339

Azaziel, 33

Azza, 33

Beit Midrash, 31, 63

Beẓalel, 31, 171, 173, 188

Body, xxviii, 6, 8, 12, 13, 17, 30, 37–41, 56, 60, 71–72, 85–86, 100, 105, 108, 115, 135–36, 137, 138, 155, 170, 227, 232, 261, 285, 287–88, 292, 297, 298, 299–301, 304, 305

Calf, xxvii, 19, 31, 40, 49, 86, 88, 89, 90, 168, 170, 171, 172, 181, 188, 194, 220, 224, 235, 239, 273–74

Color, 121–24, 126
Combinations of letters, xxiii, xxv, xxvii, xxviii, xxx, 9, 10, 11, 12, 18, 30, 31, 38, 54, 56, 58, 60, 64–65, 67, 68, 70, 71, 74, 78, 82, 85, 89, 97, 105, 108, 111, 112, 114, 120, 135, 140, 145, 148, 150, 152, 159, 162, 168, 171–73, 177–78, 181, 188, 199, 240, 242–43, 245, 248, 271, 278, 304
Covenant, 13, 22
Creator, xxvi, 5, 16, 17, 18, 50, 67, 81, 88, 131, 149, 161, 186, 230, 265, 266

Dance, 82–85, 93
David, 307
Death, 7–8, 84, 89, 108, 131, 183, 237, 285, 286–87, 289, 294, 299, 301
Dibbuk, 253
Divine Names, xviii, 11, 12, 13, 30, 31, 58, 59, 60, 61, 62, 65, 67, 68, 70, 79, 80, 82, 83, 88, 92, 98, 116, 128, 136, 138, 150, 166, 170, 172, 178, 207, 238, 239, 278, 299, 310, 311; name of 42 letters, 74, 304; name of 72:63–64, 76, 98–99, 100, 101, 105, 116, 264
Double, 101
Dust, xix, xxviii, 6, 26, 32, 34, 35, 36, 38, 42, 51, 56, 57, 61, 62, 63, 65, 67, 69, 70, 75, 76, 83, 88, 89, 91, 94, 99, 101, 102, 178, 199, 202, 210, 217, 220, 234, 249, 299, 301. *See also* Earth

Earth, 5, 8, 20, 34, 35, 36, 43, 60, 61, 64, 69, 81–82, 86, 98, 139, 167, 176, 212
Ecstasy, xix, 84, 101, 105, 112, 113, 118, 122, 168, 273, 280
Egypt, 3–4, 48, 49, 88, 192
'Ein sof, 143, 146, 150, 198
Eliyahu, 59, 286
Elisha, 59
Emanation, 136, 139, 197, 202
Embryo, 35, 36, 37, 41, 42, 71, 86, 93, 157, 202, 288, 296, 300, 301
'Emet, 4, 5, 64–65, 67, 77, 178, 208–09, 211, 212, 306–13. *See also* Seal
Enoch, 90, 179, 191
Enosh, 32, 40–41, 64, 77, 310
Eve, 62, 72
Ezekiel, 59

Faust, xx, 254
Ferdinand, King of Aragon, 176
Fire, 10, 72

Glory, 15, 89, 103, 152, 286, 292, 309, 312. *See also* Throne
Gnosticism, xxiii, 23, 43, 308, 311–12. *See also* Mandeanism
Greeks, xvii, 4, 165, 183, 184, 266

Halakhah, 28, 47, 200–201, 210, 213–31, 234–37, 263–65
Ḥamai R., 177, 179
Haran, 16, 18, 51, 56, 139
Ḥaver, Ḥavrayya, 27–28, 39, 129, 166–67
Ḥasidism, xxi, xxix, 220–24, 247–50, 252–54, 266, 279
Heikhalot literature, xxvi, 15, 32, 33, 139, 152–53, 154, 156, 162, 278, 285–86
Hermeticism, xxvii, 33, 87, 90, 169, 171, 175, 185–92
Homunculus, 185–86, 195, 257

Humanity, xx, 214
Hyle, 141, 142, 301

Ideas, 141
Imagination, 22, 50, 101, 103, 104, 124
Incest, 235
India, 88
Intellect, 99, 102, 103, 106, 107, 109, 113, 115, 131, 133, 166, 175, 176, 198, 218, 237
Isaac, 235
Isaiah, 12
Isolation, 116
Israel, 67, 88, 98, 114, 115, 151, 183, 217, 226, 236, 247, 248

Jacob, 233, 234, 235, 288, 290, 294
Jeremiah, 12, 64, 65, 66, 67, 108, 109, 112, 177–78, 192, 199, 307, 309
Jericho, 84
Joseph, 234–36, 293

Kabbalah: Christian Kabbalah, 175–80, 182, 250; Ecstatic Kabbalah, xxvi, 104, 106, 108, 116, 118, 189, 264, 276, 277, 279, 280; Lurianic Kabbalah, 244, 258, 270, 294; Practical Kabbalah, 243; Theosophical Kabbalah, 116, 117, 119, 120, 124, 134

Language, 4, 10, 12, 13, 47, 50, 87, 262, 264–65
Lavan, 86
Leah, 236
Letters, xvii, 8, 9, 10, 11, 12, 17, 21, 22, 40, 51, 54, 56–57, 60, 67, 81–82, 91, 100, 120, 123, 176, 222

Macranthropos, xxiii, 23, 33, 41, 77, 137, 150, 153, 160, 210, 277, 306–13
Magic, xvi, xvii, xviii, xxi, xxiii, xxiv, 20, 27, 28, 29, 31, 40, 47, 48, 62, 79, 86, 91, 107, 168, 171, 178–79, 181, 184, 215, 234, 251, 260–61, 265, 272, 299
Magician, xix, 129, 170, 182–83, 192, 193, 251
Malbush, 74, 148, 152–54, 159, 161, 270, 290, 298
Mandeanism, 25–26, 41
Medicine, 155, 174, 189, 287
Merkavah, 15, 16, 24, 33, 40
Messiah, 154, 246
Meṭaṭron, 30, 109
Moses, 109, 170, 173, 187, 289, 290, 293–94, 312
Mysticism, xvi, xvii, xviii, xix, xxi, xxv, 61, 107–108, 114, 166, 168, 185, 214, 259, 270, 272

Nabuchadnezzar, 297
Nature, 166, 175, 179, 180, 181, 182, 183, 189, 194, 198, 215
Neoplatonism, xxii, 24, 33, 159, 171, 278, 287, 293
Noṭariqon, 60, 122, 274

Paganism, xxii, 29, 31, 39, 47, 266
Paradise, 6, 34, 39, 84, 287, 292–93, 303
Pardes, 33
Philosophy, 66, 70, 124, 156, 165–67, 174, 183, 184, 262, 266, 274, 302
Platonism, 130
Pleroma, 137, 230
Prayer, 122–23, 170
Prophesy, 103, 105, 109, 168,

Prophesy (*continued*) 171–72, 175, 187, 198, 199
Prometheus, 4, 7

Renaissance, xxi, xxvi, xxviii, 165, 167, 169, 174, 185–215. *See also* Christian Kabbalah
Ritual, xix, 61–63, 93, 158, 201, 226, 260, 273, 291
Ruaḥ, 98, 100, 115, 131, 133, 135, 141, 142, 154, 287, 292
Ruḥaniyut (Spirituality), xvii, xxii, 189, 197
Sabbateanism, 154
Samuel, 131
Sandalfon, 109
Sarah, 16, 18, 41, 102, 147, 179
Satan, xx, 32, 229
Seal, 59, 65–66, 74, 77, 136, 154, 155, 169, 208, 300, 304, 308, 310, 313
Sefirot, 9, 14, 78, 120, 121–22, 123, 129, 130, 136, 138, 139, 140, 141, 142, 143, 144, 146, 150, 156, 158, 150, 160, 162, 168, 170, 173, 197–99, 276–78
Sex, 75, 232–41
Shekhinah, 151, 307, 319
Shem, 19
Shi'ur Qomah, 14, 23, 48, 150, 151, 152, 270, 272, 307
Solomon, 170
Soṭah, 42, 61–62, 70, 75, 76, 274
Soul, 5–6, 8, 10, 11, 12, 16, 17, 21–22, 23, 33, 34, 35, 36, 41, 51, 70–71, 80, 82–83, 85, 88, 105, 106–07, 109, 110, 128, 129, 130, 132, 135–36, 147, 154, 175, 179, 180, 182, 197, 230, 238, 287, 292
Special Cherub, 92, 93, 149, 160, 161, 267, 272, 308
Speech, xvii, 10, 12, 13, 22, 29, 55, 70–71, 89, 106, 107, 130, 135, 142
Statues, xxii, xxvii, 3–4, 5, 16, 29, 31, 32, 47, 146, 158, 169, 171, 175, 287, 299
Sufism 259, 267

Tabernacle, 31, 62, 138
Talisman, 137, 169–70, 172, 179
Technique, xix, xxiii, xxv, xxviii, xxix, 10–11, 33, 59, 61–62, 66, 67, 71, 82, 84, 93, 103–04, 156, 170, 242–46, 263–64
Tellurian powers, 36, 37, 43, 196–97, 209, 212, 280
Temple, 60–63, 75, 221, 224, 299
Throne, 14, 15, 16, 71, 80, 161
Torah, 18, 19, 40, 67, 74, 78, 115, 148, 156, 166, 235, 242–43, 246, 266, 293

Ushabti, 3
Uzza, 33

Vitality (Ḥiyyut), 65, 82–83, 91, 92, 131, 133, 197, 201, 207, 248, 250
Vowels, 56, 58, 92, 97, 100, 111, 123, 246, 274

Water, xxviii, 5, 10, 56, 61–63, 65, 76, 97, 101, 207, 234, 274, 301

Yehudah, 239
Yeẓur, 10, 12, 13, 14, 22, 23, 82, 92, 135, 154, 269–71, 300, 303, 304

Ẓaḥẓaḥot, 143, 146, 147
Ẓelem, 6, 43, 103, 142, 169, 173, 202, 240, 285–95, 299

Author Index

Abaye, 168, 188, 244
Abraham bar Ḥiyya, 305
Abraham ben Azriel, 73
Abraham ben Natan of Lunel, 93
Abraham of Esquira, 117, 274
Abu Aharon of Baghdad, 303
Abulafia, Abraham, xxi, xxii, xxviii, 22, 55, 64, 79, 83, 87, 93, 94, 96–104, 114, 115, 116, 119, 124, 161, 167, 173, 176, 179, 187, 188, 189, 190, 192, 199, 202, 239, 246, 262, 263-64, 272, 273, 275, 276
Abulafia, Meir ha-Levi, 50
Abulafia, Todros ha-Levi, 161
Agrippa, Cornelius, 179–80, 186, 188, 215
Aharon R., 143
Aharon Berakhiyah of Modena, 84
Albertus Magnus, 239
Albotini, Yehudah, 111–12
Aldabi, Meir, 133
Alemanno, Yoḥanan, 7, 8, 161, 167–75, 176–77, 179–81, 184, 185, 186, 187, 188, 189, 190, 192, 193, 195, 203, 215, 240, 281
Alexander Macedon, 298
Alqastil, Joseph, 292
Amitai ben Shefaṭiyah, 42, 300, 304
Anaqawa, Abraham, 227
Angelino, Joseph, 293
Aqivah R., 28, 39, 152, 173, 263
Archimedes, 184
Arnold, Christoph, 207
Asher ben David, 136
Ashkenazi, Joseph ben Shalom, xxi, 79, 104, 119–25, 138–44, 146, 147, 148, 156, 157, 159–60, 162, 167, 180, 184, 240, 246, 277
Ashkenazi, Joseph ha-"Tanna," 70–71
Ashkenazi, Ẓevi (he-Ḥakham Ẓevi), 201, 209, 212, 217–18, 220, 221, 222–23, 229, 236
Asud, Yehudah, 219, 230
Azriel of Gerona, 79, 120, 154, 157
Azulai, Abraham, 69, 79, 197, 199–203, 293, 302
Azulai, Ḥayyim Joseph David, HYDA', 200, 211, 212, 244
Axelrod, Alexander, 137

Bacon, Roger, 181
Baḥya ben Asher, 130, 133, 294

Bakharakh, Naftali, 153, 188, 244, 246, 280, 301
Baqi, Samson, 158
Barceloni, Yehudah, 7, 12, 20, 21, 25, 49, 50, 51, 52, 249
Barukh, Jacob, 193, 203, 240, 244
Basu, Israel, 290
Ben Amozegh, Eliahu, 231
Ben Sira, 64–66, 77, 108, 109, 110, 112, 178, 190, 199
Benjamin bar Samuel, 304
Berakh, Berakhiyah, 290
Berakhiyah ha-Naqedan, 300
Bibago, Abraham, 165–67, 173, 184, 186, 187
Bloch, Hayyim, 253, 255, 257, 290–91
Botarel, Moses, 24
Bruno, Giordano, 189

Camillo, Giulio, 181
Cordovero, Moshe, xviii, 69, 143, 196–203, 243, 256, 268, 275, 276, 287, 288–89, 292, 293

David ben Yehudah he-Ḥasid, 121, 122, 124, 125, 162
De Leon, Moses, 117, 276
Della Mirandola, Pico, 176, 182, 191, 215
Del Medigo, Joseph ben Shelomo of Candia, 153, 159–60, 184, 185, 186, 193, 230, 233, 234, 244
Del Medigo, Eliyahu, 215
Donnolo, Shabbatai, 49, 75, 304

Edeles, Samuel, 173, 222
Eleazar ben 'Arakh, 15
Eleazar ben Pedat, 242
Eleazar of Worms, xviii, xix, xxi, xxviii, 7, 20, 41, 55, 56, 57, 58, 59, 60, 64, 66, 68, 70, 74, 75, 76, 80, 82–83, 84, 93, 119, 120, 121, 122, 132, 137, 159, 169, 176, 180, 239, 271, 274, 276, 280, 292, 295, 297, 300, 303, 306–07, 308–09, 312–13
Elḥanan ben Yaqar, 92
Eliashov, Shelomo, 246
Eliyahu ben Shelomo, ha-Gaon of Vilna, 244–45, 246
Eliyahu of Helm, 77, 201, 207–12, 214, 217, 219, 224, 225, 229, 261
Emden, Jacob, 194, 200, 209–11, 218–19, 220, 221
Ergas, Joseph, 184, 187
Ezra of Gerona, 130, 136, 137, 156

Ficino, Marsilio, 193, 215

Galante, Abraham, xxvii, xxviii, 69, 70, 71, 193, 274
Gallico, Samuel, 199
Gerondi, Nissim, 195, 228
Gikatilla, Joseph, 42, 114, 276
Ginzburg, Jacob, 253
Goethe, 252
Graff, Moses ben Menahem of Prague, 188, 244, 246, 303

Ḥabbilo, David, 132, 246
Hai Gaon, 48, 49
Ha-Levi, Isaac ben Asher, 91
Ha-Levi, Yehudah, 87, 114, 188, 239, 297
Ḥamiẓ, Joseph, 113
Hamon, 'Ovadiyah, 293
Ḥananel ben Ḥushiel, 48, 49, 50
Ḥanina, 29, 30, 31, 40, 69, 194, 219, 221, 274
Ḥanina ben Teradyon, 285, 288
Hašek, Karl, 252

Ḥayyat, Yehudah, 150, 161
Ḥayyim of Volohzin, 244–45
Hiyya, 108
Horwitz, Isaiah, xx, 62, 214, 227, 233–36
Horwitz, Pinḥas Eliyahu, 237–38, 240
Hyppolitus, 43

Ibn Adret, Shelomo ben Abraham, 221, 228, 230
Ibn Avi Sahulah, Meir, 114, 301
Ibn Ezra, Abraham, 55, 75, 82, 86–87, 89, 90, 92, 94, 133, 233, 292
Ibn Gabbai, Meir, 131, 133, 182–84, 187
Ibn Gabirol, Shelomo, 233–34, 239
Ibn Ghiyyat, Isaac, 300
Ibn Ḥayyan, Jabir, 175
Ibn Latif, Isaac ben Abraham, 175
Ibn Malka, Yehudah ben Nissim, 90–91, 94, 95
Ibn Paqudah, Baḥiya, 292
Ibn Ragel, Ali, 169
Ibn Shaprut, Shem Tov, 51
Ibn Sina (Avicenna), 175, 190
Ibn Tabul, Joseph, 158
Ibn Tamim, Dunash, 49
Ibn Tufail, 167, 174, 187, 190
Ibn Ẓayyaḥ, Joseph, 151, 161
Ibn Zimra, David, 145
Irenaeus, 13
Isaac R., 12, 17
Isaac ben Abraham, Sagi Nahor, 66, 74, 80, 117, 130, 133, 135–36, 137
Isaac ben Abraham of Dampierre, 91–92
Isaac ben Napḥa, 21
Isaac ben Shemuel of Acre, xxi, 106–10, 112–13, 117, 118, 188, 196, 199, 277,
Isaac the Old, 92
Isaac ha-Kohen, 85
Isaac ben Jacob ha-Kohen, 295
Ishmael ben Elisha, 91, 152

Jacob ben Yaqar, 58
Joseph of Hamadan, 117, 276
Joseph Meir of Spinka, 257

Katz, Ephraim, 212
Katz, Isaac ben Samson, 236, 252

Lavi, Shimeon, 132, 303
Lazarelli, Lodovico, 175–77, 190
Leibush, Meir (Malbim), 219–20
Leiner, Gershom Hanoch of Radzin, xx, 133, 212, 224–26, 227, 247
Loew, Yehudah ben Beẓalel (Maharal), xx, 85, 107, 199, 207, 210, 226, 236–37, 245, 251–52, 253–54, 261, 291
Lull, Ramon, 125, 182
Lupinus Caesar, 285
Luria, Isaac, 119, 145–47, 148, 149, 244, 245, 251, 270
Luzzatto, Samuel David, 51, 52, 53

Maharal. *See Loew*
Maimonides, 103, 114, 116, 156, 214, 301, 305
Marcos the Gnostic, 13, 270
Meir R., 62
Menaḥem R., 98, 137
Menaḥem ‘Azariyah of Fano, 160, 288–89, 290, 293, 294
Menaḥem Mendel of Kotzsk, 279
Mithridates, Flavius, 176

Mordekhai Joseph of Iszbiza, 224, 226
Moses ben Eleazar ha-Darshan, 160
Muscato, Yehudah, 180, 186, 230

Naḥmanides, 78, 129–30, 133, 154, 195, 228, 243, 295
Narboni, Moshe, 187, 190
Nathan R., 99, 106–08, 110, 117, 199
Nathan of Azza, 154
Neḥunyah ben ha-Qanah, 152, 285–86, 289

Oshaya R., 29, 30, 31, 40, 69, 108, 194, 219, 221, 274
Ovid, 7

Paracelsus, 180, 185–86, 195
Phaedrus, 4–5
Plato, 42, 192
Poppers, Meir, 159, 293
Postel G., 180
Pseudo-Sa'adyah, xxviii, 22, 24, 65, 66, 68, 74, 81–87, 94, 180, 191, 193, 233, 263, 275, 297, 301
Ptolemaeus, Claudius, 169, 171

Qafman, Berakhiel, 186
Qardinal, Yehudah, 297
Qaro, Joseph, 216–17, 229

Rabad (Abraham ben David), 159, 180, 193, 233
Rashi (Shelomo Iẓḥaqi), xviii, 30, 31, 40, 50, 58, 75, 114, 131, 181, 216–17, 226, 229, 234, 235
Rava, 7, 19, 27, 28, 30, 39, 48, 50, 51, 54, 62, 76, 102, 105, 107, 111, 114, 128, 129, 130, 135, 136, 138, 139, 144–45, 150, 166, 168, 172, 181, 182, 183, 184, 188, 194, 214, 217, 225, 226, 235, 238, 244, 248
Recanati, Menaḥem, 161, 304
Reuchlin, Johannes, 176, 177–79, 180, 186, 189, 191, 192, 215
Reuven R., 280
Rocco, Shelomo, 162
Rosenberg, Judel, 85, 226–27, 234, 236–38, 245, 252–53

Sa'adiyah Gaon, 24, 48, 49, 52, 88, 94, 121, 300
Sagis, Shelomo, 158
Sarug, Israel, 13, 74, 148–54, 159, 160–61, 269–70
Shapira, Ḥayyim Eleazar, of Munkacs, 224
Shapira, Zevi Elimelekh of Dinov, 252
Shapira, Zevi Hirsh of Munkacs, 224
Shem Tov ben Shem Tov, 287–88
Shemuel he-Ḥasid, 55, 94
Shimeon ben Shemuel, 65
Shneursohn, Menaḥem Mendel of Lubavitch, 254
Simon Magus, 5–6, 8, 28, 294
Spielmann, Jacob Meir, 246
Sternbuch, Moses, 220, 230

Tam, R., 82, 92
Taqu, Moses, 58–59

Vital, Ḥayyim, 115, 145, 158, 159, 293

Wuelfer, Johann, 207

Yagel, Abraham, xxvi, 180–82, 183, 184, 186, 189, 193, 215, 216, 228

Yannai, 36, 41, 304
Yehudah ben Bateirah, 67, 79, 177, 192, 274
Yehudah ben Shemuel he-Ḥasid, 32, 55, 56, 59, 64, 66, 68, 76
Yehudah ben Yaqar, 291
Yeruḥam ben Meshullam, 216–17, 228, 229
Yoḥanan ben Zakkai, 15
Yosei ben Zimra, 16, 17, 25
Yosse ben Yosse, 43
Ẓadoq ha-Kohen of Lublin, 92, 212, 220–24, 226, 230, 231, 247–49, 250
Ẓarfati, Reuven, 104
Zeira, 4, 19, 27–28, 30, 39, 50, 51, 105, 108, 111, 128, 166, 214, 219, 220, 225, 226, 235, 238
Ẓemaḥ, Jacob, 250
Ẓioni, Menaḥem, 63, 64, 72, 76, 80, 90, 94